The International Co-operative Alliance During War and Peace 1910-1950

Second Edition

The International Co-operative Alliance During War and Peace 1910-1950

Second Edition

RITA RHODES

ISBN: 9798442147377
Publisher: Rita Rhodes

Copyright (C) Rita Rhodes 1995/2022

The right of Rita Rhodes to be identified as the author of this work has been asserted by her in accordance with the Copyright, Designs and Patents Act, 1988

All rights reserved. No part of this publication may be reproduced, stored or transmitted in any form, or by any means, electronic, mechanical or photocopying, recording or otherwise without the express written permission of the publisher.

British Library Cataloguing-in-Publication Data a catalogue record for this book is available on request from the British Library.

Typeset by Chris Waite of CW Services and Amazon Kindle Direct Publishing.

For Bernard with love and thanks…

Rita Rhodes has also written:

A Thematic Guide to ICA Congresses 1895-1995 (written jointly)

An Arsenal for Labour - The Royal Arsenal Cooperative Society and Politics 1896-1996

Cooperative Adventures
We joined the Coop and Saw the World
(Joint Autobiography)

Cooperative Insights
Essays on the Political, Economic and Social Aspects of Cooperatives

Empire and Cooperation
How the British Empire used Cooperatives in its Development Strategies 1900-1970

Author's Preface

As an International Non-Governmental Organisation the International Co-operative Alliance is distinguished by its size, its geographical spread and its longevity. The longevity is particularly remarkable because similar international working class organisations, such as the Socialist International and the International Federation of Trade Unions, did not enjoy a similar unbroken existence. Like the Alliance, they espoused peace and international fraternity but, unlike the ICA, they proved prone to the divisions that rent working class movements when war broke out.

The Alliance also succeeded in overcoming many of the difficulties that other International Non-Governmental Organisations experience. These include maintaining cohesion and identity; constructing a united policy, which can become difficult when those shaping it come from different traditions and cultures; and sustaining an effective organisation and communications. Again, all of these become more difficult when war breaks out.

How and why the Alliance succeeded where others failed provides a fascinating story. This book focuses on the two World Wars, the Cold War and the period 1910 to 1950. After describing, analyzing and interpreting events it will advance reasons why the ICA survived these crises.

Extensive use has been made of primary sources in the ICA's Archives. Not all of these originated in the Alliance and include documents from regimes that were antipathetic to co-operation and to the ICA. It seems that these documents were assembled so that the Alliance might be better able to defend those of its member movements that had come under Fascist or Nazi domination.

As far as purely internal documentation is concerned we are fortunate that much of the correspondence for the period survives; also that the Minutes and Congress Reports produced during it were virtually verbatim. These help us to see the nature of the ICA decision-making more clearly and to follow the cut and thrust of debate. Because it was the custom to agree the accuracy of Minutes at subsequent meetings we can be confident in the verisimilitude of the events and developments described.

My selection of issues and the treatment of material necessarily implies historical judgements. However, I have tried to let ICA figures speak for themselves, and they were certainly capable of doing so. Consequently, many direct quotations are included to allow us more closely into the action and to give us a better insight into the personalities who led the ICA through the crises of the two World Wars and the Cold War.

However, these people did more than that. They also tried to represent ordinary people in an international relations system where the main parties were usually Governments and supranational agencies: on a number of occasions they referred to the ICA as the 'Real League of the People'. They also brought new and challenging ideas into international relations, including the ICA proposal that world oil supplies should be brought under UN control.

Above all, they gave practical expression to the working-class ideals of association and solidarity. They tried to defend co-operative movements under attack and also gave help to those who were exiled from them. Moreover, they established ICA Relief Funds to assist in the relief and rehabilitation of co-operative movements in occupied countries.

Deservedly, such strengths earned the ICA Category A consultative status with the UN's Economic and Social Council in 1946. Generally speaking, however, the ICA has been a modest organisation. This book tries to redress this tendency and takes to heart a call by a long-standing member of the ICA Central Committee and first Director of the International Labour Organisation, Albert Thomas, in 1931:

'I am distressed to see you so restrained, so modest and so prudent. With your 70 million co-operators affiliated to the ICA you represent a force and influence which justify you in speaking with no uncertain voice - whether it concerns the economic crisis or the struggle of peace and disarmament.'

This book is a tribute to those who sought to follow this advice.

Rita Rhodes

Contents

CHAPTER ONE 2

THE IDEAS AND DEVELOPMENTS LEADING UP TO THE ESTABLISHMENT OF THE ICA 3
Introduction 3
Early Co-operative Ideas 3
The Rochdale Pioneers, 1844 7
Shift from Co-operative Communities 10
The Christian Socialists 12
Co-operation in France 13
Co-operation in Germany 14
The Founding of the ICA 15
First Congress in London, 1895 21
The Alliance 1896-1914 24
The ICA and the Peace Resolution of 1913 28
Conclusion 31
Notes 32

CHAPTER TWO 33

THE ICA'S ORGANISATION AND IDEOLOGY 1910-1950 34
Introduction 34
The ICA's Organisation 1910-1950 34
ICA Ideology 1910-1950 47
Consumer Co-operation and Socialism 47
Co-operation and Political Neutrality 51
1930s Review of Co-operative Principles 55
Peace 64
Ideological Manifestations 67
Conclusion 68
Notes 68

CHAPTER THREE 71

THE INTERNATIONAL CO-OPERATIVE ALLIANCE AND THE FIRST WORLD WAR 72
Introduction 72
Maintenance of Relations 72
Bulletin of International Co-operation 75
ICA Member Co-operative Movements During the 1914-1918 War 77
Resumption of ICA Activities after the War 81
Conclusions 86
Notes 88

CHAPTER FOUR 90

THE ICA'S RESPONSE TO COMMUNISM 91
Introduction 91
General Background 91
Background to Russian Co-operation 92
Russian Co-operation during the War and Revolution 95
The ICA's Response to Changes in the Union of Soviet Socialist Republics 100
Relations between the ICA and Centrosoyus 1921-1939 112
Old Board- New Board 112
ICA Delegation to Moscow 1922 114
Co-operative Movements in the Soviet Republics 116
Centrosoyus Subscriptions 119
Centrosoyus and the ICA's Political Neutrality 121
Conclusions 122
Notes 123

CHAPTER FIVE 127

THE ICA'S RESPONSE TO ITALIAN FASCISM AND GERMAN NAZISM 128
Introduction 128
Italian Fascism and Italian Co-operation 128
The ICA'S Response 131

The Italian Situation - Conclusions 144
Change of ICA President 145
The ICA's Response 152
Conclusions 168
Notes 169

CHAPTER SIX 177

THE ICA'S RESPONSE TO SITUATIONS IN AUSTRIA, SPAIN AND CZECHOSLOVAKIA AND OTHER QUESTIONS 178
Introduction 178
The Austrian Situation of 1934 178
Conclusions on the Austrian Situation 191
The Sino-Japanese War 192
The Spanish Civil War 196
The Czechoslovak Situation 204
The ICA and World Peace 211
Conclusions 219
Notes 221

CHAPTER SEVEN 227

THE ICA AND THE SECOND WORLD WAR 228
Introduction 228
Internal Crisis: The General Secretaryship and Presidency 228
The Wartime ICA Secretariat Staff 253
Review of International Co-operation during the War 255
Other Activities of the Wartime ICA Secretariat 257
Review Debate on Co-operatives and the State 259
The ICA and Post-War Relief and Reconstruction 267
The ICA and the United Nations 279
Conclusions 284
Notes 287

CHAPTER EIGHT 295

THE ICA AND THE COLD WAR 296
Introduction 296
The Immediate Post-War Period 296
The ICA and The Cold - Introduction 314
Communist Attempts to Determine ICA Agendas 321
Soviet Proposals for ICA Rules Revision, 1948 323
ICA Rules and Membership Applications 328
The ICA and World Peace 346
Conclusion 358
Notes 360

CHAPTER NINE 367
Suggested Reasons why the ICA Survived the Two World Wars and the Cold War 368
Introduction 368
Reasons for the ICA's Survival 376
Ideology 376
Organisation 380
Contingent Reasons for Survival 383
Location of Secretariat. 383
Reduced American Influence 384
Lack of Nationalism 385
Conclusion 386
Notes 388
Index 389

BIBLIOGRAPHY 421

Chapter one

The Ideas and Developments Leading up to the Establishment of the ICA

Introduction

The International Co-operative Alliance was founded in London in August, 1895. During the period to be studied, namely 1910 to 1950, the Alliance could be described as an international working class organisation. Unusual for such bodies - others included the Socialist International and the World Federation of Trade Unions- it survived the pressures of total war between 1914-18 and 1939-45, and the divisions of doctrine arising from the Cold War. Because the ICA has recently celebrated its 125th anniversary it is interesting to ask how and why it survived when other similar organisations did not. At the outset it would be useful to give a brief description of how the organisation came into being and to show how early co-operative ideas shaped its organisation and ideology.

Early Co-operative Ideas

Co-operative ideas evolved from various strands of history, including the period of Cromwell's Commonwealth in England and the Age of the Enlightenment in Europe, which sharpened ideas about the collective good. The Industrial Revolution which followed created further upheavals, throwing economic and social questions into sharper focus among social thinkers and intellectuals who had already been noting the calls from the French Revolution for Liberty, Equality and Fraternity.

Robert Owen (1771-1855) was a major influence on early British cooperation. His social theories appeared in a number of essays, but those with particular relevance to co-operative ideas were published in A New View of Society between 1813 and 1816. In these, Owen criticised the competitive and exploitative nature of industrialisation, arguing that it prevented people from achieving their full moral potential. To be able to do this they needed to live in a more moral environment, created by better working and living conditions and education.

Many early Owenite co-operators were particularly influenced by his ideas on community and a labour theory of value. The former encouraged experiments in establishing co-operative communities at Orbiston (1825-1827), Ralahine (1831-1833), Queenwood (1839-1845) and New Harmony in the United States (1825-1827), while the latter led to the establishment of Equitable Labour Exchanges. These used Labour Notes as the basis of monetary value and exchange, and thus gave practical expression to Owen's belief that all value derived from labour.

Whereas Owen's actions and writings suggest that he was a paternalistic figure, the co-operatives prompted into being by his ideas soon proved to be highly democratic and self-managing.

Initially they aimed to set up self-governing communities by generating the capital they required from trade rather than receiving it from philanthropists such as Owen. They had taken this idea from Dr William King (1786-1865) of Brighton who, with Dr Birkbeck (1776 1841), the founder of the Mechanics' Institutes, had opened the Mechanics' Institute in Brighton in 1825. Local Owenites attended King's classes in mathematics and natural philosophy. In 1827, he helped them to form two organisations. One was the Brighton Co-operative Benevolent Association, which collected small weekly subscriptions from its members to enable them to join co-operative communities, and the other was the Co-operative Trading Association, which began trading with the aim that its profits should be used to establish another cooperative community. Both these democratically and self-managed ventures added the concepts of self-help and mutual aid to Owen's earlier ideas for co-operative communities.

Various attempts at co-operative activity continued during the 1830s but the next big step forward came in 1844, when the Rochdale Pioneers established their society. They had learned of King's practical ideas through his journal, The Co-operator, which had a profound influence on early co-operators, particularly those in the Midlands and North of England. In his journal, King published the lessons gained from the Brighton experiments. He also emphasised the importance of unity and association, which enabled people to achieve together what they could not do individually. Important also was King's argument that such cooperation was voluntary; 'all the power in the world cannot make it compulsory, nor is it desirable that it should depend on any power but its own the interference of Governments would only cramp its energies and misdirect them.'

Three important seminal ideas were contained within this statement that later co-operators embraced. One was that co-operation should never become compulsory. The second moved co-operation away from Owen's paternalism by arguing that it should depend on no power but its own. The third was that co-operatives should avoid the interference of governments. Later, we will find that this last idea evolves into co-operatives' idea of political neutrality and their attitude to the State. All three ideas entered the mainstream of co-operative thought. They will reappear throughout this study and will become particularly relevant when we come to deal with co-operatives' relations with Fascist and Communist States.

Besides being influenced by William King, the Rochdale Pioneers' ideas were also shaped by other developments including the growth of provident or mutual benefit clubs, which had grown from the late 18th century to enable members to pay small regular sums that could be redeemed if they became sick or died. Some of these clubs also began to trade along the lines suggested by King. About the same time many craftsmen also began to produce on a co-operative basis, sometimes by setting up joint buying or marketing arrangements, and at others by establishing co-operatively owned and managed workshops.

The Rochdale Pioneers are also likely to have been influenced by the ideas which emerged from early national co-operative Congresses and a spate of regional co-operative journals. Eight of the Congresses were held between 1831 and 1835. We can perhaps note that 'Congress' was a term that came to be widely used throughout the co-operative movement. It reflected the period in which the movement began and the influences out of which it grew, congress being a term of the American and French Revolutions. Although Robert Owen chaired a number of

The Rochdale Pioneers

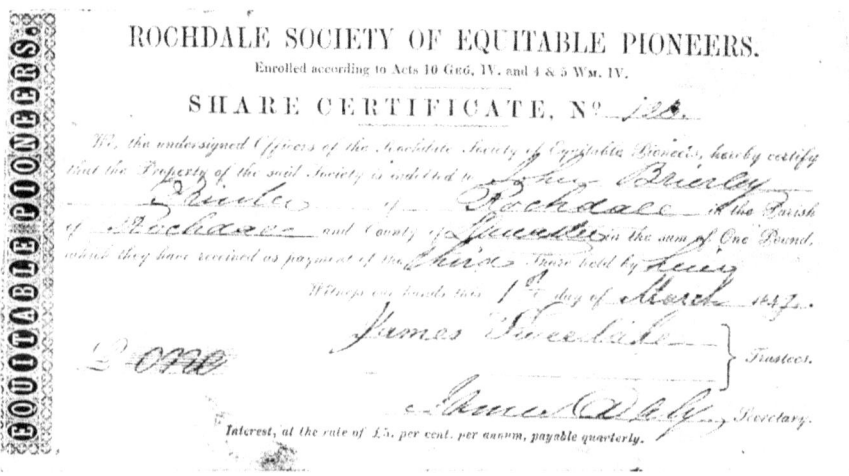
Rochdale Pioneers' Share Certificate

these early British co-operative Congresses, they reflected a move away from some of his ideas, particularly those on religion. The 1832 Congress passed a resolution that was to have historic co-operative significance. It read:

'Whereas the co-operative world contains persons of every religious sect and of every political party, it is resolved that co-operators as such, jointly and severally, are not pledged to any political, religious or irreligious tenets whatsoever; neither those of Mr. Owen, nor of any other individual.'[1]

Religious and political neutrality became a feature of Rochdale co-operation and was later enshrined in the Constitution of the International Co-operative Alliance.

The Rochdale Pioneers, 1844

Building on these early co-operative ideas, the Rochdale Pioneers added a number of their own precepts. Their practices created a formula that helped an increasing number of trading co-operatives to set up successfully. Because these practices were so widely copied they later came to be called Co-operative, or Rochdale, Principles. A guide to an early version of them can be found in the Rochdale Society's annual almanac for 1860.[2]

'The present Co-operative Movement does not intend to meddle with the various religious or political differences which now exist in society, but by a common bond, namely that of self-interest, to join together the means, the energies, and the talents of all for the common benefit of each.

(1) That capital should be of their own providing and bear a fixed rate of interest.

(2) That only the purest provisions procurable should be supplied to members.

(3) That full weight and measure should be given.

(4) That market prices should be charged and no credit given or asked.

(5) That profits should be divided pro rata upon the amount of purchases made by each member.

(6) That the principle of "one member one vote" should obtain in government and the equality of the sexes in membership.

(7) That the management should be in the hands of officers and committee elected periodically.

(8) That a definite percentage of profits should be allotted to education.

(9) That frequent statements and balance sheets should be presented to members.

At first glance these practices may seem prosaic, but closer examination reveals an underlying philosophy. For example, the Pioneers' interest in equity is reflected in a number of ways, and was underscored by the name of their society, The Rochdale Equitable Society of Pioneers. In the almanac it is shown in the practice of members' share capital receiving only a fixed rate of interest and in the payment of a pro rata dividend which resulted from charging of 'market prices'.

Like religious and political neutrality, this was a defensive mechanism. The Rochdale Pioneers did not want to compete with other traders for fear of retaliation. They therefore decided to sell the goods that they bought at wholesale prices at the prices they would pay if bought from other shop-keepers. Because these made a profit from the prices that they charged it was inevitable that the Pioneers would do so as well. Influenced by Owen's ideas, early co-operators were against profit. They believed that the quest for it led to the exploitation of workers and the sale of adulterated or poor quality food to customers. They also accepted Owen's belief that labour was the basis of value.

As we have noted, early co-operators had supported the Owenite Labour Exchanges because they gave practical expression to their belief that labour was the basis of value. This was linked to their idea of a 'just price', which was not new, having been an important Christian economic doctrine in the Middle Ages. Later, in his Wealth of Nations, Adam Smith (1723-90) acknowledged that labour had determined value in early societies, but that the emergence of the capitalist and the landlord had meant that the product of the labourer had to be divided into wages, rent and profits. Owen was influenced not so much by Adam Smith as by David Ricardo (1771-1823), who continued to argue the labour theory of value on the grounds that the capital goods used in production embodied past labour. It was this theory that entered co-operative thought through Owen and the Rochdale Pioneers and eventually underlay the ideas behind producer co-operatives and the profit-sharing schemes of consumer co-operatives.

During the early years of the Rochdale society its members performed all functions. Later, the co-operative, like others, began to employ labour, and this cost then became a charge on the surplus. Co-operatives were averse to using the term profit. They believed that members trading mutually with each other could not make a profit out of themselves. Surplus therefore became a term used to describe the difference between their costs and selling goods to themselves at market prices. It became customary to pay out of the surplus a bonus to employees on their wages. This very early form of profit-sharing thus enabled co-operatives to make an obeisance to Owen's labour theory of value.

We should return, though, to the Pioneers' ideas of equality. Their mechanism of the dividend paid pro rata to a member's purchases enabled selling at market prices without making a profit. This was equitable, but it also had the effect of encouraging members' loyalty which, in turn, strengthened their unity or association.

Equality was also reflected in the principle of 'one member one vote', as well as in the 'equality of the sexes in membership'. We should remind ourselves that Rochdale instituted these practices long before working class men, let alone women, had a Parliamentary or local Government vote. Further we should note that 'one member one vote' emphasised the low importance placed on capital. In other businesses shares would have been the basis on which voting rights were allocated. In Rochdale-style co-operatives the member had only one vote irrespective of the amount of share capital that he or she held.

It can thus be seen that, although the Rochdale practices might appear prosaic, important philosophical concepts underlined them. Besides the practices described above, the Rochdale society had longer term objectives, namely to generate through trade the capital to establish a co-operative community. In 'Law the First' of their Rules, the Pioneers stated:

'The objects and plans of this Society are to form arrangements for the pecuniary benefit of the social and domestic conditions of its members, by raising a sufficient amount of capital in shares of one pound each, to bring into operation the following plans and arrangements.

The establishment of a store for the sale of provisions, clothing etc.

The building, purchasing or erecting of a number of houses in which those members desiring to assist each other in improving their domestic and social condition may reside.

To commence the manufacture of such articles as the Society may determine upon, for the employment of such members as may be without employment or who may be suffering in consequence of repeated reductions in their wages.

As a further benefit and security to the members of this Society, the Society shall purchase or rent an estate or estates of land, which shall be cultivated by the members who may be out of employment, or whose labour may be badly remunerated.

That, as soon as practicable, the Society shall proceed to arrange the powers of production, distribution, education and government or in other words, to establish a self-supporting home colony of united interests, or assist other societies in establishing such colonies.

That for the promotion of sobriety, a temperance hotel be opened in one of the society's houses as soon as convenient.'[3]

However, Rochdale co-operation was soon to become an end in itself as a shift occurred away from the earlier ideas of the co-operative communities.

Shift from Co-operative Communities

The reasons for this change of direction were not single or simple. One was that specially created co-operative communities began to appear a less important way of securing workers' well-being. The take-off period for co-operatives based on the Rochdale Principles coincided almost exactly with the years of economic expansion in the third quarter of the 19th century. Consequently, more co-operative members were in employment. Furthermore, their spending power was enhanced by the benefits of the co-operative shop, which was situated near their homes and places of work. Consequently, the appeal of moving away to an artificially-constructed community began to decline. Another factor was that urbanisation meant that most co-operative members lived in tightly-packed streets, which constituted their own small communities and allowed them to have a close identity with the co-operative shop and the tangible benefits it provided. With such developments, retail co-operation increasingly came to be seen as an end in itself.

Out of this development emerged the 'consumer theory of co-operation'. This argued that everyone was a consumer, and that co-operatives formed to meet their needs could be all-embracing and democratic. By contrast, producer co-operatives, which had also grown in numbers, must necessarily be based on sectional interests, namely the need for their members to charge as much as possible to maximise their wages. Consumer co-operatives, though, could benefit a wider number of members by developing significant economies of scale through vertical integration, by moving back into wholesaling and into production, including agricultural production. Such economies of scale could be passed on to retail society members through lower prices, higher dividends, or both. Towards the end of the 19th century, and with the advantage of such benefits, British consumer co-operatives began to become mass membership organisations.

However, some still regarded producer co-operation as a superior kind of co-operation because it had greater affinity with Robert Owen's labour theory of value. Included among them were the Christian Socialists who, although strong proponents of producer co-operation, did much to help young consumer co-operatives, particularly in gaining their first legislative protection. One of their number, Edward Vansittart Neale, was to become directly involved in early moves leading to the founding of the International Co-operative Alliance. We should therefore make brief reference to the Christian Socialists.

The Christian Socialists

The Christian Socialists had links with producer co-operative developments in France, but perhaps their main significance in this study is that they added a liberal dimension to early British co-operative development. Although they were upper class they should not be seen as being as paternalistic as Robert Owen: they were more concerned with facilitation and animation. The former is illustrated by the help they, particularly Neale, gave in the passing of the first Industrial and Provident Societies Act in 1852, which gave young consumer societies their first legal protection. The latter is reflected in the work, particularly that of J. M. Ludlow, in the setting-up of Working Men's Associations, out of which grew a number of co-operative workshops.

Edward Vansittart Neale (1810 - 1902)

Neale was to become the first General Secretary of the Co-operative Union, established in 1869 and intended to become the national representative body of all co-operatives. However, this did not happen, and Neale became disappointed in his hopes of its becoming an agency that would facilitate trade between independent producer co-operatives and the growing number of consumer societies. The former ran into increasing difficulties, including the 35 or so which were directly assisted by the Christian Socialists. Unlike consumer co-operatives, they had no Rochdale equivalent to provide a model, or formula, for success. Moreover, the opportunities they had to supply retail co-operatives declined when these took association to a new level and federated to form two Co-operative Wholesale Societies. That for England and Wales was established in 1863, while that in Scotland was set up five years later.

The growing practical difficulties for producer co-operatives were compounded by the theoretical justification given to consumer co-operation by the publication in 1889 of the book The Co-operative Movement by Beatrice Potter, later Beatrice Webb. In this, she was critical of producer co-operation and came down firmly on the side of the consumer co-operative movement, whose success became even more marked by the added strength of the two wholesale societies. However, it was Edward Vansittart Neale, rather than Mrs Webb, who played a leading role in events leading up to the establishment of the International Co-operative Alliance in 1895. And, because he was still a strong supporter of workers' co-operatives, the embryonic Alliance was affected by the controversy between producer and consumer co-operation. Indeed, under Neale's influence the main aim of the Alliance was, initially, to 'promote co-operation and profit-sharing in all their forms'.[4] Before we look at the setting up of the ICA we should briefly note the form that co-operative developments had taken to date in other countries.

Co-operation in France

So far we have followed early co-operative developments in Great Britain because of the seminal importance of Rochdale, and of the British co-operative traditions within the International Co-operative Alliance. French co-operation was also to play an important part within the ICA, but French co-operative ideas first found expression in producer rather than consumer co-operatives. These ideas had some similarity with those in Britain and had grown out of the teachings of Saint Simon (1760-1824). He and his followers had condemned the 'exploitation of man by man' and unearned incomes as well as arguing what was to become a socialist tenet: 'From each according to his ability, to each according to his work'. Like Owen, the supporters of Saint Simon disliked competition, claiming that it led to anarchy. To counter its effects, they advocated 'associated work', going so far as to suggest that the whole of society should be seen as a vast association of producers. Such ideas were taken further by French thinkers such as Philippe Buchez (1796-1865), Charles Fourier (1772-1837) and Louis Blanc (1811-1882).

For example Fourier proposed self-supporting communities called phalanxes. These were reminiscent of Owenite communities. Indeed, they were studied in Owen's journal The New Moral World and must have been known to early British co-operators. There were also personal links between early French and British co-operative thinkers. The Christian Socialist, J. M. Ludlow, spent time in Paris, while Louis Blanc came to England. It therefore seems likely that the Christian Socialists' attempts to develop productive workshops in their working Men's Associations owed something to French ideas. We shall find shortly that French consumer co-operatives did not develop for almost another 50 years and that, when they did, they owed more to Rochdale co-operation than to early French co-operative ideas. At this point though, we should take a brief look at early German co-operation, which came from a different perspective. It also took another form, and owed little to ideas elsewhere.

Co-operation in Germany

Although German co-operation developed at about the same time as consumer co-operation in Britain and producer co-operation in France, its main form was the of thrift and credit societies. Two distinct movements emerged during the 1840s. One, founded by Hermann Schultze-Delitzsch (1808-1883), was based in urban areas and had the aim of channelling local savings to provide credit facilities to small shop-keepers, manufacturers and craftsmen. By 1859 this movement had become strong enough to hold its first Congress, and in 1864 it formed a General Union.

The second movement, founded by Friedrich Raiffeisen (1818-1888), aimed to develop similar thrift and credit facilities in rural areas to help farmers and others engaged in agriculture and horticulture. Neither Schultze-Delitzsch nor Raiffeisen was as radical as contemporary French and British co-operators. They did not wish to reorganise society and assumed the continuing existence of capitalism. Within the existing system, they viewed their co-operative activities only as a palliative, believing that if an individual was strong enough to manage a capitalist enterprise, he or she had no need of co-operation. If this were not the case, then they should join with other weak people to gain the benefits of capitalism that they could not achieve individually.

However, there were some similarities between co-operatives in the three countries. For example, German thrift and credit societies accepted the importance of association, self-help and mutual aid, and they also favoured religious and political neutrality.

As in France, German consumer co-operatives did not develop until almost the end of the 19th century and did not then contribute any new co-operative ideas.

By 1895, when the Alliance was established, three main strands of co-operative development could be clearly discerned: consumer, production and thrift and credit. While there had also been sporadic attempts to establish agricultural co-operatives, these had not yet become as significant as the other types of co-operative.

The Founding of the ICA

As we have seen, British and German co-operatives showed that they could apply the concept of association at higher levels by forming secondary societies such as Unions or Wholesales. In the 1880s the idea of creating an association at international level began to be explored. From the earliest days co-operative leaders had looked beyond their own national boundaries. For example, Robert Owen had published his plan for an 'Association of all Classes and all Nations' in an essay of that title in 1835, and had earlier gone to America to help in the establishment of the co-operative community at New Harmony. We have already noted that J. M. Ludlow spent time in France and Louis Blanc in England, while William Maxwell, Chairman of the Scottish Co-operative Wholesale Society and later President of the International Co-operative Alliance, had earlier joined Garibaldi in Italy. A British Co-operative leader, William Pare, who had been involved with the setting up of the Co-operative Union in 1869, had ties with newly emerging Scandinavian co-operatives.

Draft Outline of a Plan for an International Alliance

DRAFT OUTLINE

OF A

PLAN

FOR AN

INTERNATIONAL ALLIANCE

OF THE

FRIENDS

OF

CO-OPERATIVE PRODUCTION,

To be considered at an Inaugural Meeting at the Crystal Palace, on Monday, August 22nd, 1892, at 3 p.m.

OBJECTS.

1. The Objects of the Alliance are :—

(1.) To bring into relations of mutual helpfulness those who are seeking in different countries and in various ways to end the present deplorable warfare between Capital and Labour, and to organise Industrial Peace, based on co-partnership of the worker.

(2.) To promote the formation or aid the development in each country of Central Institutions for helping working people to establish and maintain self-governing Workshops, and for assisting employers and employed to establish just and harmonious profit-sharing arrangements.

(3.) To form an International means of connection and communication between these Central Institutions through which they may render one another mutual assistance.

(4.) Generally to promote the employment of the profits of productive industry :

(*a*) For removing the conflict of interest now existing between employers and employed.

(*b*) For permanently raising the position of the employed by the accumulation of the profits allotted to them in respect of their work.

(*c*) For promoting the use of the profits thus accumulated in ways that will most effectually conduce to the well-being of the body of workers by facilities for education, recreation, improved dwellings, provident provisions for age, sickness and death, the development of refined and elevating tastes, the care for infancy and childhood, the reward of invention, &c.

MEMBERS.

2. The Alliance shall comprise :—

(1.) All individuals ;

(2.) All firms, companies, or societies, herein called Collective Members, who signify their approval of the objects, and subscribe *not less*, annually, than—

	Dollars	Francs	Shillings	Marks
Individuals	24c.	1.25	1	1.3
Collective Members	4.75	25	20	20.5

or other equivalent money of the country where the Member resides, or is established.

(3.) Individuals who contribute shall be Life Members.

RIGHT TO ATTEND MEETINGS.

3. Members, on payment of their subscriptions, shall be furnished with cards which shall entitle them, respectively,—or, in the case of Collective Members, such person as is designated as their representative for the time being—to attend all General Meetings of the Alliance in any Country where it has been formed.

VOTING POWER.

4. Every Individual Member shall have one vote, and every Collective Member one vote, and an additional vote for each or fraction of persons represented up to a total of 10 votes for each such Member.

Neither was such impetus towards internationalism confined to individuals. The British Co-operative Congress of 1869 discussed forming an 'organisation of all Co-operative Societies at Home and Abroad'. Subsequently the Co-operative Union included Foreign Reports' in its own Annual Report, and later appointed a Foreign Enquiry Committee to enable the Union to keep up to date with co-operative developments in other countries.

Sir William Maxwell (1841 - 1929)

Fraternal relations were growing between national co-operative organisations in different countries. In 1884 French producer co-operatives established a Consultative Chamber which sent greetings to British Co-operative Congresses. These were reciprocated.

A year later, fledgling French consumer co-operatives also established contact with the British Co-operative Union. These co-operatives had first developed in accordance with earlier French co-operative ideas, but they began to shift towards the ideas of one of their leaders, Edouard de Boyve. He came from an aristocratic Huguenot family, and had an able command of English gained, no doubt, from his English mother. In 1883, at Nimes, Boyve established a retail society along Rochdale lines, influenced by his familiarity with the writings of the Christian Socialists and with various English co-operative journals. After Nimes many French consumer co-operatives began to follow the Rochdale pattern.

However, de Boyve soon became worried that these societies were concerned more with the economic advantages that they could offer their members than in proselytising co-operative ideas. Believing that this position might be rectified by forming a federation of French consumer societies along the lines of the British Co-operative Union, he sought advice from Edward Vansittart Neale, General Secretary of the British Co-operative Union. As a result of this, British and French consumer co-operatives developed closer relations, sending representatives and fraternal greetings to each other's congresses.

We could, perhaps, digress a little at this point to note that Prof. Charles Gide presided over a number of the early French consumer co-operative congresses. He was to become significant not only within the French movement, but also in the early International Co-operative Alliance, where he became a notable theorist and early historian of the ICA. The point to note is that Gide was an academic. Coming, like de Boyve, from a Huguenot family, he gained his Doctorate with a thesis on the collective law of associations and was subsequently appointed to the chair of Political Economy at Bordeaux, and later to the chair of Comparative Social Economy in Paris. Like Beatrice Webb in Britain, he illustrated the fact that co-operation, and the co-operative system, were now attracting academic interest. But we should also note that this interest came down firmly on the side of consumer rather than producer co-operation. It was at one of the French congresses presided over by Prof. Gide, and attended by British and Italian fraternal delegates, that the hope was expressed that an International Co-operative Alliance' would be set up. As a result, national committees were appointed in France and Italy to begin work towards this, while in Britain the question was passed to the Foreign Enquiry Committee of the Co-operative Union.

Despite such moves, progress towards the setting up of an International Co-operative Alliance was slow. One reason was that different co-operative movements had reached different stages of development. While fairly advanced in Britain, the movement was fragmented and spasmodic in Italy, and was developing along political and religious lines. Another reason was that over-ambitious tasks were being envisaged for the Alliance. These were not yet strictly focused on co-operation and their breadth and complexity are indicated by the fact that they included the settling of disputes in economic theories and methods; trying to bring about social and international peace; and attempting to provide a counter-balance to revolutionary socialism. It is interesting to note, though, that peace was among the earliest goals of the

Alliance. Even within a movement as advanced as the British, difficulties arose regarding how an international alliance should be set up, as a result of antipathies between the proponents of producer and consumer co-operation. On the one hand there was Edward Vansittart Neale who, although General Secretary of Co-operative Union, was dedicated to producer co-operation. On the other there was J. T. W. Mitchell, Chairman of the Co-operative Wholesale Society, who represented the Co-operative Wholesale Society (CWS) on the Union's Foreign Enquiry Committee. Neale obviously saw the proposed International Co-operative Alliance as an organisation of friends of co-operative production. Although he was responsible for convening the Union's Foreign Enquiry Committee to make plans for establishing the Alliance, he failed to do so. It seems that he feared the influence of Mitchell on the Committee.

The Committee was not reappointed in 1890 because it had not met during the whole of the previous year. Neale retired in 1891 but continued to be active in a personal capacity. His caution about the role that the Co-operative Wholesale Society might play in the Alliance is confirmed by a conversation that he is reported to have had with de Boyve in 1892, during which he blamed the lack of progress on the Wholesale Society. Both men then agreed that plans should proceed for a completely independent body, even though this could mean that it would be without the active participation of the British Co-operative Union, to which the Co-operative Wholesale Society belonged.[5] Neale and de Boyve further proposed that a Preliminary Committee of individuals, rather than organisations, should be established, to arrange the setting up of 'an international alliance of the Friends of Co-operative Production'.

The Committee was formed, and held its first meeting at Crystal Palace on 22nd August, 1892. Attending it were Neale's old Christian Socialist friend, Thomas Hughes, British trade union leaders such as Ben Tillet and Tom Mann, and representatives of the Labour Association which was concerned with co-operative co-partnership, Hodgson Pratt and Henry Vivian. Representatives from two federations of French producer co-operatives were also present. We should note the absence of consumer co-operative representatives.

Vansittart Neale was unable to attend because of ill-health and, in fact, died shortly afterwards. The Crystal Palace meeting appointed a provisional council to organise the first international congress. Two members were notable British co-operative figures, George Jacob Holyoake and Edward Owen Greening. Another member was a public figure, Albert Grey, later to become Earl Grey and first President of the International Co-operative Alliance. Two representatives from the Co-operative Women's Guild, Mrs Lawrenson and Miss Tournier, also joined the committee.

Neale's death created a practical loss. He had been a good linguist, and therefore important in maintaining contact between interested parties in different countries. It became necessary to find someone with similar skills to replace him. Neale's closest ally, Edward Owen Greening, proposed Henry W. Wolff. Although British by birth, Wolff had farmed for a long time in Germany, where he had been actively involved with thrift and credit co-operatives. He also had contacts with co-operators in France, Italy and Belgium, although he was largely unknown to the British Co-operative Union, which remained suspicious of him. Like Neale, Wolff was a good linguist, but he brought other qualities to the embryonic Alliance. One was his perception that producer co-operation and profit sharing constituted too narrow a base for a successful international co-operative organisation. He therefore made his acceptance of Neale's position as Chairman of the Preliminary Committee conditional on the proposed Alliance being made open to all that was 'genuinely co-operative'. This was accepted, and plans moved forward for the first Congress. They included a meeting of co-operative representatives from Ireland, Belgium, France, Germany, Holland, Italy and Britain. The meeting endorsed Wolff's plan for a wider Alliance and also agreed that the new organisation should be called the International Co-operative Alliance.

Thereafter, and largely at their own expense, Edward Owen Greening and Henry Wolff built up support for the first Congress, Wolff concentrating on continental co-operative organisations and Greening on those in Britain.

The delicate problem of the part that the British Co-operative Union should play remained. The Union itself continued to be aloof, having declined to join the Preliminary Committee, renamed the Executive Committee. It had done so on the grounds that the Union should be the acknowledged representative of British co-operation, and should therefore be rated more highly than individual members of the committee.

Eventually, a constitutional solution was found. The Co-operative Union was persuaded to resuscitate its Foreign Enquiry Committee, which then met the Executive Committee. The latter had by now realised that it needed the Union's support if the proposed Alliance was to be established successfully: a number of continental co-operative organisations had hesitated to become involved until the British Union did so. Eventually it was agreed that the Union should be recognised as the only legitimate representative of its member co-operative societies in Britain. In return, it added its weight to the organisation of the Alliance's first Congress.

First Congress in London, 1895

This was held in London in August, 1895, with Co-operative organisations from Belgium, Denmark, France, Holland, Italy, Russia, Serbia, Great Britain, Australia, India, Argentina and the United States being represented. In addition, co-operatives in Austria, Switzerland and Romania had indicated their future support.[6]

We should note, though, that the initial Congress was not as exclusively co-operative as later ones would become. In encouraging support for the proposed Alliance, Greening and Wolff had invited, or received, the support of many people prominent in public life, including lords, bishops, professors, social reformers, members of Parliament, delegates from the Peace Society, the Independent Labour Party, the Social Democratic Federation, the Church and the Christian Social Union.[7] The statesman, Albert Grey, now Earl Grey, presided over the first Congress and, in his address, paid tribute to Edward Vansittart Neale. The Congress went on to resolve to continue 'the work commenced by the late Edward Vansittart Neale and his friends'.

Edward Owen Greening also spoke, and emphasised that the co-operative movement was now moving into the international sphere. He reminded delegates that there was growing internationalism in many spheres of human activity,[8] and he hoped that international trade would develop between national co-operative movements. Greening's shift from the earlier and narrower views that he had shared with Neale became clear when he endorsed Wolff's proposed widening of the Alliance. Greening made a plea for toleration of 'every variety of organisation which can be fairly recognised as co-operative'.

Other parts of his speech reflect how the aims of the new organisation had been sharpened. Greening proposed that it should establish means for propaganda; that it should keep records of everything relating to co-operation at home and abroad; and that it should spread knowledge of mutuality. While the Alliance itself would not be engaged in trading, he thought that it should encourage the setting up of international committees that would help establish commercial agencies between national co-operative federations.

Despite the widening of the Alliance, which was contrary to Neale's wishes, the first ICA Congress showed its wish to acknowledge the new organisation's links with him. The resolution formally establishing the Alliance, moved by George Jacob Holyoake (Britain), seconded by Charles Robert (France) and passed unanimously, stated:

"That the organisations and individuals which have signified their adhesion be, and they are hereby constituted, the International Co-operative Alliance, to continue the work commenced by the late Edward Vansittart Neale and his friends."

A provisional Central Committee was elected to draw up a final constitution, which was to be placed before the next Congress in 1896. Guidelines for this work were laid down in a series of 12 resolutions, each embodying either the essential principles on which the Alliance was to be based or the future lines of its action.

Article 1 set up a committee to look into 'trading relations among co-operators of all nations. Article 2 echoed Rochdale when it stated simply and briefly that "The Alliance does not interfere with politics or religion'. Article 3 was more detailed:

The objects of the Alliance are defined to be:

(a) To make known the co-operators of each country and their work to the co-operators of all other countries by congresses, the publication of literature, and other suitable means.
(b) To elucidate by international discussion and correspondence the nature of true co-operative principles.
(c) To establish commercial relations between the co-operators of different countries for their mutual advantage.

Article 4, keeping in mind the earlier difficulties with the British Co-operative Union, stated that 'The Alliance will be careful to act, as much as possible, through the organisations existing in the various countries'. This presaged the Alliance's way of working and one of its subsequent organisational strengths. The next Article set up the provisional Central Committee, and appointed its members: two from Belgium, three from France, one from Germany, six from Britain, two from Italy and one from the United States. Article 6 provided for the Central Committee to elect from its own members an Executive Bureau, which should 'sit in London'. Elected to this were Earl Grey, as President of the Alliance and Chairman of the Executive Bureau, Henry Wolff, as Treasurer, E. O. Greening and J. C. Gray, as Honorary Secretaries, and A. Williams, as Assistant Honorary Secretary. We should note that J. C. Gray had succeeded Edward Vansittart Neale as General Secretary of the British Co-operative Union. This marrying of position gave practical effect to the earlier decision that the Alliance would work, as far as possible, through its member organisations.

Articles 8, 9 and 10 dealt with internal working relations, while Article 11 provided for the Alliance to have both organisational and individual members. The latter could attend and speak at congresses but only any ten of them could group together to use one vote. A final Article set the rate of subscription at 2 shillings (10 pence) per individual per year, and at least £1 for each organisation. Subscription income came to £222 in 1895, and £218 in the following year. All but a few pounds Sterling came from British subscribers, both individual and the Co-operative Union.[9]

The Alliance 1896-1914

A second Congress was held in Paris in 1896, with delegates from France, Great Britain, Italy, Belgium, Germany, Spain, Russia, Switzerland and Barbados. Attempts to finalise a Constitution ran into renewed struggles between the advocates of consumer and producer co-operation, and partly account for the long and rambling first Article:

'To study jointly, with a view to the amelioration of the lot of the working classes and to the propagation, in co-operative societies of every kind, amongst the people and public opinion of the whole world, the true principles and best methods of Co-operation in all its forms, organised without state intervention, of profit-sharing, of the associations of capital and labour and the remuneration of workers and employees taking as a basis the deliberations of the Congress of London (1895) but without claiming to impose on anyone, as a condition of admission to the Alliance, the observance of any uniform type of statutes, system of regulation.'[10]

Two aspects of this confusing text have bearing on later parts of this study. One concerns the statement 'the amelioration of the working classes'. We will argue later that throughout the period of this study, namely 1910 to 1950, the International Co-operative Alliance was an international working class organisation. This view is not unchallenged but, as early as 1896, there is evidence that the ICA saw itself as an organisation that aimed to improve the lot of the working classes. The second point concerns the phrase 'organised without State intervention'. As we have noted previously, this was a view dating from Dr William King, almost 80 years earlier, but it was the Germans who took a strong line on this at Paris in 1896, and it had been at their insistence that the phrase was inserted. This was a question that would become more controversial in the next few years.

To return, though, to the struggles between the adherents of producer and consumer co-operation, we should note that the French Consultative Chamber of Workers' Productive Societies asked the 1896 Congress to approve that profit sharing should be a prerequisite of membership of the Alliance. Had this been passed it would have proved embarrassing because a number of consumer co-operative movements were no longer paying a bonus on labour to their workers and would, most likely, have had to withdraw from the Alliance, thus weakening the organisation. However, the impasse was removed by passing an amendment stating that an object of the Alliance was to hasten the time when co-operatives of all types would extend profit sharing to all their employees.

From that time onwards, however, support weakened for producer co-operation and profit sharing. One reason was that the political complexion of ICA member movements became less liberal and more socialist. Another was that the gulf between consumer and producer co-operatives became wider, as the former proved ever more successful and the latter less and less so. As far as profit sharing was concerned, an increasing number of consumer co-operatives dropped it. A new generation of socialists was now arguing that profit sharing was a trick of capitalists to lull workers into a false sense of security that would undermine their trade union organisations, and many co-operators agreed.

Relations between co-operatives, socialists and trade unionists will be explored more fully, but we should first return to discussions at the 1896 Congress on the ICA's constitution. Whereas the Constitution drawn up at the first Congress had taken an unequivocal stand on religious and political neutrality, the new statement was more qualified. It read:

The Alliance does not concern itself with either politics or religion. Co-operation is a neutral ground on which people holding the most varied opinion and professing the most diverse needs may meet and act in common. In order to maintain this neutrality, on which the unity of the Co-operative Movement depends, every person and association in membership of the Alliance recognises that Co-operation is self-sufficient and must not serve as the instrument of any party.[11]

These sentiments were to remain constant throughout the period of this study, except that they came to be interpreted more generously in favour of political parties of the left rather than those of the right. At the time the statement was drafted, though, ICA member movements were more concerned with their relations with the socialists.

Prof. Charles Gide, the French co-operative leader referred to earlier, later described this time as the ICA's 'socialist period'. He distinguished it from an earlier bourgeois period, when the influence of the middle class Christian Socialists and the advocates of producer co-operation had been stronger. By the last years of the 19th century and the early years of the 20th century, consumer co-operation had proved the dominant kind of co-operation. Consumer co-operative movements such as the British, French, Belgian, German, Austrian and Italian had become large organisations whose memberships were urbanised and working class. It was among such members that trade unionism and socialism were also gaining significant ground.

Staying with this point, and moving forward from the 1896 Congress, we should note that consumer co-operatives became even more prominent as ICA member organisations divided over their attitudes to the State. One question raised at the Budapest Congress of 1904 was whether it was ever permissible for co-operatives to receive State aid. Agricultural co-operatives argued that it should be if such assistance were 'within moderate limits' and was a 'temporary support'. However, a majority of delegates were opposed to this, as a result of which some of the few agricultural co-operatives belonging to the ICA withdrew. The Schulze-Delitsch Unions of Germany and Austria also withdrew after their disagreements at Budapest with German consumer co-operatives. Whereas the latter wanted to change the existing order of things', the thrift and credit co-operatives 'believed in the importance of maintaining a commercial and industrial middle class and not encouraging co-operative developments which would injure that class'. [12]

As a result of these withdrawals, the predominance of consumer co-operatives in the Alliance increased its homogeneity, but there had none-the-less been a move away from the first two Congresses their emphasis that the ICA should be representative of all kinds of co-operative. An Alliance based heavily on large-scale consumer co-operatives, whose members were often members of workers' parties and trade unions, also meant that it was brought into close association with socialism. Even so, we should note that in 1910 the ICA moved strongly to retain its independence, when it resisted attempts by socialists to absorb both trade unions and co-operatives. While affinity with other working class movements was acknowledged, the ICA invoked its principle of religious and political neutrality to argue that the co-operative movement should retain its autonomy. It further argued that because co-operatives were trading organisations they were distinct in function from both trade unions and socialist parties. The issue was partially resolved when the 1910 International Socialist Congress at Copenhagen acknowledged that the Co-operative Movement had the right to act independently, though with trade unions and socialist parties when appropriate. [13]

Besides the settling of internal and external relations, the ten years between 1904 and the outbreak of the First World War in 1914 also saw the ICA become better organised. At the Cremona Congress of 1907 William Maxwell, Chairman of the Scottish Co-operative Wholesale, became President of the Alliance. Cremona also saw the appointment of Dr Hans Müller, of the Union of Swiss Distributive Societies, as the Alliance's Continental Secretary, as well as its editor of Congress Reports. Later Dr Müller also produced an International Co-operative Bibliography and the International Directory of the Co-operative Press as well as a monthly Bulletin in English, French and German. In 1910, the first Year Book of International Co-operation was published. This growing list of publications must have helped to create an identity and cohesion within the young Alliance. Müller worked from Zurich, but there was also a small administrative office based in London, which was concerned with organising congresses and meetings of the Central Committee, collecting subscriptions and compiling co-operative statistics. By 1912 it was becoming clear that the growing work load made it desirable to appoint a General Secretary and, at its meeting in Basle in June, 1913, the ICA Central Committee appointed Dr Müller. He moved to London, but soon returned to Switzerland because of ill health.

His departure, at the time when the 1913 Glasgow Congress was being organised, caused a near crisis. The location of the Congress meant that the closest national co-operative organisation that could help was the British Co-operative Union. They agreed to second their Parliamentary Secretary, Henry J. May, to take over the preparations for the Congress. The way that he did so impressed the Congress to such a degree that it invited him to become the permanent General Secretary of the Alliance.[14]

May's appointment, which he held until his death in November, 1939, was to be of great significance to the Alliance. During those years May became pre-eminent in many areas of international co-operation, and thus an important figure in this study. Considerable reference will be made to his letters and articles, and to Minutes and Reports prepared by him.

It is interesting to note May's background. He was born in July, 1867, which meant that he became ICA General Secretary at the age of 46. At the age of 13 he began work in a grocery branch of the Royal Arsenal Co-operative Society in London. Later he left to train to be an engineer, but retained his co-operative links by becoming a member of the Management Committee of the Royal Arsenal Society. His official work in the co-operative movement began when he became Secretary of the Co-operative Union's Southern Section, from which post he was promoted to become the Union's Parliamentary Secretary.[15]

Besides the appointment of Henry May as General Secretary, the 1913 Glasgow Congress had another great significance for this study: it passed a Peace Resolution which was to become the basis of the Alliance's attitudes on war and peace throughout the First World War and beyond.

The ICA and the Peace Resolution of 1913

By 1913 the ICA, like many other working class organisations, feared the increasing likelihood of war. The Alliance was apprehensive that a war could jeopardise co-operative expansion and ties at the international level. At the Glasgow Congress it took a stand on peace although, as we have seen previously, the maintenance of peace had been one of the earliest aims of the Alliance. This had taken more definite form when, in 1900, the ICA began to have informal links with the International Peace Bureau in Berne. Mr Hodgson Pratt, who, as a representative of the Labour (Co-Partnership) Association, had attended the 1892 meeting at Crystal Palace which began the organisation of the ICA's first Congress three years later, became a member of the Peace Bureau. He presided over the 11th International Peace Congress in Monaco in 1902 and forwarded copies of its resolutions to the ICA. These resolutions had urged that the International Peace Bureau and national peace societies should approach workers' organisations, including the co-operative movement, to encourage joint actions in support of peace. The ICA's 1902 Congress in Manchester passed a resolution declaring its readiness to work with the International Peace Bureau, and Hodgson Pratt became the Alliance's formal representative with the Bureau. On his death in 1907, his place was taken by Mr Aneurin Williams who, that year, had become Chairman of the ICA's Executive Bureau.[16]

The worsening international situation led the ICA Executive to pass the following resolution in 1912:

'The Executive Committee of the International Co-operative Alliance, in view of the state of war existing in Eastern Europe and the grave outlook, desires to remind Co-operators in all countries that Co-operation has peace among all nations as one of its essential principles. The Executive, therefore, in the name of co-operators generally, expresses the hope that war may not spread to any Powers not yet involved and that peace and good government may soon be established in the areas affected. Co-operators in all countries are earnestly required to use every endeavour to bring and maintain peace and concord between the nations of the world.'[17]

The Executive also decided to propose that the Central Committee should submit a resolution on peace to the Congress in Glasgow the following year. It is interesting to note that this was proposed by G. J. D. C. Goedhart of Holland, who was to become the Alliance's President in 1921. It was supported by William Maxwell (Britain), then the President of the ICA, and by Albert Thomas (France), who was to become the first director of the International Labour Organisation in 1919, and Adolf Von Elm, a German co-operative leader. The resolution passed unanimously read:

That this Congress fully endorses the action recently taken by the Executive and Central Committees of the International Co-operative Alliance in order to manifest that it is in the interest of co-operators of all countries to do their best to uphold peace. The Congress emphasises once more that the maintenance of peace and goodwill among all nations constitutes an essential condition for the development of Co-operation and the realisation of those ends which are aimed at by the movement.

The Congress further desires to impress upon the public opinion of all nations the fact that the reasons for the continuance of armaments and the possibility of conflicts will disappear as the social and economic life of every nation becomes organised according to co-operative principles, and that therefore, the progress of Co-operation forms one of the most valuable guarantees for the preservation of the world's peace. The Congress, therefore, exhorts the people of every country to join our movement and strengthen their power.

The International Co-operative Alliance declares itself in amity with all the co-operators of the world, and welcomes any action they may take in this direction or in which they may participate. Congress also welcomes all demonstrations made or to be made by other organisations with the same aim.'[18]

Such resolutions passed by the ICA or other organisations seeking peace had no effect in preventing the outbreak of war in August, 1914. Henry May then drafted a letter, which members of the ICA Executive approved by post. On 10th August it went in the Executive's name to the Central Committee. Recalling the Glasgow Peace Resolution, it went on to say:

We have therefore felt bound to consider whether any steps could be usefully taken in the present crisis to reiterate and emphasise to our co-workers the world over our determination to promote peace and amity amongst all. We do not feel that any manifestation to the world or even to Co-operators of the various countries should emanate from the Executive alone without the concurrence of the Central Committee itself. We should therefore be very glad if you will express your opinion as to whether such a pronouncement should be issued by the Alliance and if so, will you kindly send us a draft of the thoughts you would like to see embodied in it.

We assure you that the work of the Alliance will be carried on during the war as nearly as possible in the usual way. Some parts of our work may be stopped by the interruption of the postal communication and by other causes, but we shall go on with our work until such a stoppage actually occurs.

On receipt of replies to this letter, if it appears to be the desire of the Central Committee that we should do so, steps will be at once taken to issue a circular in the name of the Central Committee to all unions and societies in the Alliance.

On the other hand, if you think that this letter sufficiently expresses the attitude of the Alliance towards the present unhappy events, we shall be glad if you will communicate its contents to all the Co-operators in your own country.'

The tone of the letter is almost prosaic. Even the limited rhetoric of the Glasgow Peace Resolution is missing. The ICA, no doubt along with other organisations espousing peace, appears to have been bowing to the inevitable. As much as anything, May and the Executive seemed anxious to assure that the work of the Alliance would continue, as it did in a limited way throughout the war.

Conclusion

The outbreak of the First World War represented not only a defeat for the Alliance's policy on peace, but also the greatest threat to its survival. Three empires disappeared as a result of the war. The Socialist International and the international trade union movement were changed by it. But the ICA survived remarkably intact.

An aim of this study therefore to explore how and why the ICA managed this achievement, repeating it during the Second World War and the Cold War.

During this period, as we have already noted, ICA members were predominantly working class organisations whose own members were often active in trade unions and workers' parties. While trade unions and socialist parties espoused internationalism, the First World War generated a chauvinism that soon divided them along national lines. The ICA managed to avoid such disintegration. Its success in doing so seems to be explained in large measure by its organisation, or governance, and its ideology. The former suggests the 'how' and the latter the 'why'.

To illustrate this through a number of crises relating to war and peace, it might be helpful to establish what kind of organisation and ideology the Alliance had between 1910 and 1950. The next chapter will, therefore, briefly examine these.

Notes

1. BONNER, Arnold, *British Co-operation, Co-operative Union*, Manchester, 1961, p. 30.
2. BONNER, Arnold, *ibid.*, pp. 48-49.
3. BONNER, Arnold, *ibid.*, p. 46.
4. WATKINS, W. P., *The International Co-operative Alliance*, The International Co-operative Alliance, London, 1970, p. 39.
5. BONNER, Arnold, *op. cit.*, pp. 424-425.
6. WATKINS, W. P., *op. cit.*, pp. 30-31.
7. BONNER, Arnold, *op. cit.*, p. 427.
8. ARMSTRONG, David, *The Rise of the International Organisation - A Short History*, Macmillan Education, Basingstoke and London, 1982 pp. 3-6.
9. WATKINS, W. P, *op. cit.*, pp. 24-46.
10. WATKINS, W. P., *ibid.*, p. 48.
11. WATKINS, W. P., *ibid.*, p. 49.
12. BONNER, Arnold, *op. cit.*, pp. 429-430.
13. WATKINS, W. P., *op. cit.*, pp. 85-86.
14. WATKINS, W. P., *ibid.*, pp. 91-92.
15. International Co-operative Alliance, *Review of International Co-operation*, London, December, 1939.
16. WATKINS, W. P, *op. cit.*, pp. 64-65.
17. WATKINS, W. P., *ibid.*, p. 93.
18. WATKINS, W. P., *ibid.*, pp. 93-94.

Chapter two

The ICA's Organisation and Ideology 1910-1950

Introduction

In the first chapter we traced the growth of co-operative ideas in the 19th century. We saw how these shaped co-operative movements which, having established themselves successfully at national levels, went on to found the International Co-operative Alliance in 1895.

The treatment of this chapter will be thematic, rather than chronological, as the preceding and subsequent chapters will tend to be. Its aim is to make an initial exploration of the reasons for the Alliance's survival. Two important ones appear to be its organisation, or governance, and its ideology. While there were other reasons, these tended to be contingent or haphazard and fell into no distinct pattern.

This chapter falls into two main parts. The first examines the ICA's Constitution from 1910 to 1950, noting in particular those parts which were illumined by co-operative ideology. The second part will briefly summarise the ICA's philosophy during the period.

The ICA's Organisation 1910-1950

During this period the ICA's organisation changed little. By organisation we mean its written Constitution plus the functioning of its authorities, namely the Congress, Central and Executive Committees, General Secretary and Secretariat. In Chapter 1 we noted the main features of the Constitution which emerged from the Congresses of 1895 and 1896. The latter laid down that ICA membership comprised 'Co-operative groups, federations and associations and ... individuals who were members of co-operative associations'.[1] In other words, the ICA had both collective and individual members, all admitted by decision of the Executive Bureau and endorsed by a majority of the existing members of the Central Committee. Organisations joining were required to pass a copy of their rules and regulations to the ICA and to inform the Alliance of subsequent amendments. They were also required to let the ICA have regular copies of their journals, reports and propaganda publications.

The 1896 Constitution laid down that a member could not be expelled unless the Congress endorsed a recommendation to this effect from the Central Committee, which also had to justify the proposal. If, however, members were in arrears they could not attend, or be represented at, ICA Congresses. If the arrears exceeded six months, the member could be struck off the list of members by a resolution of the Central Committee without reference to Congress.

The 1896 Constitution laid down that subscriptions should form the basis of the Alliance's finances, together with donations, bequests and income from property. It also stated that the ICA's headquarters should be in London, and that Congresses should be held at least once every three years, with the Central Committee responsible for handling the Alliance's affairs between Congresses.

This Committee would comprise 37 members appointed by Congress with one half retiring, but eligible for re-election, at each Congress. Representation on the Central Committee would be determined by Congress according to the size of each national movement. As a result, those in France and Great Britain each had six members, Italy four, and Germany three, while the rest of the 16 countries in the Alliance had either one or two each. We should note that, at that time, the only non-European countries represented in the Alliance were Australia, the United States and the West Indies (Barbados).

The Central Committee was empowered to elect an Executive Bureau comprising chairman, treasurer and one or more secretaries. This was to handle the Alliance's day-to-day business, voting, if necessary, by post. We saw an example of this provision in action when Henry May, General Secretary, obtained the Executive's approval for a letter to go to the Central Committee on the outbreak of the First World War.[2]

No further significant constitutional amendments were made until the Manchester Congress in 1902. However, the British Co-operative Union had begun to campaign for the abolition of individual membership in the Alliance, and for members of the Central Committee to be elected only by national organisations. British delegates achieved a partial success when it was agreed:

The International Co-operative Alliance shall be a Union composed, so far as is possible, of Co-operative Societies and organisations. In respect of countries in which co-operation is, in the opinion of the Central Committee, still so insufficiently organised so to warrant such a course, it shall be within the power of the Central Committee to elect individuals as members...'[3]

By the 1902 Congress the Alliance was becoming more self-reliant. Henry Wolff, chairman of the Executive Bureau, presided; the first time that a Congress President had come from within the Alliance rather than from among eminent and external sympathizers. We should also note that the Executive Bureau, now renamed Committee, was still all-British. It was not until the Glasgow Congress in 1913 that it was considered feasible for representatives from other countries to be elected, but the First World War prevented immediate implementation of this. In addition to the British officers of the Alliance, the 1902 Congress also elected three British members of the Central Committee to the Executive. One of these was J. C. Gray, General Secretary of the Co-operative Union, while another was William Maxwell, Chairman of the Scottish Co-operative Wholesale Society.[4] Thus British co-operative leaders were now also becoming leaders of the ICA. Indeed, at the Cremona Congress in 1907, William Maxwell became the ICA's President, a position which was now permanent rather than one created for each Congress. However, it was still a ceremonial position rather than one that carried weight: the Executive Committee retained its own Chairman, who was still involved in the day-to-day running of the Alliance.

It was not until the Hamburg Congress in 1910 that the Alliance achieved a definitive constitution. This was to be one that settled the organisation's composition, structures and governance for the rest of the period of this study, and indeed beyond.

Individual membership was retained because different co-operative movements were at different stages of development. However, individuals could now be admitted only as honorary members, with the right to speak at Congresses but not to vote. The 1910 Constitution represented a move towards the British aim that the Alliance would be an association of national organisations. It provided for Co-operative unions affiliating under a new class of collective membership which covered their own member co-operatives.

Later in this study we will find that eligibility for Alliance membership became an important and contentious issue. In 1910, eligibility had only just started to be defined. Although earlier references to profit sharing or labour co-partnership had been dropped, no clear statement had taken their place. Instead, the Hamburg Constitution laid down that the principles governing member admissions should be established gradually by discussions and resolutions at ICA Congresses'.[5]

Returning to the actual governance of the organisation, it is interesting to note that, in addition to listing the Congress, Central and Executive Committees as organs of the Alliance, the position of General Secretary was also indicated, although the position was not filled until 1913. Congress remained the Alliance's highest authority, with delegates of affiliated organisations and members of the Central Committee being the only ones to have the right to speak and vote. The constitution laid down that Congress should hold the Central and Executive Committees accountable for their handling of the Alliance's work and finances. Only Congress could determine rules and amendments to them, and only it could elect the Central Committee from national organisations' nominations. The Congress also had the power to determine the seat of the Secretariat and Congress venues.

Along with this increasing power of Congress, that of the Central Committee also grew. Experience had shown that it was practicable to hold meetings of the Committee between Congresses, and these now began to be held at roughly yearly intervals. By 1910 the Central Committee could fix the date of Congresses and determine their Agenda, a power which would assume great significance during the Cold War. The Central Committee was also responsible for carrying out Congress decisions and, through the Executive Committee and Secretariat, it controlled the ICA's budget and programme. Required to meet immediately before and after each Congress, the Central Committee elected the Executive from among its own members, and later it would appoint the General Secretary and other officials, as well as determining their remuneration.

As the Alliance became more established and its work developed, the Executive Committee also increased in importance. For example, as we have seen, it made recommendations to the Central Committee as to whether or not an application for ICA membership should be accepted. It also did the initial work in the calling of Central Committee meetings and Congresses. Another function of the Executive was the responsibility for appointing an auditor and for conducting business that went to or came from the Central Committee.[6]

Thus, by 1910, the beginning of our period, the International Co-operative Alliance had taken its mature constitutional form which changed little during the years up to 1950. Subsequent amendments to its Rules only clarified the powers and responsibilities of the ICA authorities. Within that framework, however, there were some shifts. For example, the trend towards giving greater prominence to national co-operative organisations rather than to regional federations, primary societies or individuals continued. At the first Congress after the 1914-18 War (held in Basle in 1921) it was decided to recognise distinguished individual co-operators by creating a Committee of Honour, which was infact a prelude to, and a diplomatic way of, phasing out individual membership.

Another trend continued by the 1921 Basle Congress was the tighter definition of eligibility for ICA membership, not only in terms of whether existing ICA members in the same country approved, but also whether the applicants subscribed to Co-operative Principles. These Principles were those which were most closely associated with Rochdale, and therefore with consumer co-operatives. Another trend concerned the improving status of the ICA Presidency. The 1921 Basle Congress decided that, instead of remaining an honorary office, the Presidency should become an active position: not only should the President of the Central Committee preside over Congress, he should also be part of the Executive, which would now include the two Vice-Presidents and seven other members elected by the Central Committee immediately after each Congress. The position of Chairman of the Executive had been dropped. Furthermore, the 1921 Amendments to the Rules more closely defined the responsibilities of the General Secretary, delegating to him some of the functions previously carried out by the Executive, and giving him charge of the Secretariat. Once again, it was written into the Rules that the seat of the Alliance would be in London.[7]

No significant changes to Rules were made at the 1924 Ghent Congress, although the Executive increased in number from seven to eight in addition to the President and two Vice-Presidents. An important precedent was laid down when the Soviet Co-operative Movement's call to be allowed two representatives on the Executive was resisted: instead, the view advanced by Henry May, the General Secretary, prevailed. This was that election to the Executive should continue to be on an international, rather than a national, basis.[8] The position remained unchanged throughout the period of this study, including during the Cold War, although a convention developed that frequently there were Soviet Vice-Presidents of the Alliance.

Through the 1920s a distinct Soviet view emerged on a number of issues. Although the British Co-operative Movement remained the largest affiliated member of the ICA, Centrosoyus, the Soviet Central Co-operative Union, was almost as large. In any event, both the British and Soviet movements were far larger than any of the others affiliated to the ICA. Consequently, a move at the Stockholm Congress of 1927 was significant and also reflected a sense of fairness, even if it was not strictly equitable. The Rules were amended so that no country, or union of countries, could exercise more than one-fifth of the total voting power of the Congress. The Central Committee's recommendation to count the Union of Soviet Socialist Republics (USSR) as one country was also accepted.

It is important to note that, throughout the period of this study, subscriptions to the ICA were always based on membership, rather than on sales turnover. However high these might become, the 1927 Congress decided that co-operative organisations in any one country could have no more than 14 members on the ICA Central Committee. This maximum could be maintained through a system of substitution if some delegates from a country could not attend.

Moreover, if a member of the Executive Committee was unable to attend a meeting, he or she could appoint a substitute member from the Central Committee, to attend in his or her place. Throughout the whole period Soviet members made frequent use of this provision but Western representatives did not really do so until the Cold War.[9]

Thus, we can see a balancing of power taking place within the Alliance. This was to be significant for two reasons: firstly, it meant that the influence of smaller ICA member organisations was not swamped by the British and Soviet giants; secondly, conventions were developing and these would not be easily overturned twenty years later during the Cold War. Thus, the provisions of the 1927 Congress should be seen as contributory factors in helping the Alliance to avoid division.

Because Centrosoyus could exercise no more than one-fifth of the total voting power within Congress, it is perhaps not surprising that the Soviet Union sought, at the London Congress in 1934, to amend the Rules so that no organisation should have to pay more than one-fifth of the Alliance's subscription income.[10] This move was unsuccessful. However, one that was more successful was the attempt to link eligibility for ICA membership to the observance of Co-operative Principles. At the preceding Congress in Vienna in 1930 it had been decided to review the Principles, an exercise which will be considered in depth when we come to look at the Alliance's ideological base during this period. One result of the review was that the London Congress, to which its report was delivered, decided to place a moral obligation on members of the Alliance to observe all the Principles that it had endorsed, as well as the existing requirement of adherence to Congress decisions.[11]

During the remainder of the period under review, only minor changes were made to ICA Rules. For example, the 1937 Congress in Paris decided to limit representation on the Central Committee to nine from any one country or union of countries,[12] while at the Zurich Congress of 1946 this was increased to ten.[13] At Zurich a more significant amendment to the Rules was made to take into account the fact that the Alliance had been granted consultative status with the recently established United Nations, while at Prague in 1948, the Congress amended the Rules to provide for a new position, namely that of Director.[14]

It was at this Congress, though, that the most contentious debate involving amendments to ICA Rules took place. There was a heated struggle against Centrosoyus's proposals which, had they been accepted, would either have brought the ICA within the Communist sphere of influence or led to its division. A detailed study of this debate will be made when we come to consider the ICA in relation to the Cold War.

We can perhaps sum up this section by noting four characteristics of the ICA Constitution between 1910 and 1950. The first was that it reflected a co-operative ideology shaped by Rochdale. Secondly, it took account of the disparity in size of member movements by restricting the largest organisations' voting power in Congress and the Central Committee to ensure that smaller ones could also exercise influence. Thirdly, ICA authorities were clearly identified, and their powers and lines of accountability clearly stated. Fourthly, the Constitution proved workable and durable.

However, it is desirable to look beyond the written Constitution to the political framework in which it functioned. We should first quantify the financial contributions of different movements. By 1931 that from Britain had risen to £2,073, while that for the USSR, now comprising Armenia, Azerbaijan, Georgia, Russia, the Ukraine and White Russia, amounted to £2,760. The next highest subscriptions came from France at £530 and Germany at £510.[15] By 1947 Great Britain contributed £7,504 and the USSR £5,000.[16] Throughout the years, the British and Soviet movements were consistently the highest contributors. The next highest were usually France, Germany (before she withdrew in 1933), Sweden or Finland. However, these wide differences never became divisive issues. The two big movements had accepted constitutional limi-

Henry J. May (1867 - 1939)   Gertrude F. Polley (1900 - 1982)

tations on their voting rights in Congress and Central Committee, as well as the fact that they had no guaranteed places on the Executive. As we have seen, this continued to be elected on an international, rather than a national basis. For virtually the whole of the period, though, British and Soviet members were on the Executive, often at Vice-Presidential level.

We can therefore say that a fair degree of tolerance existed in the politics of the ICA. Important within these was the Secretariat, and particularly the position of General Secretary. In 1948 the post of Director was created, but for the greater part of the period studied the senior member of the Secretariat was the General Secretary. And, for 26 of the 40 years, that position was held by Henry May.

From 1932 he had an Administrative Secretary, Miss Gertude Polley, who had joined the Alliance in 1920. Like May, she came from the Parliamentary Office of the British Co-operative Union. After May's death in November, 1939, the Executive placed Miss Polley in charge of the Secretariat, but with no change of title. However, she became General Secretary in 1947, although a year later this position became subordinate to that of Director. The new position was held only briefly until 1951, by a Swede, Thorsten Odhe. A point to note is that May had wide experience of the British Co-operative Movement, while Miss Polley's experience, though more limited, was at a high level in the same movement. It was these three position holders, General Secretary, Administrative Secretary, and Director who, within the Secretariat, held any political power within the ICA. During the period in question the Secretariat rarely exceeded 15 people, and was made up largely of typists, translators and researchers, who had little or no dealings with the President, Executive and Central Committees. From 1921 to 1939 Miss Polley accompanied May to meetings of the Central Committee. She took shorthand notes of its proceedings, as well as those of the Executive Committee, and appears to have drafted their Minutes. After May's death Miss Polley became fully responsible for all Committee business and also for that of Congress.

We have already noted that the responsibilities and powers of the General Secretary, and later Director, were laid down in the ICA's Rules and May, Miss Polley and Odhe certainly worked within these. However, we will see that May in particular wielded additional political power.

He and the other office holders had responsibilities and access to all parts of the Alliance, but their most important intermediary was the ICA's President. The relations between the General Secretary and Presidency during the period are therefore important. At the beginning of the period William, later Sir William, Maxwell, Chairman of the Scottish Co-operative Wholesale Society, was President. At that time the position was more honorary and less integrated in the ICA structure than it was later to become. In 1921 Sir William retired and G. J. D. C. Goedhart, of the Dutch Co-operative Movement and an official of the Dutch Parliament, was elected President. May seemed to be particularly happy working with Goedhart. They developed a close personal friendship, which was perhaps strengthened by their shared Masonic ties. Their correspondence, which continued between the years of Goedhart's retirement and May's death, constitutes an important primary source in this study because it provides additional insights into May's views on what was happening within the Alliance.

ICA Leaders Between the Wars

T. W. Allen (UK)

Emmy Freundlich (Austria)

Albin Johansson (Sweden)

V. Klepzig (Germany)

E. Lustig (Czechoslovakia)

ICA Leaders Between the Wars

Anders Oerne (Sweden)

E. Poisson (France)

Karl Renner (Austria)

V. Serwy (Belgium)

Väinö Tanner (Finland)

Goedhart retired in 1927 and Väinö Tanner, then Prime Minister of Finland, was elected as ICA President. During the 19 years that he held the position he also held other Ministerial positions. Despite some disagreements, he and May had good working relations, although their friendship did not become as close as that which May had with Goedhart. The outbreak of war in 1939, and May's death two months later, broke a long and important relationship between General Secretary and President. However, no power vacuum developed. The Executive decided not to appoint a General Secretary until the war was over and, in the meantime, asked. Miss Polley to 'direct' the Secretariat. It also asked R. A. Palmer, Vice President of the Alliance and General Secretary of the British Co-operative Union, to help her.[17] The broken communications with Tanner, caused by the war, and the increasingly dislocated relations between. European co-operative movements and the ICA, meant that the con duct of the Alliance's business came to rest increasingly with R. A. Palmer and Miss Polley. Eventually he was to become the ICA's Acting President, subsequently becoming President in his own right in 1946. When he retired, in 1948, the position was taken by another British co-operative leader, Sir Harry Gill.

G.J.D.C. Goedhart (1857 - 1945)

We can conclude this last section on the ICA's organisation by observing that the ICA had a clear Constitution within which member organisations and the Alliance's authorities were able to work. It gave legitimacy both to the policies agreed, and to office holders. All in all it added up to the ICA being an effective organisation.

ICA Ideology 1910-1950

Having established the Alliance's constitutional base, we should now try to determine what kind of ideology drove it during this period. We have already noted that the ICA reflected co-operative ideas that predated Rochdale, including opposition to the competitive and exploitative consequences of capitalism, and support for schemes based on self-help and mutual benefit. To these the Rochdale Pioneers added ideas of democracy and equality. Although Dr William King had been the first to suggest that co-operatives were best if independent from the State, it had been the Rochdale Pioneers who developed the concept of religious and political neutrality which was carried forward into the Alliance's Constitution.

Not all the Co-operative Principles could be reflected in this. For example, it was not feasible for democracy within the ICA to be based on 'one member one vote'. Instead, voting was in line with the size of membership of an affiliated movement. However, to preserve some kind of equality of opportunity to influence the Alliance, irrespective of geographical differences and the various stages that different co-operative movements had reached, it was decided, as we have already observed, that no movement could have more than one-fifth of the votes at Congress, or a pre-determined number of seats on the Central Committee. Having said this, however, democratic ideas were reflected in other ways. The most notable of these was the system of checks and balances under which one level of ICA authority was accountable to the next.

We may be better able to identify the ICA's ideological stance during the period if we also study its policy. We shall therefore divide the following section into four main headings: co-operatives vis-à-vis socialism; the ICA's 1925 redefinition of political neutrality; the Alliance's 1930s review of Co-operative Principles; and the Alliance's attitude to peace.

Consumer Co-operation and Socialism

We have already noted that the early Alliance had favoured producer co-operation and ideas of profit sharing. But, within 20 years, it had come to be most closely identified with consumer co-operation. This change had been due not only to the relative decline of producer co-operation, but also to the fact that a number of thrift and credit co-operatives had withdrawn from the Alliance after the Budapest Congress in 1904. As a result, the Rochdale Principles, which were essentially those of consumer co-operation, became central to ICA ideology. This shift was buttressed by academic and intellectual justification.

We have already referred to Prof. Charles Gide, a prominent figure in the ICA until his death in 1932. He was one of the earliest economists to argue the importance of consumers within the economy, and in lectures and pamphlets Gide argued that this power could be enhanced by association in consumer co-operatives. Moreover, it could be further enhanced by the vertical integration which became possible if consumer co-operatives federated to form wholesales capable of moving back into primary production as the two British wholesales had done. Gide went on to argue that consumer co-operatives could eventually become the basis of a new economic order.

Of course such ideas appealed to consumer co-operative leaders, but they were also increasingly acceptable to socialists who, like those in Britain, and influenced by the Fabians, were moving more towards evolutionary, rather than revolutionary, socialism. Increasingly, consumer co-operation came to be seen as a form of social ownership that had affinity with State and municipal enterprises.[18]

We noted previously that the Socialist International Congress at Copenhagen in 1910 had agreed that the three wings of the Socialist movement workers' parties, trade unions and co-operatives - should remain independent, although mutually supportive of each other. A few days after this Congress the ICA held its own Congress in Hamburg. There, it issued an important declaration that shows the close affinity that was then felt between consumer co-operatives and socialism. The declaration began by stating that Co-operation was a social movement. Based on mutual help economic associations, it aimed to protect the interests of labour by increasing the income from labour, and by strengthening the purchasing power of workers. At the same time,

Co-operation sought to limit profits on capital, such as interest and rent which derived from the ownership of the means of production and exchange.

The ICA declaration came down in favour of consumer co-operation. Although it argued that all forms of co-operation were equally important in trying to attain the above goals, it suggested that producers' co-operatives, such as those of artisans, peasants or farmers, were liable to foster sectional interests rather than those of the whole community, which could be better represented by consumer co-operatives. Therefore, the declaration argued, consumer co-operatives held the greatest promise for a peaceful transformation of the capitalist system into one of co-operative social ownership. In moving towards this, primary consumer co-operatives could help workers and their families to combine their purchasing power and savings, so enabling them to produce goods for themselves and to create their own employment under model conditions agreed with trade unions. [19]

Later, as we shall find, the ICA returned again and again to the question of relations between co-operatives and trade unions. Certainly, consumer societies became good employers, not only because of this perceived close relationship, but also as a form of compensation to their employees for the bonus on labour that they had previously been paid.

Similar views were to be reflected in the International Labour Organisation when it was established in 1919. In the following year, the ILO created a co-operative section because it was argued that co-operatives could work alongside trade unions to improve workers' living conditions. The creation of a co-operative section within the ILO was no doubt explained by the fact that the Organisation's first Director was Albert Thomas. Besides being a leading French socialist politician, who had served in the French war-time Government as Minister of Munitions, he was a leader of the French Co-operative Movement and had been actively involved with the ICA since the Hamburg Congress mentioned above. He joined the ICA Central Committee in 1913 and, as we observed in Chapter 1, was one of the main speakers in support of the ICA's Peace resolution of 1913.

Various questions arise from this close relationship between workers' parties, trade unions and consumer co-operatives. One was how far the ICA's political neutrality might be compromised. Another was how far co-operation differed in theory from socialism.

In Chapter 1 we noted Prof. Gide's description of this time as the ICA's 'socialist period'. Obviously, he was referring to the working-class nature of consumer co-operatives, which had led the ICA to move from its earlier bourgeois, or middle-class, character. But Gide also drew an important and sharp distinction between socialism and co-operation. In an early history of the ICA he wrote:

The programme of the consumers' societies admits capitalism to a certain extent as they are societies with shares, and as they demand from the members contributions to capital and pay them an interest and it does not admit the expropriation, properly so called of the possessing class or at least it desires a different expropriation from that which would be brought about by the play of free competition if someday the co-operative enterprises show themselves superior to capitalist enterprises and get rid of them by their successful development. But these are not the characteristics of collectivist expropriation and, above all, there is this difference, that the essential article of the Socialist programme, which is the class conflict, cannot be included in the co-operative programme for the obvious reason that the consumer does not rep resent any class; he has neither difference of class nor difference of sex; everybody is a consumer.......everybody, Socialist or otherwise, has the right of admission to the association and that is a feature which suffices to give the co-operative movement its right of autonomy.[20]

Three points in this statement should be underlined. One was that, in Gide's eyes, co-operation was now synonymous with consumer co-operation. This was a view shared by other ICA leaders. Another point was that, although consumer societies worked within the capitalist system, they eventually hoped to replace private enterprise by their own successful development. The third point was that consumer co-operation was considered to be classless whereas socialists still thought in terms of the class struggle.

Despite this distinction between co-operation and socialism there were still obvious overlaps: frequently shared membership and the shared goal of improving workers' living conditions. It is therefore necessary to address the question of how far the Alliance's political neutrality could survive.

Co-operation and Political Neutrality

The Alliance itself addressed the question in the mid-1920s. It was not only a question of association with workers' parties and trade unions, but also the fact that its policy was leading the ICA to take 'political' stands on a number of international issues. For example, it warmly welcomed the setting up of the League of Nations and the International Labour Organisation under the Treaty of Versailles in 1919. Indeed, in a paper to the first post-war ICA Congress in Basle in 1921, Gide said that the Alliance's concern for world peace meant that it must support and defend the League of Nations. He even went so far as to suggest that the ICA should look on the League as a 'younger sister'. [21] This may seem presumptuous. It none-the-less reflected a long held view within the ICA, justified by its geographical spread and the nature of its membership, that it was the real 'People's League'. The claim was repeated during the 1939-45 war, when the Alliance sought to become involved in plans for post-war relief and rehabilitation, and for representation in the United Nations.

The fact that the ICA had tried to gain representation with the League of Nations and the International Labour Organisation, as well as at international events such as the World Economic Conference in 1927, meant that it was at least engaged in pressure group activities. Not all ICA members, and particularly Scandinavian co-operative movements, were happy about this, fearing that the Alliance's political neutrality would be breached.

Their fears were no doubt compounded by the fact that elsewhere in the Alliance there were co-operative leaders who were also prominent left-wing politicians. We have already mentioned Albert Thomas in France, but there was also Dr Karl Renner, who became Austria's Chancellor in 1918 and President after the 1939-45 War. In Finland, there was Väinö Tanner who, at the time of his election as ICA President in 1927, was the country's Prime Minister. There were other prominent socialists in the ICA, who did not necessarily hold Government office including Mrs Emmy Freundlich, Austria; Victor Serwy, Belgium; Ernest Poisson, France; and Emil Lustig, Czechoslovakia. Besides this overlapping of co-operative and socialist leaders, there were also two co-operative movements which had taken direct political action. In between the first and second Russian Revolutions in 1917, Centrosoyus had formed a short-lived political party. In the same year, the British Co-operative Movement formed its own political party which developed close links with the Labour Party and survives to the present day.

Internal concern about the Alliance's political neutrality came to a head in 1925. There were a number of reasons. Four years earlier the Alliance had had to take positions on Soviet Communism and Italian Fascism, and we shall deal with both questions in greater depth later. The point to note at this stage was that it began to be questioned whether the Alliance could make such judgements without breaching its neutrality. Another reason was that Scandinavian co-operative movements were uneasy about the ICA's involvement with the League of Nations and the International Labour Organisation, fearing that such association damaged its neutrality in other ways. They were particularly uneasy about the ICA's relations with the International Federation of Trade Unions in Amsterdam.[22] The Scandinavians felt that co-operatives should be non-political and concentrate only on their economic activities, and that the Alliance itself should restrict its activities to co-operative matters; the only economic questions it should consider being those with a direct bearing on co-operation.

It was never likely that the question of political neutrality would be an easy one for the ICA. As Anders Oerne, the Swedish co-operative leader, said, 'neutrality is not a very precise idea'.[23]

The question was first formally raised at the Ghent Congress in 1924, when the issue was not any of those mentioned above, but a quite different one stemming from Soviet communist propaganda in Western co-operative movements. Both the German and British Co-operative Movements had complained about this, and the latter had submitted a resolution.

The resolution asked the Alliance, while fully respecting its affiliated organisations independence, to remind these organisations that it could not allow infringements of the religious and political neutrality enshrined in its Constitution, and which they had accepted when they became members of the Alliance. Although passed by 397 votes to 183[24] the debate showed how difficult it would be for the Alliance to remain detached from political developments. A Soviet delegate suggested that when Congress had considered 'Disarmament', 'The Economic Position', 'The Conference of Genoa', 'The Position in the Near East', and 'The World Peace Congress at the Hague', as it had, it was hardly remaining politically neutral. A prophetic point was made by a Czechoslovak delegate when he said that the Alliance's concern to protect the Italian LEGA from the effect of Mussolini's rise to power would eventually lead it to pass a political judgement which would violate its neutrality.

Although the resolution was passed it settled nothing. The question was raised again when the ICA Executive met with representatives of Northern co-operative movements in Stockholm the following June. Once more, positions were stated but no hard and fast conclusions were reached and Henry May, General Secretary, was asked to prepare a memorandum to go before the next meeting of the Central Committee.[25]

The Central Committee met in Paris in October, 1925, and May's paper was passed unanimously. It included a statement that the ICA's neutrality was something that it imposed upon itself as a collective body: it was not something that it could impose upon member organisations functioning in their own countries. In this connection May's memorandum recalled that a declared purpose of the Alliance had been that people holding the most varied opinions and professing the most diverse creeds may meet and act in common'.

Obviously referring to Soviet attempts to spread propaganda among Western co-operative movements, the paper suggested that attempts by co-operative organisations in one country to influence co-operative bodies in other countries were bound to be criticised because they breached elementary good faith. However, they should not be considered to have violated the Alliance's neutrality.

In approving the Memorandum, the ICA Central Committee also agreed that the Alliance could work with other organisations without violating its neutrality, as long as such joint action was consistent with the aims and principles of the ICA, that the means employed remained free from 'party' political action or religious bias, and that the independence and authority of the ICA remained 'absolutely unimpaired'. Suggestions made about the directions in which the ICA could work without breaching its neutrality were agreed. These included representations to national international authorities on behalf of ICA member organisations which appeared to be suffering 'injustice or disability', and registering Congress and other declarations issued by ICA authorities.

In a move away from the Scandinavian position, the Central Committee accepted the Memorandum's argument that the Alliance should be free to make representations to national or international authorities on economic questions, as well as those involving conditions of labour, taxation and co-operative legislation.

On the question of relations with other international organisations, the Memorandum suggested, and it was agreed, that these should continue if they had already been approved by Congress. Thus, there could be joint action with the International Federation of Trade Unions on issues such as attempts to establish universal peace, good labour conditions in co-operatives, international fiscal policy, economic developments of mutual interest, the exchange of fraternal delegates at each other's congresses, and the mutual publication in official journals of economic, trade union, and co-operative papers.[26]

The significance of this restatement of ICA political neutrality - the issue of religious neutrality hardly ever arose - would appear to be threefold. Firstly, it attempted to reaffirm the Alliance's neutrality as far as party politics were concerned. Secondly, it reflected the fact that many national co-operative movements were politically involved, directly or indirectly, in their own countries. It was argued, though, that such actions could not breach the Alliance's political neutrality. Thirdly, the statement spelt out in far greater detail than had previously been done, those areas in which the ICA could work without breaching its neutrality. However, it is worth noting that the examples given by May in his Memorandum very much reflected the work of the ICA, and the issues that had arisen within it, since the end of the 1914-18 War. In many ways, May had been codifying neutrality within a framework of experience. It also represented a rejection of the Scandinavian position on the question.

The outcome of the 1925 debate was reaffirmed when the Alliance undertook its first major review of Co-operative Principles in the 1930s. This should be considered a major element in the ICA's ideological base.

1930s Review of Co-operative Principles

We should begin this section by noting that, by the 1920s, there were three distinct schools of thought in the ICA, with another emerging in the USSR.

The first of these schools was represented by the British tradition, which was geographically and historically close to Rochdale. The second comprised the French school of Gide, Thomas, Fauquet and Poisson, all of whom acknowledged and built upon Rochdale. Prof. Charles Gide argued that Rochdale Principles constituted a mutual aid system capable of superseding capitalism. He suggested that this co-operative system, in which co-operative societies produced mainly to meet their members' needs rather than to gain profit, would become the future mainspring of economic activity. Each co-operative society, operating within its own Rules, would be a miniature State based on justice and social benefit.[27] Ernest Poisson similarly argued that co-operative societies had the capacity to expand until they transformed the capitalist system into a co-operative one.[28] Dr Georges Fauquet, the first head of the International Labour Organisation's Co-operative Section, did not go quite so far, but none-the-less suggested that this evolutionary process could lead to a 'co-operative' sector in many economies.[29] Albert Thomas argued that the efficiency of the co-operative system would be enhanced if there were the closest possible links between different kinds of co-operative, but particularly between consumer and agricultural societies.[30]

The Swedish school of thought also subscribed to Rochdale co-operation. Its most notable exponent, Anders Oerne, believed that the Rochdale Principles should be the basis of any co-operative system. However, he did see co-operation in the Utopian terms of Robert Owen, or the rather more grandiose ones of the French. Instead, he believed that co-operation's strength lay in its appeal to self-interest.[31] Oerne held that people preferred to co-operate to provide themselves with goods and services rather than rely on the profit motive spurring others to do so for them. Oerne was critical of the profit motive in itself and of the preoccupation it caused among businessmen, politicians, and those of the left who sought protection from the competition it encouraged. Oerne argued that, because consumer co-operation was based on the welfare of consumers, it offered an alternative both to profit-making enterprises and State-planned economies. Like Gide, Fauquet, Poisson and Thomas, Oerne believed that co-operation had the capacity for limitless development.[32]

A fourth co-operative tradition was developing within the ICA, and derived from the changes brought about by the Russian Revolution. This will be considered in greater depth when we deal with the ICA'S response to Communism. At the moment, though, we should note that the co-operative system in the USSR underwent a number of changes in the 1920s, and that it was not until the mid-1930s that a more settled position emerged.

It seems that the changes brought Communism in the USSR, and Fascism in Italy, may have been one of the reasons why the French called for a review of the Rochdale Principles.

Besides these external reasons, internal ones were also developing. The 1925 debate on political neutrality had not lessened concern about the close political connections that some co-operative movements had. There was also growing doubt about how far co-operatives' secondary organisations, such as wholesales, banks and insurance societies, could observe the principles, particularly those of one member one vote and trading only for cash. Overall, there seemed to be a growing recognition that the Alliance could be facing a problem that, with its Constitution based so closely on the Rochdale Principles, it could hardly afford to ignore large-scale infringements of these Principles.

At the ICA'S Vienna Congress in 1930 the French delegation moved that a review of the Rochdale Principles should be undertaken. Its reasons included the fact that the Principles were now almost a hundred years old yet lacked a definitive statement. The French felt it desirable to agree a contemporary interpretation and definition so as to lessen the danger of different movements interpreting them in different ways.[33]

A spokesman for the Soviet delegation supported the proposal.[34] He stated that in the USSR the system of paying a dividend had been abandoned in favour of the collective utilisation of the surplus for common purposes. Centrosoyus condemned the dividend as being a capitalist principle which had led to the poorer members of a co-operative, who were the ones least able to buy, being the ones who received the smallest return.

Although the British delegation voiced reservations about the review they none-the-less agreed to it, as did the rest of the Vienna Congress. A special Committee, comprising the ICA Executive with co-opted members from Switzerland, Poland, Romania, Lithuania, Spain, Hungary and the USA, was appointed.[35] Between February, 1932 and January, 1934, the Special Committee met on seven occasions in Strasbourg, Prague, Geneva, Barcelona, Brussels, Vienna and Miramar d'Esterel. The review was administered by Henry May, General Secretary, who sent out a questionnaire to the Alliance's member organisations. It contained 37 questions under six main headings: Voluntary and Open Membership; Cash Trading; Democratic Control - One Man One vote; Dividend on Purchase - Elimination of Profit on Price; Limited Interest on Capital; and Political and Religious Neutrality.[36] The link with Rochdale was strengthened when, in an attempt to establish a 'standard by which to judge' the replies to the questionnaire, the Special Committee asked Henry May to prepare an 'objective memorandum' on the original rules and constitution of the Rochdale Pioneers' Society, as well as other existing documentation. May duly visited the Rochdale Society where he studied their 'ancient archives', and also met the daughter of one of the original Pioneers.

Not surprisingly, the Special Committee's Report came down in favour of restating the basic Rochdale Principles of Open Membership, Democratic Control, Dividend on Purchases, Limited Interest on Capital, Political and Religious Neutrality, Cash Trading and Promotion of Education. However, the report suggested that, whereas the first four were fundamental, the last three, although undoubtedly part of the Rochdale system, might have less contemporary importance. Nevertheless, the Special Committee felt that their non-observance could destroy the co-operative character of a society.[37] The Special Committee also elaborated 'Other Basic Principles of Co-operation'. Although these were not expressly included in the Rochdale Rules, it was widely believed that they were essential to the 'Co-operative System'.

The first of these was that it was necessary to trade exclusively with members if the co-operative system was to eliminate the profit-making motive. It was recognised, however, that it was difficult to sustain an 'arbitrary interpretation of this. Therefore, the Committee proposed that a 'limit as narrow as possible' should be imposed, to meet only the 'casual or accidental demands' of non-members.[38]

The second 'other basic principle' was that of voluntary co-operation. Although it was acknowledged that Rochdale Co-operation had been based on voluntarism, the Special Committee appeared to recognise that circumstances had changed. Its report noted that, although the Rochdale Pioneers had experienced hard economic conditions, they had enjoyed political freedom. They were as free as air to risk their savings in an Utopian enterprise and... the voluntary basis of their Society was, therefore, a sine qua non'[39] But it was recognised that in certain unnamed countries that had become 'virtual dictatorships' it was no longer possible for co-operatives to conform to Rochdale co-operation. However, the Committee stressed the ideal of recognising that the Principle was fundamental to the Co-operative System.[40]

Moving on to the third 'other basic principle', namely sale at current or market price, the Special Committee felt that, although the Pioneers had used this as a mechanism for convenience, and to blunt the opposition of private traders, contemporary non-observance of it could prove 'inimical to the interests of the community in general'. It therefore urged that it be retained.[41]

The fourth 'other basic principle' concerned co-operatives' 'inalienable assets'. The Special Committee noted that, while the Rochdale Pioneers, and subsequent British consumer co-operatives, had provided that, in the case of liquidation, the balance of assets over liabilities should be distributed among members holding shares, this was not always the case in other co-operative movements. Legislation applying to these often provided that societies' collective assets could not be divisible among members if liquidation occurred, but should instead be passed to other co-operatives, disinterested organisations, or public utilities. Although the Special Committee felt that, because of these opposing practices, it had been unable to come down on one side or the other, it none-the-less recommended that societies should make regular allocations to inalienable reserves. Moreover, it also recommended that national co-operative movements should work towards ensuring that their countries' co-operative legislation adequately dealt with the question of the indivisibility of collective assets.[42]

Overall, the Special Committee proposed that there should be no modification of the Rochdale Principles. It claimed that where departures from them had been made, either on grounds of helping poorer citizens or in order to keep pace with modern business developments, these had 'not been justified either on ethical or social grounds.[43]

The debate at the London Congress of 1934 on the Special Committee's Report proved inconclusive. Two stumbling blocks were quickly revealed. One was the principle of religious and political neutrality, while the other was that of cash trading. The British delegation moved that the whole report be referred back on account of these, arguing that they were practices rather than basic principles. They further argued that their co-operatives were having to operate in an economy that was increasingly planned and producer, rather than consumer oriented. It was because they had found it necessary to protect the consumer interests of their movement that they had formed their own Co-operative Party. Concerning cash trading, the British felt unable to continue supporting this because their experience showed that their two Wholesales conducted as much as 99 per cent of their trade with retail society members on the basis of credit.[44]

It is interesting to note that the Swedes, in particular, rejected the British position and took a more fundamental view. They supported the retention of cash trading on the grounds that turnover could be bought too dearly. Extending the credit system inevitably meant that co-operatives prices must rise, which could prove dangerous if competitors began a price war. As far as political neutrality was concerned, the Swedes argued once again that co-operatives were an economic, and not a political, form of organisation. Because the movement comprised people from many political creeds, engaging in party politics could eventually weaken and divide it.

A kind of middle position was taken by the French. Both Gide and Thomas had died in 1932, and French co-operative ideas were now being carried forward by Fauquet and Poisson. Fauquet joined the debate to indicate that the French supported the indivisibility of collective reserves, a principle which had been laid down in France by Buchez for workers' co-operatives and in Germany by Raiffeisen for credit societies. But, having said this, he urged that Co-operative Principles should not be so rigorously applied that they restricted co-operatives as 'living organisms': it was more important that the 'co-operative spirit' should exist within them. Swedish delegates also supported the idea of co-operatives being seen as 'living organisms' and argued that this meant trying to understand how they worked out 'in practice against the background of economic realities of today'. They felt that more should be found out about this, and therefore supported the reference back of the Special Committee's Report. This was agreed to by a large majority of the Congress.[45]

Other criticisms of the Report included the suggestion that it had been too consumer oriented and, when the reference back was agreed, the Special Committee was also asked to enquire into how other types of co-operative applied Co-operative Principles. Thus, in the second review the Committee widened their scope to include Co-operative Wholesale Societies, Workers' Productive Societies, Agricultural Productive Societies, Credit Societies and Co-operative Banks. However, it reported to the ICA's 1937 Paris Congress, that the responses from these had been disappointing and, in many cases, too vague to suggest firm conclusions.[46]

In their second report, the Special Committee concluded that consumer co-operatives were still generally based on Rochdale Principles, although 'insufficiently and incompletely' so. As far as other kinds of co-operative were concerned, the Committee believed that a less rigid interpretation of principle should be applied. For example, 'Dividend on Purchase' could become 'Distribution of the surplus to members in proportion to their transactions. Apart from this slight shift, the Special Committee appeared to have moved little in the intervening three years. It found that the seven basic principles advanced in their first report......still represent the essential basis of the Rochdale system, and that nothing in the modern developments of industry and commerce, or changes in economic method, has diminished their integrity.'[47]

From the point of view of trying to assess the ICA's ideology between 1910 and 1950, the 1930s review of Co-operative Principles leaves many questions. One obvious limitation was that the exercise had been conducted so much within the framework of consumer co-operation: too little attention had been paid, even the second time round, to how far Rochdale Principles could be applied to other kinds of co-operative. It was not only a question of defining how the surplus should be distributed. There was also the question of credit. Today we understand more clearly that agricultural, workers' co-operatives and thrift and credit societies use credit differently from the way in which consumer co-operatives do. Moreover, that 'open membership' can apply in consumer, and in some other kinds of, co-operatives. But it cannot easily do so in workers' and housing co-operatives, where either the volume of business, or the stock of housing, restricts entry. We should not perhaps be too critical. In the circumstances of the 1930s, the Special Committee's concentration on consumer co-operation is understandable, and it is necessary that we should try to understand the debate in the light of the conditions that then applied.

Included among these is the fact that the victory of consumer co-operation over producer co-operation was still recent, and ideas that consumer empowerment could transform large areas of capitalism still prevailed. Above all, there was a preponderance of consumer co-operatives within the Alliance at that time. Moreover, because the review had been firmly set within the framework of Rochdale Co-operation, its outcome was always likely to be consumer oriented. However, it is felt that neither report of the Special Committee really met the question posed by the Swedes of how co-operatives, as living organisms, operated in contemporary economic circumstances. On both occasions rather pious statements were made that the original Principles should retain their integrity, whatever economic changes had since occurred. One consequence for the Alliance was that the 1937 findings became less appropriate as other co-operative sectors increased their significance within it and that of consumer co-operatives declined. However, this process did not become marked until after 1950, although it did lead to the need for another review of Co-operative Principles in the 1960s. By virtue of its 1930s exercise, the International Co-operative Alliance became the guardian of Co-operative Principles.

Another reason to be cautious about the outcome of that first review was that it was firmly linked to a very specific place, Rochdale, at a very specific time, the mid-19th century. If the Special Committee had been able to argue that the Rochdale Principles were timeless, and that they could operate equally well in different periods and situations, there might have been some justification in retaining a static code. But it had not done so. Indeed, it acknowledged that some co-operative movements were operating under quite different regimes from that experienced by the Rochdale Pioneers. It also failed to take sufficient account of the fact that major member movements, e.g. the Soviets on dividend on purchase, and the British on politics and cash trading, were no longer observing some of the basic principles. This rather inconclusive debate might appear to weaken the case that ideology provides an important factor explaining the ICA's survival. However, it will later be argued that, from events and developments in the Alliance, it could be deduced that it was not so much a set of Principles that provided cohesion, but rather the co-operative spirit that they engendered. In other words, Fauquet had been right to call for a co-operative spirit to permeate co-operatives as 'living organisms'. The idea that there was a shared set of beliefs, however imperfectly observed, created a sense of solidarity, and encouraged goodwill and tolerance between ICA member organisations which, it will be argued, goes some way to explaining its survival.

Earlier, in Chapter 1[48] we argued that the original statement of Rochdale Principles by the Pioneers reflected certain underlying philosophical concepts such as democracy, equity, and a just price for labour. Reflected also were ideas of self-help, as distinct from paternalistic or State help, and collective action in the form of mutual aid between members. There was also a strong denial of the profit motive, which was closely linked to the underlying idea that co-operation between members was an antidote to the exploitation of worker and consumer fostered by capitalism and its emphasis on competition. It was, perhaps, a pity that the 1930s review had not brought out such underlying philosophical concepts more clearly. In fact, an example of how this might have been done had already been illustrated. In 1931, as editor of the *Review of International Co-operation*, Henry May had invited the leading British Co-operative thinker and writer, Thomas William Mercer, to write two articles under the heading of 'Foundation of Co-operation - Rochdale Principles and Methods'[49]. In these articles Mercer argued that the Rochdale Principles were practices, but he suggested that they reflected underlying Principles. These he identified as being Universality, Democracy, Economy, Publicity, Unity and Liberty. The fact that there was no sign of this approach in the Special

Committee's Reports suggests that it had found little favour. Had it done so, however, the results of the 1930s Review might have been longer lasting. So far in this section we have examined how the ICA's ideology was shaped by certain factors. These have included how far it differed from socialism, and how far it was shaped by important debates on political neutrality and on Co-operative Principles. No examination of ICA ideology would be complete, however, if we did not look at the Alliance's attitude to peace during the period.

Peace

In Chapter 1[50] we noted the ICA's links with the International Peace Bureau, and that at its Glasgow Congress in 1913 it passed its famous Peace Resolution. Before that, during the earliest discussions on the aims of the proposed Alliance, it had been suggested that these should include seeking to bring about social and international peace.[51] Thus we can see that the ICA had a long tradition of supporting peace which predates our period of 1910 to 1950. The ICA showed its concern for peace in a number of ways. One was its association with organisations such as the International Peace Bureau, the International Federation of Trade Unions and, in the late 1930s, the International Peace Campaign.

Another way was the papers it considered, and the resolutions it passed at its Congresses. Examples include the paper by Prof. Charles Gide on The Principles of International Right' presented to the ICA's Congress in Basle in 1921.[52] Essentially, this was about the Co-operative Movement's attitudes to the 1914-18 War, to future peace and to the League of Nations. At the same Congress [53] a resolution on the League was passed, welcoming it as a 'universal organisation of the people for the establishment of peace and the protection of the common interests of humanity. Later, at the Stockholm Congress in 1927, a resolution on world peace was passed.[54] Incidentally, it is interesting to observe that, although this resolution had been submitted by the British Co-operative Union, it had originated with the English Co-operative

Women's Guild, and that it was one of the ECWG's members, Mrs Barton, who moved the resolution. Throughout the inter-war years women in the ICA, mainly through the International Co-operative Women's Guild, were even more active than the ICA itself on questions of peace.

Another illustration of the Alliance's peace advocacy was its involvement with the International Conference on Disarmament which met in Geneva between 1932 and 1934. Its aim was to secure reductions national armaments in line with League of Nations Covenant. The Conference failed, partly because the French insisted that general security system should precede disarmament, and partly because more came power in Germany in 1933. In fact, later that year, Germany walked out of the conference. [55]

The ICA was involved with the Conference in two main ways. The through its request to the League of Nations appoint Observers. When this was agreed the General Secretary, President, Vice Presidents member the Executive took turns attend sessions of the Conference. The second way which the Alliance involved was through the statement that submitted the Conference President, The Right Honourable Arthur Henderson, British Foreign Secretary, 1929-31. This included passages from ICA's resolutions at the Glasgow, Basle and Stockholm Congresses, and Henderson referred the statement in his Conference address. Later the ICA circulated copies member organisations, urging their active support for disarmament. When ICA's next Congress was in London 1934, one main speakers Arthur Henderson this Congress Central Committee proposed resolution 'Peace Disarmament'. Although passed, was accepted unanimously. Centrosoyus had submitted amendment, which was lost large majority, and the Danes opposed resolution not much because they objected to disarmament, because they believed that ICA should limit itself to co-operative matters. By the time of the Alliance's next Congress, in Paris in 1937, fears of another war had deepened. Already, the Alliance had joined the International Peace Campaign [56], and the Paris Congress went on to pass a further Peace Resolution.[57]

All to no avail: the Second World War began in September, 1939. Almost immediately after its end, in 1945, the Cold War developed and threatened peace in new ways. It became more difficult for the Alliance to maintain a pro-peace stance because of its need to reconcile the views of Centrosoyus and the Eastern European co-operative movements with those of co-operative movements in the West.

Questions surrounding the issue of peace will be examined in greater depth as we proceed chronologically through the later chapters. At this point, though, we are only concerned to show that the pursuit of peace was a consistent element in ICA policy and, as such, reflected a deeper ideological concern.

That the Alliance saw itself as a serious pro-peace organisation, was illustrated by the fact that it advanced the idea that a leading co-operative figure should be nominated to receive the Nobel Peace Prize. In March, 1928, the ICA Executive decided to canvass the idea [58] and even went so far as to invite national co-operative organisations to propose nominees. However, these moves came to an abrupt halt when it was found that, under Clause 3 of the Statutes of the Nobel Foundation, the ICA had no right of nomination.[59]

We can perhaps conclude this section by noting that there were two potentially competing elements in the ICA's ideology. One was its attempt to remain politically neutral. The other was its involvement in peace promotion activities, including its support for the League of Nations. The latter was likely to lead the Alliance into taking political judgements or positions, and certainly it was unable to avoid doing so on the two great and competing ideologies of the 20th century, Fascism and Communism. The fact that the Alliance showed that it could tolerate and accommodate the latter far more easily than the former is another way in which it reveals itself to be a typical working-class organisation of its time.

Having looked at specific issues in ICA ideology from 1910 to 1950, we can perhaps close this section by noting two physical manifestations of ideology developed by the ICA.

Ideological Manifestations

An organisation which has an ideology sometimes gives physical expression to it. An obvious example is the trade unions and their banners. In the 1920s the International Co-operative Alliance developed two examples by introducing its own flag and instituting International Co-operative Day.

In 1922 the ICA Central Committee unanimously agreed a proposal by the Alliance's President, G. J. D. C. Goedhart of Holland, that there should be an annual International Co-operative Day. This was to be held on the first Saturday in July, and was intended to propagate co-operative ideals and foster co-operative internationalism. We can get an idea of the first one in 1923 from the following account.

'Telegrams of greeting passed from land to land. Artists, decorators, writers, orators, singers, athletes and, above all, simple Co-operators, joined in forming a chain of festivity and fraternity across the whole continent of Europe with extension into Asia and America, which is without precedent in the annals of voluntary associations of the workers'.[60]

A year later the Alliance adopted its own flag. Its design, suggested by Prof. Charles Gide but originally proposed by the French at the 1896. Paris Congress, contained the colours of the spectrum 'arranged in horizontal stripes of equal proportion and in their recognised order'.[61] The design of the 'Rainbow Flag', as it came to be known, reflected two elements of co-operative thinking. One was that no single colour predominated to suggest similarity with any national flag: all colours were equal. The other was the ancient folk belief that a crock of gold might be found at the end of a rainbow. It is reasonable to suppose that these two physical examples of internationalism are likely to have increased member organisations' identification with the Alliance, and also increased cohesion within the organisation. Above all, they reflected an active ideology.

Conclusion

It has been helpful to summarise the Alliance's organisation and ideology during the period 1910-1950. They provide an important back drop to the events with which we will now deal chronologically. We will find that they will illumine ICA attitudes and reactions to events and that they will permeate the rest of this work.

Notes

1. WATKINS, W. P., *The International Co-operative Alliance, London*, 1970, p. 49.
2. *ibid.*, pp. 49-51.
3. *ibid.*, p. 66.
4. *ibid.*, p. 66.
5. *ibid.*, pp. 86-87.
6. *ibid.*, pp. 86-89.
7. *ibid.*, p. 127.
8. *ibid.*, p. 149.
9. *ibid.*, p. 162.
10. *ibid.*, p. 176.
11. *ibid.*, p. 189.
12. *ibid.*, p. 205.
13. *ibid.*, p. 230.
14. *ibid.*, p. 250.
15. International Co-operative Alliance, *Report of ICA Congress, London 1934, International Co-operative Alliance, London, 1934*, Appendix VI.
16. International Co-operative Alliance, *Report of ICA Congress, Prague 1948, International Co-operative Alliance, London, 1948*, Appendix VII.
17. ICA Archives, *Minutes of the Meeting of ICA Executive, Paris, 16th March, 1940*, p. 2.
18. WATKINS, W. P., *op. cit.*, pp. 58-59.
19. *ibid.*, pp. 85-86.
20. GIDE, Prof. Charles, *The International Co-operative Alliance*, International Co-operative Alliance, London, (Presumed date of publication 1920).

21. International Co-operative Alliance, *Report of ICA Congress, Basle, 1921*, p. 137
22. ICA Archives, *Minutes of the Special Meeting of ICA Executive, with Representatives of the Co-operative Unions of Denmark, Finland, Latvia, Lithuania and Estonia, Stockholm, 28th June, 1925*, PP. 2-3.
23. ICA Archives, *Minutes of Special Meeting of ICA Executive, Stockholm*, p. 2.
24. International Co-operative Alliance, *Report of the ICA Congress, Ghent, 1924*, pp. 219-226.
25. ICA Archives, *Minutes of Special Meeting of ICA Executive and Representatives of Northern Co-operative Unions, op. cit.*, pp. 2-3.
26. International Co-operative Alliance, *Report of the ICA Congress, Stockholm,* pp. 60-63.
27. BONNER, Arnold, *British Co-operation Co-operative Union Ltd., Manchester, 1961*, p. 30.
28. *ibid.*, p. 295.
29. FAUQUET, Dr Georges, *The Co-operative Sector, Co-operative Union, Manchester, 1942*.
30. International Co-operative Alliance, *Report of the ICA Congress, Basle, 1921*, pp. 84-92.
31. BONNER, Arnold, *op. cit.*, p. 295.
32. BONNER, Arnold, *ibid.*, pp. 293-294.
33. International Co-operative Alliance, *Report of the ICA Congress, Vienna, 1930,* pp. 156-158.
34. International Co-operative Alliance, *ibid.*, pp. 158-159.
35. International Co-operative Alliance, *Report of the ICA Congress, London, 1934*, p. 131.
36. International Co-operative Alliance, *ibid* p. 132.
37. International Co-operative Alliance, *Report of ICA Congress London, 1934,* p. 155.
38. International Co-operative Alliance, *ibid.*, pp. 150-151
39. *ibid.*, p. 151.
40. *ibid.*, p. 152.
41. *ibid.*, p. 153.
42. *ibid.*, p. 156.
43. *ibid.*, p. 157.
44. *ibid.*, p. 166.

45. *ibid.*, p. 175.
46. International Co-operative Alliance, *Report of the ICA Congress Paris, 1937*, p. 145.
47. International Co-operative Alliance, *ibid.*, p. 167.
48. This Study, Chapter 1, pp. 7-10.
49. International Co-operative Alliance, *Review of International Co-operation*, London, No. 9, September, 1931 and No. 10, October, 1931.
50. This Study, Chapter 1, p. 30.
51. This Study, Chapter 1, p. 18.
52. International Co-operative Alliance, *Report of the ICA Congress, Basle, 1921*, pp. 127-143.
53. International Co-operative Alliance, *ibid.*, p. 178.
54. International Co-operative Alliance, *Report of the ICA Congress, Stockholm*, 1927, pp. 229-235.
55. PALMER, Alan, *The Penguin Dictionary of Modern History 1789 - 1945*, p. 100.
56. International Co-operative Alliance, *Report of the ICA Congress Paris, 1937*, pp. 110 - 112.
57. International Co-operative Alliance, *ibid.*, p. 126.
58. ICA Archives, *Minutes of the Meeting of the ICA Executive, Bremen, 28th-30th March, 1928*, p. 7.
59. ICA Archives, *Minutes of the Meeting of the ICA Executive, Liege, 26th-27th June, 1928*, p. 3.
60. International Co-operative Alliance, *Report of the ICA Congress, Ghent,* 1924, p. 75.
61. ICA Archives, *Memorandum on the Agenda of Meeting of ICA Executive, Paris,* 23rd - 24th May, 1924.

Chapter three

The International Co-operative Alliance and the First World War

Introduction

During the first two chapters we have been concerned to show the kind of body into which the ICA developed between 1895 and 1914. We have also tried to describe its main organisational and ideological features. Because it is felt that greater space should be allocated to dealing with the ICA during the Second World War and the Cold War, this chapter will be briefer than others.

We should begin by noting that the Alliance survived the 1914-18 War at a number of different levels. Personal links and friendships continued. Member co-operative movements survived the war, their doing so being a prerequisite of the Alliance's survival. The small ICA Secretariat continued to operate and to maintain the production of the Bulletin of International Co-operation. In addition, the ICA Executive managed to function much as before, helped no doubt by the fact that its members all came from the same country which was one that had not been overrun by war.

We will consider each of these points, and then go on to examine how the Alliance began the delicate task of resuming its activities after the war.

Maintenance of Relations

Despite the increased nationalism engendered by war, sympathetic relations continued among ICA leaders. Indirect links survived where direct ones could no longer do so, assisted by the Dutch co-operative leader, G. J. D. C. Goedhart, who acted as an intermediary. He also helped Henry May, the Alliance's General Secretary, to maintain the production of the ICA Bulletin. Their correspondence, conducted in impeccable English, but often delayed by postal and censorship difficulties, also provided interesting insights to wartime developments. Upon the outbreak of the war their despair was reflected in a letter from May:

'...our worst fears have been realised and we are plunged into the vortex of an European War. All our protestations of international friendship have gone by the board.'[1]

Throughout the war their letters were interspersed with matters of human interest. On one occasion May enclosed a letter for a friend who was anxious 'to get it through to Breslau' but was unable to post it direct. Another time he enquired on behalf of a friend whose 'daughter is a governess in Dresden', while in another letter he mentioned a lady in Hamburg whose 'sweetheart is in German East Africa'. Goedhart and May also forwarded letters on behalf of the relatives of Prisoners of War on both sides.

Once there was also an enquiry on behalf of an English co-operative society which wanted to learn if one of its employees, interned in Holland for the duration of the war, might be able to work at his trade in a branch of a Dutch co-operative society.

May and Goedhart also exchanged news concerning co-operative figures. Thus we learn that the French co-operative leader, Ernest Poisson, was serving with the French army, while the eldest son of Heinrich Kaufmann, the German co-operative leader, had been killed in the Battle of the Somme in July, 1916. Wartime division did not inhibit the paying of respects. In November, 1916, May wrote to Goedhart on the death of the leading German co-operative figure, Adolf von Elm. Three years earlier he had been one of the proposers of the ICA's Peace Resolution at the Glasgow Congress. May wrote:

'The Executive received the sad news with very deep regret and every member expressed his admiration for the work and character of Mr. von Elm. A suitable resolution will be included in the Minutes and published in the Bulletin but a general desire was expressed that some means should be taken of conveying to his friends in Hamburg, the sincere sympathy of the Committee with them in their loss.'

May also asked Goedhart if he would:

'convey these expressions of sympathy to Mr. Kaufmann and ask him to communicate them to other friends of Mr. von Elm'.[2]

International Co-operative Bulletin.

| 8th Year. | No. 2. | FEBRUARY, 1915. |

The Alliance and the War.

The Co-operative Press.

Six months ago when we were suddenly overwhelmed by the outbreak of war, the Executive of the Alliance were confronted with the task of determining the lines on which the work of the ICA should proceed during the continuance of the European upheaval.

George Jacob Holyoake had once declared that the British Co-operative Movement would hardly withstand the shock of a great war, and in the first excitement of that reversion to the barbaric arbitrament of the sword, it was felt by some that the Alliance of Co-operators in the various countries must be shattered by such an unspeakable conflict.

They remembered, with a sharp pang at thought of the change which twelve short months had wrought, the happy and successful gathering with our comrades from many lands which had taken place in Glasgow at the International Congress of 1913.

They thought of the resolution on International Peace; of the eloquent speeches with which it was supported by our colleagues from Holland, Germany, France, Norway, and Great Britain; of the wonderful demonstration with which the delegates received the announcement of the President that it had been carried without dissentient voice or vote. And as they thought of these things, there flashed through their minds an instant of doubt. Could it be that that great demonstration at Glasgow was only a "pious expression of opinion" after all, and not a consummation devoutly to be wished?

Picking up on the reference to the ICA Bulletin, we should note that its continued publication, on a monthly basis, throughout the war should be considered a remarkable achievement and an indication of the ICA's capacity for improvisation and organisation. May and Goedhart played central roles.

Bulletin of International Co-operation

When war broke out the British Government issued a regulation for bidding the publication of any journal in the language of a country that was at war with Britain. This made it impossible to continue printing the German edition of the Bulletin in London.[3] Thus, at a meeting in May, 1915, the ICA Executive asked Henry May:

'To communicate with Mr. Kaufmann through Mr. Goedhart, suggesting that the German Union might undertake the sole responsibility of publishing the German edition for the time being; the manuscript could be sent on from the office of the Alliance, the translation completed and published by the German Union which could collect the Bulletin subscriptions from the subscribers.'[4]

Goedhart had already anticipated this request and had made an informal approach to Kaufmann in Hamburg, who had responded favourably. Kaufmann also expressed other views which Goedhart forwarded to May:

'...his long letter, in which he says much about the chance of the ending of the war, that he and his friends advocate "CO-OPERATIVE NEUTRALITY"* and do not feel themselves in private war against the co-operators of other countries, but that they do most earnestly hope that the co-operative organisations of the other warfaring nations are doing as well as the German ones. The letter ends with this sentence. "So we do wish that after the war the former friendly relations between various co-operative organisations shall be restored in order that we may be able to take up again our work for the promotion of co-operative ideals?" I think that you will be glad to read this; for as I, you will have been afraid that the war will have put a stop to the development of our Alliance.'[5]

*author's capitals

May later wrote to Goedhart that he had conveyed Kaufmann's sentiments to a co-operative conference in London, where they had been received with 'considerable approval'. Moreover, William Maxwell, President of the Alliance, had not only expressed his 'appreciation of the message', but had asked 'us to convey a similar expression of our sentiments to Mr. Kaufmann'[6].

By November, 1915, the German edition of the Bulletin was being published. In the following February, the Swiss Co-operative Union began to print the French edition, which it then sent to its counterpart in France for distribution to French subscribers.[7] May retained overall editorial responsibilities. However, these were complicated by his wish to preserve both the Bulletin's neutrality and co-operative orthodoxy.

'Our friend Daude-Bancel* has been away a good deal...so that we have had very little information from France, and of course none from Belgium except scraps from the Swiss papers. Emancipation, the paper of de Boyve, and in which Gide writes so much, comes in regularly to hand, but it is so full of war and politics that I cannot use it for the Bulletin just now, not only on grounds of Censorship but also because the views expressed are often very strong.'[8]

* responsible for French arrangements for the Bulletin

May treated other articles with caution, even if they did not relate directly to the war but might upset co-operative leaders in belligerent countries. An example concerned an article that he received from the Austrian, Mrs Emmy Freundlich, in 1916, in which she advocated an international co-operative women's organisation. May wrote to Goedhart:

'...it was decidedly premature to discuss just now...Mr. Kaufmann need not be afraid that I shall go too far in finding space for such articles'.[9]

May also had problems of paucity of material. In the same letter, he told Goedhart that he had had difficulty in getting any material for the Bulletin from Norway, Denmark and Russia.

Despite such difficulties, the Bulletin continued to be published throughout the war. It is likely to have helped maintain member organisations' identity with the Alliance, and also to have assisted internal cohesion.

We have already observed that a prerequisite of the Alliance's survival during the 1914-18 War was the survival of its member co-operative movements. All survived the turbulent period, but with varying degrees of success. We should therefore take a brief look at the main ways in which the war affected them and its ramifications for the ICA.

ICA Member Co-operative Movements During the 1914-1918 War

Official ICA Minutes and correspondence give a good insight, but a more graphic account can be found in a report published by the ICA, Reports of the Central Organisations On Their Activities During the War.[10] The idea for this report came from Ernest Poisson, France, and it performed the useful function of allowing ICA member movements to reintroduce themselves to each other during the period between the end of the war and the resumption of ICA meetings.

Running to 94 pages, the Report includes accounts of wartime experiences from 20 ICA member organisations in Armenia, Austria, Belgium, Canada, Czechoslovakia, Denmark, Finland, France, Georgia, Germany, Great Britain, Holland, Hungary, Italy, Norway, Russia, Spain, Switzerland, the Ukraine and the United States. Reports varied in substance and length, those of Canada and Spain each being one page while that of Russia ran to 13.

Generally speaking, because of what they brought to the national war effort, co-operative movements improved their standing with their national Governments. In Britain and Germany co-operative-owned facilities such as bakeries, butcheries, horses, and co-operative halls, as well as foodstuffs, were requisitioned to provision the armed forces. Elsewhere, Governments used consumer co-operatives to channel rationed goods, though a number of movements, such as the British one, introduced rationing among their own members before this so as to ensure an equitable distribution of goods which were rapidly becoming scarce. As far as Governments were concerned consumer co-operatives, with their mass memberships, provided a firm base for a war time system of distribution. Moreover, they were most closely identified with the working classes and Governments found it increasingly necessary to work with these as the war intensified.

There were a number of consequences for consumer co-operatives becoming large-scale distributors of government-rationed goods. One was that, in some countries, their membership widened to include the middle classes, who were not traditionally members. Where co-operative movements, such as that in Austria, limited their trade to members only, it meant that people had to join the co-operatives to receive rationed goods. In other countries, though, such as in Russia and Norway, Governments compelled consumer co-operatives to trade with non-members, thus causing them to break a Co-operative Principle, about which both movements expressed their regrets in reports to the ICA.

However, the widening of co-operatives' membership was likely to benefit the ICA, because its subscription was based on the national movements' membership rather than on their trade. Co-operatives' assistance to Governments meant that, at least during the war, they improved their standing with them. The French even went so far as to say in their report: 'Our influence became such that in all questions of food distribution no reforms were introduced without our being consulted.'[11]

Such developments were likely to raise questions about co-operatives' political neutrality, particularly as a number of co-operative leaders were brought into war-time administrations or, like Goedhart in Holland, Aneurin Williams in Britain and Väinö Tanner in Finland, were elected as Members of Parliament. More notably, Dr Karl Renner in Austria and Albert Thomas in France both became wartime Ministers. Despite closer relations with Governments, some co-operative movements felt that they were unfairly treated. In Britain dissatisfaction with what was believed to be preferential treatment for private traders led to action by the British Co-operative Congress. In 1917 it decided to attempt to secure direct representation in Parliament and local authorities.

Subsequently, the National Co-operative Parliamentary Representation Committee was formed. It later became known as the Co-operative Party and still exists today. At the 1918 General Election it ran 10 candidates, including Henry May, General Secretary of the Alliance, although he and the nine others were unsuccessful.

In passing, we can perhaps note that direct political action was also attempted in Russia, although this seems to have been more of an attempt to increase co-operatives' political standing between the first and second Russian Revolutions than to seek to redress war-time in justices. We read from the Russian report:

'In October (1917) a conference of the representatives of co-operative unions held in Moscow, in spite of the protests of many prominent co-operative workers, came to the conclusion that Co-operation, as such, should participate in the Constituent Assembly putting forward its own list of candidates and entering into political agreements with other political parties. This POLITICAL SIN* of Russian Co-operation, dictated though it was by the laudable intention of saving democracy and Socialism from the onslaught of the demagogues, ended in decisive failure. Not a single candidate on the co-operative lists was elected. It must be pointed out that the Centrosoyus (Central Co-operative Union) as an organisation abstained from taking part in the elections. That step, however, made it possible for the adversaries of Co-operation to accuse it of adopting a "counter-revolutionary" character and very much enfeebled its position in the ensuing struggle for its economic independence.' *author's capitals

This report indicates, like a number of others, that co-operative movements had to respond to revolution as well as to war. Immediately after the war many also had to adjust to changes in their national boundaries, which had a direct impact on the ICA. Under the Peace Settlements countries such as Poland, Czechoslovakia, Armenia, the

Ukraine, Georgia, Estonia, Lithuania and Latvia became independent and the co-operative movements within them applied for ICA membership. Before the war the Alliance, because it did not accept applications from movements whose countries lacked national identity, had rejected applications from the Polish and Czechoslovak Co-operative Unions.[12] As we saw, under their new status Armenian, Ukrainian and Czechoslovak Co-operative Movements submitted reports to the ICA on their war-time experiences. Consequently, at the end of the war, the ICA needed not only to bring together co-operative movements whose countries had opposed each other in war, but also to adjudicate which movements had the right of representation in the ICA.

At the end of the war there may have been some in the Alliance who regretted that subscriptions were based on membership rather than on member movements sales. The reason was that during the war, many movements had made large sales increases: Austria 600 per cent, Finland 500 per cent, Czechoslovakia and France 300 per cent, Britain almost 200 per cent and Switzerland 50 per cent. Often these increases: were due not only to new members trading with co-operatives because of rationing schemes, but also to war-time inflation.

It was more difficult to establish how co-operatives' capital base had changed. The German movement reported that theirs had improved because food shortages had crippled sales and surplus spending power had found its way into co-operatives' savings which rose from 60 million Marks in 1914 to 177 million in 1918.

'This substantial increase is due chiefly to the increase in savings deposits of members. Very high wages were paid in the war industries. The general scar city of provisions was responsible for a fundamental lowering of the standard of living. Workmen were unable to buy the requisites they needed, simply because they were not to be had. In consequence, considerable savings were effected, which were deposited in the savings banks of the co-operative societies.'[13]

By contrast, Belgian co-operatives found that their savings banks were besieged with demands for the repayment of members' shares.

'Between 1914-1915, the greater part of the share capital had been reimbursed to co-operators, all of whom had been hard hit by the stoppage of industry'.[14]

Elsewhere, co-operative movements exploited new opportunities. Although part of their movement had been overrun, the French acted on Albert Thomas's suggestion that new co-operatives should be formed to provide stores and restaurants for the workers massed in war-production factories. The French National Federation of Consumer Co-operatives also decided to undertake propaganda among French soldiers. Where these were being exploited by wartime profiteers, it urged its member societies to supply those at the front with goods by means of 'travelling bazaars'.[15]

One can perhaps conclude this section by noting that although ICA member movements experienced different things during the war all managed to survive. This helped to ensure that the Alliance itself would survive. But the ICA had other problems to overcome, including how it was to resume its activities after the war.

Resumption of ICA Activities after the War

It can be argued that the ICA's survival of the First World War owed quite as much to how it resumed its activities as to how it managed its business during the war. Despite ties of personal friendship and co-operative loyalty and neutrality, the war had brought strains between ICA member movements, particularly between those in Belgium, France, and Germany, which were core members of the Alliance. This goes some way to explaining the ICA Executive's caution about calling a meeting of the Central Committee or convening a Congress.

We should remind ourselves that the ICA Executive was still all-British and that such caution might well have been a national characteristic. Having said that, we should also note that an Executive comprising just one nationality helped the Alliance to avoid the kind of damaging split that could have occurred had its membership been wider and included, for example, French, German and Belgian members. In all probability, an international executive would not have been able to have met during the war whereas the all-British Executive did so, thus providing a measure of continuity that was important in a relatively young organisation.

Another benefit derived from the Alliance having been based in a country which, although at war, was not overrun. In 1910 there had been the possibility that the ICA would move to Hamburg.[16] Had that materialised it is likely that, given the part that Germany played in the 1914-18 War, it would have been more difficult to sustain even the limited functions that did continue through the war. Moreover, the resumption of ICA activities would probably have been more difficult.

While the all-British Executive and small Secretariat were cautious throughout the war, and in its immediate aftermath, they at least acted constitutionally and with the wider interests of the Alliance in mind. This can be seen in a number of ways. One was with the question of financial assistance to co-operative movements devastated by war. The most badly affected was the Belgian movement, which had appealed for ICA help as early as the end of 1914.[17] Although sympathetic, the Executive decided not to mobilise ICA member movements' help at that stage. One reason was that they could not know how many others would seek similar help: they already thought that societies in north eastern France were likely to make a similar appeal. Instead, the Executive asked the British Co-operative Union if British societies could be approached with a view to their assisting Belgian co-operatives until the Executive could agree a more definite line. The question was delayed further when, at an Executive meeting in March, 1915, it was suggested that the setting up of a relief fund should be delayed until the end of the war, when the position would be clearer. [18]

It is debatable quite what the Executive could have done in a European war which was to widen into a world war, and which became ever more dislocating and bitter. The Alliance still had only limited organisational capacity, with a small Secretariat which was unlikely to have exceeded three or four during the war. Moreover, Henry May combined the position of General Secretary with that of Parliamentary Secretary to the British Co-operative Union, and did not become the ICA's full-time General Secretary until after the war. Furthermore, as we have seen, he held parliamentary ambitions. Perhaps it is not surprising, therefore, that the Minutes of the Executive's meetings during the first year of the war show that routine and fairly mundane matters were still uppermost in members' minds: arrangements for the Congress due to be held in Berne in 1916, but which was never convened; applications for membership; and Alliance representation at ICA member movements' Congresses. Financial reports and staff matters were also discussed. Moreover, the full devastation that the war would bring could hardly have been anticipated. In these circumstances the caution about raising a relief fund becomes more understandable.

Despite the constraints upon it, the ICA Executive always acted constitutionally. An example was its attitude to three conferences called by the French National Federation of Consumer Co-operatives.

The objective of the first, held in 1916, was to 'prepare the way for the resumption of the work of the Alliance at the conclusion of the war'.[19] Nevertheless the Executive declined the French invitation to participate on the grounds that:

...as the conference will represent not even neutral countries they fear that their attendance would be inconsistent with their position as the Executive Committee of the Alliance and of the co-operative organisations of all countries, and might be capable of misinterpretation. [20]

This Inter-Allied Conference, as it came to be known, was to be held at the same time as the Congress of the French National Federation of Consumer Co-operatives and, while the ICA Executive appointed the President and Secretary to attend that on their behalf, they requested them to take no part in any of the official proceedings, social or otherwise, in connection with the Inter-Allied Conference'.[21]

While the ICA Executive took a cautious but constitutionally correct position with regard to this conference, and the two which followed in 1919, we should none-the-less consider them in some detail because they helped to shape the Alliance's post-war Agenda. Before doing so we should note that they illustrate the point made elsewhere that, at different times, different ICA member movements made the intellectual running in the Alliance. At this time it was the French. The 1916 conference considered three main subjects: Economic policy during and after the War', 'Our responsibility towards co-operative societies which have suffered during the War', and 'The organisation of an international wholesale'. These questions were taken further at the second Conference in Paris in February, 1919, which also considered The Influence of the Peace Treaty on Economic Relations between the Peoples and on Co-operation. Attendance at the third Conference, held in Paris in June, 1919, was widened to include representatives from organisations in neutral countries, and this enabled Aneurin Williams, Chairman of the ICA Executive, and Henry May, the General Secretary, to attend on behalf of the ICA. The fact that the conference was attended by co-operative representatives from 'no less than 20 States suggests that an enthusiasm existed for the resumption of international co-operative relations, an impression underlined by the topics considered. These were International co-operative policy after the war and the economic relations of the peoples'. The organisation of commercial relations between the Co-operative Wholesale Societies, and When, how, and under what conditions international relations should be resumed [22]

The last item may have been an attempt to get a cautious ICA Executive to call the first post-war meetings of the Alliance. Certainly, it led to the proposal that a special meeting of the Executive be called in August, 1919, at which the date, place and agenda for a meeting of the Central Committee should be considered. Geneva was suggested as was further suggested that this meeting of the Central Committee should include discussion on the resumption of the ICA's work, arrangements for the first post-war Congress, and consideration of the three Inter-Allied and Neutral Conferences held in Paris.

The third Paris conference also recommended that members of the Central Committee be informed of the proposed meeting of the Executive in August, 1919 so that they might attend if they were able to be in London.

When the Executive meeting was held, in addition to members of the Executive there were also members of the Central Committee from Great Britain, Belgium, France, Switzerland, Russia and Finland, a further indication of the interest in resuming ICA activities. Linked to the question of when and where the ICA should hold its first post-war meetings there were the proposals from French and American co-operative organisations that Co-operation, 'either through the Alliance or its national sections', should be represented at the Peace Conference at the end of the war. The Co-operative League of the USA, which had joined the Alliance in 1917, further suggested that an International Co-operative Congress should be held at the same time.

The Executive did not act on the first part of this suggestion. Instead it focused on the difficulties of calling ICA meetings. Its views were summed up in a memorandum prepared by Henry May.

'Men's minds will necessarily be full of war bitterness and very difficult questions with regard to territory, nationalities, annexations or no annexations, indemnities or no indemnities, will have to be decided. These questions do not directly concern the Alliance as such. At the co-operative gathering serious friction might arise with consequent great injury to the future harmony and usefulness of the Alliance.

It is therefore suggested that a declaration by the Co-operators of the world in favour of a League of Nations would be more useful than the immediate meeting and that, after an interval of time, a meeting of the Alliance might be held with the excellent hope of the re-establishment of relations between Co-operative bodies in various lands.[23]

Quite apart from these reasons, there were also practical difficulties in calling a meeting of the Central Committee. When it was suggested that it be held in Geneva, in December, 1919, Heinrich Kaufmann, Germany, asked for a delay because of:

'difficulties of travel to Geneva in December in view of the coal shortage, there would be neither heating nor lighting in trains in addition to which the journey from Hamburg would take at least five or six days'.[24]

These difficulties were taken into account, and the Central Committee's meeting was delayed until April, 1920[25], while the first post-war Congress followed in Basle in August, 1921[26]. It is perhaps fitting to view that Congress through the eyes of the American delegate Dr James Peter Warbasse. His observation suggests that it had indeed been wise to go slowly in bringing the ICA together again after the First World War. He said:

'At that Congress I saw Frenchmen greet Germans, and I saw a German salute Henry May, its Secretary, and felicitate him upon the event. On that occasion I realised what Mr. May had done. It had been his organising ability that had accomplished this union of estranged people.'[27]

Dr Johnson once wrote that 'no man is on oath when writing a lapidary inscription', and perhaps we should be careful of Warbasse's judgement, penned almost two decades later. The quotation comes from a special edition of the *Review of International Co-operation*, which was published as a Memorial to May after his death in November, 1939. None-the-less, it suggests that May had helped to shape the ICA Executive's cautious approach in the resumption of ICA activities after the war, and that this approach had been justified.

Conclusions

We might perhaps note that many International Non-Governmental Organisations failed during the First World War. Before 1895, the year in which the ICA was founded, the number of International Non-Governmental Organisations never exceeded 50. Between 1895 and 1914 their number rose sharply to around 130. Probably as a result of the war, that figure fell back to approximately 50.[28] The Alliance had therefore gained something of an achievement by surviving. Some of the reasons for its doing so were merely fortuitous, like being based in Britain and having an all-British Executive. Others, however, stemmed from the nature of its organisation and ideology.

The Alliance also exhibited some detachment from the war, stemming no doubt from the fact that it saw itself as an international working class organisation. Like other left-wing movements, it believed the war to be an imperialistic war. In November, 1939, Henry May wrote about the differences between the origins of the First and Second World Wars. He held that the former had been an imperialist war arising from secret diplomacy in which ordinary people had no part or knowledge. [29] In other words, while ordinary people could not avoid involvement, the war was not of their making. Such detachment might help to explain why goodwill and tolerance could survive at a personal level among ICA figures, as illustrated by the greetings from Heinrich Kaufmann and conveyed by G. J. D. C. Goedhart in 1915.

The war strengthened another element evolving within ICA ideology. This was its belief that it, rather than the League of Nations, was the real League of the People. In Chapter 2 we noted the somewhat high flown attitude to the League of Nations when Prof. Gide suggested that the ICA should welcome it as a 'younger sister'.[30]

While the ICA's claim that it was the 'Real League of the People' may seem grandiose, we should keep in mind its geographical spread, and the comment by Judge and Skjelsbaek that, at one time, only three nations could boast higher populations than the ICA could affiliated individual members.[31]

As we shall see in later chapters, the Alliance, having kept together through the First World War, became organisationally stronger. It also developed an ideology that enabled it to decide its attitude to both Communism and Fascism, which were about to develop.

Notes

1. ICA Archives, Letter from Henry May to G. J. D. C. Goedhart 11th August, 1914.
2. ICA Archives, Letter from Henry May to G. J. D. C. Goedhart, 3rd November, 1916.
3. WATKINS, W. P., *The International Co-operative Alliance*, The International Co-operative Alliance, London, 1970, p. 102.
4. ICA Archives, *Minutes of the meeting of the ICA Executive, London*, 21st May, 1915, p. 2.
5. Letter from G. J. D. C. Goedhart to Henry May, 16th April, 1915.
6. Letter from Henry May to G. J. D. C. Goedhart, 27th April, 1915.
7. *Minutes of the meeting of ICA Executive*, London, 23rd February, 1916.
8. Letter from Henry May to G. J. D. C. Goedhart, 15th December, 1916.
9. Letter from Henry May to G. J. D. C. Goedhart, 15th August, 1916.
10. International Co-operative Alliance, *Reports of the Central Organisations On Their activities During The War*, International Co-operative Alliance, London, 1921, p. 34.
11. *ibid.*, p. 75.
12. GIDE, Prof. Charles, *The International Co-operative Alliance*, London, 1920, footnote 9.
13. International Co-operative Alliance, *Reports of Central Organisations*, op. cit., p. 42.
14. *ibid.*, p. 13.
15. *ibid.*, p. 34.
16. GIDE, Prof. Charles, *The International Co-operative Alliance op. cit.*, pp. 9-10.
17. ICA Archives, *Minutes of meeting of ICA Executive, London, 14th December, 1914*, p. 2.
18. ICA Archives, *Minutes of meeting of ICA Executive, London, 15th March, 1915*, p. 1.
19. International Co-operative Alliance, *Report of ICA Congress, Basle, 1921*, p. 22.
20. ICA Archives, *Minutes of meeting of ICA Executive, London, 26th July, 1916*, pp. 1-2.
21. *Minutes of meeting of ICA Executive, London, 19th September, 1916*, p. 1.

22. International Co-operative *Alliance, Report of the ICA Congress 2 Basle, 1921*, pp. 22-24.
23. WATKINS, W. P., *op. cit.*, p. 108..
24. ICA Archives, *Minutes of the meeting of ICA Executive, London, 21st October, 1919*, p. 2.
25. ICA Archives, *Minutes of meeting of ICA Central Committee, Geneva, 12-14 April, 1920*.
26. International Co-operative Alliance, *Report of ICA Congress Basle, 1921*.
27. International Co-operative Alliance, *Review of International Co-operation*, No. 12, December, 1939, p. 602.
28. JUDGE, Anthony J. N. & SKJELSBAEK, Kjell, *Transnational Associations and Their Functions*, pp. 182-183.
29. International Co-operative Alliance, *Review of International Co-operation*, No. 11, November, 1939, p. 514.
30. International Co-operative Alliance, *Report of ICA Congress Basle, 1921*, p. 137.
31. JUDGE, Anthony J. N. & SKJELSBAEK, Kjell, *Op. cit.*, p. 184.

Chapter four

The ICA's Response to Communism

Introduction

Having examined how the ICA faced up to problems created by the First World War, we should turn now to two which arose in the aftermath of the war, namely Communism and Fascism. Each of these affected ICA member movements and thus, eventually, the ICA. In most cases, the Alliance attempted to help the co-operative movements concerned. For nearly all of them the question arose as to whether they should have continued membership of the Alliance. In connection with those that did, the further question arose as to who should represent them: their old or the new leaders.

Thus, organisational problems were created for the Alliance. Equally, there were also ideological difficulties. Communism and Fascism, including Nazism, represent the major popular ideologies of the 20th century. Separately, and in their opposition to each other, they threatened world peace and thus one of the ICA's objectives.

If we construct a spectrum of ideologies we find that Fascism is at the extreme right and Communism to the extreme left. Near to centre left come the gentler creeds of Socialism and its close relation, Co-operation. In a century noted for its clashes of ideologies, it was inevitable that a minor one like Co-operation would find it difficult to remain neutral or, indeed, unaffected by the consequences of those clashes.

We therefore need to analyse the ICA's responses to Fascism and Communism. This Chapter will be concerned with the latter and will trace the ICA's actions from the Russian Revolution in 1917 to the outbreak of the Second World War in 1939. Although largely chronological, the chapter will also reflect distinct themes.

General Background

It should be underlined that changes arising from the Russian Revolution, and their effect on co-operatives, became apparent only in stages in the ICA. One reason was that Soviet Communism itself changed as circumstances around it changed. There were also shifts in policy when Stalin followed Lenin as Soviet leader. The result was that it took time for the ICA to determine its position on Russian Communism. We will find that, in comparison, it decided its response to the rise of Fascism elsewhere far more quickly. We can trace its relations with Soviet Communism during the inter-war years from a number of extant primary sources. One is the Russian Report in *The Reports of the Central Organisations in the Various Countries on their Activities During the War*, to which we referred in Chapter 3. Others include ICA Minutes, reports and correspondence, as well as Congress reports which included verbatim accounts of debates.

Two main secondary sources have been consulted. One is the book by the Soviet Co-operator, A. I. Krasheninnikov, *The International Co-operative Movement - Past, Present and Future*, published in 1988 by Centrosoyus, Moscow, and printed in the then German Democratic Republic. Its purpose was to review and evaluate the ICA 'from a Marxist-Leninist point of view'. The other book is the history of the Alliance by W. P. Watkins, *The International Co-operative Alliance 1895-1970*, to which we have already made a number of references.

Background to Russian Co-operation

It is from Watkins' book that we learn that, during the 1914-18 war, the ICA Secretariat had greater difficulty in keeping in touch with the Russian Co-operative Movement than with any other co-operative movement.[1]

This was partly remedied when, at its meeting on 11th June, 1918, the Executive received a Dr Harold Williams and Mrs Williams, who were visiting Britain from Russia. We gather from the Central Committee's Report to the ICA's Congress of 1921 in Basle that Dr Williams was a 'well-known journalist' and that his wife was Russian.[2] It is not known on what authority Williams was able to speak about Co-operatives in Russia. Neither do the Minutes of the Executive's meeting record Dr Williams' comments. It seems likely that these were important, because they led to a further meeting in August, 1918, this time between Williams and the Executive, with representatives of the British Co-operative Union, Co-operative Wholesale Society and the Co-operative Productive Federation. At the meeting:

'Dr. Williams.........stated at length HIS* views of the present position in Russia from the co-operative standpoint and suggested that a useful purpose might be served by encouraging Russian co-operation at the present time. The best means of doing this at the moment and the need was urgent - was by communicating with Russian co-operative organisations and then by sending a mission to Russia to convey moral encouragement and propaganda of co-operative principles and, if found practicable to arrange that any help given to the population should be passed through co-operative channels.'[3]

* author's capitals

Williams's advice that any help given to the Russian population should be passed through co-operative channels was acted upon. When, in January, 1920, the Allied Supreme Council at Paris lifted its blockade of Russia it encouraged the reopening of certain trade relations between Russia and allied and neutral countries. In this connection it decided to 'give facilities to the Russian Co-operative organisations, which are in direct touch with the peasantry throughout Russia, so that they may arrange for the import into Russia of clothing, medicines, agricultural machinery, and other necessaries of which the Russian people are in sore need, in exchange for grain, flax etc. of which Russia has surplus supplies'[4]. To conclude such arrangements a Russian Co-operative Trade Delegation was appointed. It was based in London and received considerable help from the ICA.

Not much else can be gathered about Dr Williams's visit apart from the fact that it led to consultations with Russian co-operative organisations in London and 'Mr. Tschaikowsky at Archangel' regarding how best the ICA could organise help. The feasibility of sending a co-operative delegation to Russia was also explored, and enquiries made at the British Foreign Office about the granting of travel facilities.[5]

For information on the actual conditions in Russia we need to examine the report referred to in Chapter 3 on Russian Co-operation During the War and Revolution, which formed part of the Reports of the Central Organisations in the Various Countries on Their Activities During The War, published by the ICA in 1920.

Unfortunately, the Russian report is unsigned. We do not know, therefore, the author, or from which standpoint, or on what authority, he wrote. However, the mass of detailed information contained within the thirteen closely-typed pages suggests that he was a figure of some importance. Although obviously knowledgeable on recent co-operative developments in Russia, he may already have gone into exile. By 1919 or 1920 a number of Centrosoyus leaders had done so, including two members of the ICA Central Committee, Selheim and Totomianz. Because of this link it would be reasonable to suppose that one of these two was the author of the Russian Report, particularly as its internal evidence suggests that it was written by someone away from Moscow since it contains phrases such as 'facts and reports that have reached us recently', and 'according to recent information'. Besides Russian co-operative leaders who were exiled, there were others, such as Korobof, Lavruklin and Musnetsof who were imprisoned.[6]

From the above it seems reasonable to conclude that the reporter was unlikely to have been a Bolshevik or supporter of Lenin. Before looking at the report in detail, it might be helpful to trace Russian co-operation before the 1914-18 War and the 1917 Revolution.

A kind of consumer co-operative, 'Big Artel', was founded in Transbaikal in 1825. This anticipated some of the Co-operative Principles such as voluntary membership, and democratic management and control. In the 1830s a number of mutual aid societies were formed and, by the 1860s, there was growing interest among 'progressive intellectuals, professors, doctors and teachers.' About this time the ideas of Schulze-Delitzsch had spread to the Baltic region, where German influence was strong. A short-lived consumer co-operative was also established in Riga, and became a model for consumer co-operatives in the Baltic and elsewhere in Russia. Many of these early societies did not survive long, and it was not until the last years of the 19th century that three main kinds of Russian consumer co-operatives developed successfully.

One of these was the factory consumer co-operatives'. Between 1875 and 1905 these numbered between 250 and 300 and came to form the majority of consumer co-operatives. Their membership was limited to workers of a particular factory or enterprise whose wives were unable to join. Moreover, the management of these societies was heavily influenced by the factory owners, which meant that their members were at a disadvantage during industrial disputes.

The second kind of co-operative was the 'special associations', comprising Government officials, army officers and civil servants. Like the factory consumer co-operatives, these were heavily influenced by their respective authorities, on whose direct orders they were established. Consequently, they were also only semi-independent. The third kind of co-operative was the consumer societies that were organised more along the lines of retail co-operatives in Western Europe, with a more mixed and proletarian membership.

It was on this third kind of co-operative that, in October, 1898, the provincial Moscow Union of Consumer Societies was founded. This became the 'spiritual centre' of the consumer co-operative movement in pre-Revolutionary Russia, eventually becoming the All-Russian Union of Consumers' Societies (Centrosoyus), which joined the ICA in 1903.[7]

Russian Co-operation during the War and Revolution

By the outbreak of the war, in addition to consumer co-operatives, agricultural and credit societies had also developed. They went on to achieve a considerable degree of success with 'large masses' of the rural population.

This success was due partly to the fact that 'private capitalistic industry in Russia was as yet undeveloped, the methods of private trading being comparatively primitive'. Before the 1917 March Revolution 'Co-operation had become one of the most significant manifestations of Russian economic and social life, with the Tsar's Government veering between support out of necessity, and hostility because of its suspicions that some co-operatives had revolutionary tendencies. Nevertheless, under the Tsar's regime, Co-operation was the only form of democratic organisation that was allowed.

In the short-term the March Revolution increased the Movement's status. More than fifteen Co-operative leaders became Cabinet Ministers or Assistant Ministers in the Government of Lvoff and Kerensky. Co-operatives became even more important when increasing economic and political chaos began to paralyse capitalist businesses. By mid-1917 some 10,000,000 Russians belonged to approximately 25,000 consumer co-operatives federated into around 300 unions.

After the March Revolution, the Government set up Food Committees which had 'dictatorial powers in all matters concerning food supply'. One half of the membership of these Committees was elected by traders, manufacturers and big landowners. The other half comprised representatives of Workmen's and Peasants' Councils, Trade Unions and Co-operative Societies. It was after this that the Russian co-operatives began to face increasing difficulties.

Bolsheviks began to favour the increased extension of the economic functions of the Food Committees. Initially there were only 'casual' attacks on Russian co-operatives, which were allowed to continue despite the 'cessation of all political and social life brought about by Bolshevism, the abolition of municipal institutions, the suspension.... of the Trade Union Movement, and the closing of the Law Courts....... ' As in the time of the Tsar, co-operatives remained the only free institutions which were allowed to operate. The Co-operative Movement's People's Bank was, apart from the nationalised State Bank, the only institution allowed to accept deposits, which now flowed into it.

However, the Movement experienced increasing difficulties, including the proposal by the Food Commissariat to create 'consumer' communes which, the Report to the ICA suggested, would have transformed

'Russia by a stroke of the pen into a realm of communism'. The Report went on to observe that as fantastic as this proposal was, it found many supporters among the People's Commissaries Council, including 'Lenin himself'. Centrosoyus managed to negotiate a temporary compromise under which no more than two consumer co-operatives should exist in any locality, 'one of the citizens in general and another for the workmen'. It soon proved to be that the latter type became the vehicle for communist infiltration and was used as a means of 'getting possession of Co-operation' from below, with the eventual aim of changing the nature of Centrosoyus.

The increasing friction between Government and the Movement was compounded by the worsening economic position and the failure of new State mechanisms to provide essential services. This led the Communists to press for greater centralisation and nationalisation, including that of co-operatives.

In October, 1918, a decree on nationalisation was issued. It excluded co-operatives but nevertheless laid down that representatives of the Supreme Economic Council and the Food Commissariat should sit on the board of Centrosoyus and 'co-operatives in general' with the right of veto over their decisions. This move was resisted by the following arguments:

'Co-operators tried to bring home to Communists that Co-operation would retain its superiority compared with the Soviet bureaucracy only so long as the technical apparatus of Co-operation was managed directly by the elected boards and were responsible to the meetings of members, whose needs and interests were looked after by Co-operation. Co-operators also pointed out that Co-operation was based in all its stages on strict democratic principles, that almost the whole population were members of co-operative societies, and that the only way of introducing Communists into the administrative board would be through the bringing forward of their candidature at the general meeting of the members.'

This plea was unsuccessful, and representatives of the Food Commissariat were appointed, with the right of veto, to the Board of Centrosoyus and co-operatives generally.

The Government then announced its intention to amalgamate the Co-operative People's Bank with the Soviet State Bank, which had the effect that deposits into the former almost came to a halt. At the same time an injunction was issued to all Soviet institutions ordering them to transfer their deposits and banking accounts from the Co-operative People's Bank to the State Bank. There followed a remarkably strong and spirited Co-operative rearguard action.

'...the deposits just mentioned ran into as large a sum as 250 million roubles, while the whole balance of the bank totalled 1,200 million. Still, the bank with the assistance of its members, succeeded in mobilising up to 100 millions out of which the incoming demands could be satisfied; shortly afterwards it succeeded in getting the order revoked.'

Such resistance was only temporary and the Government soon made it clear that, if the People's Bank did not voluntarily consent to the amalgamation, it would be liquidated. Even so, in November, 1918, a general meeting of People's Bank shareholders unanimously rejected the proposal 'as being contrary to co-operative principles and harmful to the economic interests of the country'. The meeting appointed a special deputation to meet with Lenin, as President of the People's Council, but it was unsuccessful. Ten days later the People's Bank was transformed into a Co-operative Department of the State Bank. From being the financial centre of Co-operation' it had become a 'mere agency for distributing amongst the co-operative societies the subsidies assigned to them by the State Bank'.

An even more alarming development occurred in March, 1919, when, by decree, co-operatives were transformed into Consumer Communes. These were to comprise all the inhabitants of a locality, and would be managed by means of general meetings. The functions of credit and agricultural co-operatives were also subsumed into the Consumer Communes. The Communes would appoint delegates to Centrosoyus, and its Board would be elected from among these. In addition, the Soviet Government would be represented on the Board by a number appointed from the People's Commissaries' Councils. As the Russian Report to the ICA concluded, the decree virtually meant the destruction of consumers' co-operation in Russia 'in general and ... Centrosoyus in particular'. It added the hope that foreign co-operative organisations and the International Co-operative Alliance would continue their relations with Russian Co-operation, as long as its representatives abroad are not self-styled representatives appointed by the Soviet Government.'[8]

At this stage we should perhaps note the Soviet regime's justification for its moves. We have already seen that its policy, including that for co-operatives, often shifted as circumstances changed in the aftermath of war and revolution. In May, 1923, at the end of the Russian Civil War, the New Economic Programme was introduced in the hope of reducing peasant resistance to Communism. As a result, the Government's policy on co-operatives was becoming clearer and Lenin wrote two articles in Pravda in May, 1923, outlining it.[9] One of these included the statement that the co-operative movement had become one of great significance' under the New Economic Policy, which also offered a new view of co-operation.

'There is a lot of fantasy in the dreams of old co-operators. Often they are ridiculously fantastic. But why are they fantastic? Because people do not understand the fundamental and rock-bottom significance of the working class political struggle for the overthrow of the exploiters. We have overthrown the rule of the exploiters, and much that was fantastic, even romantic, even banal in the dreams of old co-operators is now becoming unvarnished reality.'

Lenin classed Robert Owen as one of the 'old co-operators'. He also positioned co-operatives in different systems. ...in the capitalist state, co-operatives are...collective capitalist institutions'. Under the new Soviet system, 'co-operative enterprises differ from private capitalist enterprises because they are collective enterprises but do not differ from socialist enterprises if the land on which they are situated and the means of production belong to the state, i.e. the working class.'

Lenin went on to suggest that it was possible to build a complete socialist society on co-operatives alone, because these could assure the proletarian leadership of the peasantry. He felt that they could also constitute a social system, but observed that a 'social system emerges only if it has the financial backing of a definite class'. Consequently, co-operatives should receive preferential State loans and have economic, financial and banking privileges to enable them to involve large masses of the population.

The Lenin articles provide us with some insights. A. I. Krasheninnikov, in his book, *The International Co-operative Movement - Past, Present and Future*, gives others when he describes Soviet conditions in the early 1920s. Fourteen countries had intervened in the Russian Civil War in support of anti-revolutionary forces. Critical food shortages were made worse by the occupation of important grain growing areas, and also by landowners sabotaging the sale of grain. Financial and transport systems were also severely dislocated. Against this background, co-operatives were required to provide the population with rationed commodities. As we have seen, the decree of 10th April 1918, required everyone to join existing co-operatives or form new ones. Credit and agricultural functions were added to the existing co-operatives, effectively making them multi-purpose societies.

Whatever the mix of ideology and expediency in the Russian situation, an important fact was that a long-time member movement of the International Co-operative Alliance had changed its philosophical base and organisational structure. We need now to examine the ICA's response to such changes.

The ICA's Response to Changes in the Union of Soviet Socialist Republics

The ICA's immediate response appeared to be clear, but later became less so. At its meeting in Geneva in April, 1920, the Central Committee passed the following resolution:

'That this Central Committee approves of the immediate raising of the blockade of Russia, which is necessary in the interests of the populations of Russia and of all other countries. It considers it essential that the co-operative organisations should participate in the re-establishment of trading relations with Russia. Moreover, it protests against the loss of the independence and full autonomy of the Russian co-operative organisations and against the intervention of the

Government in the matter of the freedom of co-operative organisation. The Central Committee considers as representatives of Co-operation only such persons as have received their mandate from free democratic co-operative organisations.[10]

The Central Committee reaffirmed this position at its next meeting at the Hague in October, 1920, but went further to justify the existing Russian members of the Central Committee remaining on the grounds that they were 'appointed from one Congress to another, in accordance with the rules of the ICA, and therefore remain in office.'[11]

This aspect of the situation was already becoming caught up with that of trade. Throughout this study trade forms a kind sub-theme and, as far as the USSR is concerned, we can trace it through the Central Committee's Report to the ICA Congress in Basle, 1921.[12]

From this we learn that three days after the Allied Supreme Council in Paris lifted its Russian blockade and began encouraging trade between Russia and allied and neutral countries, four Centrosoyus representatives in Paris sent a telegram requesting the ICA's moral assistance in establishing co-operative trading relations. It seems likely that the four - Selheim, Berkenheim, Yakhimstroff and Mme Lenskaya - were part of the old Centrosoyus Board in exile. Henry May, General Secretary wrote to Mr Korobof, 'president of Centrosoyus' in Moscow, asking him to confirm that co-operative organisations would be authorised to export goods in exchange for raw materials, and whether Russian representatives in London could accept responsibility for the safety of the goods sent to Russia. May also asked what goods were required, what could be sent in exchange, and whether Russian co-operatives were ready to export on a large scale. The reply, under the 'duly authenticated' signatures of A. Lezhava (President), Dr. Korobof (now Vice-President) and M. Paretchny (Secretary), confirmed that the Soviet Government had given Centrosoyus permission to enter into direct commercial relations with co-operative societies and firms in other countries. On 26th February, 1920, Mr Berkenheim, presumably still in Paris and in some kind of representative capacity for Centrosoyus, received a message from Lezhava, President of Centrosoyus in Moscow, announcing the appointment of a Trade

Delegation which was to be based in London and empowered to conduct negotiations and conclude transactions. Its members were Litvinoff, Krassin, Nogin, Rosovsky and Khintchouk'.

May subsequently reported to the Basle Congress that it was obvious that this delegation was not only authorised by, but consisted largely of, direct representatives of the Soviet Government', which must therefore increase doubts about the 'liberty and independence of the voluntary co-operative organisations from Russia, and the genuineness of the delegation representing them'.

Once in London, members of the Russian Trade Delegation pressed that they should be considered the rightful representatives of the Russian Co-operative Movement in the ICA. This raised the question of whether Centrosoyus remained eligible for ICA membership, the first time this question had been raised regarding any ICA member movement. From all that had gone before - Central Committee resolutions and May's statement - it might have been expected that the issue would be settled quickly, but this was not to be the case.

The ICA Executive invited both the existing Centrosoyus members on the Central Committee and the members of the Russian Trade Delegation to a meeting. This was declined by both parties, on the grounds that each had the prerogative of representation. The Executive then passed the following resolution to go before the Central Committee at its meeting on the eve of the Congress at Basle. It read:

'That, having fully considered in all its bearings the question of the representation of the Russian co-operative organisations in the International Co-operative Alliance, this Executive finds itself unable to come to any other conclusions than the following:

1. That the only authority which can properly nominate representatives of Russian Co-operation to serve on the Central Committee of the ICA, or appoint delegates to the Congress at Basle, is the Board of the Centrosoyus at Moscow.

2. That the form and constitution of the Board and of the All-Russian Central Union is primarily a matter for the decision and approval of the Russian co-operators in Russia.

3. That, therefore, the Executive have no alternative but to accept any properly authenticated nominations for the Central Committee, or appointment of delegates to Congress, which may be forwarded to the Alliance by the Board of the Central Union at Moscow, in accordance with the rules of the ICA and that the General Secretary be instructed to act accordingly.

4. Finally, that the Congress at Basle be strongly recommended to adopt these conclusions as the solution of the present deadlock in our relations with the Russian co-operative movement.'

Not only did the Central Committee fail to endorse the Executive Committee's proposal, it went on to pass its own resolution. This regretted the absence of Centrosoyus delegates which, it stated, prevented it from coming to a definite position on the question. The Central Committee's resolution went further to suggest that, in view of the division in the Russian co-operative Movement, no final decision could be reached. It therefore recommended that Congress be asked to remit the question back to the Central Committee so that it might be considered at a subsequent meeting. In the meantime, it proposed that the Russian seats on the Central Committee should be left vacant.

This, then, was the confused background to what must be considered one of the most significant debates in the Alliance as far as this study is concerned. Had the outcome been different it could have meant that the ICA split in 1921. The occasion was one of the few times that the Central Committee took an opposing view to that held by the Executive. In Congress, the debate was complicated by procedure as well as by issue. For example, May was delegated to propose both the Executive's report and the Central Committee's resolution.

'I have the rather difficult task...to attempt to place before you the reasons upon which the Executive based the report which is before you...and to do that in the face of the fact that the Central Committee - not the Central Committee as a whole, but a majority of the Central Committee - have taken the

extraordinary course of proposing an amendment to their own report, prepared in their name by the Executive and with their knowledge and consent.'

May was soon interrupted by Albert Thomas (France), who questioned the General Secretary's authority to speak against a motion passed by the majority of the Central Committee. Goedhart, presiding in place of William Maxwell, who was ill, justified May's statement by the need for delegates to be fully informed before coming to a decision. Goedhart also argued that May was entitled to inform Congress and to speak under Article 35 of the Rules dealing with the duties of the Secretary, including the power to 'advise'. 'Yes, to advise but not to controvert', interrupted Thomas once more.

May resumed, and pointed out that the Central Committee's recommendation to leave the Russian places vacant until its next meeting was contrary to the Rules of the Alliance. Neither the Central Committee nor Congress itself had the right to withhold an existing member organisation's right to nominate representatives to the Central Committee. May reminded Congress that Centrosoyus had been an Alliance member since 1903, and that until the early part of 1920 there had been no question at all as to the existence of Centrosoyus, its membership in the ICA and its full right to the privileges of membership. Moreover, its subscriptions for the current year had been accepted, in addition to which it had a representative at the Congress. For these reasons, the Executive believed that Centrosoyus had the right to nominate representatives to Congress and to the Central Committee. What appears to have been at issue, although largely unspoken, was the question of whether the ICA had the right to test an existing member's right to continued membership.

Poisson (France) was the first speaker in the debate which followed. Speaking in support of the majority view of the Central Committee, and thus against the Executive, he reminded Congress that the Centrosoyus delegates appointed in 1913 had declared that the organisation was no longer co-operative. However, he continued:

'Whatever your decision this amendment (to the Executive's recommendation) must not be interpreted as showing enmity to the Central Russian organisation or in any way as a desire to exclude the Russian Co-operative Movement from the Alliance, nor as a condemnation of Bolshevism. That does not concern us, but it is for us to know whether Centrosoyus, as it exists today, is co-operative or not. That is the only matter of interest to us. If it is a co-operative organisation it has a right to a place in this assembly. If it is not a co-operative, there is no place for it in the Co-operative Alliance.'

Poisson regretted that the delegates who could answer these questions were not present, whereas the one lady from Centrosoyus who was in the Congress, 'does not know the present position of the movement in Russia'. The questions he would put to Centrosoyus were:

'Are you co-operative or not? Do you accept the statutes of the Alliance or do you wish to establish A RIVAL INTERNATIONAL?'*
* author's capitals

Poisson believed that a proper decision could only be taken when the answers to these questions had been received.

Like Thomas (France), Lorenz (Germany), challenged May's position. He pointed out that the Central Committee's amendment had been passed by a two-thirds majority.

'If the General Secretary, in reporting on this resolution (the amendment to the Executive's recommendation), had fulfilled the whole of his duty he would not only have presented to you the side of the minority, but he should also, in an objective manner, have given the reasons of the majority ...If it had been supposed that he would not do so, the Central Committee would probably have appointed someone to report specially on the question.'

Lorenz continued and said that, like Poisson, he was not concerned with the political situation in Russia. But twice, at Geneva and at the Hague, the Central Committee had taken a negative attitude on Centrosoyus's continued representation in the ICA. He wondered, therefore, if something had occurred in the Russian situation of which Congress was not aware but which could perhaps justify a different attitude being taken. Until it was known whether there had been any change he believed that it was necessary to retain the amendment in order to allow the Central Committee to hear Russian delegates before coming to a final decision. Otherwise, it was impossible for Congress to form a correct idea of conditions in Russia.

There were obvious difficulties in obtaining a clear picture from Centrosoyus. Its delegates to the Congress, including Lezhava, Acting Commissary of Foreign Trade, had travelled as far as Germany, but had to remain there because they had been unable to obtain visas to enter Switzerland. The only Centrosoyus delegate to arrive was a Dr. Polovtseva who, when she went to the rostrum, spoke of the honour of representing one of the mightiest of all existing co-operative organisations, but also apologised for 'the inadequacy of my knowledge and the difficulty of discharging the task in the absence of my comrades'.

Her contribution did, however, reflect the turbulent events in Russia. She confirmed that the Russian Co-operative Movement was linked to the Russian Government's policy, particularly its economic aspects, which had been forced to shift because of famine and constantly changing conditions. Russian Co-operation now had the 'task of exchange in order to regulate the relationships between town and village, to increase the productivity of the peasant masses, and thus increase export so as to put foreign trade on a more normal footing'.

Dr. Polovtseva went on to liken Centrosoyus's development to that of Marxist dialectic. The 'thesis' of its existence had lasted until the beginning of the Revolution 'during which it proved its capacity for work within its own limited sphere'. Then came the period of 'antithesis' when Russian Co-operation and Centrosoyus were enlarged through the incorporation of all Russian consumers. At this point, and no doubt in an effort to win friends, Mme Polovtseva quoted two leading Co-operative figures. She recalled a Congress paper by Victor Serwy (Belgium), in which he had said 'there is no better means of improving the economic conditions of the people, and no surer guarantee of world peace, than the grouping of all consumers in co-operative societies'. She also quoted Anders Oerne's view that 'distribution is the key to the whole system'. The enlarged Centrosoyus enshrined these points and was now entering its period of 'synthesis', under which 'it receives back its nationalised assets and becomes the collaborator of the State Power'.

Although Goedhart, as President, reminded Mme Polovtseva that she had exceeded her allotted time, Congress agreed to allow her extra time but even then Mme Polovtseva still failed to satisfy Congress on the position of Centrosoyus.

When she had not finished at the end of extra time, Albert Thomas intervened once again. He claimed that Dr. Polovtseva had told the Congress many things, but she had not given a clear answer to the one question that mattered: namely, was Centrosoyus a genuine co-operative organisation conforming to the statutes of the Alliance, or not. Thomas therefore felt it necessary to warn against making a hasty decision.

'I consider it is morally impossible to close our ears to the complaints we receive from Moscow. If a Co-operative society, of production, for example, had become a capitalistic society, would the fact that an invitation had been sent to it by the Alliance be sufficient to justify its delegates being accepted without question at this Congress? I venture to think no one could support such a view. '

Thomas urged that a decision be remitted to the next meeting of the Central Committee, by which time the Russian position might have become clearer. We should perhaps remind ourselves that, although Thomas was Director of the International Labour Organisation, he was participating in the Congress as a member of the French delegation. When he died suddenly at the age of 54 in 1932, the *Review of International Co-operation* noted:

At each Congress of the ICA since the war he has been, by turns, on the floor of the Congress speaking as a member of the French delegation, or on the platform addressing the Congress as Director of the I.L.O., or again, contributing a special report on some aspect or other of international co-operative development, but always with the one purpose of moulding the Co-

operative Movement into that superlative weapon of economic advance, social reform and human betterment, which he profoundly believed it was destined to be.'[13]

On this occasion Thomas was not able to persuade Congress, which decided that it wished to vote on the question without hearing further speakers. A card vote followed and resulted in the surprise defeat of the Central Committee's amendment to the Executive's recommendation by 474 votes to 733.[14]

In view of the importance of the decision, which meant that Centrosoyus would remain a member of the Alliance, it would be interesting to know more about the vote. Unfortunately, no official details exist other than in the record of the Congress. We can only speculate, therefore, on who voted for what.

It was unusual for the Central Committee not to be able to secure a majority in Congress. We should remind ourselves that it was not until the Stockholm Congress of 1927 that the ICA Rules were changed to ensure that no country, or union of countries, had more than one-fifth of the votes in Congress.[15] In these circumstances it seems likely that the British delegation played a decisive role. Although they had only seven members on the Central Committee, the British had 111 delegates at the Basle Congress out of a total of just over 400. In his book *The International Co-operative Movement - Past, Present and Future* Krasheninnikov lists, besides the British, the American, Italian and Czechoslovak 'and some other co-operators' as voting in favour of the Executive's position, while the German, French and Swiss delegations voted against it.[16]

In addition to a large Congress delegation, British influence was also likely to have been felt through the Alliance's all-British Executive Committee, as well as its British General Secretary. Deducing strong British influence is one thing. Establishing motives for it is quite another. It seems likely, as Lorenz (Germany) had speculated, that something had occurred in the Russian situation which was too sensitive to make known more widely, perhaps something involving the British Government which was party to the Russian-British Trade Agreement.

This seems a reasonable supposition to explain the shift from a previously unambiguous position, which had been shared by the Central Committee, Executive and General Secretary; it also helps to explain the strange procedure whereby Henry May, the General Secretary, rather than a member of the Executive, moved the Executive's resolution.

In looking for other motives, and doing so on both sides of the debate, it might help to summarise their main arguments. The Executive argued that, under Rule 28, it was out of the power of the Central Committee, and even of Congress itself, to deprive an existing affiliate of its right to nominate representatives. It further argued, on the question of whether Centrosoyus still existed, that the Central Committee had itself decided at the Hague that it did because it had allowed the Russian representatives nominated in 1913 to remain until the Basle Congress. Finally, the Executive made much of the fact that Centrosoyus's current subscription had been paid. The Executive's arguments were heavily based on procedure. Only Sir Thomas Allen, a member of the Executive and shortly to become a Vice-President of the Alliance, touched upon a non-procedural point when he urged caution in rejecting Russian Co-operation. *'Politically we know...that the Allied Governments presumed a certain condition of things prevailing in Russia, and they took a certain course, and we know what the consequences have been to the world at large. If co-operatively a certain condition of thing prevails in Russia, and it is decided to act on that presumption, we say, as an Executive, it is conceivable that we may make a very regrettable mistake.'*[17]

The opposition's arguments were more philosophical and about legitimation. Was Centrosoyus a genuine co-operative organisation? If it were not, then there was no more place for it in the ICA than there would be for a capitalist enterprise. As Lorenz (Germany) had said, 'the important question to us is the co-operative character of our Alliance, the principles of which are expressed in our rules'.

This kind of analysis does not take us very far. Turning, therefore, to reasoned speculation and the role of the British delegation, we should note that the British Co-operative Movement had strong pro-Soviet sympathies at that time. For example, in a letter to ICA President

William Maxwell reporting on the 1920 Co-operative Union Congress, Henry May wrote, 'The Russian representatives, and in fact, any mention of Russia, secured an immediate response from the Congress'[18]. May actually became Chairman of the British Joint Labour Aid Committee of the Workers' International Russian Relief. Although he held this position in a personal capacity, a letterhead refers to his being the General Secretary of the International Co-operative Alliance'. [19] Later British labour and co-operative attitudes to Russia became more suspicious and cautious, and in January, 1925, May resigned the chair. [20]

Another factor that may have influenced the delegations voting in favour of the Executive's position may have been the fear of a rival International Co-operative Alliance being set up by the Communists. As we have seen, Poisson actually mentioned the possibility.

Henry Faucherre, in his 60 *Jahre Internaitonaler Genossenschaftsbund*, refers to proposals in 1921 to establish an 'International Union of Red Co-operatives', which was to convene in Moscow following contacts with supporters in 'England, Italy, Germany, Spain and Belgium. Faucherre observes that nothing further was heard of this proposal after the Basle Congress of the ICA had decided to recognise the Russian Co-operatives and their Communist representatives in the ICA'.[21]

We should note that the Third Socialist International had only a brief life after the 1914-18 War. The reason was Lenin's establishment in 1918 of the Communist International (COMINTERN), which claimed leadership of the world socialist movement, and excluded non-communist socialists from its membership. Its establishment not only split the Socialist International but also the International Federation of Trade Unions. Faucherre speculates that the International Co-operative Alliance had been next in line. It seems reasonable that those voting for the Executive's position could have believed that to suppose, therefore, they were voting to pre-empt this COMINTERN action.

Another factor influencing them could have been the expectation of the trade that their co-operatives might do with Soviet co-operatives. This could have been a particularly strong motivation for the British, not only in view of the potential role of their two Wholesales, but also because of the role that the British Government had played in the Trade Agreement: its signatories were R. S. Horne for the British Government and L. Krassin, who subsequently became a member of the ICA Central Committee, for the Russian Trade Delegation.[22]

Although it was a British-Russian Trade Agreement, the agreement seemed to have a wider significance to the ICA, as we can see from the fact that it was widely reported to Executive and Central Committees. For example, at its meeting in Copenhagen in April, 1921, the Central Committee received a report from Henry May describing the various stages of negotiations that led to the Trade Agreement. Such procedure seems to be explained by the fact that May, and the Executive, hoped that, besides leading to large contracts', the agreement could help to ease the position of Centrosoyus vis-à-vis the Soviet Government. In his Memorandum to the Central Committee, May reported that there seemed to have been a 'modification of State Control of Co-operative Organisations, which we have always urged would take place as and when the Government of Russia tended to become "stabilised". May also said that in the previous December (1920) 'Mr. Korobof, Vice President of Centrosoyus and Messrs. Lavruklin and Musnetsof, Co-operative leaders serving long sentences of imprisonment, were suddenly released.'[23]

It seems likely, therefore, that May and the ICA Executive were being humanitarian and far-sighted when they looked beyond the immediate upheavals and hoped for a more settled period, under which Soviet co-operatives would return to something like their previous position. The trade factor brings us once again to possible influence by the British Government: it had been one of the Allied Governments that had imposed the trade blockade against the USSR but, when this was lifted, it was keen to re-establish trade. The agreement of March, 1920, although including private enterprise, appears to have been heavily dependent on British and Soviet co-operatives.

It is possible that British Government interests went far beyond trade, and were concerned in keeping routes open to the USSR through non-governmental organisations such as the ICA. We know that in the early 1920s Governments were still coming to terms with the Russian Revolution, and making various adjustments. For example, there was the view that the setting up of the ILO was 'a means of appeasing restive elements in the trade union movement who might otherwise be attracted to Communism.'[24] We should also note that, as early as the Basle Congress in 1921, the League of Nations was appointing one or two Observers to attend ICA Congresses, a practice which continued throughout the inter-war years and which suggests that the importance of the ICA as an International Non-Governmental Organisation was becoming recognised.

If the British Government had interests that went beyond trade, Henry May was obviously a good intermediary. As Parliamentary Secretary of the Co-operative Union he had been used to dealing with Government officials while, as General Secretary of the ICA, he had links with Soviet co-operation.

All the above go to show that the question of whether Centrosoyus should be allowed to remain a member of the ICA was indeed a complex one. Yet it was crucial as far as this study is concerned. Had the Soviet Co-operative movement left the ICA, international co-operation would have been divided in the early 1920s.

The fact that Centrosoyus remained a member of the Alliance meant that the ICA's attitudes to a number of issues had to change. We will now examine these in turn.

Relations between the ICA and Centrosoyus 1921-1939

Old Board- New Board

The decision at the Basle Congress had an effect on the ICA's attitude to a number of related issues. These included its relations with the 'old' Centrosoyus Board, as well with other co-operative movements in what had now become the USSR. There were also questions concerning representation and subscriptions.

As far as the 'Old' Board was concerned, it will be recalled that two of its members had been elected to the ICA Central Committee at the Glasgow Congress in 1913, and they remained until the 1921 Congress despite the fact that Centrosoyus had been re-styled after the Revolution and that they were now Soviet exiles. After Basle, however, the ICA needed to develop formal relations with the 'new' Board of Centrosoyus. It soon became apparent that, while there might be personal sympathy for members of the 'old' board, the ICA Executive no longer recognised it. An example was the question of the transfer of external assets and liabilities from Centrosoyus's 'old' Board to its 'new' Board.[25]

The transfer was eventually made under an agreement reached in January, 1922, but part of that agreement was that the 'old' Board could make a Declaration explaining why they had resisted making the transfer. One reason was their fear that the new Centrosoyus was based on compulsion, with co-operative structures being changed by decree rather than by the decision of their members.

The 'old' Board was also apprehensive that the majority of the population would not feel that the new co-operatives belonged to them. They had also resisted demands to transfer Centrosoyus's foreign assets on the grounds that these represented the property that had been entrusted to them by co-operative organisations, and that it was to these bodies that the property should be returned. Another fear was that because Centrosoyus had been incorporated into the Ministry of Food, any goods and monies handed over to the 'new' Board would become caught up in the 'general mass and...completely lost to the Co-operative Movement'.[26]

A final condition of the transfer was that the 'old' Board should be allowed to send a copy of their Declaration to the ICA Executive which was due to meet shortly in Brussels. From the point of view of orthodox co-operative ideology, it would have been surprising if members of the ICA Executive were not moved by the 'old' Centrosoyus Board's Declaration. The fact that the Declaration exists in the ICA Archives indicates that it was received. But there is no record of its ever having been considered by the Executive either at their meeting at Brussels or later.²⁷ This seems to underline the legitimacy that the ICA now accorded the 'new' Board of Centrosoyus, and also its recognition that it was with this Board that it must now deal.

A point that we should note is that for whatever reasons - humane, political, or expediency - from this point onwards the ICA's dealings with the new Centrosoyus meant an ideological compromise. It was one that the organisation managed to live with for over two decades, but the fudging of the issue would compound the problems that arose in the Cold War.

ICA Delegation to Moscow 1922

The fact that the ICA was working with the new Centrosoyus Board was emphasised in another way when, at its meeting in Brussels in January, 1922, the Executive decided to send an international co-operative delegation to the USSR. It laid down two objectives. One was that the delegation should enquire into the present position of co-operative organisations in Russia; the other was that it would explore possible economic relations with Russia through co-operative channels. For this reason, two representatives from the Committee of National Wholesale Societies were invited to participate. May was the only actual Alliance representative, but each member of the Executive was invited to join the delegation as long as their organisation on the Central Committee met their expenses.²⁸

A 30-day visit took place during February and March, 1922. Afterwards the delegation affirmed its belief that the economic resources of Russia, relative to its needs and to those of the rest of Europe, made it desirable to develop mutually advantageous economic relations. It suggested that these would best be developed through an international co-operative wholesale and bank. It also urged that there should be direct and indirect trade between Russia and the other European countries.²⁹ Of direct significance to the Alliance was the statement that:

'The evidence we saw convinces us that a complete internal transformation of the movement is being accomplished in the direction of uniformity in principle

with the movements in other countries. There is, therefore, no longer any reason for discussing the relations of Russian Co-operation to the ICA, in which we believe it is entitled to the fullest rights and privileges of all members, and there is the greatest necessity for Co-operation everywhere to support Russian Co-operation in order that it may be able to fulfil its great role in the universal movement and accentuate and continue its evolution.'

The delegation therefore recommended:

'That the Central Committee should at once take steps to give Russian Co-operation a representative on the Executive of the ICA'.[30]

With the benefit of hindsight, such a ringing endorsement would appear to have been misplaced. However, the 1922 ICA delegation obviously hoped that the Soviet movement was being brought back in line with those in other countries. It could hardly know that the Soviet regime and Centrosoyus would pass through a number of phases, or that Stalin would follow Lenin.

Moreover, the delegation seems to have been excited by what it saw of the Russian Revolution. Manuscripts in the ICA Archives include a draft article signed by Henry May which recounts how, since his return from the USSR, he had used the salutation 'comrade', recalling that nearly every civilised country had:

'...an equivalent expression of that universal "fellowship" described so beautifully by William Morris: "Fellowship is heaven and lack of fellowship is Hell." There is a fellowship today amongst the Russian proletariat which is heaven in comparison to the hell which Czarism produced........'[31]

The writer of an unsigned typescript was similarly enthusiastic and naive:

'...Co-operation is the State, and the State it is Co-operation. This has been the consummation to be wished for, let us not, therefore, shrink from its realisation.'[32]

As a result of the delegation's report, the ICA Central Committee agreed to invite a Centrosoyus representative to join the Executive, but only in a consultative capacity until elections at the next Congress.[33]

Co-operative Movements in the Soviet Republics

ICA endorsement of the new Centrosoyus affected not only its links with the members of the previous Centrosoyus Board but also its relations with co-operative movements in the Soviet republics. A Soviet Declaration in November, 1917, had proclaimed the equality and sovereignty of the nations of Russia, and gave them rights of self-determination and of even possible independence.[34]

As a result, for a few short years, co-operative movements in Lithuania, Estonia, Latvia, the Ukraine, Georgia and Armenia had direct representation in the International Co-operative Alliance. But growing Soviet domination in their countries later caused problems for them in their relations with the Alliance. An example was the case of Georgia, which proved that, although the ICA was far from lacking sympathy, it nevertheless took a constitutional line which, after the Basle decision, favoured Centrosoyus.

Like the Soviet Co-operative Movement, the Georgian movement also invited an ICA delegation to visit, ostensibly to hand over a contribution from the ICA's Famine Relief Fund, but also to study the conditions under which the Georgian Co-operative Movement was operating. The ICA Executive discussed the invitation at its meeting in Brussels in January, 1922, but, being divided, decided to adjourn the question.[35] When the Georgians continued to press the invitation, the Executive, at its meeting in Milan in April, 1922, compromised by appointing Victor Serwy (Belgium) as a one-man delegation.[36]

There was strong and immediate Soviet reaction to Serwy's report, which was presented to a meeting of the ICA Executive in Essen in October, 1922. On behalf of Centrosoyus, A. A. Kissin lodged a 'strong protest' and demanded that consideration of it be adjourned until Centrosoyus had an opportunity to submit a reply. Ever constitutional, the ICA Executive decided that, having appointed Serwy, his report was their property and that they should now receive it. But, after doing so, they decided to refer it to the next meeting of the Central Committee.[37]

By the time that took place Henry May had been to Moscow for a second time. The occasion was the celebrations of Centrosoyus's 25th anniversary, to which he and Prof. Gide had been invited. On his return May reported that he and Gide had met Georgian representatives, who had reassured them about the well-being of the Georgian Co-operative Movement.[38] Moreover, Gide and May agreed that there had been a great advance in the economic life of Russia and they believed that the Co-operative Movement was being allowed increasing freedom.[39]

Other documentation in the ICA Archives relating to Georgia shows that, like Centrosoyus, its Central Co-operative Union now had a 'new' Board which changed its delegates to a number of bodies, including the ICA. It is reasonable to suppose that it had been the representatives of the 'new' Board that May and Gide met in Moscow. The significant thing is, however, that May's account of his second visit to Moscow prompted the ICA Central Committee to pass a pious resolution. This hoped that Centrosoyus would help the ICA to establish a voluntary co-operative organisation in Georgia, but assured the Georgian Central Union that any representatives it appointed to the ICA would be accepted.[40]

The Georgian question, however, had raised the issue of the rights of co-operative movements in the Soviet republics, including that of their representation in the Alliance. After discussion at several meetings of the ICA Executive during 1925, May was asked to prepare a memorandum, which would be presented to the meeting of the Central Committee in Paris in October, 1925. In it, May noted two opposing points of view: one acknowledged that the USSR was a national unity, which meant that its component States lacked autonomy and independence and were therefore effectively controlled by the Soviet Government in Moscow; the other, which had initially been taken by Centrosoyus, was that the 1917 Declaration referred to earlier, meant that the former Russian empire had been divided into independent countries, namely Russia, the Ukraine, White Russia, Georgia, Azerbaijan, Armenia, Finland, Poland, Estonia, Latvia and Lithuania.

Leaving aside for the moment the Baltic States (Poland, Estonia, Latvia and Lithuania), May went on to note the circumstances and conditions under which the co-operative movements in the other countries had joined the ICA. All, except Centrosoyus and the Union in White Russia, had affiliated since 1919 and had been admitted according to the Alliance's procedure and 'upon the basis of an equal national status in their respective countries.'[41] Their combined representation on the Central Committee numbered 14. Although they had been properly admitted, and were from countries that Centrosoyus claimed were independent under the 1917 Declaration, May argued that subsequent changes in Russia made their position uncertain. For example, if the ICA used the yardstick suggested by Poisson (France) that a country's status should be determined by the nature of its diplomatic representation with other countries, it would be seen that Poland, Finland, Estonia, Latvia and Lithuania, remained independent under the 1917 Declaration. But since March, 1924, Russia, the Ukraine, White Russia, Armenia, Georgia, and Azerbaijan, had come under the unified diplomatic representation of the USSR. Moreover, co-operative organisations in these countries had been increasingly brought within the control of Centrosoyus, which now appointed their representatives to the Alliance. Consequently, May suggested, these movements should no longer be treated as belonging to separate countries 'any more than the nations which constitute Great Britain or the German States, or those of Yugoslavia, should be regarded as separate countries'. The Central Committee endorsed this view and, as from 1st January, 1926, the USSR, and its republics listed above, were treated as one country in the ICA.

The question of representation was, of course, closely linked to that of subscriptions, and this soon became an area of difficulty between Centrosoyus and the Alliance.

Centrosoyus Subscriptions

The question of subscriptions could not be settled as smoothly as that of representation had been. There were a number of complicating factors.

Soviet membership increased dramatically as voluntary membership was augmented by compulsory membership among large sections of the Soviet population. Other increases resulted from the addition of co-operative membership in the smaller republics. By 1934, combined Soviet membership had risen to 73 million, out of a total ICA membership of 100 million, but Centrosoyus was reluctant to increase its affiliation fees proportionately.

At the ICA Congress in Vienna in 1930, Centrosoyus proposed an Amendment to Rules under which the maximum subscription of any country, or union of countries, should not exceed one-fifth of the Alliance's total subscription income. This was rejected by a large majority[42]. We should remind ourselves that voting was determined by the Rules changed at the Stockholm Congress in 1927, under which no country, or union of countries, could command more than one-fifth of the total votes at a Congress.

It seems likely that reluctance to accede to Centrosoyus's request was due to the adverse effect of the crash of 1931 on ICA subscription income. As a result many Governments embargoed overseas payments, in addition to which the devaluation of British Sterling in September, 1931, meant that ICA subscriptions had become payable in a currency that had lost three-eighths of its purchasing power.[43]

Despite Congress's rejection of the Centrosoyus proposal, May and the Executive tried to ease the position by a compromise under which Centrosoyus's subscriptions would remain at the 1931 figure of £2,750 until the next Congress. This was still an increase of £238 on the figure paid in 1930, but was considerably less than what would have been the figure under the existing Rules. In return for this accommodation, the Executive stipulated that Centrosoyus should make the payment for a current year on the basis of the rate of exchange applying at 1st

January, and that the arrangement would not prejudice any decision by the next Congress.[44]

Centrosoyus did not respond to the proposed compromise. Only £1,000 was paid on account in December, 1931.[45] Not only did they refuse to pay any more, but they also refused to discuss the question[46]. This situation, and the fact that Centrosoyus was also making 'continuous unjustifiable attacks and misrepresentations' on the Alliance, led the Executive to pass a resolution at their meeting in Geneva in October, 1932, threatening that if the attacks continued they could place the 'Soviet Organisations outside the limits of membership of the ICA'[47] A similar threat was made the following year, when Centrosoyus had still not paid its full subscription.[48] Despite these provocations, the threat was not carried out and Centrosoyus remained in ICA membership.

We do not know how the question of subscriptions was resolved, but the Report of the ICA Congress held in London in 1934 shows that Centrosoyus eventually paid its full subscriptions of £2,760 for 1931 and £2,750 for each of the following two years.[49] This figure was then paid each year until 1936,[50] increasing to £3,500 per year between 1937 and 1939.[51]

Only Great Britain paid a comparable figure. We can see, therefore, that Centrosoyus had considerable financial significance for the ICA. There would be the risk of over-simplification if we concluded that this was why the Alliance retained its Soviet member. However, this is difficult to understand for other reasons also. We have already noted, from the 1930s review of Co-operative Principles, that Centrosoyus had fundamentally changed the principles relating to Open (or voluntary) Membership and the payment of dividend. Democracy in its co-operatives had also been altered by virtue of the appointment of Soviet Government representatives to their boards, and that of Centrosoyus, with the right of veto. However, the change of principle that led to direct confrontation within the ICA was that concerning political neutrality.

Centrosoyus and the ICA's Political Neutrality

Throughout the inter-war years we find that, at each ICA Congress, Centrosoyus took distinctive points of view on many questions, shaped always by its extreme proletarian views. Centrosoyus sought to proselytise these views not only in the Alliance, but also among its member organisations.

It is interesting to note that at this time the British Co-operative Union still had a Propaganda Department.[52] A possible factor in its being dropped was that 'propaganda' took on new and unwholesome connotations following Soviet propaganda among co-operatives, trade unions and workers' parties. In this connection, one must recall the neutrality debate in the ICA in 1925 and remember that it had arisen because of British and German objections to Soviet propaganda among their co-operatives. When he moved the British motion at the Ghent Congress, 1924, W. R. Rae had spoken of his movement's fears that it was becoming the 'stalking horse' or 'catspaw' of Moscow Communist Co-operators, who obviously saw co-operative societies as being vehicles for revolutionary propaganda, and for giving moral and material support to trade unions and proletarian campaigns. Rae also drew attention to a recently issued manifesto which, besides explaining Communist policy, urged people to join co-operative societies so as to use them as weapons in the class war. Strong exception was taken to this being circulated among British societies. Rae continued:

'British Co-operators have always favoured the right of the Russians or any other nationality, to determine their own form of Government. When other Britons thought they ought to interfere in Russia, British Co-operators dissented strongly, and we are, therefore, entitled to claim the same liberty to work out our own political future at home.'[53]

Nevertheless, Soviet propaganda continued throughout the decade before the Second World War and reached the point where the ICA protested at 'unjustifiable attacks and misrepresentations'.

In view of all these difficulties, the continuation of Soviet membership becomes even more of an enigma, particularly if we take into account the view, expressed at the highest level of the Alliance in 1936, that no proper co-operative movement remained in the Soviet Union.

In March, 1936, Henry May wrote an article in the *Review of International Co-operation* entitled 'Is the Co-operative Movement Extinct in the USSR?'[54] It looked at different stages in the Soviet Movement's subjugation within the Communist system from 1918 and, in a closely illustrated and argued article, concluded that the Soviet co-operative movement was indeed extinct, claiming that it was no longer distinguishable from the 'super Socialist State nor recognisable according to the approved standards of Co-operation'. Even so, it did not lead to the suggestion that Centrosoyus should leave the Alliance.

Conclusions

This Chapter, although one of the most interesting, has been one of the most difficult to write because of the problem of arriving at conclusions. It is difficult to make a definitive judgement of what lay behind the decision at the 1921 Basle Congress. Then, in view of the subsequent problems, and particularly the verdict of Henry May on the Soviet movement in 1936, it is difficult to establish why Centrosoyus was allowed to remain a member of the Alliance.

Further research might provide some answers, particularly if it was made in the archives of Centrosoyus, the British Co-operative Movement and other ICA member organisations. Unfortunately, there was not sufficient opportunity to undertake it during the present project. However, it is felt that the answer perhaps lies not so much in specific incidents or situations, but in the shared values and identification with the working classes. The ICA undoubtedly saw itself as a working-class movement: May's enthusiasm after his first visit to Moscow comes easily to mind. Therefore, there was an underlying affinity with an avowedly proletarian regime that survived despite the strains that arose.

Practical considerations remain, however. In an interview with W. P Watkins in September, 1989, the author posed the question of why

Centrosoyus had been allowed to remain in the ICA. After long thought Watkins replied rhetorically, 'What alternative was there? '.

His advanced age made it difficult to establish whether he meant that Centrosoyus's withdrawal would have created financial difficulties or whether there was no alternative Soviet co-operative organisation that could have joined the Alliance. It seems that both reasons may have played their part in deciding the ICA's response to Soviet Co-operation.

Notes

1. WATKINS, W. P., *The International Co-operative Alliance*, The International Co-operative Alliance, London, 1970, p. 117.
2. The International Co-operative Alliance, *Report of the ICA Congress Basle*, p. 27.
3. ICA Archives, *Minutes of meeting of ICA Executive with Representatives of British Co-operative Organisations, 14th August, 1918*, p. 2.
4. The International Co-operative Alliance, *Report of the ICA Congress Basle*, pp. 27-28.
5. ICA *Archives, Minutes of the meeting of ICA Executive with Representatives of British Co-operative Organisations, op. cit.*, p. 2.
6. International Co-operative Alliance, *Reports of the Central Organisations in the Various Countries on Their Activities During the War - Report on Russian Co-operation During the War and Revolution*, 1920, p. 84.
7. KRASHENINNIKOV, A. I., *The International Co-operative Alliance Past, Present and Future, Centrosoyus,* printed in German Democratic Republic, 1988, pp. 21-25.
8. International Co-operative Alliance, *Reports of the Central Organisations. op. cit.*, p. 84.
9. Lenin articles appeared in Pravda Nos. 115 and 116 on 26th and 27th May, 1923, but republished by Novosti Press Agency Publishing House, Moscow, 1969, under the title of "V. I. Lenin on Co-operation".

10. International Co-operative Alliance, *Report of the ICA Congress Basle, 1921*, p. 29.
11. *ibid.*, pp. 29-30.
12. *ibid.*, pp. 27-32.
13. International Co-operative Alliance, *Review of International Co-operation, No. 6 June, 1932*, p. 219.
14. International Co-operative Alliance, *Report of the ICA Congress Basle, 1921, op. cit.*, p. 55.
15. This study, Chapter 2, p. 47.
16. KRASHENINNIKOV, A. I., *op. cit.*, p. 64.
17. International Co-operative Alliance, *Report of the ICA Congress Basle, op. cit.*, p. 51.
18. ICA Archives, Letter from Henry May, General Secretary, to William Maxwell, President, ICA, 28th May, 1920.
19. ICA Archives, Letterhead from Workers' International Russian Relief, letter from Secretary to Henry May, 20th April, 1923.
20. ICA Archives, Letter from Mrs H. Crawfurd to Henry May, 1925.
21. ICA Archives, Faucherre, Henry, Proof version, *60 Jahre Internationaler Genossenschaftsbund 1895-1960*, p. 351.
22. ICA Archives, *British-Russian Trade Agreement, 1921*.
23. International Co-operative Alliance, Memorandum on the Agenda of the Meeting of the ICA Central Committee, Copenhagen, April, 1921, p. 1.
24. ARMSTRONG, David, *The Rise of the International Organisation -A Short History*, Macmillan Education, Basingstoke, Hampshire, p. 17.
25. ICA Archives, An Agreement between the Old and New Boards of Centrosoyus, signed in Berlin, 25th January, 1922.
26. ICA Archives, Declaration made by Old Board, Centrosoyus appended to above Agreement.
27. International Co-operative Alliance, *Minutes of the meeting of the ICA Executive, Brussels, 28-29 January, 1922*.
28 Members of the International Co-operative Delegation to the USSR were Henry May on behalf of the ICA, Sir Thomas Allen, A.W. Golightly, J. English, J. Hawkins, (Great Britain), E. Poisson, (France) and Victor Serwy (Belgium).

29 International Co-operative Alliance, *Report of the ICA Congress, Ghent, 1924*, pp. 66-67.
30. *ibid.*
31. ICA Archives, Typescript headed: "The International Co-operative Delegation to Russia" with the name of H. J. May underneath.
32. ICA Archives, Unsigned typescript headed "The International Co-operative Delegation in Russia" - Moscow - its Mosques and Museums".
33. International Co-operative Alliance, *Minutes of meeting of ICA Central Committee, 10-11 April, 1922*, Milan, p. 4.
34. International Co-operative Alliance, Memorandum on the Status of the National Co-operative Organisations in the Union of the Soviet Socialist Republics, With Special Reference to Representation on the Central Committee, p. 1, presented to meeting of ICA Central Committee, Paris, 5th and 6th October, 1925.
35. International Co-operative Alliance, *Minutes of meeting of ICA Executive, 28th and 29th January, 1911*, p. 5.
36. International Co-operative Alliance, *Minutes of meeting of Executive Milan, 9th - 10th April, 1922*, p. 1.
37. International Co-operative *Alliance, Minutes of meeting of ICA Executive, Essen, 30th September to 2nd October, 1922*, p. 3.
38. WATKINS, W. P, *op. cit.*, p. 138.
39. International Co-operative Alliance, *Report of ICA Congress..1924*, p. 68.
40. *ibid.*, p. 69.
41. International Co-operative Alliance, Memorandum on Status of National Co-operative Organisations ...., *op. cit.*, p. 3.
42. International Co-operative Alliance, *Report of the ICA Congress, Vienna, 1930*, p. 148.
43. WATKINS, W. P, *op. cit.*, p. 176.
44. International Co-operative Alliance, *Minutes of meeting of ICA Executive, Paris, 27-29 September, 1931*, pp. 1-2.
45. ICA Archives, Letter from Henry May, General Secretary to Väinö Tanner, ICA President, 16th December, 1931.
46. ICA Archives, Letter from Väinö Tanner to Henry May, 22nd March, 1932.

47. International Co-operative Alliance, *Minutes of meeting of ICA Executive, Geneva, 28th October, 1932*, p. 3.
48. International Co-operative Alliance, *Minutes of meeting of ICA Executive, Vienna, 6-8th October, 1933*, p. 3.
49. International Co-operative Alliance, *Report of ICA Congress London, 1934*, Appendix vi.
50. International Co-operative Alliance, *Report of ICA Congress, Paris, 1937*, Appendix iv.
51. International Co-operative Alliance, *Report of ICA Congress, Zurich, 1946*, Appendix v.
52. ICA Archives, Letter from R. A. Palmer, General Secretary, Co-operative Union to Miss G. Polley, Administrative Secretary, ICA, 25th November, 1940-letterhead listing the Union's Departments as being: - Agriculture- Education- Finance- Labour- Legal Propaganda- Publications- Research
53. International Co-operative Alliance, *Report of the ICA Congress, Ghent, 1924*, pp. 220-221.
54. International Co-operative Alliance, *Review of International Co-operation, No. 3, March, 1936*, pp. 82-86.

Chapter five

The ICA'S Response to Italian Fascism and German Nazism

Introduction

Having examined the ICA's response to Communism we now turn to the study of its reaction to the other major and competing ideology of the 20th century, namely Fascism. The first manifestations of this occurred shortly after the 1914-18 War. Indeed, the ICA's Basle Congress in 1921 passed a resolution condemning Fascist violence in Italy.

This Chapter, and the one that follows, will trace the impact of Fascism on co-operative movements in Italy, Germany, Austria, Spain and Czechoslovakia. Besides describing how the ICA tried to protect its member organisations in those countries, we shall also note the position it took on the Sino-Japanese War. In effect, these two Chapters will describe events leading to the Second World War and will, therefore, be largely chronological. The first Chapter will take us through events from 1921 until 1934, and deal with those in Italy and Germany. In both cases the Alliance took an immediate anti-Fascist line because it argued that Fascism was against Co-operative Principles and encouraged violence against co-operatives, their property and their members. Inherent in the ICA's response was a sense of solidarity, and by the 1930s the Alliance had developed sufficient organisational capacity to give practical expression to this. The ICA's response was also buttressed by close personal friendships among many ICA leaders, as well as an efficient central office and good postal communications. International telephones were not used, and telegrams only in emergencies. Instead, there was the fast overland transport of letters, and the convention was that they were answered by 'return of post'. Often it is surprising to find how quickly letters moved, for example between London and Hamburg. All these factors will be seen at work in the following account of the Italian situation.

Italian Fascism and Italian Co-operation

Italy was the first country to set up a Fascist dictatorship and, in doing so, reflected a shift to the right which took place throughout Europe in the postwar years. There were a number of possible reasons for this. One was the fear of the westward spread of Communism from the Soviet Union: there had, in fact, been brief Soviet-style Governments in Budapest and Munich, while others had almost formed in Vienna and Berlin. Another reason, cited by J. M. Roberts in his book, Europe 1880-1945, was the rejection of the whole of liberal civilisation - capitalism and the market system, individualism and rationality, the belief in progress and the faith in politics as a way of meeting society's needs without violence'.[1] Indeed, apart from Czechoslovakia, which maintained a democratic constitution until her absorption by Germany in 1938, and 1939, all the new states created by the post-war settlements developed right-wing or dictatorial regimes.[2]

We should note, therefore, that the post-war world was unlikely to be one in which the ICA, as an international working-class movement with a number of prominent socialists among its leaders, was going to feel comfortable. This was particularly the case where right-wing regimes threatened national co-operative movements to whose aid the ICA felt that it had to come.

The first clash came with the new Italian Fascist regime: the issue was not to prove as divisive within the ICA as that of Centrosoyus had been. Nevertheless, it showed that the ICA needed to take into account the regimes of the far right quite as much as it did that of the extreme left in the USSR.

The first sign of the Italian crisis appeared within the ICA at its Congress in Basle in 1921. Their concern was registered about violence against Italian co-operatives in a protest tabled in the names of Goedhart (Holland), Sir Thomas Allen and Prof. Hall (United Kingdom), Poisson and Prof. Gide (France), Prof. Staudinger (Germany), Prof. Totomianz (Russia)* and Dr. Suter (Switzerland). It read:

Elected to ICA Central Committee at the Glasgow Congress, 1913, and remained on the Committee until the end of the Basle Congress, when a new Central Committee was elected.

"That this International Co-operative Congress, having learned of the acts of brutality, of violence, and of devastation done in Italy by the hordes of people paid by the capitalists, with the complicity of the police, against the co-operative institutions and their employees, who have been killed, wounded, and chased from their offices, protests against these barbarous and criminal manifestations, and expresses the hope that the indignation of honest people may procure peace for the Italian Co-operative Movement".[3]

The resolution passed was in support of the ICA's Italian member organisation, the Lega Nazionale, established in October, 1886. Then named the Federazione fra le Co-operative Italiane, it became one of the ICA's founding members when its leader, Luigi Luzzatti, became a member of the 1895 Provisional Central Committee. By the early years of this century, though, the Lega had moved closer to the Italian Socialist Party and thereafter remained left-wing.

This shift to the left seems to have been one reason for the formation of non-Socialist co-operative organisations. In January, 1919, the Catholic Confederazione delle Co-operative was set up, followed shortly afterwards by the Sindacato Nazionale delle Co-operative, which became a forerunner of the Italian Fascist Co-operative Movement. Both the Confederazione and the Sindacato sought relations with the ICA, but the Alliance's Executive ruled that the Lega should remain the ICA's Italian organisation.[4] When the left-wing Lega became a target for Italian Fascists the ICA felt that it had to defend it. Hence the resolution at the Basle Congress, the tone of which illustrates the working-class sympathy of the Alliance. It should be noted, though, that the resolution had been proposed by middle-class leaders. Attacks on the Lega's co-operatives should be seen within the context of Italy's political fragmentation and post-war convulsions. Despite being on the winning side the country had been weakened by the Great War. Demobilised troops returned to unemployment and inflation. Politically and socially, the country was bitterly divided between right and left, the former fearing the threat of Communism spreading westward. The Italian Communist Party was formed in January 1921, [5] while the Fascio di Combattimento, which had preceded it some two years earlier, became known as the Fascist Party. Headed by Benito Mussolini, the latter drew financial support from industrialists afraid of the spread of Communism, and membership from among discontented war veterans and the unemployed. It soon numbered 300,000 and included the violent 'black shirts' who attacked co-operative property and personnel.[6]

Violence against co-operatives, as well as against trade unions and socialists, increased after Mussolini came to power in October, 1922. In January, 1924, the Government made all associations, including co-operatives, subject to the provisions of provincial authorities: these had the power to inspect or to dissolve organisations. In this way, in November, 1925, the Lega was dissolved by the Prefect of Milan, on the grounds that it had engaged in 'anti-national activity aimed at subverting the institutions and the regime'.[7]

The ICA'S Response

From the time of its resolution at the Basle Congress, the ICA sought to help its Italian affiliate. We should note the influence of close personal relations, particularly between Henry May, ICA General Secretary, Dr. A. Suter, of the Swiss Co-operative Union, and Antonio Vergnanini, the Lega's General Secretary from 1912. Born in 1861 into a bourgeois family, Vergnanini went to university and developed considerable literary ability, later writing plays and operettas. He also became a Socialist, but Italy's laws against Anarchists and Socialists forced him into exile in Switzerland for seven years. After his return in 1901 he devoted most of his time to the co-operative movement, and attended all ICA Congresses between 1907 and 1927, except that in 1910. He also served on the Central Committee between 1913 and 1927.[8] Besides translating the works of Charles Gide into Italian, Vergnanini wrote extensively for Co-operative journals.[9]

The resolution passed at the Basle Congress was forwarded to the Italian Government, which made no response. In May, 1922, in a Memorandum sent to May in London, Vergnanini updated the position and attributed many of the current problems to the 'war crisis' which had destroyed the old cohesiveness of Italian co-operation, dividing it into 'opposing currents: Socialists, Nationalists, Catholics, ex-soldiers,

Republicans, Communists, Trade Unions, Fascists and autonomous independents'.[10] As a result, the hegemony of the Lega had been broken and its members had become increasingly 'subjected to encroachments, acts of violence, massacre of hundreds of our best men, burning of property, devastation and pillage which have been experienced in nearly all our provinces....... '[11] Vergnanini ended by calling upon the International Co-operative Alliance to assist the Italian movement with 'political and moral protection'.

The ICA's response was quick and positive. It was the first time it had intervened in a situation arising between a member movement and its national Government. No similar action had been taken over Centrosoyus, but neither had it been sought.

As in all the crises which followed - Germany, Austria, Spain and Czechoslovakia - Henry May responded quickly and decisively. Various references suggest that he was a 'little man' in physique, but he was obviously robust in other ways. As soon as he received the update from Vergnanini he contacted Dr. Suter who, as a Swiss member of the Central Committee, had been elected to the ICA Executive in 1921. May asked if Suter could travel to Milan to see at first hand what the position was and then report to the ICA Executive. Suter visited Milan between the 30th September and 2nd October, 1922, and did so at his own expense. His report to the Executive,[12] made in excellent English, like all his handwritten letters to May, showed that he had first gone to the headquarters of the Lega in Milan, where he had been given the statistics of the co-operatives 'destroyed or invaded'. Later he visited many societies, and largely verified the facts and figures he had been given. Suter concluded that 'approximately one-third' of the Lega's affiliated societies had been destroyed, while another third were no longer able to pay their subscriptions to the central body, which could then have difficulty in paying its membership fees to the Alliance.

Suter added that he was 'certain that often private interests are hidden under a political mask with a view to attempting to destroy the Co-operative Movement. ' The situation was virtually one of civil war, but Suter reported that co-operative leaders argued that all attacks should be received with passive resistance, and that they no more wished for civil war than they did for war with other countries. Suter ended his report with three proposals. First, that the Co-operative Press in all countries should vigorously denounce the Fascist attacks on Italian co-operatives. Secondly, that members of the Alliance should give financial aid to the Lega. Thirdly, that the co-operative banking organisations should give sympathetic consideration to any requests for loans made by Italian societies.

In December Suter travelled to the Hague to meet May and Goedhart to discuss his report.[13] As a result of that meeting, and assured of the agreement of the Executive, May sent the following letter of protest to Mussolini on 20th December, 1922:

"At the request of the Executive Committee of the International Co-operative Alliance, which represents about thirty States and nearly twenty-five millions of Co-operators throughout the world, I have the honour to forward for your consideration the following resolution expressing the views of this Alliance as to the present sad state of Co-operation in Italy, and asking your powerful and friendly intervention to prevent the extension of the damage, both personal and material, which the Movement in Italy has suffered during the past year. The International Co-operative Alliance, which is bound by its Statutes to act independent of all party spirit whether religious or political, has carefully examined the facts submitted to it by reliable authorities as to the action of the Italian Fascisti towards the Italian Co-operative Movement. It has also now had the great advantage of studying the report received from its special envoy, Dr. A. Suter, of the conditions which he had witnessed during a recent tour of the devastated Co-operative Societies in Italy.

It has learnt with great regret of the outrages inflicted on Co-operators and the property of Co-operative Institutions in that country where Co-operation was organised and inspired by leaders such as Luigi Luzzatti, Ugo Rabbeno, Leone Wollembourg, and upheld in the Councils of the Government and also in Parliament by Statesmen such as G. Giolitti.

Outrages, assaults on persons, the destruction of property, which should be excluded from social conflicts in civilised times, are inexplicable to Co-operators throughout the world in a country whose Government only recently, on the occasion of the Economic Conference held at Genoa in the Spring of 1922, greeted the Co-operative Movement in such lofty and courageous terms. The International Co-operative Alliance wonders how, in a highly civilised country, it is possible with impunity to threaten, terrorise, assault and even kill the administrators of the Co-operative Societies, pillage and burn their establishments, and illegally seize their property.

The International Co-operative Alliance has always held aloof from ALL interference with the internal policy of States but its mission is to defend Co-operative Principles and also the Institutions which apply those Principles. In the fulfilment of its mission it has received encouragement from the most eminent politicians in Italy. For this reason the International Co-operative Alliance, being proud to count Luigi Luzzatti among the members of its committee of Honour, and gratefully remembering the hospitality extended to its Seventh Congress at Cremona in 1907, feels that it is not only justified, but has a duty to express to the Italian Government the deep pain and indignation felt by Co-operators throughout the world. It further expresses the hope that the Co-operative Movement may receive reparation for the damage to which it has been subjected in a country where the Government, the political parties and the civil community have hitherto agreed to assure to Co-operation a more and more important part in the national life and international relations'.

Mussolini made no reply, although May tried hard to elicit one. The ICA's letter and resolution were eventually forwarded by the Italian Foreign Office to its embassy in London, which invited May to call to discuss it.[14]. However, no date for a meeting was suggested and, when May wrote requesting one,[15] no reply was received. May then called in person at the embassy, but failed to gain either an appointment or a reply to the original letter to Mussolini.[16]

At its meeting in Ghent in February, 1923, the ICA Executive declared its wish to continue helping the Lega [17] but, by this time, Vergnanini and his colleagues had become more hesitant about what moves to make.[18] They may have believed, as many others did, that Fascism was a temporary phenomenon and that they should wait for the 'Fascist Cyclone' to pass.[19] If it did not, they had reason to believe that they could expect little from the Mussolini regime: this conclusion emerged from a meeting with Il Duce in November, 1922, despite the fact that Mussolini had apparently shown goodwill.[20]

In his book on the Lega, John Earle speculated whether this goodwill had been prompted by the protest of the ICA at its Basle Congress the previous year. Quite apart from that, it does seem that the Italian Government wanted to maintain some kind of relationship with the Alliance. This is suggested by the fact that, two years later, it sent three representatives to the Congress in Ghent in 1924. This was the first of the Alliance's Congresses to which Governments had been invited to appoint observers. Ten Governments did so, each sending one representative, apart from the Belgian Government, which sent two, and the Italian, which sent three.[21] The Italian Government also encouraged the mounting of the Italian stand at the Co-operative exhibition that was held in conjunction with the Congress. W. P. Watkins observed that those who had seen the Italian exhibition 'might have been pardoned for believing that Italy was the European country par excellence where Co-operation was favoured.....'[22]

It is also possible to detect Italian Government influence behind a move made by the old Italian co-operative veteran, Luigi Luzzatti, who was still a member of the ICA's Committee of Honour. He had written to May, proposing that the International Co-operative Alliance and the Association of Italian People's Banks, should call a 'confidential meeting in order to lay the foundation of a European People's Bank'.[23]

This proposal received a cool reception or, rather, no reception at all. Although May reported Luzzatti's letter to the Ghent Congress, Goedhart as President, moved directly on to the next business, so allowing no opportunity for comment or discussion.[24] The matter was not even raised when Gaston Levy (France) presented a paper shortly afterwards on closer relations between member movements' banking organisations. It seems likely that, in ICA eyes, Luzzatti had already become compromised by allowing himself to become a figure-head for Italian co-operation under the Mussolini regime. When the Lega was dissolved in the following year the Italian Government created a new organisation, the Ente Nazionale della Cooperazione, and appointed Luzzatti to be the President of its Supreme Council.

It seems unlikely that good relations with the ICA could have been a long-term aim of the Italian Government. Although its representatives at the Ghent Congress delivered a formal invitation to the Alliance to send a delegation of enquiry to Italy,[25] the arrangements were never finalised. The invitation was accepted, but May expressed his private doubts to Dr. Suter[26] and to Goedhart.[27]

He was further worried when he heard from Suter that Italian refugees in Switzerland believed that the ICA visit would be 'useless' because anyone seen to give it information was likely to be killed, some days afterwards.[28]

The Italians did not finalise the date or other arrangements for the ICA visit. Eventually May accepted Vergnanini's view that the invitation had been simply an expedient to avoid an adverse vote of the Congress' at Ghent.[29] Events speeded up once more with the dissolution of the Lega on 14th November, 1925.[30] Vergnanini had been stopped when leaving the office by 'a party of Fascists accompanied by the carabineri and the police' and compelled to return to hand over keys. He managed, however, to send a postcard with the news to Dr. Suter in Lausanne, who immediately sent a telegram to May in London. As soon as he received this, May sent the following telegram to Mussolini:

'International Co-operative Alliance learns with great regret of seizure by Fascists of offices and material of Lega Nazionale delle Co-operative Milan on Saturday last Stop Lega Nazionale affiliated to this Alliance nearly thirty years as purely economic organisation with active collaboration Luzzatti Buffoli and other eminent Italians Stop This Alliance profoundly convinced that Lega Nazionale and its constituents are no way inimical to Italian administration and equally not concerned in plots Stop We confidently appeal to your Government to afford Lega Nazionale Milan the protection accorded to all law abiding citizens.*

Goedhart, President
Poisson, Vice President
May, General Secretary' [31]

This was followed by a letter to Mussolini from Goedhart and May [32], while the ICA Executive agreed that May should write to all ICA affiliated organisations urging them to lodge their own appeals.[33] ICA Archive material also shows that May canvassed for support among members of the British Government. On 4th December he wrote to the British Prime Minister, Stanley Baldwin, asking for 'the aid of your intervention with the Italian Government on behalf of the Co-operative Movement of Italy..... ' and informed Baldwin that ICA affiliates in 33 countries had 'forwarded protests and appeals both direct and through their governments'[34]. May was later able to report to the ICA Executive that Baldwin had acknowledged the letter and that it had been 'personally mentioned between the Prime Minister and some of our friends in Parliament'. [35]

May also kept in close touch with Suter and Vergnanini, letters to the latter being sent 'in duplicate and to different addresses as a precaution',[36] and canvassed personal friends in the British Government. [37] and [38] His personal feelings were summed up in one of his letters to Suter, when he said that he had done his utmost to give effect to dignified appeals and protests but continued: 'It is with great difficulty that I am able to restrain myself to fitting language, but of course I realise that only by doing so can there be any possible hope of aiding our friends.'[39]

Examining the wider impact of Italian developments on other parts of the Alliance, we should note that because Centrosoyus had remained a member of the Alliance, its views had to be taken into account on the Italian question. These soon became apparent when Khinchuk, leader of the Centrosoyus delegation to the ICA and a member of the Alliance's Executive, proposed, together with Lozovsky, General Secretary of the Red International Labour Unions, that Centrosoyus, with the non-communist International Federation of Trade Unions and the ICA, should hold a joint conference. The purpose of this would be to organise joint action in defence of Italian co-operatives and trade unions.[40]

May handled the matter adroitly. When reporting to Khinchuk that Executive Committee members opposed the proposal on the grounds that they felt each organisation should work in their own spheres 'for

Dr. Anton Suter, Switzerland
1863 - 1942

Bernhardt Jaeggi (CH)
President Coop Suisse
1869 - 1944

Albert Thomas, ILO Director
1878 - 1932

the object we commonly desire', he added two further considerations. One was the fact that the 1924 Congress of the ICA had decided that the Alliance should not engage in joint activities with the International Federation of Trade Unions (IFTU) without the prior agreement of the Central Committee; the other was that the IFTU had itself decided to have no relations with its Moscow counterpart.[41]

Besides receiving Centrosoyus's views, May also found it politic to take into account the views of the International Labour Office: Albert Thomas, its Director, was still a member of the ICA Central Committee. On 5th December, 1925, and about to leave for Paris to meet Poisson to review the Italian situation, May had 'an interview with Albert Thomas who promised to make presentations from the ILO to the Italian authorities'. Thomas was visiting London and supported Suter's view that the ICA should send a delegation to Milan to speak directly with Vergnanini.[42] However, May and Poisson, when they met in Paris, took a more cautious view. Both men were worried that such a delegation might increase the danger for Vergnanini, and felt any meeting would be better held outside of Italy, possibly in the Swiss town of Lugano.[43]

The ICA Executive disagreed, and took the rather surprising decision that May should make the visit to Vergnanini and members of the Lega Council by himself. It also earmarked the sum of £1,000 to help 'Italian Co-operators to keep together the remnants of their Organisation'[44]. May left for Milan on 1st March, 1926. En route, he met Albert Thomas again, but this time at the ILO in Geneva, and also Dr. Suter in Lausanne. After earlier developments in the Italian situation, and no doubt because of geographical proximity, the Swiss Co-operative Union had decided that it did not wish to be involved in any direct representations to, or objection to, the acts of the Italian Government, as it was not in the national interests to do so'.[45] Consequently, it was no longer appropriate for Dr. Suter to accompany May, although he indicated that he still wished to do so. May doubted, however, whether Suter would be allowed into Italy after the bitter attacks Fascists had made on his report to the ICA three years earlier. Uncertain, also, whether he himself would be allowed to cross the border, May carried a letter of introduction to the branch of a British firm in Milan to make it easier for him to do so.[46] Even so, he believed that he had come under surveillance.[47] Italian friends also thought this, but felt that there should be little danger as long as May behaved himself and expressed no anti-Fascist sentiments. They warned him, though, to be careful while eating and drinking because 'even waiters have ears and that some waiters are Fascists'.[48]

For reasons of security May had not advised Vergnanini of his arrival. Thus, Vergnanini was out when he called. However, he joined May shortly afterwards and they spent much of the next two days in talks, joined by those members of the Lega Council who could be assembled at short notice.[49]

Like Suter three years earlier, May tried to establish how many Lega affiliated societies had disappeared; how many had become private undertakings; how many had joined the Ente Nazionale, forcibly or otherwise; and the extent of Lega's financial losses. May concluded, 'The loss which the Movement has sustained by confiscation, incendiarism, and other forms of destruction is......enormous, and at present incalculable.[50] The Lega believed that 4,000 of its affiliated co-operatives had been destroyed. Approximately a further 3,000 societies had been forced to join the Fascists'. 400 more had become private traders, while the remainder had so far escaped Fascist control. Lega officials estimated that the present membership of the new Ente was between 5,000 and 6,000 co-operatives.

May went to some lengths to obtain corroboration of the Lega's claims of violence against co-operatives. He reported to the ICA Executive that he had consulted sources independent of the Lega leaders, and that they had indeed verified these claims. May concluded that there were no reasons to doubt these observers' statements 'that the reign of Fascism is to a great extent a reign of terrorism, and that thousands have donned the Fascist badge as a measure of self-defence'.

In receiving May's report, the ICA Executive could not know that events in Italy would be repeated in Germany and Austria. Consequently, their responses were probably made in the belief that this was a one off situation which would set no precedents. They were thus receptive to the idea that the remnants of the Lega should be formed into a sort of agency of the ICA in Italy, or a statistical bureau of the ICA'.[51] May reported that the Lega leaders had supported the idea that their President, Vergnanini, should set up a consultative and statistical office, which would be able to keep in touch with loyal elements in Italy and also with the ICA.[52] The ICA Executive agreed to this suggestion.[53] However, we should note that little was ever heard of the office, which was initially based in Milan but later in Rome.[54] Vergnanini became its head but made no regular reports to the ICA Executive.

As we have already noted, the Italian Government set up the Ente Nazionale della Cooperazione in 1926 and this became the national and controlling organisation of all co-operatives, including those affiliated to the Catholic Federation. The President, appointed by the Government, was the ageing Luigi Luzzatti. Writing of these events in his history of the ICA from 1895 to 1970, W. P. Watkins observed: Mercifully, he did not long survive this indignity, but died on 29th March, 1927. [55]

ICA Archives reveal that the Alliance maintained a good research capacity, which allowed it to follow events in countries where member movements came into conflict with their national regimes. This process began with the Italian crisis. Many items were collected, including the Model Rules of the Ente under the heading of Fascist National Party, Ente Nationale Della Cooperazione, Milan [56] and letters from the Mayor of Milan, concerning the administration of co-operative societies.[57]

The ICA Archives also filed a report of an interview with Luigi Luzzatti in which he claimed that, with the help of Mussolini, he had been able to bring all forms of co-operation together within the Ente. But he complained about the foreign protestations' by 'foreign associations', among which he no doubt included the International Co-operative Alliance.[58]

From 1926 the Italian Government and the Fascist Ente on the one hand, and the ICA on the other, became engaged in propaganda campaigns against each other. The ICA's main vehicle was its *Bulletin*, renamed the *Review of International Co-operation* in 1928.

However, we should now turn to the question of Italian membership in the Alliance. Until the Stockholm Congress in 1927 the Lega, or its subsequent Consultative Office, was taken to be the ICA's Italian affiliate, and Vergnanini remained on the Central Committee. Thereafter, the affiliation lapsed and the Ente did not apply to join. Nevertheless, the Ente sought to gain credibility with, and to develop relations with, co-operative organisations outside Italy. It even invited the ICA Executive to several events, but these invitations were not accepted.[59]

This situation continued throughout the late 1920s. By 1931, however, it began to change, although it is not clear why. In March of that year May attended the World Wheat Conference in Rome, and, in a surprise move, Vergnanini suggested that he should meet Roasario Labadessa, Director General of the Ente Nazionale. May's personal note[60] indicates that 'Vergnanini and his friends.....desired to see the Italian Movement once more a member of the international co-operative family'. It seems that Albert Thomas of the ILO also took this view. When May reluctantly agreed to a meeting, arrangements for it were made by Dr. Georges Fauquet, who was then Head of the Co-operative Section of the ILO and also a French member of the ICA's Central Committee: indeed, May recorded, the meeting was held in 'Dr. Fauquet's room at the Clinic'. Present were May, Labadessa, Vergnanini and his niece, and a 'local representative of the ILO', M. Cabrini. Its aim was 'to have a friendly conversation on neutral ground', although May recorded that he had only accepted the invitation on the understanding that the others, and not he, had sought the meeting.

Both sides reviewed past events, but came to the conclusion that there was little purpose in repeating past hostilities. Labadessa went on to refer to the possibility that the Ente would apply to join the Alliance, but 'made no definite proposition'. He indicated that, unless they had some assurance that it would be accepted, 'they could not support the humiliation of refusal'. May replied that no such assurance could be given but, in any event, the matter could not be considered in the absence of an application. He suggested that 'the time was not yet ripe for their admission', but felt that both sides' difficulties might be eased by exchanging information, documentation, and ideas purely objectively. The first step, though, should be the 'cessation of personal attacks upon the leaders of the ICA, upon the work and policy of the ICA, and incidentally, upon the General Secretary'.

Relations seemed set to improve when May accepted an invitation to visit the offices of the Ente Nazionale the following evening. Fauquet accompanied him and they were shown around by Labadessa and a large group of Fascist members of the personnel. It is interesting to note that May was somewhat impressed. He recorded that the offices were well organised and gave 'full evidence of serious and useful work', with publications being numerous and well distributed. May said:

'...I came away with the conviction that the Co-operative Movement in Italy today possess many features which would rightly excite the approval of the members of the ICA Executive if they could see them in operation!'

Although May seemed to be moderating his views there were others in the Alliance who were not yet prepared to do so, including the leaders of the German Co-operative Movement. Everling, Head of the Grosseinkaufs-Gesellschafts D. Consumvereine, wrote to the ICA on 28th July, 1932:

'In view of the fact that the Italian Co-operative Societies or their Central Organisation are not members of the ICA, it has recently aroused our astonishment that Dr. Labadessa was able to publish an article in the June issue of the ICA Review entitled: "Credit Trading". From this it seems that your attitude towards the Fascist Co-operative Organisations of Italy has changed. We may, therefore, be allowed to ask for an explanation and the attitude to be adopted towards the visit of Italian co-operators. We would like to observe that we are prepared to allow Italian co-operators to visit our factories, if such a procedure would not give the impression to the opposing side that we received Italian co-operators unconditionally and with the same sentiments of friendship which we have towards members of the International Co-operative Alliance.'[61]

May replied, assuring Everling that there had been no change in the situation as far as the admission of the Ente Nazionale into membership/ of the Alliance was concerned. However, relations between the two organisations had been modified since his meetings with Labadessa and the Executive's acceptance of his recommendation that there should be a greater exchange of information 'without prejudice to the question of membership'. Concerning the publication of the Labadessa article, May made a double defence. First, it had not been written for the Review, but for a Fascist Co-operative Journal from which it had been reprinted because it supported a line that May wished to urge. Secondly, it had never been the practice of the Review to exclude articles from persons who were not members of ICA member organisations.

May added that, while he hoped that Italian visitors to German co-operatives would be received in the spirit of relations agreed to by the Executive last year....I do not suggest for a moment that you should treat them on the same plane as members of the ICA but only that they should not be refused information which is generally accorded to any enquirer, or a sight of your operations'.[62]

When the Executive held their next meeting in Geneva the following October, they endorsed the views summed up in May's reply to Everling. Thus, there would be 'no change in the attitude of the Alliance with regard to the admission of the Italian Co-operative Movement to membership of the ICA, but there seemed to be no reason for refusing the desire of the Italian leaders for information concerning other Co-operative Movements'.[63]

This remained the position until the outbreak of the 1939-45 War.

The Italian Situation - Conclusions

To conclude this section on the Italian situation we should underline certain aspects. The first is to make a comparison with the ICA's response to Communism. Whereas the Alliance had been divided or ambivalent at its Basle Congress about the Centrosoyus situation, on the Italian question it was hostile to Fascism from the start. Divisions only began to appear in 1931, when some, like the Germans, believed that some kind of rapprochement was developing. An element in the ICA's hostility to Fascism was the fear that it encompassed attempts by private traders to undermine co-operatives through political action. We will see this recur in the Austrian situation.

Another interesting point is that, despite coming from quite different ends of the political spectrum, both the Communist regime in the USSR and the Fascist regime in Italy appeared to have wanted some kind of relationship with the International Co-operative Alliance. This suggests that the ICA was seen as an important international forum, and its working-class member co-operative movements as fertile ground for propaganda.

The final point to underline is that the Alliance reacted immediately and robustly to Italian Fascism. This was not only at the level of the Congress, Central and Executive Committees, but also at personal levels among ICA leaders. Moreover, such a response was united. When we come to consider the impact of Nazism on co-operative movements elsewhere, we will find that the ICA became less sure of its responses, possibly for two main reasons: how to preserve political neutrality and how to resist the overwhelming tide of events.

We could perhaps end this section on the Italian situation with a postscript illustrating again the close personal ties among ICA leaders. When Vergnanini died in April, 1934, his widow was unable to meet the full cost of a 'permanent sepulture'. Cabrini, the ILO representative in Rome, present at the 1931 meeting between May and Labadessa, appealed to the ICA for financial help. In an unusual gesture it made a gift of 2,500 lira towards the cost of the grave stone.[64]

Change of ICA President

Before moving on to the rise of Hitler in Germany and its repercussions on German co-operation, we should note an organisational change within the ICA. This came when G. J. D. C. Goedhart (Holland) resigned at the Stockholm Congress of 1927 and Väinö Tanner (Finland) was elected in his place.

As early as 1925, Goedhart had indicated his wish to retire because of ill-health.[65] May, and the Executive tried to persuade him to remain, and he did so for nearly two years but, in February, 1927, felt that he must finally withdraw.[66]

The search for a new President is revealing about the internal politics within the ICA at the time. For example, it showed that May was not automatically pro-British. He obviously had ideas about who should succeed Goedhart, and was aghast when he heard from the German leader, Heinrich Kaufmann, that Goedhart was suggesting that the British should nominate the next President. Despite their personal friendship this news led May to remonstrate with Goedhart.[67] He wrote saying that, although he himself was British, he hoped that Goedhart would not pursue the idea.

May's relations with his own Movement had not always been smooth, stemming perhaps from his view that the English Co-operative Wholesale Society was not as helpful as he thought it should have been in attempts to form an International Co-operative Wholesale Society. In May, 1922, he had written to Goedhart saying:

'I cannot tell you the depression I feel since....our meetings at Milan. I regard the position of the co-operative leaders of Britain as being exactly comparable with the attitude of M. Poincare** towards the Genoa Conference, that is to say, they are all the time protesting their sympathy with the ideal and their decision to make progress, but much more strenuously standing in the way of any advance.'[68]

While not wanting a British President, May had another candidate in mind, Dr. Bernhardt Jaeggi of the Swiss Co-operative Movement. In his letter to Goedhart regarding the Presidency May had said:

'I do not care whether he comes from the smallest country and the smallest organisation in the whole Movement so long as he is a man* in the widest sense of the word.'[69]

* May's underlining
**Prime Minister of France

The Swiss Movement was not necessarily small. Of 35 countries represented in the Alliance at the 1927 Stockholm Congress, it came ninth in terms of subscriptions.[70]

Together with Dr. Suter, who had been so active on the Italian question, Dr. Jaeggi was a member of the Central Committee. He was not, however, a member of the ICA Executive Committee, from where it might have been supposed that the next President would emerge. Both of the existing Vice-Presidents, A. Whitehead (Great Britain) and E. Poisson (France), had declared their interest in succeeding Goedhart.

After the Executive's acceptance of Goedhart's resignation at its meeting in Strasbourg in February, 1927, May travelled to Basle to meet Dr. Jaeggi. It is interesting to note that he was accompanied by Miss Gertrude Polley. As we have noted, she had joined the Alliance in 1920, coming, like May, from the Parliamentary Office of the British Co-operative Union. It is likely that she had been at the Strasbourg meeting. At its meeting in August, 1920, the Executive agreed that, at future meetings, May should be assisted by a member of staff.[71]

May justified his approach to Jaeggi on the grounds that many members of the ICA sought the advice and opinion of the General Secretary, which it is laid down in the statutes of the ICA, is one of his duties to give'[72]. He continued that he believed that Jaeggi 'would be acceptable to a large proportion of the members of the Central Committee', as he was to May himself. May also indicated that he would have liked to have found our new President in Switzerland.[73] However, Jaeggi declined to let his name go forward.[74]

It is not clear how Väinö Tanner (Finland) emerged as the Presidential front-runner. Like Jaeggi, he was not a member of the ICA Executive. His name was first suggested by Heinrich Kaufmann (Germany). At the beginning of his career Tanner had been a protégé of Kaufmann in Germany. However, Kaufmann subsequently changed his mind and had written to members of the Executive urging, as Goedhart had done, that 'the British should find a President'.[75]

It therefore seems likely that the Scandinavian co-operative movements played a large part in Tanner's election. He was known to have a high standing among them, and they were becoming effective as the first geographical pressure group within the ICA.

At the time of his election as ICA President, Väinö Tanner was Finland's Prime Minister. Possibly, because of commitments arising from this office, he was not present at the Stockholm Congress and was therefore elected in his absence. However, his involvement with the ICA predated the First World War; he had joined the Alliance as an individual member in 1905. In 1919, he had written to the ICA Executive asking if he could retain his seat on the Central Committee. The Executive had had to refuse because Tanner had left his then nominating body, the Union Keskuskunta, so was no longer entitled to a seat on the Committee [76]. In a very short time, though, Tanner brought the new Union, Kulutusosuuskuntien Keskusliitto (KK) representing 'workingmen's co-operative societies', which he had helped to form, into the Alliance[77] and was therefore able to return to the Central Committee.

The election of the new President has been described for two main reasons. One is that it illustrated the organisational capacity of the Alliance to effect the change smoothly. As in the case of Centrosoyus at the Basle Congress, 1921, a decision of Congress legitimised the outcome. The matter was settled. Although there had been room for the General Secretary to seek a candidate to his liking, May immediately accepted the Congress vote. However, he was never to become as close to Tanner as he had been to Goedhart. That friendship survived until May's death. Although Goedhart had withdrawn on grounds of poor health he outlived May by three years. Their correspondence, which continued during the inter-war years, provides some useful insights into May's views of the ICA and international affairs.

The other reason for describing the change of Presidency was to help set the scene for subsequent developments in the Alliance. Through the election, we have seen various interest groups operating within the Alliance. The Presidency had now moved to a Scandinavian co-operative movement that operated within the shadow USSR close links with the German, as well as Nordic movements meant that Väinö Tanner's view of events differed somewhat from of May. We see this shortly on the question

German Nazism and German Co-operation rise Hitler has been well documented elsewhere. For the purposes this study should merely remind ourselves he became Chancellor Germany January, 1933. An Enabling Act passed two later allowed Hitler become virtual dictator of new National Socialist State. In addition, Service purged, Party system abolished, and State Governments the old Federal were dissolved. In June, 1934, Hitler also purged rivals and opposition within his Party. His rival, Rohm, was murdered along with hundreds of other influential Nazis, and this followed the purging of the Judiciary when Hitler declared himself Germany's Supreme Judge. Through demand that should take an oath to serve him, Hitler paved the way political interference were party in July, 1933.

Along with this dismantling of the constitutional framework, trade unions and co-operatives were subsumed into gigantic Labour Front (Deutsche Arbeitsfront, DAF), whose chief was be Robert Ley[78] features in ICA records of the period, the place that operatives took within it, will made later.

From the description we have given of Hitler's takeover of the German State it is immediately obvious that the German Co-operative Movement, like its counterparts in the USSR and Italy, stood very little chance of surviving. The main interest in this section will therefore be to examine the ICA's response. We will find that, whereas the Alliance had been united in reaction to events in Italy, it became divided over those in Germany. This pattern was repeated, to varying degrees, in all the other crises that mark the count-down to the Second World War.

At the outset we should perhaps recall the early development of the ICA's German affiliate. In Chapter 1 we noted the rise of credit societies formed by Schultze-Delitzsch and Raiffeisen in mid-19th century Germany. By the end of that century, though, consumer co-operatives were also becoming established in significant numbers.

Initially, consumer co-operatives joined the General Union of Industrial and Economic Societies but, as in Finland and elsewhere, political divisions grew. We may recall that the leader of the General Union, Dr. Cruger, had withdrawn the Union from the ICA in 1904 over its disagreement with the Budapest Congress's decision to support State assistance to young co-operative movements in countries where help from stronger co-operative movements elsewhere could not easily be received. Cruger argued that this decision represented 'a victory for the representatives of co-operative socialism'.[79] Back in Germany he secured the expulsion of around 100 consumers' societies from the General Union on the grounds that they had breached political neutrality.[80] It was these societies that then joined with the Co-operative Wholesale, (GEG), to form the Central Union of German Consumer Societies. This new organisation joined the ICA in 1904, the same year that the General Union of Industrial and Economic Societies had left.

We will see later that the new Union urged its members to observe political neutrality. It is likely, though, that in common with other consumer co-operative movements of the time, their membership was proletarian. The new Union's leaders, Kaufmann and Lorenz, became prominent within the Alliance's Central Committee and, from 1921 until his death in 1928, Henrich Kaufmann served on the ICA Executive. He was followed by Vollrath Klepzig, who was to become a central figure in the difficult question of relations with the ICA after Hitler came to power in 1933.

We noted in Chapter 3 that members' savings in German consumer co-operatives rose from 60 million Marks in 1914 to 177 million Marks in 1918. That position was temporarily threatened by the hyper-inflation of 1923, but was restored when trade revived. The period that followed was later described as 'prosperity on credit', and ended with the collapse of one of Germany's largest banks, the Darmstadter and National bank, in July, 1931.[81]

At the Central Union's 1932 Congress, Heinrich Lorenz claimed that co-operatives, unlike private trade, had not financed their trade through borrowing. While they had had to increase their investments to maintain a turnover that had trebled between 1924 and 1930, they had done so without prejudicing the liquidity of their members' deposits. A rule of the Central Union required its member co-operatives to keep liquid at least 50 per cent of their members' deposits. In 1932 this requirement had been observed while 95.3 per cent of development costs had been met from societies' own funds. This was despite the run on members' savings triggered by the 1931 banking crisis. Lorenz was therefore able to claim that consumer co-operatives had not financed their expansion on credit.[82]

Lorenz's statement is important, and has been quoted in some detail because it helps to contradict the Nazis' later claim that German co-operatives had been weakened by bad financial management.[83] Despite their relatively healthy state in 1932, Hitler's rise to power in early 1933 caused a new run on societies' deposits. Väinö Tanner, the ICA's President, visited Germany in April, 1933, and found that the Nazis were calling on co-operative members to withdraw their society deposits. They were also demanding that State and municipal employees should even withdraw their actual membership. As a result, members' savings had declined

'...from 419 million German Marks to 240 million Marks at the moment. Without going into difficulties the Societies have paid out this sum. According to Mr Klepzig's calculations at least one-half of the remaining deposits will still have to be paid out and this the Societies cannot do without aid.'[84]

This need for assistance, and attempts to obtain it from the German Government, were the initial leverage that the Hitler regime used to gain control of the German consumer co-operative movement.

The ICA's Response

Attacks on co-operative property soon followed. The ICA in London kept a close watch on developments. In March, 1933, May wrote to Tanner expressing his disquiet at reports of these attacks appearing in the German co-operative paper, the Rundschau. He had also received first-hand accounts from an English CWS Director, who had returned from Leipzig and had spoken of damage to co-operative premises, which had prompted fresh cash withdrawals.[85]

May kept in touch with Klepzig in Hamburg. When the first reports of trouble appeared, he wrote:

'You seem to be the centre of very stirring events in Germany generally and this week particularly in Hamburg. I most earnestly hope that no harm may come to the Co-operative Movement by the activities of the new regime or any of its extreme supporters.'[86]

Klepzig replied that trade carried on as usual, although there had been 'individual unlawful attacks' on societies. He added:

'Our Societies have for decades past been instructed that violation of political neutrality involves expulsion from the Central Union..... Should special events occur in the near future, I will inform you in my capacity as a member of the Executive of the ICA, in so far as you are not already informed through the Konsumgenossenschaftliche Rundschau'.[87]

By 'special events', Klepzig may have had in mind the petition that the Central Union was then preparing to present to Hitler.[88]

This was to try to correct misleading statements appearing in the press about consumer co-operatives' attitudes towards the changed German

State. Co-operative leaders also wanted to use the petition to remind Hitler of the part that the Central Union, and consumer co-operatives, had played in improving Germans' living standards in the previous 30 years, and to emphasise that co-operatives' aim was to increase the welfare of all, rather than the profits of a few. The petition went on to claim that the 2,800,000 German families in consumer co-operative membership came from all trades and professions, as well as wage and salary earners. It also emphasised that consumer co-operatives were purely economic organisations', a line of defence that the ICA had used in respect of the Italian Lega ten years earlier. The petition concluded by asking for 'recognition and legal protection on the part of the Government of the Reich'.

German co-operative leaders appeared anxious to reach an accommodation with the new regime. Consequently, they were nervous that any support from the ICA might imply criticism of the German Government and so prejudice their chances with the new regime.[89]

In March, 1933, those interests were firmly centred on obtaining credits from the Government to shore up the societies' capital base, weakened by the run on capital precipitated by the Nazis. German consumer co-operative leaders did not feel that they were being unreasonable in calling for Government help because Agricultural co-operatives had already successfully applied for, and had received, some 30 million Marks to protect them against panic withdrawals. Indeed, the State Bank had earmarked a further 8 million Marks for the Distributive Movement', anticipating that similar help would be forthcoming for consumer co-operatives. However, the Hitler Government continued to block their release.[90]

Klepzig emphasised the importance of obtaining the credits when writing to Henry May:

'Owing to the serious financial and economic position of important sections of the German Consumers' Movement the Central Union has found it necessary for some time past to appeal to the Government for credits, such as have been given to other economic sections in Germany. These appeals have

been effective and credits are still available, and cannot be dispensed with for some time to come by the Societies and their Central Economic Organisation. For this reason the Central Union must strive to establish the same relations with the existing Government, as have existed between the Union and previous governments'.[91]

Thus it can be seen how and why the leaders of the German Central Union tried to accommodate themselves within Germany's changed political framework. Unlike Vergnanini and his colleagues in Italy ten years earlier, they made few if any protests and did not appeal to the ICA for help. This meant that the Alliance's response to the German situation had to be different from that made on behalf of the Lega. From the outset, May was more circumspect, due in part to the caution of the German Movement but also to differences in the ICA Executive on the question.

These soon showed themselves. In June, 1933, the Alliance held a Special Conference in Basle. Klepzig had missed two previous Executive meetings, cautious no doubt about being asked about events in Germany and giving answers that might compromise his position at home. However, May had visited Hamburg in May, 1933 and was able to keep the Executive informed. His arrival at the offices of the Central Union was not propitious. It coincided with a Nazi storm troopers' raid on the offices of the joint trade union and co-operative insurance society, Volksfusorge, housed in an adjoining building. Because some of the insurance staff worked in the offices of the Central. Union, a storm trooper guard was also placed outside that building and May was challenged as he entered.

In these circumstances, it is perhaps not surprising that board members of the Central Union and Wholesale persuaded May that outside intervention was unlikely to help and could, in fact, make their position worse. When the ICA Executive learned of this it quickly agreed that no criticism of the German movement should be made. Instead, it decided that the Special Conference in June, 1933, should underline the importance the ICA attached to voluntary and autonomous co-operation.[92]

The conference was 'special' inasmuch it replaced Congress that should have been held 1933. That had been postponed because of continuing economic crisis. Several countries had difficulty obtaining foreign currency enable their delegates attend, a number co-operative leaders it necessary concentrate their own movements.[93]

Instead, was decided hold Special Conference which would attended those to travel Basle, which would as its main business review the position national co-operative movements, including in Germany. However, conference became known the storm it produced about changes German Co-operative Movement.

Initially, Klepzig thought unlikely German delegates would attend when May arrived Basle found two telegrams announcing a German delegation, comprising Klepzig, Erich Grahl Robert Scholesser,[94] would participate after all..

Because status of the delegation uncertain, ICA Executive refused accept automatically the meeting the Executive held immediately the Special Conference, Klepzig was asked to brief members of the Committee on the position in Germany. He replied that the Movement was still in a state of suspense, the German Government not having yet decided its final form of reorganisation.[95]

The Executive became divided in what its response should be. Its British members - Sir Thomas Allen, Sir Robert Stewart and R. A. Palmer - joined Jaeggi (Switzerland) in suggesting that the German delegation be accepted, but Emmy Freundlich (Austria), Lustig (Czechoslovakia), Poisson (France), and Serwy (Belgium) opposed this. However, all members of the Executive felt that the ICA needed to make a 'proper enquiry' into the changes occurring in the German Movement. Thus, one of May's early problems was to find a way out of the impasse arising from a divided Executive. He attempted to do so by drafting a Declaration which was eventually accepted by the Executive and the Special Conference. It read:

'The Executive, having heard the explanations of Mr Klepzig of the present situation of the German Co-operative Movement and the efforts which are being made to prevent its destruction, accepts the nomination of its representatives to this Conference in the spirit of the constitution of the ICA, but reserves its conclusion upon the character of the changes which are now taking place in the organisation of the German Movement, the full character of which must, in any case, become the subject of enquiry on the part of the ICA and consideration at its next Congress.

But the Executive declares again its determination to maintain the voluntary and democratic character of co-operative organisation which is open to all without respect of their religious faith or political opinion; it protests against all interference by the State or other authority which would limit the freedom, abrogate the rights of voluntary organisations to develop under their own control, or interfere in their direction.

The Executive expresses the hope that the delegates will accept, without discussion, this solution of the situation for the purposes of this Conference and in the interests of the vital questions which it is called upon to consider.'[96]

The final paragraph suggests that a temporary solution was being proposed, one that would apply only to the Special Conference but would facilitate the questions that the Alliance needed to ask about the German situation. However, it is believed that the Executive's proposition that there should be no discussion on its proposal was unique. No similar case comes easily to mind. It was certainly most unusual, and suggests that delegates to the Special Conference were likely to be as divided as the Executive and that there was a wish to avoid a split that discussion might encourage. Any such split could prejudice remaining links with the German Movement.

Although the Executive and Special Conference fell in with May's suggestion, his compromise soon rebounded on him. When the German delegation took their place at the Conference and their leader, Robert Schloesser, rose to speak, he did not keep to the diplomatic niceties of the occasion. Instead, he launched into a propaganda statement about the benefits that National Socialism was bringing to Germany,[97] outraging many delegates, who considered it a breach of ICA hospitality.

Perhaps on their behalf, but quite as likely out of his own disappointment, May made an immediate and strong reply. This so offended Klepzig and Grahl that they walked out of the Special Conference and left Basle almost immediately. Schloesser, however, remained, perhaps in an attempt to try to retrieve something from the situation. May later reported to the Executive that Schloesser had asked him,

'...with some passion, to make a statement that would relieve the situation. He asked me what, in the circumstances of my speech to the Conference, he could REPORT TO HIS GOVERNMENT* whose confidential agent he declared himself to be and also 'CHIEF OF THE GERMAN DELEGATION'* to Basle.' [98]

* May's capitals

Despite events in Basle, it is clear that May wanted to keep links open to the German Movement from the way that he tried to appease Schloesser. Before he left Basle, May wrote to Klepzig, regretting that he had 'quite unintentionally' caused the German withdrawal. He expressed

'...sincere regret that certain words and phrases in my speech should have given you offence and caused you all to withdraw. I admit that under the pressure of my disappointment at the effect of Mr. Schloesser's speech on my paper, which not only turned the discussion of the Conference into a political channel but also has left a very painful impression on the delegates, I used expressions which were not appropriate to the occasion.' [99]

May reminded Klepzig of the efforts that he had made to get the German delegation admitted to the Special Conference. He believed that these should have assured Klepzig, and the German Central Union, of his goodwill.

Klepzig's reply shows that, either under pressure or of his own free will, he now fully identified with German events.[100] He said that May's speech had produced equally strong reactions with all three German delegates', and that divisions in the Executive and Special Conference over the German delegation had caused 'unbearable damage to the prestige' of that delegation whose 'national feelings....had...not been spared during the discussions'. Even so, Klepzig had agreed with Schloesser and Grahl that, if May sent the ICA Executive a copy of the letter which he had written to Klepzig, 'the Basle incident will be considered closed'. [101]

May did this, but the question of the relations between the Alliance and the German Co-operative Movement would not be so easily settled. One reason was that the position in Germany was still unfolding. A new national co-operative organisation, the Reichsverband, was created with similarities to the Ente Nazionale in Italy. Like the Ente, it could not be assumed to have automatic admission to the Alliance. Moreover, the repercussions of the Basle incident continued to reverberate within the ICA itself, both among members of the Executive and within some affiliated co-operative Movements. They included criticisms of the way that the President, Väinö Tanner, had handled the situation, with some believing that he had allowed Schloesser to continue his speech for too long. [102]

It is perhaps worth mentioning at this point that Väinö Tanner was to become a controversial figure during the Second World War when he became closely identified with the pro-German, anti-Soviet foreign policy of the Finnish Government. From study of Väinö Tanner in the ICA during the inter-war years it would seem that, while he was undoubtedly anti-Communist, he was certainly not pro-Nazi. Indeed, as we will see later, he fell foul of Finnish Nazis shortly before the 1939-45 war. Any suggestion of pro-German sympathies seem to have stemmed mistakenly from two sources. The first came from his personal qualities of gentleness and tolerance, though he proved capable of firm action. The second derived from his long-established links with the German Co-operative Movement, dating from the time when he had been a protégé of Heinrich Kaufmann, with whom he had worked in his youth.

Research has found a number of indications that, in 1933, Tanner wanted to give the German movement the benefit of any doubts there might be about the predicament in which they found themselves after Hitler came to power. We have seen that May also understood and sympathised with those difficulties. But he seems to have been more sensitive than Tanner to the feelings running through the Alliance over the German question. A month after the Basle Special Conference he wrote to Tanner:

'Quite personally...and amicably, I would say that I do not think you fully appreciate the attitude of the members of the Executive towards this question, and, equally frankly, I think it is necessary that you should do so in the interest of the Alliance and its immediate future'.[103]

Tanner had already justified his handling of events on the grounds that it had enabled the Special Conference to get a clearer picture of the real situation in Germany. He also believed that this would not have happened had he stopped Schloesser's speech earlier. In any event, Tanner argued, he had acted in a way that was quite customary in Scandinavia.[104]

Within the Executive there had been some movement. Emmy Freundlich (Austria), Lustig (Czechoslovakia), and Serwy (Belgium) remained anti-German. But Poisson (France), who had originally voted with them to exclude the German delegation from the Special Conference, had already changed his position at Basle. There he had told the Conference, 'If we admit the Bolsheviks...we must also admit the National Socialists'. Such comments led the German Rundschau to view Poisson as being 'very objective in his utterances'. [105]

Later Poisson suggested that the German situation raised fundamental organisational questions for the Alliance, including the possible need to restructure its membership base. In July, 1933, he wrote to Tanner outlining two alternatives that he believed faced the ICA. One was to contract and become only 'an institution of statistics and of contacts, without international action'. The other was to maintain the Alliance's present character and increase its activities, while remaining faithful to its traditions and its constitution'. [106]

Poisson believed that, by adopting the more limited first course, the ICA might hope to retain most of its members, including the Germans and the Russians in addition to the possibly readmitted Italians, and be able to resume 'its important activities' when brighter days returned. If, however, the second course were adopted, Poisson feared that the ICA would have to rely on a smaller membership. That was likely to include the British, Scandinavian, Belgian, Czech and Austrian movements, but the effect of this would be that the Alliance would become 'too Socialist in character'.

Throughout this study we are often reminded of the backdrop of contemporary international relations. Poisson's further comments provide another example:

'The fact that the Czechs have written that they will not attend any future meeting of the Alliance if the Germans are present creates, for certain countries such as our own, an extremely delicate situation. Although, as you saw at Basle, we did not wish to exclude the German Co-operative Movement, following in this respect the same policy as towards Russia, the alternative of having to separate ourselves either from Germany or from Czechoslovakia would force the French delegation to choose in favour of the Czechs.'

Poisson's ideas were not taken up. Although his proposal that the President should meet the two Vice-Presidents and General Secretary was accepted, there were difficulties in arranging a date. In the middle of these attempts Sir Thomas Allen was suddenly withdrawn from the English CWS's delegation to the ICA and automatically ceased to be one of the Alliance's Vice-Presidents. [107] In addition, May cast doubts upon how much weight Poisson's ideas carried and whether his own French movement supported them.

'I have talked to him a little about the situation and in reply he had promptly said that the Alliance is going to die. Naturally, I have laughed at him and assured him that his abilities as a prophet were weakening visibly. He then jumps off at another angle with the suggestion that the Alliance should abandon its principles, democracy, voluntarism, autonomy etc. for the time being (whatever that may mean) in order that it may continue to fold to its bosom

the Co-operative Organisations of Soviet Russia and not refuse representatives of Fascism. It is impossible in a letter to describe fully the mental gymnastics through which our discussion passed and his proposals turned. I am satisfied of this, that many of his colleagues in the F.N.C.C. are totally opposed to his point of view.

Another of May's letters, which underlined the repercussions from the Special Conference, led to a quite unconstitutional move by May which was undoubtedly intended to avoid the kind of split that might occur if German members remained active in the ICA. We have already learned through Poisson that the Czechs were threatening to attend no more meetings if German representatives were present. May suggested to Tanner that, for the time being, it might be 'wiser if the German Movement did not participate in the Committees of the Alliance'. [108]

Tanner appreciated the delicacy of the situation. While agreeing with May's proposal, he urged that Klepzig should be approached privately rather than in the name of the Executive.[109] However, the speed of events obviated the need for such action. Within weeks May could write to Tanner that there was 'abundant proof' that the German Central Union no longer existed as a 'free, independent and democratically controlled Organisation'.[110]

This was confirmed almost immediately when the 'Reichsbund of German Consumer Societies' was created and the Central Union was dissolved.[111] May immediately wrote to Klepzig, but the reply came from Müller and Everling to the effect that

'..the future collaboration with the International Co-operative Alliance now devolves upon the Reichsbund der deutscher Verbrauchergenossenschaften, which will, therefore, have to appoint its representatives in the ICA.'[112]

The letter indicated that the previous German representatives on the ICA'S Central Committee, Heinrich Lorenz, Hugo Bastlein and Georg Buchlein, were being withdrawn and their places taken by Karl Müller, Erich Grahl and Robert Schloesser: Everling and Klepzig retained their nominations, with the latter continuing to 'collaborate' on the ICA Executive. May was informed, however, that Klepzig would be unable to attend the next meeting of the ICA Executive in Vienna because of the 'travelling difficulties between Germany and Austria'.

Thus the question of avoiding German representation at the next Executive meeting was settled without May's needing to take any action. It also seemed to be settled in the longer term, because doubts increased about the eligibility of the new German organisation for ICA membership. At the Executive's meeting in Vienna, May reported the dissolution of the Central Union. He went on to argue that this had

'...juridically terminated the affiliation of the German Movement with the ICA. There could be equally no doubt about the creation of a new Organisation comprised in part of Organisations not affiliated to the Alliance. In such a case the rules of the ICA required an application for membership from the new Organisation.'[113]

Some members wished to postpone adoption of May's report because to accept it would automatically end the German Movement's affiliation to the ICA. Before this happened they felt that the enquiry into the German situation, agreed upon in Basle, should be held. May's report was finally accepted, but was hedged around with the following resolution:

That, in view of the expressed desire of the German Union to continue in membership with the ICA, and after a full discussion of the report of the General Secretary on the present situation of the German Co-operative Movement - which was approved - the Executive of the ICA is of the opinion that a first-hand investigation of the constitution and the practice of the German Movement may be necessary to ascertain whether the German Co-operative Movement now conforms in principle and practice to the rules of the ICA, and, therefore, asks the German Union whether, in the event of the ICA desiring to send a deputation of investigation to Germany, they will grant all necessary facilities and guarantees to enable a complete investigation to be made.

However, events were quickly overtaking any action that the ICA might take in support of German co-operation.

For example, in July, 1933 a circular letter from the Minister of Economic Affairs to the Governments of Individual States stated that, 'in agreement with the Chancellor of the Reich', it was now 'exclusively the task of the Government of the Reich to decide all questions of principle relating to Consumers' Co-operative Societies.[114]

In the following September an 'Official Decree of the German Workers' Front' laid down that consumers' societies should be 'administered in the National-Socialist sense'. [115]

In the same month Robert Ley, Leader of the German Workers' Front, announced a plan to combine 1,200 consumer co-operatives with private traders to form a National Consumers' Organisation.[116]

In passing, we should note that Ley was close to Hitler and the centre of the Nazi Party. From 1928 he had been Gauleiter of Cologne, from where he became the head of the Nazi Party's organisation in 1932. A year later Hitler appointed him leader of the German Labour Front (DAF), into which the offices and assets of all trade unions and co-operatives were subsumed. Ley remained close to Hitler until the end. After the war he was captured and put on trial with the major German war criminals at Nuremburg, but hanged himself before judgement was passed.[117]

The implementation of the Ley plan blurred the distinction between co-operative and private trade in Germany. Bodies called 'Consumers' Societies continued to exist, but as an integral part of the German Labour Front, and it was difficult to disentangle what had previously been private and what had been co-operative. The Anschluss in 1938, which merged Germany and Austria, created a further difficulty in deciding what had belonged to German or Austrian co-operatives Ley decreed that anyone who criticised the new Consumers' Societies would be considered an enemy and be treated accordingly'.[118]

These moves heightened concern not only in the ICA itself, but also among its member movements. The ICA Archives contain a number of English translations of articles appearing around this time in the national co-operative journals of other countries, all showing concern at the deteriorating position of consumer co-operatives in Germany. [119]

Not surprisingly, the new Reichsbund found the ICA's proposal for an 'on the spot' enquiry incompatible with its dignity, although they indicated that they were prepared to invite two members of the ICA Executive as long as they could choose who these would be. [120]

When the Executive met at Miramar D'Esterel in January, 1934 it was still divided. It adopted the following resolution:

'The Executive of the ICA, in considering the application of the Reichsbund for membership of the ICA, have also taken into account the conditions under which the Co-operative Movement in Germany at present functions, and they are not convinced that the fundamental conditions of Co-operation as laid down in the Rules of the ICA can be fulfilled. They are therefore, unable to admit the Reichsbund to membership in the present circumstances.

In view of that decision, and in acknowledging the opportunity offered in the letter of Herr Müller* for representatives of the ICA to meet the Board of the Reichsbnund at Hamburg, the Executive are of the opinion that no useful purpose would be served by such an interview.

The Executive, nevertheless, express the hope that the time will arrive when the German Co-operative Movement will again freely take its place in the Alliance in conformity alike with its own traditions and Rochdale Principles of World Co-operation.'[121]
*Letter from Muller, Hamburg, dated 9th November, 1933

Although the ICA had seemed to close the door on German membership, Väinö Tanner, in particular, tried to keep links open to German co-operative leaders and visited Everling and Klepzig in Hamburg on his way home from the Executive's meeting in Vienna. He later admitted to May that he had been among those who had wanted to postpone a decision about the German movement, but after his visit to Hamburg he recognised that this was 'impossible' and he no longer felt that there was any point in sending representatives to make an on the spot enquiry. [122]

There was not total opposition to German developments. In Switzerland, Dr. Bernhardt Jaeggi suggested that they were not as bad as many believed, thus causing May to write:

'I thank you for your further letter of the 2nd instant, with reference to the German Co-operative Situation, in which you express your personal opinion that co-operative principles are being observed in the German Co-operative Movement today and, further, that in other lands there is much misrepresentation of the position in Germany'. [123]

May went on to say how much he regretted that 'on any grounds, personal or official', he should disagree with Jaeggi, on a 'matter of such vital interest to the ICA, and to International Co-operation'.

The Jaeggi correspondence raises the question of what might have happened had Jaeggi, as May had wanted, been elected ICA President in 1927. As it was, from 1934 Jaeggi became a member of the ICA Executive, and therefore part of the Alliance's decision-making process.

Tanner visited Everling and Klepzig in Hamburg again when en route to Paris for a meeting of the ICA Executive in February, 1935. He reported that he had also had an informal meeting with almost the full Board of the Reichsbund, which expressed regret about the broken relations with the ICA. While no resumption of membership had been proposed, the Reichsbund Board had asked whether the ICA might not agree to help them make representations to the German Government in Berlin. As we shall see in the next Chapter, the ICA had recently made a successful similar appeal on behalf of the Austrian Movement to its Government. It would seem from the suggestion that the Reichsbund, even though it was a Nazi creation, was not fully easy in the National-Socialist system. Indeed, Tanner reported that Everling and Klepzig now realised that they had been wrong ever to believe that they could save the German Co-operative movement by working with the Nazis. Even so, the ICA Executive was uncertain what to do. Apart from Lustig, Czechoslovakia, its members agreed to take any action that might be possible to aid the German Co-operative Movement' [124] There was uncertainty about what form this might take. Poisson proposed, and Jaeggi seconded, that the 'Bureau be instructed to comply with the request of the Reichsbund....to intervene in Berlin with the German Government...', but this was rejected by four votes to six.

In passing, we should perhaps note the decisive move of the British which foreshadowed similar actions in the Alliance during the Cold War. On this occasion an alternative to the Poisson-Jaeggi motion was proposed by Sir Fred Hayward and seconded by R. A. Palmer, and was accepted by seven votes to one against, with two abstentions. A short, pithy motion shifted the onus for action onto the President rather than to the Secretariat.

'That the President be instructed to inform the German Co-operative movement that if they address a request for the ICA to approach the German Government to restore the democratic basis of their organisation and permit them to conduct propaganda etc., for the development of the Principles of Co-operation, the request will receive sympathetic consideration.'[125]

The wording of the motion virtually pre-empted German acceptance which was, no doubt, the intention.

However, this intervention caused friction between the ICA President and General Secretary. Tanner believed that May had colluded in the British proposal. [126] May strongly denied this, explaining that Hayward, on coming to his first meeting of the Executive, had *'revealed himself to be an enthusiastic proposer of resolutions which Mr. Palmer drafted on his instigation. I had nothing whatever* to do with the drafting of the resolution concerning the German question.'*[127]

*May's underlining.

Tanner still visited Everling and Klepzig in Hamburg on his way home from Paris, and reported their disappointment at the Executive's response. They believed that to ask the German Government to restore their democratic basis would be 'as to wave a red cloth in front of a bull'.[128] Tanner added that, nevertheless, Karl Müller had promised to speak to Dr. Ley, 'who would be consulting with Mr. Hess and he again would ask for the opinion of Mr. Hitler,[129] thus revealing the hierarchy into which the remnants of the German co-operative Movement had become tied.

May made plans to visit Everling and Klepzig in Hamburg in the spring of 1935. Tanner approved, and suggested that 'an open and kindly discussion would certainly make them more trustful'. He was also sure that they would be 'exceedingly glad to get some breath of wind from abroad in their present isolated position'.[130] Tanner continued:

'There is no doubt about Everling's loyalty towards his old ideals. I would neither distrust the other leaders, having remained in their positions. I, however, at a confident moment with Everling took up the rumours moving about Klepzig abroad. He laughed heartily and was wondering how even small things could pass their well watched borders. He was himself assured that Klepzig was the same as before, but however blamed him for many a thing... for having too eagerly delivered the Nazi-greeting in unnecessary places and sung too eagerly the new songs.'

May visited Germany in May, 1935, and while he was there the new Decree Law completed the implementation of the Ley Plan and the virtual destruction of the German Consumer Movement. Both Everling and Klepzig were compulsorily retired.[131]

There was nothing further that the ICA could do. At its meeting in Prague in October, 1935, the Executive delegated Tanner, Sir Fred Hayward, the enthusiastic motion drafter, and Victor Serwy, to draw up a resolution to go before the Central Committee. This deplored developments in Germany, but expressed the hope that the Co-operators of Germany would eventually have restored to them the liberty to develop their co-operatives within their 'well defined limits of...economic and social purpose', [132] The resolution was forwarded to Hitler and to Dr. Schact, Reichs Finance Minister, but the Alliance received no acknowledgement.[133]

In July, 1940, the ICA produced an 'impartial' account of Consumers' Co-operation Under the Nazi Regime. The section on Germany summed up the Alliance's attitude towards the German Co-operative movement in a quotation taken from the last article that Henry May wrote for the ICA Review in the month of his death, November, 1939.

'The Peace we look for is one that will restore to the Alliance all its lost members - German, Austrian, Czechoslovakian, Polish - and will thus contribute to the realisation of the Co-operative Federation of Mankind.'[134]

The loss of the German movement was the first in this series, and we could perhaps draw an analogy by imagining what would be the impact if a region, such as that of S. E. Asia, withdrew from the Alliance today. In the smaller international movement of the 1930s, which was more heavily concentrated in Europe, the loss of Germany was likely to have represented a blow of similar magnitude.

Conclusions

Ten years had separated the Italian and German crises. Whereas in the former the Alliance and its Executive had been united in their responses, in the latter they were divided. Within these divisions emerged Poisson's ideas about the possible need to re-structure the Alliance. Although never consciously adopted, these ideas presaged, to quite some extent, the shape of the Alliance during the 1939-45 War.

On several occasions the German situation also brought tensions between the ICA President and General Secretary. We should note that these stemmed partly from different traditions within the Alliance. But, equally, we should observe that in a weaker, or less tolerant, organisation they might have had more severe consequences.

The ICA's response to what happened in both countries has been dealt with at length for two main reasons. The first is that the advent of Fascism in Italy and Nazism in Germany threatened world peace and, therefore, one of the aims of the Alliance. They also eventually led to the Second World War. The second reason is that these events also helped shape subsequent patterns in ICA thinking and action. Having dealt with their genesis in this Chapter should enable us to cover subsequent developments more briefly in later ones.

Notes

1. ROBERTS, J. M., *Europe 1880-1945*, Longman Group, UK Limited, Harlow, Second Edition, 1989, p. 442
2. ROBERTS, J. M., *ibid.*, p. 439.
3. International Co-operative Alliance, *Report of ICA Congress Basle*, 1921, p. 188.
4. International Co-operative Alliance, *Minutes of Meeting of ICA Executive, London, 9th April, 1921*, p. 2, and *Minutes of meeting of ICA Executive, London, 31st May, 1921*, p. 5.
5. EARLE, John, *The Italian Co-operative Movement, Allen and Unwin Ltd., London, 1986*, p. 22.
6. EARLE, John, *ibid.*, pp. 24-25.
7. EARLE, John, *ibid.*, p. 29.
8. ICA Archives, Notes prepared by Henry May for Obituary of Antonio Vergnanini, April, 1934.
9. ODHE, Thorsten, Obituary of Antonio Vergnanini, published in *Kooperatoren*, No. 7, 1934, the technical journal of Kooperativa Forbundet.
10. ICA Archives, Memorandum by Antonio Vergnanini on The Position of the National League of Italian Co-operative Societies (Lega), Milan, 23rd September, 1922, p. 1.
11. ICA Archives, *ibid.*, p. 1.
12. ICA Archives, Report *to the ICA Executive on The Position of the Co-operative Movement in Italy, 20th November, 1922*
13. International Co-operative Alliance, *Minutes of Meeting of ICA Executive, Ghent, 3rd & 4th February, 1923*, p. 4.

14. ICA Archives, Letter from Henry May to G. Preziosi, Italian Embassy, London, 10th February, 1923.
15. ICA Archives, Letter from Henry May to G. Preziosi, Italian Embassy, London, 10th February, 1923.
16. ICA Archives, Letter from Henry May to G. Preziosi, Italian. Embassy, London, 20th March, 1923.
17. International Co-operative Alliance, *Minutes of meeting of ICA Executive, Ghent. 3rd & 4th February, 1923*, p. 4.
18. International Co-operative Alliance, *Report of ICA Congress, Ghent, 1924*, p. 70.
19. ICA Archives, "Fascist Cyclone" was a term found in May's handwritten notes used in preparing the obituary of Antonio Vergnanini.
20. EARLE, John, *op. cit.*, pp. 27-28.
21. International Co-operative Alliance, *Report of the ICA Congress, Ghent, 1924*, p. 13
22. WATKINS, W. P., *The International Co-operative Alliance 1895-1970, op. cit.*, p. 139.
23. International Co-operative Alliance, *Report of ICA Congress, Ghent, 1924*, pp. 37-38.
24. International Co-operative Alliance, *ibid.*, pp. 37-38.
25. International Co-operative Alliance, *Report of the ICA Congress, Ghent, 1924*, pp. 171-172.
26. ICA Archives, Letter from Henry May to Dr. A. Suter, Lausanne, 10th September, 1924.
27. ICA Archives, Letter from Henry May to ICA President, G. J. D. C. Goedhart, 11th September, 1924.
28. ICA Archives, Letter from Dr. A. Suter, Lausanne, to Henry May, 5th October, 1924.
29. ICA Archives, Letter from Henry May to Dr. A. Suter, Lausanne, 3rd November, 1924.
30. ICA Archives, Letter from Henry May to ICA Member Organisations, 23rd November, 1925.
31. ICA Archives, Typed copy of telegram addressed to Prime Minister, Italian Government - no date on copy but believed to be 18th November, 1925.
32. ICA Archives, Letter from ICA President, G. J. D. C.

Goedhart and General Secretary Henry May to Italian Prime Minister, dated 24th November, 1925.

33. ICA Archives, Letter from Henry May to ICA affiliated organisations, dated 23rd November, 1925.

34. ICA Archives, Letter from Henry May to the Rt. Hon., Stanley Baldwin, British Prime Minister.

35. International Co-operative Alliance, Memorandum on the Agenda of meeting of ICA Executive, the Hague, 30th and 31st January, 1926.

36. ICA Archives, Letter from Henry May to Dr. A. Suter, Lausanne, 18th November, 1925.

37. ICA Archives, Letter from Henry May to I.H. Mitchell, Labour Department, Whitehall, London, 28th November, 1925.

38. ICA Archives, Letter from Henry May to The Rt. Hon. G. M. Barnes, PC., 28th November, 1928.

39. ICA Archives, Letter from Henry May to Dr. A. Suter, Lausanne, 26th November, 1925.

40. ICA Archives, Telegram from Lozovsky, General Secretary, Red International Labour Unions, to ICA 25th November, 1925, and Letter from L. Khinchuk, ICA Executive Member, to Henry May, 23rd December, 1925.

41. ICA Archives, Letter from Henry May to L. Khinchuk, 12th December, 1925.

42. International Co-operative Alliance, Report by Henry May 2 on the Italian Situation made to meeting of ICA Executive, the Hague, 30th and 31st January, 1926.

43. ICA Archives, Letter from Henry May to Dr. A. Suter, Lausanne, 10th December, 1925.

44. International Co-operative Alliance, Memorandum on the Agenda of the meeting of ICA Executive held in the Hague, 30th & 31st January, 1926.

45. International Co-operative Alliance, *ibid*.

46. ICA Archives, Letter from Henry May to Dr. A. Suter, Lausanne, 13th March, 1926.

47. ICA Archives, *ibid*.

48. ICA Archives, *ibid*.

49. ICA Archives, Second letter of 13th March, 1926; from Henry May to Dr. A. Suter, Lausanne.
50. International Co-operative Alliance, Report of Henry May's visit to Italy to meeting of ICA Executive, Antwerp, 1st & 2nd May, 1926, p. 2.
51. ICA Archives, Letter from Dr. A. Suter, Lausanne, to Henry May, 16th November, 1925.
52. International Co-operative Alliance, Report of Henry May's visit to Italy, op. cit. p. 5.
53. International Co-operative Alliance, *Report of ICA Congress, Stockholm 1927*, p. 78.
54. International Co-operative Alliance, *Minutes of meeting of ICA Executive, the Hague, 24th & 25th November, 1927*.
55. WATKINS, W. P., *op. cit.*, p. 140.
56. ICA Archives, Fascist National Party, Ente Nazionale Della Cooperazione, Milan, English translation of Model Rules, presumed date late 1925.
57. ICA Archives, Letter from the Mayor of the Province of Milan to Co-operative Societies dated 1st December, 1925, and Fascist National Party, Ente Nazionale della Cooperazione, communication to the Co-operators of Milan, undated.
58. ICA Archives, Undated English translation of a statement 'Italian Co-operation According to Luigi Luzzatti'.
59. International Co-operative Alliance, *Minutes of the meeting of ICA Executive, Bremen, 28th-30th March, 1928*, p. 6 and *Minutes of ICA Executive, Geneva, 7th November, 1928*, p. 6.
60. ICA Archives, Henry May's personal note of the meeting between himself and R. Labadessa of the Ente Nazionale on 30th March, 1931.
61. ICA Archives, English translation of letter from H. Everling, Grosseinkaufs-Gesellschaft d. Consumvereine, to ICA, 28th July, 1932.
62. ICA Archives, Letter from Henry May to H. Everling, 3rd August, 1931.
63. International Co-operative Alliance, *Minutes of meeting of ICA Executive, Geneva, 28th October, 1932*, p. 1.

64. ILO Archives, Correspondence between M. Colombain, Head of the Co-operative Section of the International Labour Office, Geneva, Cabrini, ILO Office, Rome, and Henry May, ICA, London, April, 1936.
65. ICA Archives, Letter from G. J. D. C. Goedhart, ICA President, to Henry May, 5th August, 1925.
66. International Co-operative Alliance, *Minutes of meeting of ICA Executive, Strasbourg, 10-11 February, 1927*.
67. ICA Archives, Letter from Henry May to G. J. D. C. Goedhart, 13th February, 1927.
68. ICA Archives, Letter from Henry May to G. J. D. C. Goedhart, 8th May, 1922.
69. ICA Archives, Letter from Henry May to G. J. D. C. Goedhart, 13th February, 1927.
70. International Co-operative Alliance, *Report of ICA Congress, Stockholm, 1927*, (Appendix ii).
71. International Co-operative Alliance, *Minutes of meeting of ICA Executive, London, 24th August, 1920*.
72. ICA Archives, Letter from Henry May to Dr. Bernhardt Jaeggi, Switzerland, 9th March, 1927.
73. ICA Archives, Letter from Henry May to Dr. Bernhardt Jaeggi, 4th March, 1927.
74. ICA Archives, Letters from Dr. Bernhardt Jaeggi to Henry May, 7th and 16th March, 1927.
75. ICA Archives, Letter from Henry May to G. J. D. C. Goedhart, 21st February, 1927.
76. International Co-operative Alliance, *Minutes of the meeting ICA Executive, London, 21st October, 1919*, pp. 1-2.
77. International Co-operative Alliance, Minutes of meeting of ICA Executive, London, 16th December, 1919, p. 2.
78. CRAIG, Gordon A., *Germany 1866-1945, Oxford University Press, Oxford, 1987*, reprint, pp. 575-583.
79. WATKINS, W.P., *op. cit.*, p. 74.
80. WATKINS, W.P., *ibid.*, pp. 73-74.
81. ICA Archives, Paper headed *The Present Situation of the German Consumers' Co-operative Movement and Its Causes*.
82. ICA Archives, *ibid*.
83. ICA Archives, *ibid*.

84. ICA Archives, Letter from Väinö Tanner, Finland, ICA President, to Henry May, 18th April, 1933.
85. ICA Archives, Letter from Henry May to Väinö Tanner, 17th March, 1933.
86. ICA Archives, Letter from Henry May to Vollrath Klepzig, Germany, member of ICA Executive, 11th March, 1933.
87. ICA Archives, Letter from Vollrath Klepzig to Henry May, 13th March, 1933.
88. ICA Archives, English translation of the petition of the German Central Union to the German Chancellor, Adolf Hitler, 27th March, 1933.
89. ICA Archives, Letter from Vollrath Klepzig to Henry May, 29th March, 1933.
90. ICA Archives, Letter from Väinö Tanner to Henry May, 18th April, 1933.
91. ICA Archives, Letter from Vollrath Klepzig to Henry May, 29th March, 1933.
92. International Co-operative Alliance, *Minutes of the meeting of ICA Executive, Paris, 20-21 May, 1933* and *Review of International Co-operation, No.7, July, 1933*, p. 242.
93. ICA Archives, Letter from Henry May to Members of the ICA Central Committee, 17th January, 1933.
94 International Co-operative Alliance, *Minutes of the meeting of ICA Executive, Basle, June, 1933*.
95. International Co-operative Alliance, *Minutes of meeting of ICA Executive, Basle, 8th June, 1933*, p. 2.
96. International Co-operative Alliance, *ibid.*, p. 3..
97. ICA Archives, English translation of report appearing in German co-operative newspaper the *Rundschau*, 8th July, 1933.
98. ICA Archives, Letter from Henry May to members of ICA Executive, 13th June, 1933.
99. ICA Archives, Letter from Henry May to Vollrath Klepzig, written at Basle, 11th June, 1933.
100. ICA Archives, Letter from Vollrath Klepzig to Henry May, 21st June, 1933.
101. ICA Archives, *ibid*.

102. ICA Archives, Letter from Henry May to Väinö Tanner, 5th July, 1933.
103. ICA Archives, Letter from Henry May to Väinö Tanner, 18th July, 1933.
104 ICA Archives, Letter from Väino Tanner to Henry May, 5th July, 1933.
105. ICA Archives, English translation of report from the "Rundschau", 8th July, 1933.
106. ICA Archives, Letter from Ernest Poisson, ICA Vice President, to Väinö Tanner, ICA President, 27th July, 1933.
107. ICA Archives, Letter from Henry May to Väinö Tanner, 11th August, 1933.
108. ICA Archives, Letter from Henry May to Väinö Tanner, 28th June, 1933.
109. ICA Archives, Letter from Väinö Tanner to Henry May, 5th July, 1933.
110. ICA Archives, Letter from Henry May to Väinö Tanner, 18th July, 1933.
111 ICA Archives, English translation of report in the *Rundschau*, 19th August, 1933.
112 ICA Archives, Letter from the Reichsbund to the ICA, 5th September, 1933.
113. International Co-operative Alliance, *Minutes of meeting of ICA Executive, Vienna, 6-8 October, 1933*.
114 ICA Archives, English translation of report in the *Rundschau*, 22nd July, 1933.
115. ICA Archives, English translation of report in the German co-operative paper, the *Konsumgenossenschaftliche Praxis*, 1st September, 1923.
116. ICA Archives, English translation of report of the Ley Plan in the *Rundschau*, 16th September, 1933.
117. TAYLOR, James and SHAW, Warren, *A Dictionary of the Third Reich, 1988*, Grafton Books, a Division of the Collins Publishing Group, Glasgow, pp. 212-213 and 216-217.
118. ICA Archives, English translation of report in the Rundschau, 16th September, 1933.
119. ICA Archives, English translation of reports from *Le Cooperateur Suisse*, 20th September, 1933; Die

Konsomgenossenschaft, Prague, 25th September, 1933; *Schweiz Konsumvereine*, 23rd September, 1933; *Andelsbadet*, (Denmark), 15th December, 1933.

120. International Co-operative Alliance, *Minutes of meeting of ICA Executive, 16-18 January, 1934*, p. 3.

121. International Co-operative Alliance, *ibid.*, p. 4.

122. ICA Archives, Letter from Väinö Tanner to Henry May, 17th November, 1933.

123. ICA Archives, Draft letter sent for translation from Henry May to Dr. Bernhardt Jaeggi, Switzerland, 3rd November, 1933.

124. International Co-operative Alliance, *Minutes of meeting of ICA Executive, Paris, 8-9 February, 1935.*

125. International Co-operative Alliance, *ibid.*, p. 2.

126. ICA Archives, Letter from Väinö Tanner to Henry May, 18th March, 1935.

127. ICA Archives, Letter from Henry May to Väinö Tanner, 27th March, 1935.

128. ICA Archives, Letter from Väinö Tanner to Henry May, 5th March, 1935, p. 2.

129. ICA Archives, *ibid*.

130. ICA Archives, *ibid*.

131. International Co-operative Alliance, Report of ICA Congress, Paris, 1937, pp. 87-89.

132. International Co-operative Alliance, *ibid.*, pp. 88-89.

133. International Co-operative Alliance, *ibid.*, p. 89.

134. International Co-operative Alliance, Paper entitled *Consumers' co-operation Under the Nazi Regime - An Impartial Statement of Facts based Upon Authentic Documents in the Records of the ICA*, published by the ICA in London in 1940, p. 11.

Chapter six

The ICA's Response to Situations in Austria, Spain and Czechoslovakia and other Questions

Introduction

This Chapter will be shorter, and will aim to examine the ICA's responses to later situations where national co-operative movements became subject to Nazi or Fascist regimes. It will therefore act as a linking Chapter between the major examples of Fascism and Nazism in Italy and Germany and the outbreak of the Second World War in 1939. In particular, we shall examine the ICA's reactions to events in Austria, Spain, China and Czechoslovakia, which represented the countdown to the Second World War. We shall end the Chapter by noting the ICA's stance on the question of peace as events propelled the world towards war once more.

The Austrian Situation of 1934

With the Italian situation, we saw the ICA acting decisively but to little effect. Its approach to the German crisis had been more cautious, but was equally ineffectual. Its one success came in Austria in 1934, when it was able to persuade the Dollfuss Government to restore the freedom of the Austrian consumer co-operative movement. Even that victory was to be short-lived, lasting only until Germany and Austria were united in the Anschluss of 1938.

Two figures at the centre of the ICA were involved in the Austrian troubles. One was Dr. Karl Renner, past Chancellor of Austria and a member of the ICA Central Committee. The other was Emmy Freundlich, Austrian Socialist Member of Parliament and a member of the Alliance's Central and Executive Committees.

Renner had been a member of the Central Committee since 1922 and a prominent figure at ICA Congresses from 1921 to 1930.[1] Dr. I. Nitobe, who attended the 1921 Congress as an Observer and Guest of Honour from the League of Nations, recorded that Renner was among the 'delegates of great eminence'.[2]

First and foremost, Renner was a leading Austrian politician, although he was also President of the Austrian Co-operative Central Union and of the Wholesale Society. However, Mrs Freundlich, although prominent in the Austrian Socialist Party and a Member of Parliament, was more important within the Alliance. By 1934 she had been a member of its Executive for ten years, as well as being President of the International Co-operative Women's Guild for the same period. She had also represented the Alliance on a number of bodies, and her links with the League of Nations and the International Labour Organisation are well documented in the archives of both bodies.[3] When writing to Albert Thomas, Director of the ILO, she addressed him as 'Cher comrade Thomas'.

Both Dr. Renner and Mrs Freundlich were imprisoned in February, 1934, when conflict broke out in Austria. Reasons for this conflict can be traced back to the 1914-18 war and Austria's subsequent loss of territories. The resulting economic and social problems are well described in an article which Emmy Freundlich wrote for the *Review of International Co-operation in May, 1932*.

> *'In no country has the economic crisis been so persistent since the conclusion of the world war as in Austria. Apart from general difficulties of the war and post-war periods, there have been special structural obstacles which were bound to arise in a small economic territory which had been artificially cut out from a larger economic body.'*[4]

A republican Government was established in Vienna in November, 1918, headed by Karl Renner as Chancellor. In the following March, it voted in favour of Austria joining a Union with Germany. However, this was not possible under the Peace Treaties, and a new constitution, passed in October, 1920, provided for a federation along Swiss lines. Little cohesion emerged in the new Austria, and Vienna, constituting a quarter of the country's population, suffered the worst economic effects, and became steadily more socialist. Elsewhere, the population remained more clericalist, with political affiliations that were regional, Pan-German or pro-Hapsburg. There was a number of political parties ranging from the Fascist Heimwehr on the right to the Socialist

Schutzbund on the left. Both of these had private armies, which clashed in serious riots in Vienna in July, 1927. That trouble was smoothed over, but the underlying economic problems remained and worsened with the economic depression of 1931-32. During this a leading bank, the Credit Anstalt, collapsed [5], reminding us of the failure of the Darnstadter und National bank in Germany during the same period.[6]

In May, 1932, Englebert Dollfuss became Chancellor. Although he had links with agricultural co-operatives, he was strongly anti-socialist. Believing that the existing Austrian constitution favoured the socialists, he suspended it in March, 1933. Eleven months later, following a demonstration by socialist workers, Dollfuss ordered the army to attack huge socialist housing estates on the outskirts of Vienna. Five days of civil war followed before the socialists were defeated and many of their leaders arrested, including Karl Renner and Mrs Freundlich. Some consumer co-operatives and their members were also attacked.

Before that, Austrian retail societies had had a more chequered history than many of their counterparts in other countries. Some had developed as early as the 1860s, but no Co-operative Union was established until 1903 and no Wholesale Society until 1906. Within a few years further progress was hindered by the First World War and the subsequent dismemberment of Austria.

Austrian consumer co-operatives later suffered from a collapsed currency, as well as inflation and deflation, but from 1925 onwards they consolidated and grew.[7] However, by 1933, the Austrian movement still ranked only 11th in the ICA in terms of subscriptions.[8] In passing, we should note that the movement's central organisation was the Union of German-Austrian Consumers' Societies,[9] its name suggesting that it tended to be pan-German. It is interesting to note in passing that a German Co-operative Union also existed alongside a non-German one in Czechoslovakia, both affiliated to the ICA.

May was unusually pessimistic about the violence in Vienna. He wrote to Tanner:

'You are doubtless as fully acquainted with the terrible events of the past week in Austria. It is difficult to discuss them: some aspects of the matter seem to me to be unspeakable and to indicate that the human race, at least in Europe, is slipping back to barbarism. I am wondering how our work is to proceed in the near future with the belt of nationalism complete from Baltic to the Mediterranean'. [10]

May telegraphed Emil Lustig, the Czechoslovak member on the ICA Executive, in Prague to ask what news he had. Lustig replied the following day that Mrs Freundlich and Dr. Renner had been arrested and that the Labour Bank had been placed under a State Controller although he believed that co-operative societies were 'functioning normally'. He appealed to May to seek help from the British Government on behalf of our friends'.[11] May did so, speaking to two leading Labour politicians and to the British Foreign Minister.

May asked Tanner whether he thought that an emergency ICA Congress should be convened, but the ICA President thought that this was unnecessary unless it was used to express solidarity. He agreed with May that if one were held it would mean that:

'Our friends in the east of Europe will have to take their courage in both hands and travel through Germany'. [12]

May's appeal to the British Foreign Minister had some effect. He was summoned to the British Foreign Office, where he was given 'official assurance' that action had been taken in obtaining clemency for co-operative victims, and for Dr. Karl Renner and Mrs Freundlich in particular.[13] May was assured that both were in first class prison quarters. Besides having access to books, they were able to obtain food from the outside. The British Foreign Office promised to keep in touch with the situation and to give all possible help 'within the limits of diplomatic representation'.

Following the precedent of asking Dr. Suter to report on the Italian situation in 1922 May now asked Lustig in Prague if he would go to Vienna to get first-hand information on the position there. Unable to go himself, Lustig asked Anton Dietl, who was also a member of the ICA Central Committee, to go instead. In the meantime, May had written to Andreas Korp, Director of the Austrian Co-operative Wholesale Society, to say that he himself 'was prepared to go to Vienna if his presence was desired'. [14]

On 23rd February, eleven days after the outbreak of the troubles, May received a detailed report from Dietl. It enclosed copies of an appeal by the Austrian Union and CWS to the Austrian Government as well as notices to co-operative societies, and copies of Government Decrees concerning consumer co-operatives. These enclosures no longer survive, but we can learn of the wording of the Memorandum which the Austrian Central Union, the Co-operative Wholesale Society and the Vienna Co-operative Society addressed to the Federal Government on 15th February from another source. It was reproduced in a report entitled *The Austrian Co-operatives Under Dictatorship*, prepared by Austrian socialists who were opposed to what they believed was the sell-out of the consumer co-operative movement to the Dollfuss Government. They quoted the memorandum as follows:

'The present directors of the under-mentioned headquarter offices pledge themselves to observe, with the utmost strictness, all legal regulations now in force and to restrict the co-operatives conscientiously to their pure economic tasks.'

Should special measures be thought necessary in order to attain the desired end of maintaining the economically important values of our enterprises and to reassure the mass of our members, we shall collaborate loyally in the execution of such measures. Seeing that questions are involved which will have to be decided within a few hours, we request that our application for an immediate interview with a representative of the Federal Government may be treated with the utmost urgency.

For the Central Union of Austrian Consumers' Societies: Dr. Andreas Vukowitch: for the Co-operative Society of Vienna and District: Beck, Schnopf for the Wholesale Society of Austrian Distributive Societies: A. Korp, F. Lessiak. '[15]

The authors of the report from which this quotation was taken pointed out that the signatories to the Memorandum were all members of the Austrian Socialist Party and castigated them for promising total submission to a Government that was sending their party comrades to prison and to the gallows.[16]

Opposition from Austrian socialists to an accommodation by Austrian consumer co-operatives with the Dollfuss Government reflects the dilemmas that were facing socialists throughout Europe as they attempted to respond to right-wing regimes. These dilemmas were sharp in the ICA, whose leaders included many socialists.

May was also a socialist, but he obviously believed that his main objective should be the saving of the Austrian consumer co-operative movement. He therefore responded to an urgent call from Andreas Korp, Director of the Austrian Co-operative Wholesale Society, 'to come at once' to Vienna, despite the fact that he was busy preparing for an imminent meeting of the Central Committee and the Congress to be held later that year. Dietl also urged, 'Start at once for Vienna. Viennese friends wish urgently to speak with you'.[17]

Travelling by train, May arrived late at night on 28th February, and was met by Dr. A. Vukowitch, General Secretary of the Austrian Co-operative Union, and Andreas Korp. They went with May to his hotel, where they discussed the position until midnight and again for two hours the next morning.

May learned that on 12th February, the day that violence had broken out, the Central Union had urged its member societies to keep clear of the fighting, to keep their shops open and staffs at their posts. However, the Government had ordered the closing of all socialist organisations by country or local authorities, and many had interpreted this order as applying to co-operative societies also. As a result, a number were closed, or taken over, or had their cash confiscated. Some co-operatives had been used by the socialist military forces which led to 'Many co-operative officials' being among the socialists arrested. Co-operative trade had been affected in other ways, including the decision of the Board of Trade to stop sugar supplies to societies, and merchants' refusal to make deliveries except for cash.

Vukowitch and Korp advised May that, within two days of the outbreak of violence, Commissioners had appeared throughout the provinces claiming to exercise control on behalf of a variety of authorities. Some seemed to have been self-appointed and were trade competitors or officials of Traders' Organisations. The CWS headquarters in Vienna had almost been closed by the police, but Andreas Korp managed to persuade them that they had authority only to close the branch of the Labour Bank which was housed in the same building.

However, help for consumer co-operatives had come from surprising sources.

'While the guns were still firing, endeavours were made to save the movement from breakdown. Prompt action was taken by the Neutral Co-operative Union; the Agricultural Co-operative Movement to induce the Government to act, which they succeeded in doing'.[18]

We should note in passing that neither of these organisations was socialist or a member of the International Co-operative Alliance. On the 16th February, the Government had issued four Decrees. The first announced that the Chancellor's Office would appoint a Committee Administration for the Austrian Co-operative Wholesale Society, which would take over the powers of the General Meeting, the Board of Directors and the Supervisory Council. All subsidiary organisations of the Wholesale were suspended. The second Decree brought the General Consumers' Society of Vienna under the Wholesale, and thus under the direction of the same Committee of Administration, while the third Decree provided for the appointment of similar Committees of Administration for local consumers' societies. The fourth Decree dissolved and liquidated the Labour Bank.

On 18th February the Union and Wholesale had written to consumer societies and advised them that the Government had withdrawn all

Commissioners and, in their place, had appointed the Committee of Administration for the CWS with which the Central Union had agreed to collaborate'. The Union and Wholesale had sent another circular, asking societies to withdraw completely from politics and instructing them to take no part in politics or to allow political discussions in societies meetings. Moreover, no political posters or leaflets were to be exhibited in co-operative shops or premises.

By the time that May had arrived in Vienna the implications of the Government's Decrees were becoming clearer. The dissolution and liquidation of the Labour Bank meant considerable financial disruption. However, efforts were being made to handle credits through the Girozentrale, which was the financial centre of the Agricultural Co-operative Movement. Morale in consumer co-operatives had also been adversely affected by the 'combing out of old officials' by the Heimwehr, Patriotic Front and others. There were also political uncertainties, including a possible change of Government.[19]

From May's report we learn that, following their intercessions with the Austrian Government, the Neutral Co-operative Union and the Agricultural Co-operative Movement were invited to appoint representatives to sit on the Committee of Administration of the Wholesale and General Consumers' society of Vienna. Dr. Ludwig Strobl, President of the Agricultural Movement, became a member, and it was he who had created the links with the Girozentrale to arrange credits for consumer societies. Dr. Otto Maresch, Vice-President of the Neutral Consumers' Union, also became a member, together with Professor Obreggor of Graz, who belonged to that Union too. The fourth member of the Committee, Director Müller, was Director of the Control Department, Vienna Municipality. At the time of May's visit, three further members had still to be appointed, but May had been given reason to believe that these would be 'favourable to Co-operation'.[20]

Already, it will be seen that circumstances existed in the Austrian situation that had not applied in Italy or Germany. One was the readiness of other, and non-socialist, co-operative federations to assist the consumer movement by attempting to 'induce the Government to act' to prevent its breakdown. Another was the fact that the Dollfuss Government was open to such persuasion. A third difference was the quick capitulation of the Austrian Central Union and Wholesale, which contrasted with the equivocation of their German counterparts and the long drawn out struggle of the Lega in Italy.

Perhaps the biggest difference was that the Austrian Government was willing to receive the representations of the International Co-operative Alliance. A factor in this readiness appears to have been Austria's need to find export markets, and a belief that the ICA might be able to help in this.

A further difference in the Austrian situation from that in Germany was that, like the Lega in Italy, the Austrian Union and Wholesale had appealed to the ICA for help. This meant that the Alliance, through May, could intervene positively. Dietl's fact-finding mission had been the first step, while May's arrival in Vienna was the second. Vukowitch and Korp appealed to him to 'accept the responsibility of stating their case to the Chancellor, Dr. Dollfuss'[21]. May agreed to do this and, in sharp contrast with Hitler and Mussolini, Dollfuss agreed to receive him.

Before their meeting on 2nd March, 1934, May had other meetings with Dr Otto Maresch, Vice-President of the Neutral Consumers' Union, and Dr Ludwig Strobl, President of the Agricultural Co-operative Movement, both members of the Government-appointed Committee of Administration. May also met Dr Schüller, the Austrian Ambassador in Geneva, and it is from this meeting that we learn of the Austrian Government's concern to find export markets through co-operatives abroad. The tone of all meetings was good. May recorded that he was received 'warmly' or 'cordially' or with 'charming courtesy' [22]

It was Schüller who accompanied May when he was received by Dollfuss. Of that meeting May recorded that:

'Dr. Dollfuss received me with charming courtesy and at once plunged into the subject of my visit. He reminded me that for many years he had given his energies to the Co-operative Movement in the agricultural sphere and had

contributed its literature personal interest close the life peasantry, sympathetic towards the Co-operative Movement consumers.'[23]

Dollfuss confirmed that the Movement had become closely associated with the activities of the Socialist Party. Consequently, it had to be 'freed from its political character and kept to its real economic purpose'. To achieve that, the Government had imposed control, but Dollfuss hoped that the autonomy of the Austrian consumer co-operative movement would be 'restored as soon as possible'.

May reported that, because the Chancellor had anticipated in his remarks most of the questions that he had planned to raise, he had limited himself to asking for a brief interview with Mrs Freundlich. Presumably, although Renner was a member of the ICA Central Committee, May judged that his political eminence as a past Chancellor made it unlikely that a request on his behalf would succeed. Even as far as Mrs Freundlich was concerned, Dollfuss refused permission on the grounds that he had had to turn down similar requests, even from Ambassadors of other countries, on behalf of other prisoners. Significantly, though, May records that Dollfuss added:

'........that he would convey to her my good wishes, and if I wished to write to her there and then he would see that the letter was delivered'.

When the meeting came to an end May thanked the Austrian Chancellor for the 'honour he had done to the ICA' by receiving him. May was pleased to have been given assurances about the intended restoration of the autonomy of the Austrian consumer movement, but indicated that this was only what we had anticipated in view of the Chancellor's well-known connection with the Co-operative Movement'. He assured Dollfuss of the satisfaction there would be 'to the authorities of the ICA to know that the Co-operative Spirit and Principles would be safeguarded.'

That was putting a diplomatic gloss on the situation. May reported to the Executive and Central Committees in Rotterdam nine days later, where the latter Committee passed the following resolution:

'The Central Committee of the International Co-operative Alliance having received and approved the report of the General Secretary concerning the present situation of the Co-operative Movement in Austria;

Having taken note of the assurances given to him by the Austrian Chancellor, Dr. Dollfuss, that the intention of the Government in assuming the temporary control of the Co-operative Organisations is not to impair but to assure the Co-operative Economic Structure and that they will restore the complete autonomy of the Movement;

And while regretting that the Austrian Government have deemed it necessary to deprive, even temporarily, the Co-operative Organisations of their autonomy - expresses its solidarity with the Co-operators of Austria and its conviction that they will collaborate in any measures which are calculated to maintain Co-operative Principles in their integrity and to restore the complete autonomy and independence of their Movement.' [24]

A motion of sympathy proposed by Dietl and supported by Lustig (Czechoslovakia) was also passed. This read:

'The Central Committee of the International Co-operative Alliance, assembled at Rotterdam on the 11th March, extends its heartfelt sympathy to its colleagues of the Central Committee and fellow workers in the world Co-operative Movement Dr. Karl Renner, Emmy Freundlich, and their co-operative co-workers in their present distressful position.

The Central Committee also expresses the sincere wish that these Pioneers of Co-operation, national and international, may soon be set at liberty to resume their collaboration with the ICA in the cause of Co-operation. We should perhaps note that the stronger line taken by the Czechs was consistent with the position that they had taken over the German situation. '

More substantial divisions arose over the ICA Appeal Fund for Austrian Relief, which the Central Committee agreed to launch at Rotterdam. The sum raised was £5,268, which May referred to as a 'very modest sum' in the Central Committee's Report to the Paris Congress, 1937.[25]

In a letter to Tanner in April, 1934, May advanced the view that the appeal had suffered from two opposing views. One, typified by the political elements of the British Movement, suggested that the ICA had 'delivered the Austrian Movement to the Dollfuss Government and was favouring Fascist tendencies'. The other view was that, by contributing to the fund, countenance was being given to socialist activities.[26]

The Czechoslovak view at the Rotterdam Central Committee meeting could have been shaped in part by the fact that the Czechs had become heavily involved in helping Austrian co-operative refugees. To help meet the heavy additional costs incurred by the Czech Central Union and the German Economic Union in Prague, £1,000 of the ICA Appeal Fund was sent directly to them.[27]

Back in Austria events improved somewhat. Renner and Mrs Freundlich were released from prison and on 10th November, 1934, the Austrian Government issued an amended Decree contemplating 'the early restoration of the autonomy of the Co-operative Movement.......' [28] The condition attached to it was 'the exclusion of political action from their assemblies' and, when this was accepted, the Decree restoring the autonomy of the General Consumers' Society of Vienna was adopted in May, 1935. That of the Austrian Co-operative Wholesale Society was restored the following December by another Decree.

Thus the Austrian consumer movement was able to stay within the ICA and was represented at the London Congress in September, 1934 by six delegates, three of whom were Strobl, Korp and Vukowitch.[29]

Things, however, could not be as they had been before. Both Renner and Mrs Freundlich were barred from co-operative work, and they were replaced on the ICA Central Committee by Dr Vukowitch and Andreas Korp. It is interesting to note that, after the Second World War and the rehabilitation of the Austrian Movement, both men returned to the Central Committee, thus providing some measure of continuity between the Austrian movement and the ICA during the 1930s and 1940s.

Mrs Freundlich's departure from the Central Committee meant that she lost her seat on the ICA Executive. She was allowed, however, to retain her Presidency of the International Co-operative Women's Guild and it was in this capacity that she attended the ICA's 1937 Congress in Paris as a Guest of Honour[30]. Her work in the Austrian co-operative movement appeared to provide its own testimony. When the Vienna society became autonomous once more and elections were held for its Supervisory Board, 16 of its 32 members were women.[31]

May kept in touch with both Mrs Freundlich and Dr Renner. At one point Vukowitch and Korp proposed that Mrs Freundlich should come to work for the ICA in London. Although he had some reservations about a then-member of the Central and Executive Committees working in the Secretariat, May nonetheless wrote to Dollfuss to see whether Mrs Freundlich would be allowed to leave Austria[32]. The idea came to nothing because of Mrs Freundlich's subsequent exclusion from co-operative work.

In June, 1934, May attended the Swiss Movement's Congress and later another in Prague. En route he stopped in Vienna and wrote to Tanner.

'Mrs. Freundlich and Dr. Renner are now definitely excluded from renewing their co-operative work: on the other hand, their material needs are provided for, and each of them will receive a pension. I am arranging to see them during my visit and to pass some time with them.'[33]

Renner and Freundlich fared better than Dollfuss, who was assassinated in an abortive Nazi putsch only four months after May had met him. This event provided a graphic illustration of the continuing uncertain nature of Austrian politics. Final Nazi success did not occur until the Anschluss of March, 1938, under which Austria became a province in 'Greater Germany' until the end of the Second World War in 1945[34], and the co-operative movement that May had helped to save became 'Nazified'[35] Renner fared better, becoming Austria's President in 1946 until his death in 1950. Today, part of Vienna's main thoroughfare, the Ring, is named after him.

Conclusions on the Austrian Situation

The Austrian situation resolved itself satisfactorily, at least in the short term, and could therefore be considered the one success for the ICA in this series of situations involving right-wing authoritarian regimes. In neither the Italian nor the German crisis had May been able to make direct representations to Mussolini or Hitler in the way that he was able to do so with Dollfuss. As we have seen, though, the success lasted only until the Anschluss in 1938 but was, in any event, considered by socialists in Austria and Great Britain to have been achieved at too high a cost.

We can see that in each of the Italian, German and Austrian situations an organisational pattern was emerging in which the ICA Secretariat, and particularly the General Secretary, Henry May, led ICA action. The Executive and Central Committees kept to their usual roles of determining policy and approving, or otherwise, May's reports. ICA Archives testify to the fact that May's reports were backed by good intelligence. He also used personal contacts to augment this knowledge. In the Italian situation he had called upon Dr Suter to help him gain a clearer picture, and in the Austrian situation May employed Lustig and Dietl in Prague in a similar fact-finding capacity. In every case the people used were members of the ICA Executive or Central Committees.

Moving on to the Austrian Government's side of the situation, we should note that Dollfuss's agreement to meet May probably owed much to two factors that had not been present in the two earlier situations. The first was the readiness of other Austrian co-operative organisations to intercede on behalf of Austrian consumer co-operatives. The other was the state of flux of Austrian politics which, during the period, veered between German Nazism and Italian Fascism. This competition was not resolved until the Anschluss in 1938. In the meantime, an organisation, such as the ICA, that could help to neutralise the political power of the consumer co-operatives yet provide possible trading links with co-operative movements in other countries, was not one to be spurned.

Before moving on to the Spanish situation we should note that the ICA took a position on the Sino-Japanese War, 1937.

The Sino-Japanese War

At its Congress in Paris in 1937, the ICA acknowledged that Fascism and Nazism had become a worldwide force.[36] It went a stage further when, for the first time, it took a hostile attitude to a Government irrespective of the fact that it had a member organisation in that country. The occasion was the Sino-Japanese War, 1937, and ICA archive material reveals that the Alliance, under strong leadership from Henry May, became firmly opposed to Japanese militarism. Moreover, that it took a pro-Chinese stand, although it had no Chinese affiliate.

The stand was justified in the following terms:

................the Alliance..........took an attitude with regard to the Sino-Japanese war which clearly indicated its general attitude towards aggression of every kind; not only did the Alliance fully realise the general threat to peace which such actions of a military nature or backed by a military power involved, it also felt the moral urge to stand by the victims in defence of their right.[37]

By the time of the war's outbreak in 1937, Japan had been a member of the ICA for over a decade. From an ICA 'Report on the Activities of National Co-operative Organisation'[38] we learn that Japanese societies were divided into Rural Producers' Societies, Urban Credit Societies and Urban Consumers' Societies. These numbered 15,459 in 1936 and had a combined membership of 5,825,000.

According to a Chinese report in ICA archives, Consumer, Supply, Utility, Credit, Productive, Marketing and Insurance Co-operatives had developed in China after the First World War. When the Sino-Japanese War broke out, 46,983 societies existed with a combined membership totalling 2,139,634.[39]

Thus the affiliated Japanese movement was roughly twice the size of the unaffiliated Chinese movement. Nonetheless, the ICA considered organising a co-operative consumer boycott of Japanese goods, as can be seen from a memorandum that Henry May sent in early 1938 to the members of the ICA Central Committee. This sought their views on whether the ICA should organise such a boycott among member co-operative movements. The forty-two replies received from Central Committee members in 18 countries reflected a split. Fifteen favoured a boycott. A further 11 supported the proposal in principle but did not believe that the ICA should organise it, while the others were opposed.[40]

It is not surprising that the Central Committee should be divided, because here was a proposal that would, if implemented, have adverse consequences for an ICA member movement. More than that, the idea of a trade boycott took the ICA far away from its belief in political neutrality. We will see shortly that, around this time, the Alliance struggled over how far it could remain politically neutral over events in Spain. It can be argued that, in the countdown to the 1939-45 War, the Alliance's working class allegiances challenged its ideological stance of political neutrality. However, the weapon envisaged was the movement's economic power.

Writing in the *Review of International Co-operation* in March, 1938, on the destruction of democracy by the 'Dictatorships of Europe and Asia', Henry May urged that co-operators should attempt to save democracy through their citizenship and economic power.

'In my opinion, it is urgently necessary that the whole Co-operative Movement should bind itself in a solemn covenant to use all the Economic Means at its disposal to stop Japanese aggression'.

He continued:

'The Co-operative Movement has not the means of Government at its disposal, and cannot exercise Governmental powers. But the organised Movement of Consumers in every country has in its possession a weapon of the most effective kind in the economic forces at its disposal and probably the only one which, in the present critical circumstances, is capable of being understood by either the Japanese military authorities or the misguided Co-operators of this country'.[41]

While May realised that a co-operative boycott alone would not stop Japanese aggression in China, he did feel that it might 'put a little backbone into the actions of Governments'. He also drew a distinction between co-operatives and trade unions.

The Co-operative Movement is in a different and infinitely stronger position to adopt such an attitude than the Trade Union Movement. As an economic organisation, self-constrained and self-controlled, it is, in effect, a State within the State, having ideals of association in the pursuit of economic and social equality amongst all people and races, which constitute the real antidote and remedy for the insane nationalism which afflicts the world today, whether in Europe or Asia or America'

May's reference to the 'misguided Co-operators' of Japan seems to have stemmed from the fact that they seemed to be almost totally behind the Japanese Government, apart from one notable exception. In an article printed elsewhere, but reported in the *Review of International Co-operation*, February, 1938, ICA Executive member Victory Serwy, Belgium, wrote:

'for several years past...Kagawa, the Japanese co-operative leader has been preaching to the working classes that Co-operation is essentially Christian in character and pursues the reign of Peace on Earth. Today, however, his voice is stilled! During a meeting at which he was present recently he sat with bowed head, taking no part in the proceedings. Suddenly, he raised himself and said, "It is not Kagawa who is here with joy, but only his shadow. The real Kagawa is across the ocean in China, with the suffering mothers and children, mutilated and rendered homeless by the war"'.

Serwy continued:

'Under the pressure of the militarist Government of Japan the co-operators numbering several millions, are obliged to make themselves at one with the authorities in the fratricidal struggle against the Chinese people, and to bow before the will of the Mikado..' [42]

It has not been possible to trace what position Kagawa held in Japanese co-operation, or how he came to have links with Serwy in Belgium.

He was not one of the Japanese delegates to ICA Congresses between the two World Wars. However, he may have been significant in prefiguring the staunch pro-peace attitudes that Japanese co-operators took after 1945.

In October, 1937, May sent a telegram to the ICA's Japanese affiliate, expressing horror and detestation of the crimes against humanity wrought on the Chinese by the Japanese forces.[43] The Japanese Union replied by sending a copy of a resolution that it had passed in which it stated its belief that:

'................the Imperial Military Forces were enhancing the national prestige of Japan throughout the world by making brilliant records of victory in all places in China, on land, sea and in the air'.

It continued that Japanese co-operators would give every possible aid to the prosecution of the war in China and 'to strengthening and perfecting national defence behind the guns'.[44]

Strangely enough, in the light of the strong statements on both sides, Japan did not withdraw from the Alliance, neither was her membership cancelled. It continued until May, 1940, when the following letter was received by ICA Head Office from the Central Union of Co-operative Societies of Japan:

'We informed you in 1937 that our opinions were very different from yours regarding the new order in the East, the mission of Japan, and the national function of the Co-operative Movement. We have never considered it necessary to alter these opinions of ours since then. Furthermore, we think we should make more our attitude clear under the present international state of affairs. Therefore, we make the formal statement of our secession from the ICA.'[45]

Japanese membership of the ICA was renewed in 1952,[46]

Events elsewhere moved towards war and, from 1937 onwards, international crises dominated ICA business. That arising out of the Spanish Civil War formed a large and poignant part of the ICA's last pre-war Congress held in Paris in 1937.

The Spanish Civil War

The ICA's links with Spanish co-operation were far more tenuous than those with Italian, German or Austrian co-operation. Initially, it had been on a personal basis between Juan Salas Anton, the veteran Spanish co-operator, and Henry May. Their correspondence dated back to 1914, when May had hoped to participate in a demonstration in Barcelona but had been prevented from doing so by the outbreak of the First World War.[47]

In February, 1915, in impeccable English, Salas Anton advised May about the setting up of the Regional Chamber of Co-operative Societies of Catalonia and Balearic Islands [48], of which he became President. He resigned five years later because of:

*'indifferency of our co-operators for the great co-operative ideals..........
......most of our workers have put their hopes only in syndicalism, they being generally opponents to Co-operation.'*[49]

Salas Anton's resignation could have broken his links with the ICA but, in view of the high regard in which he was held, he went on to become a member of the Alliance's Committee of Honour.[50]

By 1924, the Regional Chamber of Co-operative Societies and Balearic Islands had joined the ICA and appointed Mr J. Ventosa Roig to become their representative on the Central Committee. He remained the Spanish representative when the Spanish National Federation of Co-operatives in Madrid took over from the Regional Chamber as the ICA'S Spanish member.[51]

The ICA's London Congress in 1934 noted:

'the steadily increasing Co-operative Organisations of Spain were conspicuous by their number and enthusiasm.'[52]

However, growth was soon to be hampered by the brief civil war of 1934, during which Ventosa Roig, a Catalonian representative in the Madrid Parliament, joined the exiles who fled to France.[53]

Moreover,

> '........a number of the Societies in Oviedo and the Asturias incurred considerable loss and damage, and in several cases destruction by fire. In Catalonia and the other provinces the Societies experienced a paralysis of their activities resulting from the imprisonment of many members and the disappearance of others in flight or hiding from the military forces responsible for the war.'[54]

May kept in close touch with the situation throughout.[55] The Civil War in 1934 was brief, and co-operative societies were soon able to resume their activities. They believed that they had escaped worse problems because they had maintained political neutrality. Ventosa Roig returned from exile in France and the Spanish Congress, delayed by the 1934 troubles, went ahead in the spring of 1935. Henry May attended, representing the ICA, and later reported:

> 'We were able to convey to the Congress, one of the best organised and most seriously deliberative assemblies that the Spanish Movement has ever held, the encouragement and solidarity of the ICA....'[56]

In the relatively more settled conditions, the National Federation of Consumers' Societies established a Central Wholesale Society in 1936.
But when the main Spanish Civil War broke out in July, 1936, co-operatives' political neutrality could not save them a second time from the 'hatred felt by the revolting military for all forms of democracy'[57] and the brief period of progress was brought to a halt.

The 1936 conflict stemmed from the election of a Popular Front Government comprising republicans, socialists, communists and anarchists. The army intervened under Franco when it became concerned at the growing disorder and the social reforms being introduced by the Popular Front Government. The notoriety of the Spanish Civil War lay in its heavy loss of life, with three-quarters of a million killed, and the involvement of external

Germany, Italy and the USSR.[58]

P. M. H. Bell, in his book The Origins of the Second World War in Europe has argued that:

'................here was a strong inclination for men to project their own fears and hopes upon the Spanish Civil War. Outsiders created the war in their own image, and saw it as an extension of their own struggles.'[59]

This was certainly the case as far as the ICA was concerned. The Paris Congress of 1937 noted that:

'Very soon the Co-operators of other countries became convinced.........that their fellow Co-operators were in need of material help for their personal needs as well as for their societies, and insistent demands were made for evidence of the solidarity which the International Co-operative Alliance is organised to manifest. Even before the Spanish Co-operators asked for our help, we were pressed to take action to render them aid'.[60]

£33,737 was raised through the ICA, of which £21,750 was used to buy food that was distributed through the recently-established Spanish Co-operative Wholesale Society.[61] The balance was used to support Spanish co-operators who had taken refuge in France or emigrated to Latin America.[62] In France, the main co-operative body involved was the National Federation of Consumer Co-operatives, which took over two thousand Spanish children under their care[63]. We had already noted the similar help that had been given to Austrian co-operative refugees by co-operative organisations in Czechoslovakia.

An early point that should be noted is that because the Spanish co-operative movement was caught in a Civil War, there was no scope for the ICA to make representations on its behalf as it had sought to do in the cases in Italy, Germany and Austria. The Alliance was therefore limited to expressing solidarity and to channelling aid. While there was no difficulty in the latter, there were problems about the former. For example, how to draft a resolution which the 1937 Paris Congress could pass without breaking the ICA's political neutrality. This question arose initially, and was discussed at great length by the Executive at its meeting in Paris in September, 1937.[64]

The motion finally emerging, and approved by the Central Committee to go to Congress, read as follows:

The Congress receives with deep concern the report on the situation of the Co-operative Movement in Spain, and expresses its profound sympathy with the Societies and their members who have suffered in the fratricidal conflict in the country for more than a year past.

The Congress also approves the action taken by the Central and Executive Committees of the Alliance in launching appeals for funds to aid the Spanish Co-operators in their distress. The need for this support is even more urgent at the present time and will surely be afforded.

The representatives of the Co-operators of the world assembled at Paris express the fervent hope that effective measures may speedily be found for ending this dreadful conflict and restoring Peace to the Spanish People.[65]

Despite such a pious motion, a vigorous debate followed, in which three main issues emerged. What effective help could the Alliance give to Spanish co-operators? How could it take a stand that was not political and therefore in breach of its principle of political neutrality? How should it respond to the increasing dangers of wider war?

The second point was the most contentious, while fear of the third can clearly be seen running through the debate. It was perhaps prophetic that this debate was the very last business that an ICA Congress discussed before the outbreak of the Second World War.

A feature to note about the debate itself was that it was largely led by politicians. For example, the main British delegate to speak and lead the debate did not do so on behalf of the Co-operative Union or the Co-operative Wholesale Society, but spoke instead for only 31 of the 109 British delegates. The speaker was Alf Barnes, Chairman of the Co-operative Party and a Labour and Co-operative Member of Parliament. Supported by the '31 other members of the British delegation', he had tabled an amendment which had not been accepted by the Congress Committee because of its political nature. However, Barnes was allowed to speak, and when he did so he mentioned the two main points of the rejected amendment. One was that the policy of non-interference by many Governments had acted to the detriment of the elected Spanish Government. The other was that it was necessary to restore 'to the Spanish people and their Government all the rights under established international law'.

Barnes criticised the Central Committee's resolution for being 'a mere pious expression of sympathy'. Sooner or later, the Alliance would have to 'grapple differently' with such grave international problems. He continued:

'We are supposed to represent here today 70,000,000 citizens of the world, and yet we are faced by the body responsible for collecting the opinion of International Co-operation, with a futile resolution of this character on a matter of supreme importance to workers throughout the world. What is the use of a gathering of this description if we cannot take these grave problems that divide the peoples of the world and have an opportunity of discussing them freely and fairly, and differing where necessary?

Surely in our international conferences we must learn the art of differing without creating national enmity and national bitterness. If our working class movement cannot establish that standard of debate, how do you imagine that you are going to create peace throughout the world, through your various capitalist instruments of discussion? '

Barnes's intervention led to the reference back of the Central Committee's resolution and to the request that Barnes's amendment be circulated to Congress.

Back in the Central Committee, the motion got bogged down in semantics until Tanner suggested that:

'Perhaps the best way out would be that the Central Committee should decide not to submit any Resolution at all concerning Spain, for the simple reason that it appeared impossible to obtain unanimity of view. It would be detrimental to the Spanish cause if the Congress were divided into a small majority and a large minority'. [66]

This was about expediency rather than political neutrality, but Tanner's proposal was seconded by A. Juell, Norway, suggesting that the Scandinavian movements might have taken a concerted line. However, it was defeated by 22 votes for to 27 against.

Ventosa Roig, Spain, then proposed two amendments. The first, which deleted 'fratricidal' from paragraph 1, line 4, was accepted, but the second was not. It proposed to delete the words after 'conflict' in paragraph 3 and substitute instead:

'in conditions which would fully restore International Law and the constitutional institutions which the Spanish people have freely chosen'.

However, an amendment proposed by Poisson (France) went part of the way to meeting Ventosa Roig's sentiments by adding at the end of the resolution the words 'with due respect to International Law'. While this amendment was accepted by the Central Committee, the proposal that Barnes's amendment should be circulated to the Congress was not.

The resumed Congress debate reflected an inherent ideological tension within the Alliance: how to aim for world peace, which involved making political judgements and taking stances on political issues, while at the same time preserving the Alliance's political neutrality. Until the end we find that Ernest Poisson (France), one of the Alliance's Vice-Presidents, was attempting to reconcile both, but that others, such as the Spanish, some British and Soviet delegates, believed that a more political stand had become necessary if the worldwide threat of Fascism was to be averted.

When the amended resolution returned to Congress one of the finest, yet one of the most tortured, debates in ICA history began. The Spanish strongly believed that the resolution did not go far enough, and were disappointed that the Ventosa Roig amendment had not been accepted. Barnes made another hard-hitting speech in which he set the Spanish situation in the context of:

'the worsening situation right throughout Europe and the world today, that is dragging every nation and every people again to a conflict far greater, far more devastating, than that which we went through from 1914 to 1918'.

He repeated his view that the question was not being addressed forcefully enough because of the ICA's political neutrality, but asserted that elsewhere the Congress had taken a number of political positions on questions such as currency protection and peace. Barnes continued:

'........the application of collective security embodies sanctions, which is one of the great political controversies of this particular period, and on its decision the success or failure of the League of Nations will be written. Now, international law is not a political issue, any more than the civil law of any country is a political issue. International law is the common right of every nation, as civil law is the common right of every citizen within that nation, and I request the Central Committee now, before it is too late, to insert at the end of the resolution "right of international law to the Spanish people". At this last moment of Congress I appeal to every delegation not to look at international law as a political matter, but to look at international law as the very safeguard of our civilisation itself.'

Mr J. H. H. Codd (Great Britain), who had moved the motion for the reference back of the original resolution and the distribution of the Barnes's amendment, rose to regret that 'the Central Committee had defied the decision of Congress'. He now moved an addendum of five words, namely 'and Right of International Law', to the final paragraph of the resolution. The final sentence would thus read: '............that effective measures may speedily be found for ending this dreadful conflict and restoring Peace and Right of International Law to the Spanish People', thus reflecting Barnes's proposal.

It is interesting to note that Codd's proposal was seconded by Alf Robens, who, although attending Congress as a delegate from the English Manchester and Salford Society, was later to become a British Labour Cabinet Minister.

The Soviet view was expressed by Mr A. P. Kukhtin, who stressed the global nature of the Spanish problem:

'We are living in a stormy period, World war is threatening us. Fascists are pursuing a policy of open aggression; they threaten Spain and China; they are attacking merchant vessels on the open sea. At this moment no progressive man can remain neutral; everybody must pronounce himself clearly and distinctly for or against fascism.........

A Congress which represents nearly 80,000,000 Co-operators can say and must say to the Governments of all the nations that, in order to defeat fascism, the Spanish Republic must receive effective support'.

Ernest Poisson (France) made two main points. One underlined the fact that different delegations viewed the Spanish question differently. For example the British had their Co-operative Party which opposed the British Government on the question, and from whom it was easy and even necessary to disassociate itself. However, in France, the Co-operative Movement took no part in politics, even though the great majority of its members were 'republicans of the Popular Front, radicals, socialists, and even communists......'

Poisson's second point was that, while he did not dissent from adding 'international right' to the final sentence, he felt that it weakened the resolution. Although the Spanish rebels led by Franco had violated international right, they had above all violated national right. Some delegates might then feel it was better to refer to both in the resolution but Poisson argued

'............that is not possible, because you could not obtain in this Congress a sufficient majority on the question of violations of constitutional right............that is an opinion of a political character, and, until the Alliance alters its Rules in this respect, we are not authorised to interfere in questions relating to the national policy of any country'.

He therefore asked the British and Spanish delegations to adopt the resolution submitted by the Central Committee.

Surprisingly, in view of the earlier split votes in the Central Committee, the Congress was of a different view and the Codd-Robens addendum was adopted without dissent' when put to the vote. Even more surprisingly, the amended resolution was carried 'unanimously' when put to the vote. [67] Thus Congress came to a united position on Spain in the end.

Something that we should keep in mind was the fact that the crises which we are examining in this chapter often overlapped with each other, and therefore had a cumulative effect. We have already seen how the new German co-operative organisation had observed the ICA's success in representing the Austrian movement to its Government in 1934, and wanted the Alliance to attempt something similar on its behalf. We should now observe that the Spanish Civil War and the Sino-Japanese War began within a year of each other and reinforced fears of the worldwide threat of Fascism. It was to be in Europe, though, that the immediate events leading to the Second World War occurred and, in particular, Nazi Germany's annexation of Austria and Czechoslovakia in 1938 and 1939. In respect of both countries there was still time for the ICA to make its protests, but this luxury could not apply to Poland after the German blitzkrieg of September 1939 led directly to the Second World War.

We have already observed that the ICA's success in helping to save the Austrian co-operative movement could last only until the Anschluss of 1938. The penultimate section of this Chapter will therefore examine briefly the Alliance's role in the Czechoslovak situation. Now, in the absence of any ICA Congress, the lead had to be taken once more by the Executive and Central Committees, and in particular by Henry May and the ICA Secretariat.

The Czechoslovak Situation

There was little that Alliance could do in the crisis that overwhelmed the Czechoslovak State in 1938 and 1939. The country had been created in 1918 from former provinces in Austria and Hungary.

J. M. Roberts, in his book Europe 1880-1945 suggested that 'Czechoslovakia was abhorrent to Hitler as the one stable democracy and capitalist society in Central Europe'[68]. Such stability emerged despite the fact that the Sudetenland comprised many people of German stock, whereas the rest of the country was made up largely of Slavs. Throughout the 1930s there were Sudeten demands for autonomy, but always within Czechoslovakia. However, the Munich Agreement of September, 1938, provided for its complete secession to Germany. Then, six months later in March, 1939, the Czechoslovak Government was inveigled into asking Hitler to give Germany military protection to the rest of the country.

In these circumstances there was little that the International Co-operative Alliance could do except show sympathy and solidarity through visits by its General Secretary, and through the establishment of a relief fund.

Before examining the impact of these events on the Czechoslovak co-operative organisations it might be helpful to describe their backgrounds.

From the document Consumers' co-operation under the Nazi regime - an impartial statement of facts based on authentic documents in the records of the ICA showing the treatment of the consumers' co-operative movement in Germany, Austria, Sudetenland and Czechoslovakia, published by the ICA in July, 1940, we learn that the Union of German Economic Societies, formed in 1919, brought together German co-operatives in the provinces of Bohemia, Moravia, Silesia and Slovakia in the German speaking part of Czechoslovakia. Before the collapse of the Austro Hungarian Empire they had been part of the Austrian Co-operative Union. By 1938, the Union of German Economic Societies had its wholesale and Head Office in Prague, although the 140 co-operatives constituting the Union were predominantly located in the Sudeten region.

Elsewhere in the country, the consumer co-operative movement was made up by a number of other unions. Two of the largest were the Central Union of Czechoslovak Co-operative Societies, and the Union of Czechoslovak Co-operative Societies. In 1937 the former, also with a wholesale and headquarters in Prague, had 214 member societies with 380,600 members, while the latter brought together 122 societies with 155,700 members. Besides these two unions there were smaller ones such as the Union of Ex-Service Men's Co-operative Societies, and the Co-operative Union of Moravia and Silesia.

As early as April, 1938, six months before the ceding of the Sudetenland to Germany, May wrote to Väinö Tanner of his fear that the ICA could lose Czechoslovak membership if what the world generally conceives to be the purposes of the Fuehrer are given effect'.[69]

May had just visited Prague to attend the 30th anniversary of the Czech Co-operative Union. While there he had been received by Dr Edward Benes, the President of Czechoslovakia.[70] Of his co-operative business, May wrote to Tanner to say that:

'My first care after meeting the Czechs was to visit the Germans, who I found in a condition of great depression and tension.....'[71]

When the Germans urged him to attend their Congress a few weeks later he agreed. We should perhaps remind ourselves that at this time Henry May was nearing 71 years of age, yet the records show that he was remarkably active. In addition to these two visits, May returned to Prague in October, 1938. Earlier that month the ICA Executive had held a Special meeting in Amsterdam to consider the Czechoslovak co-operative position in the aftermath of the Munich Agreement.

The Executive allocated £2,000 to help Czechoslovak co-operators and launched an appeal for additional funds. They also agreed to appeal to national co-operative organisations to try to employ exiled Czechoslovak officials. They particularly wanted information regarding the actual position in Prague and asked May to go and, while there, make arrangements for the distribution of ICA relief funds.

It seems likely that May was busy with other work, because the Executive had also asked him to prepare, for their next meeting, a 'survey of the Co-operative movement in each country in relation to the State'. This provides a strong indication that the Executive recognised that recent events demanded some kind of reappraisal by the ICA.[72]

Despite the pressure of work, May left for Prague within six days of the Executive's Special meeting. Before doing so he had made representations at the British Foreign Office on three points. One was that the British Government might intervene to prevent 'Germans being forced out of Czechoslovakia back to the Sudeten areas'. Another called for the British Government to make representations to the German Government to safeguard the economic interests of co-operatives in the Czech and Sudeten areas by safeguarding their members' assets. The third request was for assistance from the British Minister in Prague for May's imminent visit, particularly in regard to advice on the safeguards necessary for the distribution of ICA relief funds. Only on this last point had May received a positive response.[73]

He also spent most of the 24th October being briefed in London by Mr S. Schrier, President of the Union of German Economic Societies. It had been hoped that Schrier would attend the Executive's Special. Meeting in Amsterdam but, that very day, he left Prague for London, where the British Government had offered him asylum. Once in London he lost no time in briefing May on the up-to-date position in the Sudetenland and how the German Union had been affected.

May arrived in Prague on 30th October, 1938[74], after long delays because frontier changes had disrupted transport routes. He found the leaders of both the Czech and the German co-operative movements in a very depressed state. In an apparent reference to the Munich Agreement, May observed that:

'Their excess of bitterness arose from their conviction that they had been betrayed by those who had been their friends, and who had encouraged them in the confidence that those same friends would stand by them in defence of justice, liberty and their democratic state'.

On his first day May spent between four and five hours with co-operative leaders, but also visited the British Minister in Prague, the first of three such visits. In the evening, and on the three subsequent days, he met the Directors of the Czech and German Co-operative Wholesales, as well as the boards of both Unions, and the Manager of the General Co-operative Bank, Karl Komeda.

We can gather from his report to the ICA Executive that May had become strongly anti-German. He denounced the 'delusion' that Germany's right to Czechoslovakia could be based upon an error of the Peace Treaties at the end of the 1914-18 War and that she had only been retrieving what had been improperly taken from her. For example, the greater part of the territory ceded to Germany had not been within that 'Empire during 1,000 years'. May underlined the fact that the Sudeten Germans had not demanded incorporation in the German Reich, but rather self-determination within the Czechoslovak Republic, and he reported a strong sense of grievance among Czechoslovak co-operators that the Western Powers had supported the German claim for the cession of all areas with 51 per cent of Germans in their population, 'no matter by what census they were counted'. A further grievance was that 'the victim had no part or voice' in the settlement.

May went on to describe how co-operative leaders kept a daily watch 'on a huge map specially prepared' to show the day-to-day frontier changes decided by the International Commission of Ambassadors, or by the actual occupation of German troops. Regarding the new frontiers May commented:

........it would be difficult to imagine a more fantastic line than that which has been achieved. The redrawing of the frontiers in 1918 had at least the merit of seeking to make a logical and convenient division of territory. In Czechoslovakia today the new frontiers are masterpieces of cunning and rapacity, designed to reserve for the raiders the vital economic resources, as far as that is possible, of a little country which was, a few short weeks ago, one of the most richly endowed lands in Europe. Scores of towns and villages have had their means of transport cut, so that now they must travel many miles, without railway connections, to reach a market hitherto easy of access and a fraction of the distance away. The lines of a "jig-saw puzzle", in many cases, enclose lands of considerable extent, the former properties of members of the Sudeten German aristocracy, which were purchased by the State under the Land Reform Act of 1910'.

May learned that, while he was in Prague, a new Berlin decree had restored these lands to previous owners and he concluded that the new frontiers had indeed been drawn to facilitate their return.

May's report to the ICA Executive went into great detail about the losses that the Czech and German co-operative movements had sustained and the problems they were facing: safeguarding members' savings; obtaining credits, possibly from other ICA member movements, with which to buy raw materials; and the problems of finding employment for an increasing number of co-operative refugees. May described how the offices of the German Union and Wholesale had become a rendezvous for displaced co-operative officials and how, while he had been there, one of these had come in to 'bid an affecting farewell'. He had just received authority to leave the country, thus avoiding, May observed, being returned to Germany to the concentration camp, or possibly death'.

Moving onto uses for the ICA's relief fund, May said that he believed German refugees numbered some 43,000 with whom 'Our charge is, of course, with the co-operators...... Immediate relief was required the form of clothing, but financial assistance was needed for those forced to leave Czechoslovakia. Such help could be expensive, covering not only actual fares but financial support in a new country.

May reported to the ICA Executive that two Directors of the German Wholesale Society had agreed to handle applications for assistance, while Mr Emil Lustig, President of the Czech Union and Wholesale and a member of the ICA Executive, together with Mr Karl Komeda, General Manager of the Co-operative Bank, would act as a Control Committee. Contributions to the Fund should be placed in a separate account with the Co-operative Wholesale Bank in London.

A touching note came at the end of May's report. The Board of the Czech Union had unanimously agreed not to take any money from the fund. Instead, they believed, it should be 'used for the benefit of the German co-operators who are either fugitives from the Sudeten areas or are in distress and danger as the result of the ceding of the Sudeten areas to Germany'.

By the time that the ICA Executive and Central Committees met in Zurich in January, 1939, £10,230 had been paid into the ICA's Czechoslovak Relief Fund. £6,000 of this had already been forwarded to Prague[75]. May reported that ICA member movements, particularly the British, were active in trying to find work and housing for Czechoslovak co-operative refugees.

Two months later, on 15th March, 1939, the new Czech President was inveigled into inviting German troops to enter Czechoslovakia on the grounds that it faced civil war and had become ungovernable. Three days later Emil Lustig resigned the Presidency of the Czech Co-operative Union and Wholesale Society and, with the help of the Swedish co-operative leader, Albin Johansson, fled the country. He later emigrated to Argentina, where he became the Manager of a co-operative and representative of Sweden's Kooperativa Forbundet.[76]

We should end this section on the Czechoslovak crisis by reiterating the point made earlier that there was little the ICA could do except provide sympathy and solidarity. However, as we have seen, both were given generously. We should also note that the crisis occurred in the growing shadow of the coming war. To some extent this can be sensed in the changing tone of May's writing. He no longer avoided, as on earlier occasions, emotive phrases or sentiments.

A similar shift can be seen elsewhere in the ICA, particularly in the Executive's call for a paper from May on the position of the Co-operative Movement in each country in relation to the State'. May presented the paper at the meetings of the Executive and Central Committees in Zurich in January, 1939. No resolutions were tabled on it, which suggested that discussion was intended to continue at later meetings. This, however, was not to be, because the Central Committee did not meet again until 1946. We can only note, therefore, that the Alliance had become conscious of a need to analyse the implications for co-operatives functioning in different political and economic systems, including those of Communism and Fascism. To some extent this debate had begun at the 1937 Paris Congress when Alliance President, Väinö Tanner, had presented a paper on *The Place of Co-operation in Different Economic Systems*.[77]

During the coming war a debate would occur in the pages of the *Review of International Co-operation* between American, British and South

American co-operative leaders on the dangers to co-operative organisation from the State becoming too involved in business and welfare in the post-war world. It is therefore possible to view May's 1939 paper, which proceeded no further than an analytical stage, as part of a continuum by which the international co-operative movement repositioned itself in a changing world.

The Alliance was finding it necessary also to reappraise some of its longest held beliefs, including support for the League of Nations and how best to campaign for world peace. This Chapter will close with a brief look at these issues as the count-down to the Second World War accelerated.

The ICA and World Peace

We have noted earlier occasions when ICA leaders were not necessarily united in their perception of events, or how best to respond to them. Further examples occurred on the eve of the 1939-45 war. One was a heated exchange between Emmy Freundlich and Ernest Poisson. Although no longer a member of the ICA Executive, Mrs Freundlich was still President of the International Women's Guild, whose report was included in the main report to ICA Congresses. The Guild's 'Notes' also featured prominently in each issue of the *Review of International Co-operation*. It should be noted that, in many respects, the Guild had been more militant in its support of peace during the 1930s than the rest of the ICA. It had also adopted the white poppy of peace, as distinct from the red memorial poppy for those fallen in the First World War.

In August, 1938, Mrs Freundlich wrote to the ICA Executive, protesting at remarks that Ernest Poisson, Vice-President of the Alliance, was reported to have made at a meeting of the French Guild at Avignon. The occasion and location of the remarks prompted the ICA Executive to decide to take no action[78]. However, from the point of view of this study it is useful to note the arguments that were involved. Poisson's charges can only be inferred from Mrs Freundlich's letter, but seem to have arisen from a circular and 'confidential private letters' that she had written. She told the ICA Executive that in the circular she had said that:

'....the changed situation would compel us to reconsider our attitude to various questions, as for instance, our policy with regard to the League of Nations. Should we continue to support this or would it be wiser to try and build a new organisation based on similar principles? Apparently this had been interpreted that I am prepared to betray the democratic ideals of our Co-operative Movement.

Yet nearly all the smaller powers, the Oslo Group, Switzerland, Belgium and Poland, have revised very considerably their former attitudes to the League, and should it not be the duty of every international organisation to re-examine its policy from time to time? Surely it is only by doing this that it can find the best method of serving the cause of Peace and democracy.

I also remarked that at one of our Committee Meetings we had already discussed the question as to whether future events might not compel us choose between our ideals. Some of our member organisations stand for absolute pacifism and believe that no circumstances can justify war.

What would the decision of these organisations be, I wondered, if they had to choose between abandoning democracy, because its only defence was war, or sacrificing Peace in order to save Democracy? These are questions that must be thought out beforehand if one is not to be taken unawares when the decisive moment comes.[79]

Two points should be taken from Mrs Freundlich's letter. The first is that it reflects growing disenchantment with the League of Nations and its ineffectualness during the 1930s. In passing we should note that similar doubts had been expressed elsewhere in the Alliance. For example, the Executive, at its meeting in Glasgow in May, 1938, had noted an 'open letter' published in Accion Cooperatista, the official journal of the Catalonian Co-operative Federation, the previous month. While expressing gratitude for help received through the ICA's Relief Fund for Spain, the letter continued:

'...........we cannot consider that the International Co-operative Alliance, in failing to call attention to the crime which is being committed by the League of Nations, with England at its head, against the Spanish Republic, has arisen

to the heights of moral and official intervention which the circumstances demand'[80].

The second point of note in Mrs Freundlich's letter was her belief that events were forcing co-operators to face the stark choice of 'abandoning democracy because its only defence was war, or sacrificing peace in order to save Democracy'.

In the final months before the war the Alliance, at least in terms of rhetoric, made strong efforts to preserve the peace. We should note, though, that it was Henry May, rather than the Executive and Central Committees, who made the running in this.

Two main elements emerged in the ICA's campaign for peace. One was to work closely with the International (previously 'Universal') Peace Campaign. The other was to increase comment and reporting on peace issues in the *Review of International Co-operation*.

In 1936 the International Peace Campaign, whose President was Edward Benes, President of Czechoslovakia, invited the ICA to become 'associated' with its work. Although a number of other international organisations were already supporting the Campaign, the Alliance hesitated. The reasons for this are not clear. At its meeting in Vienna in June, 1936, the Executive decided to adjourn without a decision, but agreed that Ernest Poisson should attend the Campaign's first International Conference at Geneva in September, 1936.[81] The conference became a 'Congress' and took place in Brussels rather than Geneva. Poisson reported to the ICA Executive when it met at Warsaw later in September, 1936. Despite the fact that he recommended affiliation, and that a number of other co-operative representatives attended the Congress, forming themselves into a Co-operative Commission, the ICA Executive still delayed a decision. In passing, we can perhaps note that recommendations of the Co-operative Commission at the Peace Congress were as follows:
1. The inviolability of treaty obligations
2. The reduction and limitation of armaments by international agreement; the suppression of profits by the production of, and the trade in arms

Meeting of ICA Executive, Warsaw, September 1936

3. The strengthening of the League of Nations in order to prevent and to stop wars by the organisation of collective security and mutual assistance

4. The creation within the framework of the League of Nations of efficient machinery for remedying international situations likely to provoke war.[82]

Affiliation to the Peace Congress was also urged. Finally the ICA Executive, at its meeting in Strasbourg in February, 1937[83], agreed to affiliate to the International Peace Campaign. Ernest Poisson became the Alliance's representative on the Campaign's Council.[84] It was reported that he was 'extremely well received' and appointed to the committee drafting resolutions for the London Congress of the Peace Campaign held in October, 1937. May was asked to preside over its Co-operative Commission at the Congress.[85]

In the October, 1937, edition of the *Review of International Co-operation*, May wrote an editorial entitled 'Why I Support the I.P.C. (International Peace Campaign)[86]. It was unusual for May to use the personal pronoun in his articles in the Review and his doing so on this occasion could suggest several things. One was that there were still reservations in the Alliance about joining the Peace Campaign, and we shall see shortly that the British Co-operative Union appeared not to support it. The other was that May was now making the pursuit of peace a personal campaign. Certainly, from now on he devoted much of his energies to the question of how the peace could be saved.

When he reported to Tanner on the IPC's London Congress, May said that over 600 delegates attended but that:

'There would have been many more co-operative representatives from Great Britain had it not been for the lukewarm attitude of our friends at Manchester' [87]

By Manchester he was obviously referring to the British Co-operative Union. The letter also provided an insight into the working of the Congress.

'Poisson came together with three other French representatives who pushed him into a rather reluctant support of the memorandum and Resolution which I had prepared for the Co-operative Commission. We made him the Rapporteur for the Co-operative Commission, while the I.P.C. appointed me to the chair, in spite of my objection'.

May recounted that the resolution was passed with:

'Absolutely the whole of the essential points of my text embodied'.

Details of this resolution can be found in the *Review of International Co-operation* for March, 1938,[88] from which it can be seen that heavy emphasis was laid on co-operatives' boycotting Japanese goods. Apparently the International Peace Campaign welcomed ICA support. Its leader, Lord Cecil, later went on record as saying:

'Without the wholehearted support of the entire Co-operative Movement I feel that it is impossible to think of the International Peace Campaign developing at the necessary rapid pace'.[89]

Of course, the pace was not rapid or successful enough. The approach to war was reflected in the increased number of peace articles which May wrote in the *Review of International Co-operation* throughout 1938 and 1939.

In January, 1938, he wrote a general article headed 'The Pursuit of Peace,[90] in which he looked at what co-operators could do at local, national, and international levels to try to save peace. Two months later, in March, 1938, his leader article in the Review asked 'What should be the role of the ICA in the Present World situation?[91] In this May advocated a co-operative Peace Campaign that, presumably, would have been complementary to the International Peace Campaign. He argued that Co-operative action should be based on the principles of tolerance, equity and justice; respect for the rights of others, whether individuals, races or nations, and the inviolability of national territories; the settlement of disputes by reason rather than by armed conflict; the honourable fulfilment of all contractual obligations; the adjustment of economic inequalities; and the satisfaction of economic needs between nationals by means of freely constituted international authorities. May ended by urging national co-operative organisations to pass resolutions embodying these principles at their Congresses.

The ICA Executive was more cautious. When it met in Glasgow in May, 1938, it 'entirely approved' May's action, but hesitated over mounting a separate ICA peace campaign. Instead, it decided that the Alliance should continue its work with the International Peace Campaign, while May pursued questions of peace in the *Review of International Co-operation*.[92]

Already in April, 1938, May had written a leader reminding readers that 'The policy of the International Co-operative Alliance has, as its keynote, the necessity of maintaining peace amongst the nation.............'[93] Two months later he wrote the leading article under the heading of 'Peace, Pacifism or Passivity', in which May held that The Peace Principles of the ICA have nothing in common with pacifism as it is commonly understood'. The article ended with the International Co-operative Day Declaration, headed 'Peace Through Co-operation' [94].

By March, 1939, it appears that May was becoming impatient with the rest of the Alliance. In a Review article entitled 'Does the ICA Still Stand for Freedom?' he said that he raised the question for the following reasons:

The first of these is the simple fact that, during the past two years of increasing tension in international relations and unexampled progress of forces of aggression towards the destruction of the foundation of our Movement - Liberty, Independence, Justice and Peace - the International Co-operative Alliance has not made one definite and clear stand in the defence of its own Principles or the support of human principles of Government compatible with its professions.

Steadily and continually it has found the time inopportune, the circumstances too confused, the risks uncertain, and the possibility uppermost of 'doing more harm than good'. The policy of impotent 'neutrality' towards all the great and vital interests of humanity and civilisation is a policy of feebleness which awaits, if it does not provoke, the inevitable disaster'.[95]

From this it might seem that the ICA was palsied by the worsening international situation. If so, it was in the company of many other organisations, and even Governments, in being divided on how to react to increasing Nazi and Fascist aggrandisement. Within the Alliance, however, we should note that May had consistently taken a stronger line than his Executive and Central Committees on the question of peace.

Mrs Freundlich had asked if one of the Alliance's aims, namely that of peace, had to be sacrificed to ensure another aim, that of democracy. May's attitude and utterances on the eve of the war suggest that he recognised that political neutrality was no longer feasible. This is borne out by disparaging comments in a letter that he wrote to G. J. D. C. Goedhart, past President of the Alliance, and still a close personal friend of May, in May, 1939.

'Entre nous, the ultra neutralism in political matters amongst certain members of the Committees of the Alliance increases as the world situation becomes more acute'.[96]

May reflected his own view regarding neutrality on another occasion when, writing in the Review, he quoted Mrs Eleanor Roosevelt, wife of the United States' President:

'It may be safe to be neutral, but I am not sure that it is always right to be safe. I am beginning to think we undermine our backbone when we do not have to make up our minds between right and wrong'. [97]

In April, 1939, May called for a 'United Peace Effort' in the *Review of International Co-operation* [98], repeating it two months later, when it preceded the International Co-operative Day Declaration headed 'Freedom, Co-operation and Peace are Indivisible'.[99] In the same issue of the Review May called on two earlier leading co-operative figures, in an item called 'Echoes'. He quoted from a speech that Sir William Maxwell, then President of the ICA, had made on peace at Hamburg in 1910. Then he recalled Albert Thomas of France, first Director of the International Labour Organisation, as saying in Paris in 1931:

'I am distressed to see you so restrained, so modest and so prudent. With your 70 million co-operators affiliated to the ICA you represent a force and influence which justify you in speaking with no uncertain voice whether it concerns the economic crisis or the struggle for peace and disarmament'.[100]

The last ICA peace declaration before the outbreak of war came in the *Review of International Co-operation* in July, 1939. Signed by Tanner, as President, and May, as General Secretary, it was 'An Appeal to the Co-operators of the World' [101]

Repeating May's earlier arguments, it is significant because it was not addressed to ICA member organisations, as was customary, but to all Co-operators, who were urged to mobilise their material and moral resources in a supreme effort to prevent the world conflict. The appeal reiterated the essential characteristics of the Co-operative Movement: its universal character, which overcame frontiers, colour, race or creed; and its equitable economic system, which shared nature's resources according to man's needs. Co-operators faced the challenge of averting war and working to achieve equity, justice and freedom.

Such exhortations proved useless when war finally broke out on 3rd September, 1939.

May had unsuccessfully striven for peace. Nevertheless, he showed that he had the mental agility to turn round and face a different challenge. His first article in the *Review of International Co-operation* after the start of the War was entitled 'This War for Freedom and Right' and showed that he was reappraising the situation now that the Alliance was once again on a war footing.

Conclusions

The developments that we have described in this Chapter would seem to suggest that the Alliance had not been particularly successful in helping to maintain world peace, or in saving member organisations from Fascism and Nazism. Against this, however, it can be argued that the massive forces represented by the extreme right-wing ideologies were far greater than any non-Governmental organisation or any single Government.

It can also be argued that within this framework of worsening international relations the Alliance remained an effective organisation. Although ICA representations had only been effective in the case of Austria, and only then for a limited period, May's energetic intercessions, the maintenance of a good research capacity that kept ICA authorities informed of developments, and the swift organisation of relief funds had allowed the Alliance to show its sympathy for, and solidarity with, the co-operators in the Austrian, Spanish and Czechoslovak movements. Such responses were typical of an international working-class organisation.

However, we have also noted some increase in ideological ambivalence. Suggestions that the ICA should mount a Japanese Trade Boycott or a separate ICA Peace Campaign brought fears that its political neutrality would be weakened. On the one hand, we have seen that throughout the period May consistently argued for stronger action, as did some others at the 1937 Paris Congress. On the other, we have seen that the Scandinavians and Poisson (France) urged the preservation of the Alliance's political neutrality. It was likely, though, that in the approach

ÚSTŘEDNÍ SVAZ ČESKOSLOVENSKÝCH DRUŽSTEV V PRAZE

1908-1938

ZA PRÁCI A POCTIVOST!

Představenstvo Ústředního svazu československých družstev v Praze osvědčuje, že

Mr. Henry J. May

zasloužil se o družstevní podnikání, soustředěné v Ústředním svazu

československých družstev v Praze jako

generální tajemník
Mezinárodního družstevního svazu v Londýně,
svým celoživotním dílem ve službách družstevní idee

A PROTO BYLA MU JAKO DRUŽSTEVNÍ UZNÁNÍ UDĚLENA

ZLATÁ PLAKETA

ČÍSLO REJSTŘÍKU

1

V Praze, dne 3. dubna 1938

ÚSTŘEDNÍ SVAZ ČESKOSLOVENSKÝCH DRUŽSTEV V PRAZE

předseda

ústř. tajemník

Certificate featuring the Gold Medal presented to Henry J. May by the Czechoslovak Co-operative Movement as recognition for his services to the co-operative movement, to which he devoted his lifetime's work (April 1938).

to war and, as we have seen, in the case of the British delegation at the Paris Congress, national delegations within the ICA did not necessarily hold unanimous views on how to respond to Fascism and questions of war and peace.

The issues seemed to have been well summed up by Emmy Freundlich and Henry May. Might not peace have to be sacrificed to ensure the eventual survival of democracy, and might not neutrality also have to be gainsaid in order to fight the threat of Fascist world domination? In the next Chapter we shall find that ICA membership fell broadly in line with the Allied countries fighting against Germany, Austria and, initially, Italy in Europe, and Japan in the Far East in the 1939-45 War. We will also find that the war aims of the Allies, summed up in the Atlantic Charter, 1941, were ones that the Alliance could wholeheartedly support. This meant that the ICA's period of ideological ambivalence had largely passed, at least until the Cold War.

Notes

1. International Co-operative Alliance, Report of the 1921 Basle Congress, p. 93 and p. 187, plus Report of the 1930 Vienna Congress, p. 129, p. 141, pp. 253-54.
2. League of Nations Archive, Dossier 3763.
3. Archives of the League of Nations, Geneva, Dossiers or Series Nos. 143, 40641, 34652, 46893, 1032, 40567, 39791, 61275 and 62254. Archives of the International Labour Office, Files: C01011, C01000/1/3 and Dossier 7-501.
4. International Co-operative Alliance, *Review of International Co-operation, No.5, May, 1932*, p. 198.
5. Palmer, Alan, *Dictionary of Modern History 1789-1945*, Penguin Reference Books, London, Second Edition, reprinted 1988, p. 37.
6. This study Chapter 5.
7. International Co-operative Alliance, *Report of the 1930 Vienna Congress*, International Co-operative Alliance, London, 1930, p. 33.
8. International Co-operative Alliance, *Report of the 1934 London Congress*, International Co-operative Alliance, London, 1943, Appendix VI.

9. International Co-operative Alliance, *Report of the 1937 Paris Congress*, International Co-operative Alliance, London, 1938, p. 93.
10. ICA Archives, Letter from May to Väinö Tanner, 16th February, 1934.
11. ICA Archives, *ibid*.
12. ICA Archives, Letter from May to Väinö Tanner, 16th February, 1934.
13. ICA Archives, Unsigned and undated report of 'The Austrian Situation', an internal report, p. 1.
14. ICA Archives, Report of *'The Austrian Situation'*, *op. cit.*, p. 1.
15. ICA Archives, *The Austrian Co-operatives Under the Dictatorship - Report to the International Co-operative Congress at Paris, September, 1937, on the Tasks of the Socialist Opposition. Groups in the Co-operative Organisations of Austria*, pp. 27-8.
16. ICA Archives, *ibid.*, p. 28.
17. ICA Archives, Letter from May to Väinö Tanner, 20th February, 1934.
18. ICA Archives, *Internal report on The Austrian Situation'*, *op. cit.*, p. 3.
19. ICA Archives, *ibid.*, p. 5.
20. ICA Archives, *ibid.*, p. 4.
21. International Co-operative Alliance, *Report of the 1937 Paris Congress*, International Co-operative Alliance, London, 1938, p. 94.
22. ICA Archives, Internal report on *'The Austrian Situation'*, *op.cit.*, pp. 6/8/12 and 14.
23. ICA Archives, *ibid.*, p. 14.
24. International Co-operative Alliance, *Minutes of the meeting of the Central Committee, Rotterdam, 11-12 March, 1934*, p. 4.
25. International Co-operative Alliance, *Report of the 1937 Paris Congress, International Co-operative Alliance, London, 1938*, p. 95.
26. ICA Archives, Letter from May to Väinö Tanner, 12th April, 1934.
27. International Co-operative Alliance, *Minutes of the meeting of the Executive, London, 1st September, 1934*, p. 4.
28. International Co-operative Alliance, *Report of the 1937 Paris*

Congress, International Co-operative Alliance, London, 1938, p. 95.
29. International Co-operative Alliance, *Report of the 1934 London Congress*, International Co-operative Alliance, London, 1934, p. 17.
30. International Co-operative Alliance, *Report of the 1937 Paris. Congress*, International Co-operative Alliance, London, 1938, p. 15.
31. International Co-operative Alliance, *ibid.*, p. 95.
32. ICA Archives, Letter from May to Väinö Tanner, 12th April,1934.
33. ICA Archives, Letter from May to Väinö Tanner, 11th June, 1934.
34. Palmer, Alan, *op. cit.*, p. 38.
35. Nazification' was a term used in the ICA and can be found in its internal report, *Consumers' Co-operation Under the Nazi Regime*, July 1940, p. 12.
36. International Co-operative Alliance, *Report of ICA Congress, Paris, 1937*, pp. 129 and 229.
37. International Co-operative Alliance, *Report of ICA Congress, Zurich, 1946*, pp. 17-18.
38. International Co-operative Alliance, Report on the Activities of Fifteen National Co-operative Organisations in twenty-seven Countries, *International Co-operation 1930* 1936, Volume 111, pp. 162-163.
39. Co-operative League of China, *The Chinese Co-operators*, Vol.1. No.1. February, 1942, p. 5.
40. International Co-operative Alliance, *Minutes of the meeting of the ICA Executive, Glasgow, 16th and 17th May, 1938*, p. 3.
41. International Co-operative Alliance, *Review of International Co-operation, No.3 March, 1938*, p. 108.
42. International Co-operative Alliance, *Review of International Co-operation, No.2. February, 1938*, p. 53.
43. International Co-operative Alliance, *Minutes of meeting of ICA Executive, Lausanne, 1st/2nd December, 1937*, pp. 6-7.
44. International Co-operative Alliance, *Review of International Co-operation,* No.12, December, 1937 p. 508.
45. International Co-operative Alliance, *Minutes of the meeting of*

the ICA Central Committee, Manchester. February, 1941, p. 3

46. ICA Archives, List of Membership Admissions, p. 4.
47. ICA Archives, Letter from May to Juan Salas Anton, 17th August, 1914.
48. ICA Archives, Handwritten letter from Juan Salas Anton to May, 8th February, 1915.
49. ICA Archives, Handwritten letter from Juan Salas Anton to May, 7th March, 1920.
50. International Co-operative Alliance, *Report of the 1921 Basle Congress,* International Co-operative Alliance, London, no date of publication, p. 126.
51. International Co-operative Alliance, *Report of the 1927 Stockholm Congress*, International Co-operative Alliance, London, no date of publication, p. 23, and *Report of the 1930 Vienna Congress*, p. 27.
52. International Co-operative Alliance, *Report of the 1937 Paris Congress*, International Co-operative Alliance, London, 1938, p. 85.
53. International Co-operative Alliance, *Minutes of the meeting of the Executive, Paris, 8-9 February, 1935*, p. 7.
54. International Co-operative Alliance, *Report of the 1937 Paris Congress*, International Co-operative Alliance, London, 1938, p.85.
55. ICA Archives, Letter from May to Väinö Tanner, 17th November, 1934.
56. International Co-operative Alliance, Report of the 1937 *Paris Congress*, International Co-operative Alliance, 1938, p. 85.
57. WATKINS, W. P., op. cit., p. 199.
58. ROBERTS, J. M., op. cit., p. 448.
59. BELL, P. M. H., op. cit., p. 212.
60. International Co-operative Alliance, Report of the 1937 Paris Congress, International Co-operative Alliance, London, 1938, p. 86.
61. WATKINS, W. P., op. cit., p. 213.
62. ibid., p. 213.
63. International Co-operative Alliance, *Report of the 1937 Paris Congress*, International Co-operative Alliance, London, 1938, p. 86.

64. International Co-operative Alliance, *Minutes of the meeting of the Executive, Paris*, 4th September, 1937, pp. 2-3.
65. International Co-operative Alliance, *Report of the 1937 Paris Congress*, International Co-operative Alliance, London, 1938, PP. 127-8.
66. International Co-operative Alliance, *Minutes of the meeting of the Central Committee*, Paris, 8th September, 1937, p. 4.
67. International Co-operative Alliance, ibid., p. 302.
68. Roberts, J. M., op. cit., p. 537.
69. ICA Archives, Letter from May to Tanner, 21st April, 1938, p. 2.
70. International Co-operative Alliance, *Review of International Co-operation*, No.6, June, 1937, p. 267.
71. ICA Archives, Letter from May to Tanner, 21st April 1938.
72. International Co-operative Alliance, *Minutes of Special Meeting of ICA Executive*, Amsterdam, 21st October, 1938, p. 3.
73. ICA Archives, Letter from May to Tanner, 25th October, 1938, p. 1.
74. ICA Archives, Report of the General Secretary on the Czechoslovak Situation, November, 1938.
75. International Co-operative Alliance, *Minutes of meeting of ICA Central Committee, Zurich, 12-13 January, 1939*, pp. 4-5.
76. ICA Archives, Letter from May to G. J. D. C. Goedhart, 29th October 1939.
77. International Co-operative Alliance, *Report of ICA Congress Paris, 1937*, pp. 185-210.
78. International Co-operative Alliance, *Minutes of meeting of ICA Executive, Zurich, 10th January, 1939*, p. 7.
79. ICA Archives, Letter addressed to members of ICA Executive from Mrs Emmy Freundlich, President, International Women's Guild.
80. International Co-operative Alliance, *Minutes of meeting of ICA Executive, Glasgow, 16th & 17th May, 1938*, p. 3.
81. International Co-operative Alliance, *Minutes of meeting of ICA Executive, Vienna, 25-26th January, 1936*, p. 4.
82. International Co-operative Alliance, *Minutes of meeting of ICA Executive, Warsaw, 22nd September, 1936*, p. 4.
83. International Co-operative Alliance, *Minutes of meeting of ICA Executive Strasbourg, 10th-11th February, 1937*, p. 6.

84. International Co-operative Alliance, *Minutes of meeting of ICA Executive, Ostend, 12th April, 1937*, p. 3.
85. International Co-operative Alliance, Memorandum on Agenda of Meeting of ICA Executive, Lausanne, 1st-2nd December, 1937, p. 10.
86. International Co-operative Alliance, *Review of International Co-operation* No.10, October, 1937, p. 393.
87. ICA Archives, Letter from May to Tanner, 21st February, 1938.
88. International Co-operative Alliance, *Review of International Co-operation* No.3, March, 1938, pp. 110-112.
89. International Co-operative Alliance, *Report of ICA Congress, Zurich*, 1946, p. 18.
90. International Co-operative Alliance, *Review of International Co-operation*, No.1., January, 1938, p. 1..
91. International Co-operative Alliance, *Review of International Co-operation*, No.3, March, 1938, p. 105.
92. International Co-operative Alliance, *Minutes of Meeting of ICA Executive, Glasgow, 16th-17th May, 1938*, p. 3.
93. International Co-operative Alliance, *Review of International Co-operation*, No.4, April, 1938, p. 157.
94. International Co-operative Alliance, *Review of International Co-operation*, No.6, June, 1938, p. 264.
95. International Co-operative Alliance, *Review of International Co-operation*, No.3, March, 1939, p. 105.
96. ICA Archives, Letter from May to G. J. D. C. Goedhart, past President of ICA, 19th May, 1939.
97. International Co-operative Alliance, *Review of International Co-operation*, No.3, March, 1939, op. cit.
98. International Co-operative Alliance, *Review of International Co-operation*, No.4, April, 1939, pp. 157-159.
99. International Co-operative Alliance, *Review of International Co-operation*, No.6, June, 1939, pp. 261-264.
100. International Co-operative Alliance, *ibid.*, p. 263.
101. International Co-operative Alliance, *Review of International Co-operation*, No.7, July, 1939, p. 313.
102. International Co-operative Alliance, *Review of International Co-operation*, No.9, September, 1939, pp. 417-419.

Chapter seven

The ICA and the Second World War

Introduction

This Chapter will follow the ICA through the 1939-45 War and will be divided into two parts. The first will examine the internal ramifications of the war, while the second will look at the external ones.

Internal Crisis: The General Secretaryship and Presidency

The war itself represented a major crisis: important ICA member movements were seriously affected by bombardment or invasion, and organisational problems were created by the inability to hold meetings and the dislocation of communications through censorship or postal difficulties. Simultaneously, two other large problems arose within the Alliance itself. The first was that, within a very short time, the ICA's President, Väinö Tanner, became cut off from the rest of the organisation by the Russo-Finnish War of 1939-40, and later the main war. The second was that, within two months of the outbreak of the war, Henry May died suddenly. We begin this Chapter by looking at May's death and its organisational implications. The way that the problems it created were overcome suggests that the Alliance, now nearing its half centenary, had become a mature and even sophisticated organisation. May died of cancer after a very brief illness. He went into hospital at midday on 15th November, 1939 for an exploratory operation, having been to work at the ICA office that morning. Four days later he died.[1] No one in the ICA had realised that he was so ill. In the year of his death he had maintained a busy work schedule, having attended Executive meetings in Holland, Switzerland and Finland. The second of these had been followed by a meeting of the Central Committee referred to in the last Chapter. May had also visited co-operative organisations in Estonia,[2] Latvia,[3] Denmark, Sweden, and France in the months before the outbreak of the war. As we saw in the last Chapter, he also wrote extensively in the *Review of International Co-operation*, remaining its Editor until his death.

May had recognised that war would disrupt the Secretariat, and had written to Tanner that he was even considering moving it away from London and the risk of air raids.[4]

Once war was declared, May turned his full attention to it. Together with Väinö Tanner he wrote to members of the Central Committee proposing plans for the war-time work of the Alliance[5]. He went into greater detail about these plans in the *Review of International Co-operation*. In his last article, published in the November, 1939, edition of the Review and headed The War-Time Tasks of the ICA[6], May urged the Alliance to learn from its experiences in the First World War. Whereas that had been an 'Imperialist War', resulting from secret diplomacy, and had taken the populace unaware, the new war was the:

'last stand against an avalanche of barbarism which, let loose upon the world six or seven years ago, has destroyed the liberties, ruined the lives of millions'.

Unrestrained aggression and lawlessness had become a menace to the world. Attempts at peaceful solutions had only seemed to provoke the aggressors to further outrages. Now it was necessary to 'meet force with force as the alternative to destruction'.

May pointed out that during the 1914-18 War co-operators had been able to help each other across frontiers, without hindrance from their Governments.

'Political neutrality on the part of our movement was imposed by the character and circumstances of the war, and 'Each for All and All for Each' was the unchallenged motto of Co-operation.'

In the new war, however, co-operators should remember that National Socialism had restricted or destroyed the voluntary character and autonomy of co-operatives. Therefore, and perhaps anticipating the nature of the total war that was beginning, May argued that:

'The interests of citizenship in any State are sufficient to call for the whole hearted support of measures that are calculated to break the power of any system of government which so threatens the Rights of Man'.

The co-operative aim remained the same: it was to change the present capitalist system of society with a simple plan of 'equitable association', which would 'collectivise natural resources, co-ordinate economic activity, and outlaw war and tyranny'. To achieve this change, and to ensure the continuance of the Co-operative Movement, it was necessary to support 'those fundamental principles of liberty for which the war is being waged'.

May moved on to postulate the ICA's main tasks during the war in a way that was remarkably forward-looking and wide. He suggested that they should be:

'I. To maintain communications and, as far as possible, personal contacts with the membership, i.e. the national Affiliated Organisations.

II. To maintain the publication of the Official Journal, the Review of International Co-operation, and the several News Services, with the special features of a chronicle of information on matters of war-time importance to the National Movements.

III. To consider and prepare the main lines on which full activities may be renewed after the war.

IV. To seek agreement on the principles and considerations which should govern a World Settlement calculated to ensure Freedom, Security, and Universal Peace.

V. To determine what should be the contribution of organised Co-operative Movements to the adoption and realisation of such a programme.

VI. To institute a more intensive campaign of recruitment to the ranks of the Alliance of Movements of Co-operation now developing on other Continents than Europe.'

When May elaborated each of these points he revealed that the war had already had some impact on the Alliance's workings. Whereas in the 1914-18 War the British Government had not introduced controls on the contents and despatch of printed matters until 14 months or so after the outbreak of the War, they had introduced them within the first month of the Second World War. May hoped that the *Review of International Co-operation*, and the ICA's three News Services, could be maintained, though he anticipated that they would be disrupted by paper shortages and difficulties in obtaining news from member co-operative movements. Correctly, he anticipated problems in holding meetings of the Executive and Central Committees and the Congress due to be held in 1940.

Besides these internal questions, May was also concerned about external ones such as the Peace Settlement at the end of the war and the rebuilding of the post-war world; and the international co-operative movement's participation in both of these.

May pointed out that the Alliance had made no attempt to be involved with either during the previous war. Reminding readers of the valuable work that had been done by the Inter-Allied, and Inter-Allied and Neutral, Conferences in Paris, organised by the French Co-operative Movement in 1916 and 1919,[7] May hoped that similar discussions could be held this time on the Alliance's post-war activities and he suggested that these could be assisted by the 'Special Enquiries, and Congresses' held in the inter-war years when the 'grandes lignes' of the Alliance's programme had been laid down. But ICA member movements should also be invited to offer their contemporary views. May recognised that 'Revolutionary changes' would occur during the war, and would affect social and economic life.

Moving onto the World Settlement at the end of the war, May hoped that it would have a broad basis capable of bringing 'Freedom, Security, and Universal peace'. Above all, May argued:

'..........*the making of the Peace should not be left, as it was at Versailles, in the hands of those who made the war, or were responsible for its military conduct. It may well be that they cannot all be excluded, but in the next Peace Conference there should be no hegemony of any nation, whether victor, vanquished, or neutral*'.

As far as co-operatives being associated with the Peace Settlement was concerned, May acknowledged that:

'............the World Co-operative Movement made no attempt to contribute to the Peace of 1919. It may also be said that the war of 1914-1918 made no direct threat to the Co-operative Movement..... All the belligerents encouraged it and most used its organisation as a national economic instrument............ The principles and freedom of the Movement emerged intact, at least so far as the Peace Treaty was concerned'.

May also suggested that:

'.............it has proved a great mistake that the Co-operators of the World neglected the opportunities of making their claim to recognition, and a place in the League of Nations, and of setting the seal of permanence to the ascendancy which the Movement obtained while the war was in progress. Seven years later we sought, with some success, recognition in the World Economic Conference and the organism that resulted from its deliberations. But we missed the way to the Peace Conference, and have never regained the lost ground'.

'If the ICA repeated this mistake at the end of the present war it would mean that the failure

'to make the will of the people prevail would be that we should win the war and lose the Peace'.

Concerning the anticipated Peace Conference, May emphasised that common action on the part of Co-operators would be necessary because:

'The organisations of capitalism, private trade and industry will not meekly remain in the background to accept the crumbs that fall from the Conference table. Neither should we, but rather take all action to present the claims of the organised consumers and the superlative value of the co-operative economic system as an equitable means of sharing the world's resources and guaranteeing good relations between all people'.

The sixth and final point in May's war-time tasks looked equally to the future. It concerned the Alliance's recruitment of younger co-operative movements in other continents, including South America. May pointed out that:

'The misfortunes of our friends in the lands conquered or confiscated,' might help. Some of the Spanish Co-operators, exiles from tyranny, who have emigrated to South America, have already exhibited enthusiasm for this work'.

But, equally, May looked to new Alliance members in 'Australia, New Zealand, South Africa and Asia'.

Ever since May had become General Secretary of the Alliance he had also been the Editor of its *Review of International Co-operation*. As such, he had written hundreds of articles, editorials and notes. There is poignancy in the fact that in this final article his very last sentence was:

'Co-operation should play its full part in the revolution of tomorrow'.

May's death on 19th November, 1939, added to the upheaval that the outbreak of the war had caused the ICA. Something of a mystery exists about arrangements for the succession. Despite May's advancing years, the Alliance had taken no steps to appoint a new General Secretary. Now the war made this difficult to do.

It is open to speculation whether May hoped that Miss Gertude Polley would follow him. It will be recalled that he had recruited her from the Parliamentary Office of the British Co-operative Union in 1920.[8] People who knew Miss Polley refer to her great attachment to, and admiration of, Henry May.[9]

Whatever their relationship, May undoubtedly had a high regard for Miss Polley's ability. From 1921 she accompanied him to Executive and Central Committee meetings. As we have seen, she was even present when May tried to persuade Bernhardt Jaeggi to accept nomination as the ICA President following the resignation of G. J. D. C. Goedhart in 1927.[10]

As early as 1928, in a letter to Goedhart, May referred to Miss Polley as the 'Assistant Secretary' to the Alliance.[11] Almost a year later, and in another letter to Goedhart, May referred to his increasing workload, but said that he was helped by Miss Polley's taking a large share of the burden'.[12]

It was not until the Executive's meeting in Geneva in October, 1932, however, that May proposed that this unofficial position be formalised and Miss Polley appointed as the Administrative Secretary of the ICA.[13] His grounds were that she had assisted him for some years past, and had been 'chief of the Staff, taking full responsibility for the work of the office in his absence'. Because of the Alliance's increasing workload, he wished her position in the office to be officially recognised.

It is intriguing to speculate on May's motives. At an age when he could have been expected to retire, he showed no signs of doing so. If, at this point, the ICA Executive and General Committees appointed someone to eventually succeed him May's position might have become less firm. He may, therefore, have thought that Miss Polley's appointment as Administrative Secretary could delay such action. However, May might actually have wanted her to succeed him, an impression reinforced by the Executive's decision:

'That Miss G. F. Polley be appointed Administrative Secretary of the ICA, acting in all matters under the instructions of the General Secretary, but that this appointment carries with it no right of succession to the General Secretaryship when that post becomes vacant'.[14]

If May really had wished Miss Polley to succeed him he was being rather unrealistic. He had been nominated by the British Co-operative Union to become General Secretary, and nomination by ICA member movements for this, and other senior positions, became the practice after the Second World War, such a process being in keeping with the federal and international nature of the organisation. It was thus unlikely that someone from ICA office ranks could have been eased into that position. This was even less likely if that person was a woman, particularly in the culture of the 1930s. Moreover, the ICA was an organisation in which men held all the leading positions. Mrs Freundlich was the only woman to have become a member of the ICA Executive, and remained so for almost another fifty years. In 1932, when Miss Polley became Administrative Secretary, there were 63 members of the Central Committee, but only two of these were women. [15]

Whatever the reasons for the 1932 decision, the crisis conditions created by the outbreak of the war and May's death meant that Miss Polley became de facto head of the ICA secretariat. When the Executive met in Paris in 1940, it decided to delay the appointment of a General Secretary until after the end of the war.[16] This decision will be examined in greater detail shortly, but in the meantime we will look at other events surrounding May's death.

One was the remarkable production of a special memorial edition of the *Review of International Co-operation*. Despite early dislocations caused by the war, the issue appeared within a month of May's death and contained 26 tributes, twenty coming from overseas co-operative leaders.[17]

The following March, the ICA Executive met in Paris, its last meeting until after the war. It is therefore interesting to note who participated. Tanner could not attend, but the two Vice-Presidents, Ernest Poisson (France) and R. A. Palmer (Great Britain), were present, as was Dr Bernhardt Jaeggi (Switzerland), K. de Boer (Holland), and J. Downie and N. Beaton (Great Britain). Miss Polley attended as Administrative Secretary.

Besides Väinö Tanner (Finland), I. S. Khoklov (USSR), Prof. Rapacki (Poland) and E. Lustig (Czechoslovakia) were absent.[18] Poisson chaired the meeting.

Tributes were made to Henry May and the many letters and telegrams of sympathy received by the Alliance were noted. R. A. Palmer then raised two points on behalf of the British Co-operative Union. One was a proposal that there should be an international memorial to May, [19] while the other was to report on discussions with Mrs May about a possible pension. However, Palmer reported that Mrs May was 'not in any need of financial help', and he believed that it would not have been May's wishes to have used the Alliance's funds in this way.[20] The Executive conveyed their deep sympathy to Mrs May, and, as a token of the Alliance's respect, agreed to commission a bronze bust of Mr May to be presented to her. This was eventually passed back to the ICA and is now housed in its Geneva Head Office.

As we noted earlier, the question of a new General Secretary was deferred, since the Executive was

'..............unanimously of the opinion that it would not be advisable to appoint a new General Secretary during the period of the war. It was agreed that the work of the Secretariat should continue to be directed by Miss Polley, Administrative Secretary, and Mr. Palmer, Vice-President, was asked to continue the close contact which he had maintained with the administration since the death of Mr. May, and to give all necessary advice'.[21]

R. A. Palmer, General Secretary of the British Co-operative Union, thus moved into a more central role in the Alliance, a move that was to become even more important as troubles now befell the Alliance's President, Mr Väinö Tanner.

Of all ICA leaders he was the one caught most cruelly, and most directly, between the opposing forces of Communism and Fascism. A leading Finnish politician, he had been involved in Finnish attempts to avert the Russo-Finnish War of 1939-40. Before examining the plight in which he found himself, let us try to establish what kind of man he was.

In Chapter 5[22] we traced Tanner's election as President of the ICA, and we also noted the positions that he took on a number of issues such as Germany[23] and Spain. From the papers that Tanner presented to ICA Congresses, including his Presidential addresses at the Vienna (1930), London (1934) and Paris (1937) Congresses, we find that he was an educated man, knowledgeable in history, and in economic and political theory, which was shown by his paper to the 1937 Congress on 'The Place of Co-operation in Different Economic Systems'.[24]

It is more difficult to deduce his attitudes to events. From the German and Spanish examples quoted above, he seems to have been cautious. But this may have been due more to tolerance than to timidity, as suggested by his handling of the German issue at the Basle Special Conference in 1933.[25]

Another possible example was his reply to a letter that May had written complaining about slow decision-making within the ICA. While Tanner regretted this, he replied that he 'tried to understand it as a sign of the present difficult time', during which Co-operators were focusing more on home, than on international, issues.[26]

There may have been political calculation in Tanner's toleration, but it does seem to have been in line with his gentleness and modesty, as well as his enjoyment of simple pleasures. Writing of a return journey to Helsinki, he wrote to May 'It was a great joy to me to travel in new localities and see the sights through the window of the motor car'.[27]

Of his summer holiday in 1932 he wrote, 'I used to be running about in the mountains looking at the beautiful sights' and 'I have been able to enjoy...splendidly my chief work....... the digging of ditches in the forest to have them dried'. [28]

In June, 1933, he asked if May could find him accommodation in London for a visit that he was making as a Finnish Government representative at an economic conference. Tanner indicated that he would prefer to stay with a family as he would be lonely in a hotel, and he wanted to improve his English.[29]

Tanner's correspondence with May reveals that he kept a close watch on international developments, and that he had strong links with Scandinavian and Baltic co-operative Movements.

His letters also revealed that he was probably not a nervous person. During 1933 May had been concerned at news reports that Tanner was to be prosecuted by the Finnish Minister of Justice for remarks which were critical of the country's Administration. May expressed surprise that freedom of speech seemed threatened, and that even a former Prime Minister had been given no latitude.[30]

Tanner's reply gives us an insight into the growth of Fascism in Finland. He recounted how he had spoken at a couple of labour festivals. about the contemporary political situation in Finland, pointing out that, in the recent general election, the Fascists had received only 5 per cent of the votes and

'not more than 1/6 of the whole Parliament. Thus it should be easy to maintain a thorough Democratic command in our country, but thanks to the Government, this has not been the case. I particularly directed my criticism against our auxiliary army, the members of which are very badly mixed up with Fascist plottings, but who as a rule so far have not been punished for their criminal activities.

Such was the essence of the said speech. It was considered that I had given a wrong picture of the truth when I stated that the Government had sheltered persons belonging to the auxiliary army for the crimes they had committed...

..........In trying to follow a policy of political equilibrium the Government has, evidently, thought it necessary to institute legal proceedings also against a representative of the left, as this has happened fairly often with regard to the Fascist Press.[31]

This incident should be kept in mind when we come to consider the charges against Tanner for supposed pro-Nazi sympathies. In the mean time we should now return to the question of the Russo-Finnish War and the ICA.

The *Review of International Co-operation* for November, 1939, reported that Väinö Tanner had been one of the 'Ministers Plenipotentiary of Finland' engaged in negotiations with the Soviet Government, which amounted 'to a defence of the freedom and sovereign independence' of Finland.

'We are naturally proud that the President of the ICA should be chosen for a task that is so fully in keeping with his headship of the International Co-

operative Family, and we wish that he will succeed in averting anything that could be interpreted as a display of force on the part of the Soviet Government'.[32]

The report continued:

'Our interest in these momentous proceedings lies still more in the fact that the Soviet Co-operative Organisations, with the full knowledge and consent of the Supreme Soviet Executive, are members of the International Co-operative Alliance and, therefore, pledged to that reasoned and mutually tolerant manner of settling differences which is the essential basis of Co-operation and the foundation of our hopes for Peace.'

Both through Centrosoyus and the Finnish Legation in Moscow, May sent telegrams wishing Tanner success in his mission.[33] He also sent a telegram to I. S. Khoklov, Vice-President of Centrosoyus, saying:

'International Co-operation hopes strongly for your support to Tanner in obtaining a true co-operative solution'.[34]

All of this was to no avail. Two months later the *Review of International Co-operation* reported on the impact of war on Finnish Co-operatives. While being 'aghast at the forces of aggression which have been hurled unprovoked against the valiant and peace-loving Finnish nation,[35] the Review made no condemnation of Soviet aggression. In other circumstances, and if there had not been a more important war raging elsewhere, it is interesting to speculate what line the ICA might have taken had the Russo-Finnish War lasted longer. Would it have supported its President's country or that of its second largest member movement? As it was, the war lasted only 15 weeks, although Finland surrendered some 16,000 square miles to Russia.[36]

Sympathies for Finland existed in a number of ICA member organisations. The Secretariat reported receiving many letters on the question, including one from the Co-operative League of the USA indicating that it was making an appeal to its affiliated societies. In addition, the Executive agreed to mount its own Finnish Appeal among ICA member organisations, and began this by contributing £2,000 from ICA funds.[37]

However, support for Finland soon disappeared when she later allied herself to Germany and supported Germany's attack on the USSR in June, 1941.[38] This move seems to have been made for two reasons. One was to try to get back the areas she had been forced to cede to Russia. The other was to attempt to offset the threat arising from the eight or nine divisions of the German army based in Finland.[39]

Tanner left the Finnish Government after the signing of the Peace Treaty with Russia, supposedly as a result of Russian pressure. His return to Government after the alliance with Germany was interpreted in friendly circles as his attempt to keep a Finnish Government in power and avoid Germany's placing a quisling in charge.[40]

Even so, these actions naturally concerned the national co-operative movements whose countries were at war with Germany. Such concern would have made an impact in the ICA had it been possible to call meetings of the Executive and Central Committees. Soon it was not possible to do so, and a power vacuum could have developed for the duration of the war had not the ICA Secretariat been in an unoccupied country, and had it not been possible to develop an alternative device whereby the British members of the ICA Central Committee met as both Executive and Central Committees.

This arrangement had evolved from the Executive's last meeting in Paris in March 1940, where it had anticipated some of the war's effects on the Alliance's activities and income. Previously, May had proposed economies in staff and publications, and to give effect to these the Executive appointed a Sub-Committee comprising the President, two Vice-Presidents and Sir Fred Hayward, Chairman of the British Co-operative Union.[41]

It soon became clear that Tanner and Poisson could not participate in the Sub-Committee, leaving only the two British members, Palmer and Hayward. Thus, meetings of the British members of the Central Committee helped to legitimate their handling of the ICA's financial affairs. However, the work of the meetings widened almost immediately. While the first meeting in Manchester in February, 1941, certainly considered staff and financial matters, it also received reports about

Publications, Economic Research, and the implementation of the Alliance's war-time tasks. The meeting also agreed to try to ascertain the position of co-operative movements in Poland, Norway, Denmark, Holland, Belgium and France, as well as how the ICA, the British Co-operative Union and co-operative organisations in Allied countries, could stimulate interest in Co-operation amongst the Allied forces based in Britain.[42]

Meetings of the British members continued. It should be underlined, however, that such a device had no constitutional basis within the ICA. At the end of the war the group reported to the rest of the Alliance, which accepted its work as having been that of a de facto Executive. Membership of the group, with an average membership of around eight, was determined by the British Co-operative Union, which continued to nominate representatives on the same basis as it had previously done to the ICA's Central Committee. The ICA Secretariat also became accountable to the British members in the same way that it had done to the Executive. Prime movers in ICA business had therefore become Miss Polley and Mr R. A. Palmer, rather than Henry May and Väinö Tanner.

Later, it will be argued that this ability to innovate to the constitutional satisfaction of the rest of the Alliance was an important reason why the organisation survived the dual crisis of disruption from war and the coincidental, but simultaneous, loss of its General Secretary and President.

During the war the British members of the ICA Central Committee conducted a wide range of business, but without doubt the most difficult and delicate question was what position to take regarding Väinö Tanner.

The matter was raised formally by the Co-operative Union at the meeting of the British members in October 1941. One reason for this was the following motion from one of its members, the Methil Co-operative Society:

Sample Press Cuttings 1940 - 1944

NAZI "PEACE TERMS" FOR FIN[LAND]

Release from Fighting When Lening[rad] is Captured

Mannerheim's Policy Worries U.S.

Washington, Tuesday. — The United States Government is believed to be seriously concerned at the direction which Finni[sh] policy has taken lately. U[nless] some change in that policy be discerned soon it is regar[ded] as likely here that Washingto[n's] attitude towards Helsinki w[ill] rapidly change.

It is reported here that Finnish armistice talks actually took place, but that Field-Marshal Mannerheim's statement that Russian Karelia must be incorporated into Finland caused the Russians to break the talks off.—Reuter.

FINNISH MINISTER GOING TO GERMANY

The Finnish Minister of Commerce, Mr. Tanner, will visit Germany on September 17 with a delegation of the Finnish Foreign Trade Association, says a Helsinki dispatch to the German News Agency.—Reuter.

...ter Guardian' Service

HELSINKI COMMENT

According to the Helsinki correspondent of the Vichy News Agency, the Finnish Foreign Minister has received a communication from the British Government concerning the attitude of Britain to the Finnish-Soviet war.

It was stated (says the correspo[ndent]) that the text communicated [to the] Finnish Government is not i[n con]formity with that published in [press] and broadcast [by the] B.B.C[.] official co[mmuniqué]...

BRITISH WARNING TO FINLAND

PENALTY OF INVADING RUSSIA

FROM OUR DIPLOMATIC CORRESPONDENT

A message has been passed from London d[irect] to Helsinki warning the Finns that if they [go] on to invade purely Russian territory, [we] shall have no option but to treat them [as] as open enemies both now and when the [time] comes for making peace.

Many Finns themselves hoped that a truce could be arranged when the Finnish and German armies reached the ol[d] Finnish frontiers, but their hopes ha[ve] been disappointed. Field-Marshal Ma[nnerheim] has declared that the fight m[ust] go on and the Germans are offering fr[esh] bribes for a continued campaign. Hith[erto] the Finnish Ministers have declared they were not taking part in Germ[an] war, but were merely taking the o[pportunity] of recovering the land that w[as lost] 18 months ago. Such attempts to [distin]guish between the various Rus[sian cam]paign[s] against... Germany's campaign and now [in] order... Each yard that the [Finns advance] beyond their old frontiers is [...] validity. [...] pure and simple.

The British message was sen[t to the] Finlan[d in] consultation with the Soviet G[overnment ...] conside[rs] America as a dem[ocratic] nation, [a]nd enjoys great popula[rity] having been the only country [to pay] her war debts and for having b[een the] only little country to defend he[r inde]pendence."—Reuter.

242

'Owing to the prominent part being taken by Väinö Tanner in endeavouring to procure supplies from Britain and the LL.S.A. to Petsamo, Finland, such supplies being destined to be used by German fascists in their war aimed at world conquest and suppression of all peoples to the German monopolists and barons, we call upon the ICA to define its attitude to Väino Tanner and repudiate his activities as being contrary to the progressive and democratic ideas and practices of the Co-operative Movement'[43].

R. A. Palmer reported that the Union was finding that other member societies were also refusing to pay their dues to the ICA while it was thought that Tanner had any control over the Alliance's activities and funds.

These reactions occurred at the critical period of the war and were heightened by adverse press coverage. ICA archives have kept numerous press cuttings from 1940 to 1944 relating to Väinö Tanner. Those from mid-1941 indicate why anti-Tanner feeling had grown in British co-operative circles.

Despite this adverse press coverage, British members tried to take a balanced view. They received a report of a recent meeting of the National Council of Labour, the body representative of the British Labour Party, Trade Unions and Co-operatives, at which a more tolerant view had been taken of Tanner, and Finnish trade unionists and co-operators. They were thought to be 'just as democratic now as they always were': but the trouble was that 'Germany was obviously in control'[44]. Palmer reported that the National Council of Labour had thought it desirable to learn the views of the Labour members of the British War Cabinet on the Finnish situation and a deputation, including Palmer and two other co-operative members, had met Mr Attlee, Leader of the Labour Party, Lord Privy Seal, and, from February, 1942, Deputy Prime Minster; Mr E. Bevin, Minster of Labour; and Mr A. Greenwood, Minister without Portfolio. They had proven 'quite sympathetic' to the difficulties of Tanner, the Finnish trade unions and co-operators. Palmer added:

'I think that it was Attlee who suggested that, as in the case of the Methil Society, those who were now anti-Tanner and anti-Finland were, until Rus-

sia was forced into the war, anti-war in this country, and that, therefore, their attitude towards Mr. Tanner was dictated entirely by what was the communist policy. The Labour members gave the impression that Mr. Tanner and Finland were in an extremely difficult situation, and that we should not take too harsh a view with regard to what he was doing'. [45]

Palmer warned that that view 'may have changed since', because it had become clearer that Tanner was rejecting a separate peace with Russia, although still claiming that Finland was not fighting Germany's war. Press reports of the time indicate the pressures brought on Finland to agree peace with the USSR. The Manchester Guardian's Special Correspondent in Stockholm wrote, on 25th September, 1941,

'Today, when the situation has become critical for the Soviets, it is sought to force Finland to cease hostilities to bring relief to the besieged city of Leningrad by depriving the Germans of the possibility of using Finland as a base for their operations and by retaining the port of Murmansk in order to continue supplying the USSR.'

The Manchester Guardian further reported a visit that Tanner, now Finland's Minister of Trade, had made to Germany, and an interview he had given in Stockholm, during which he had confirmed that Finland would not make a separate peace with the USSR. Tanner had added 'that his visit to Germany had given him the opportunity to confirm this standpoint, which was also his own personal one'.[46]

Despite such reports, R. A. Palmer led the British members of the ICA Central Committee towards a strictly constitutional view of Tanner's position within the Alliance. This was:

'..... that Mr. Tanner was elected President of the ICA by the Central Committee after the Congress at Paris; in the normal course of events there would have been another Congress at Prague in 1940, when he would either have been re-elected or another President appointed. But he is the elected President of the Alliance, and apparently he will hold that position until such time as the Central Committee of the Alliance can determine that he shall be relieved of his office and a successor elected, or until they re-elect him. It is only the Central Committee who can elect the President of the Alliance and, in the *present circumstances, it is quite impossible to call the Committee together - indeed it is impossible even to communicate with the majority of the members. We, here, have no power to relieve Mr. Tanner of his office, and we cannot even send a message to him suggesting that he should resign, simply because it would not reach him.'*[47]

Having said this, Palmer believed that it was desirable that the British members of the ICA Central Committee should express their views on the position of Väinö Tanner.

The discussion following Palmer's statement seemed designed to 'placate hostile British opinion' in general, as well as that of ordinary co-operative members. One member, who wanted a statement strong enough to 'stifle these enquiries' from British co-operators, said:

'I quite agree with what Mr. Palmer has said as to the source of these communications which the Union has received, but these people, though not numerically strong are strong vocally and have a fair nuisance value'.

Another member stated his view that:

'Finland hated Germany as much as anybody, but there were eight German divisions in Finland, and possibly nine I feel that while we want to express the feeling that the Finns did wrong, we should deal lightly with them at the present time.'

Palmer had proposed a draft statement, which after one amendment and some rearrangement, read:

'This meeting of British Members on the Central Committee of the ICA, having considered the question of the attitude of the Alliance towards Mr. Väinö Tanner, referred to them by the Executive of the British Co-operative Union, and having taken into consideration the various statements which have appeared in the press concerning the part which Mr. Tanner has played in the decision of the Finnish Government to ally herself with the anti-democratic and aggressive forces of Nazi Germany, expresses most profound regret that such an eminent co-operator in both the National and International Move-

ments should appear to act in a manner so contrary to the principles and interests of Co-operation.

Throughout the period of the war, Mr. Tanner has been almost cut off from the life and work of the ICA, and it categorically declares that no action which he has taken, or may take, as a member of the Finnish Government can in any way prejudice the position of the International Co-operative Alliance.

According to its Rules Mr. Tanner retains the position of President of the Alliance until such time as a meeting of the Central Committee, by whom he was elected, and which consists of representatives of the 35 countries affiliated to the Alliance, can be convened.'[48]

That this statement was primarily intended for British public opinion was underlined by the fact that it was agreed to communicate it only to the British co-operative press and the general press, and that it should not '*be given publicity in the publications of the Alliance*'.

Next day the statement was reported in the Manchester Guardian,[49] but the British members' views became known elsewhere in the Alliance and proved contentious. An article appearing in the Swedish co-operative journal VI on 6th December, 1941, criticised British members of the Central Committee and led Palmer to write to Albin Johansson, of Sweden's KF, regretting its tone and contents. He also enclosed the text of the British statement in an effort to *'dispel and correct the false impression which the article must have made upon Swedish co-operators'*.[50]

Johansson replied, expressing 'real pleasure' at receiving Palmer's letter, and stating that it was important that he should acquaint Swedish co-operators with the attitude of English co-operators to Tanner. He continued: *'It is creditable to the co-operators in England to look so dispassionately on this question'*.[51]

Elsewhere, though, criticism of Tanner surfaced, and there was disquiet that he remained President of the ICA. Mr Keen, General Secretary of the Canadian Co-operative Union, sent the ICA copies of articles appearing in two Canadian co-operative journals, *Western Producer* and *Canadian Co-operator*, both critical of Tanner. [52]

The article in the Western Producer', headed 'V. Tanner - Traitor', argued that:

'As a citizen of Finland Mr. Tanner may do as the likes about the policy of his country; as president of the International Co-operative Alliance he has no right whatever to follow a policy which is not only contrary to co-operative principles but positively injurious to the Movement everywhere.' [53]

The British Government may have believed that co-operative pressure could be brought to bear on Tanner to sue for a separate peace with the USSR, because time was found on BBC radio for Palmer to broadcast to Tanner in Finland in October, 1941. During the broadcast Palmer *'appealed to the Finns to withdraw from a war beyond their own frontiers'*. Tanner's broadcast reply was reported by the French Vichy News Agency. He reiterated that Finland was fighting for her own interests; she was carrying on a defensive war which had nowhere gone beyond her former frontiers. Responding to the USSR's claim that its initial air attacks had been made because of German troops in Finland, Tanner admitted that they had been there, but'.... *they were in limited numbers and only in the extreme north.*' He continued:

'Finland has not been occupied by Germany. There is nothing we in Finland hope for more than that peace should return to Europe. Then we could turn our energies to constructive work'.

While we cannot be certain how Tanner really felt about Germany there could be no doubt about his feelings for the USSR when he reiterated *'We remain the enemy of the Soviet Union'.*[54]

From this point onwards, the press and popular Allied feelings became more hostile to Tanner. An undated Evening Standard article, referring to him as 'the Finnish Minister of Trade and Commerce' and 'the head of the International Co-operative Movement', reported:

'British co-operators would like to remove him from that office because of the part he and his Government have been playing towards our Russian ally. In fact, he has been kept in office by Hitler, and for this reason. Since Germany over-ran Europe it has been impossible to convene a meeting of the Alliance, and the machinery for putting him out cannot be brought into operation. There is no doubt that if it could Tanner would have been told to go before now.'[55]

A kinder interpretation of Tanner's actions was suggested by The Times in September, 1941, when it reported 'German Blackmail of Finns', and suggested that this was why, in a recent speech, Tanner had said that the Finns would fight on. The Times also reported that several members of 'his Socialist-Democratic Party' had been arrested because they had advocated an early peace.[56]

It was probably in connection with the incident that, six months later, *the Scottish Co-operator* reported a news item from the *Soviet War News* to the effect that five Finnish Members of Parliament had been sentenced to long terms of hard labour.

'These deputies were prominent members of the Finnish Social Democratic Party and leaders of the left opposition in the movement. In the autumn of 1940 they were expelled from the party by Tanner..... because they had exposed the connection between Finland's present rulers, including Tanner, and the Nazis'.

'This group of deputies was against Finland's entering the war on Germany's side. Last September they were flung into prison. Only in December were they summoned before a court, which held its sittings in camera, as the authorities feared the revelations of the accused.'[57]

The Soviet Weekly News was likely to be biased, but the imprisonment of the Finnish Members of Parliament 'for alleged pro-Russian activities' is confirmed in other sources, including a report in The Times of 24th October, 1944. Seven months earlier, the British left-wing journal, Tribune, had referred to the incident in 'The Story of Väinö Tanner' which had also said:

'Väinö Tanner is shrewd and skilful. His record is by no means wholly negative. He has done much for the improvement in the standard of living of the man-in-the-street in Finland; his skill in internal politics was a by-word in all Scandinavia; his powers of organisation made him one of the most successful men in the Co-operative movement of any country; his personal courage during the growth of Lappo Fascism was the subject of countless anecdotes in Finland.'

'But Tanner is thirsty for power, merciless against his adversaries and brutal against his opponents in his own movement.'[58]

These reports indicate that Tanner was at the centre of Finnish Government during Finland's alliance with Germany, with which he was very much identified. However, Tanner's real position in Finland, and his relations with the USSR and Germany between 1939 and 1944, must be left to other researchers to determine. This study is primarily concerned with the implications of Tanner's wartime activities on the ICA. The point to note is that Tanner, in the heat of War, had become a very controversial figure and that was causing embarrassment to the Alliance.

Although not formally on the agenda, the question was raised again at the meeting of the British members of the Central Committee in London in June, 1943, when the Declaration for the coming International Co-operative Day was discussed. Because of their constitutional ambiguity, a member queried whether it was within the competence of the British members to issue such a statement on behalf of the ICA. He recalled the recurring criticism that:

'..... while there are certain matters which the British members on the Central Committee consider themselves competent to deal with, there were others, particularly the removal of Mr. Tanner from the Presidency of the Alliance, with which they did not consider themselves competent to deal'.[59] He referred to reports in American journals out Tanner's supposed close personal relationship with Hitler. While this was unlikely to be true, it does indicate public hostility to Tanner. By way of digression, it is interesting to note a report in the Daily Herald of 15th February, 1944, which referred to Tanner as having saved *'Stalin's life in 1905 by hiding*

*him from the Tsar's police'*⁶⁰. The President of the ICA seems to have associated with the 20th century's most powerful men!

At their meeting in June, 1943, British members of the Central Committee were well aware that they were coming under fire because of their reluctance to tackle the question of Väinö Tanner's Presidency. For example, the Scottish Co-operative Wholesale Society reported that when it had recommended that £36,000 be allocated to the ICA's Freedom Fund, a number of Scottish co-operatives had been opposed because they feared that Mr Tanner might influence the use of the fund after the war.⁶¹

It was eventually agreed to discuss the matter formally at the next meeting and, in the meantime, seek the views of those overseas members of the Central Committee who could be contacted and who would be asked *'whether any steps should be taken during the war to remove Mr Tanner from the Presidency of the Alliance'* ⁶²

A letter to this effect was sent by Miss Polley on 13th July, 1943.⁶³ After quoting the 1941 statement in full, Miss Polley referred to the criticisms of Tanner in co-operative boardrooms, in co-operative meetings and conferences, and among members of the Central Committee and officials of the Alliance:

'........ the attitude which is taken by many British co-operators is that by using his influence to keep Finland in the war on the side of Germany, by his friendship with Hitler and the help which he is personally giving to Hitler, Mr. Tanner has betrayed the fundamental principles that ICA and all the Co-operation stands for, and that he should be removed from the Presidency of the Alliance'.

However, Miss Polley drew a distinction between popular criticism of Tanner and the more cautious view of the British members of the Central Committee.

'While all the members definitely refrain from passing judgement upon Mr. Tanner and are not disposed to accept many of the reports about his activity which have appeared in the press in this country and also in the USA, they

cannot but realise that the fact that he is still, in name at least, its President casts a reflection upon the Alliance. This is particularly regrettable at the present time when the ICA is known to be considering contribution to post-war relief and reconstruction; when it is pressing its claim to participate in the Peace Conference; and has launched an Appeal on behalf of the Co-operative Movements in the occupied and war ravaged countries which have suffered damage and destruction at the hands of the Nazis.'

Reiterating the view of British members that no action could be taken regarding the Presidency until a post-war meeting of the Central Committee, Miss Polley came to the punch line:

'.... but that meanwhile Mr. Palmer should be recognised in all the communications, etc. of the Alliance as Acting President'.

It is not clear where the authority came from to make this statement. Certainly, the suggestion had not been made at the lasting of the British members, whose constitutional position, in any event, was unclear. Moreover, it is interesting that such an important proposal was made almost as a throwaway suggestion, with no supporting arguments other than that implied in the reference to 'communications'. Having said this, however, we should note that in the unparalleled circumstances created by the war, Palmer, by virtue of his Vice-Presidency, had been acting as de facto President. Moreover, there was obviously an increasing need to have a leader who could sign ICA initiatives to become involved with post-war relief and reconstruction, the Peace Conference and the financial appeal for Co-operative Movements in occupied countries.

Replies to Miss Polley's letter were received from Albin Johansson (Sweden), the Hon. V. Ramadas Pantulu (India) and Dr J. P. Warbasse (USA). All three approved the British members' view of the constitutional position that only the Central Committee could replace Tanner, but Dr Warbasse did not agree that Mr Palmer should be recognised as the Acting President, arguing that there was no provision in the ICA Rules for such an office. Moreover, Warbasse urged that there should be a 'reservation of judgement as well as of action', and an attitude of tolerance towards Tanner. He was confident of Tanner's devotion to the Co-operative cause.

Notwithstanding Warbasse's reservations, the British members, when they met in Manchester in January, 1944, confirmed R. A. Palmer as 'Vice-President and Acting President.' It was not merely the case that Johansson and Ramadas Pantulu supported this, but that endorsement came also from Tanner himself. Johansson, Managing Director of 'Kooperative Forbundett' and member of the ICA Executive, had been able to contact Tanner and could confirm his agreement to the move.[64] However, Warbasse continued to disagree and made this public in the *Co-operative Builder*, the official journal of The Central Co-operative Wholesale, Wisconsin, much to the upset of the British members of the Central Committee.

Finland finally sued for a separate peace with the USSR in 1944. *The Times* of 24th October, 1944, reported a 'serious' rift within Tanner's Finnish Social Democratic Party, over the attitude to be adopted towards the leaders who had been responsible for the party's wartime policy.[65] It shows that leading party members called for the resignation of leaders who had advocated territorial aggrandizement and had opposed a separate peace.

'Though no names are mentioned the description is patently worded to fit the party's actual leader the former Finance Minister, Mr. Tanner, and his closest associates.'

However, The Times reported that Tanner had scored a 'clear victory' after a seven hour debate, winning a vote taken on the party's policy, and refusing to resign. His luck would not last, however. The centenary of his birth was celebrated in Finland in 1981. A potted unsigned biography in English then stated:

'When the war was over, Väinö Tanner was sentenced to five and a half years in prison at the trial arranged in accordance with the demand of the allied powers in 1946 but was released two years later in 1948'.[66]

By the time he died in April, 1966, Tanner had been rehabilitated. Rafael Passio, who succeeded him as Chairman of the Finnish Social Democratic Party, said of him:

'Without this upright and straightforward pipe and cigar smoker, many things in present day Finland would certainly be different. And probably not better.
[67]

As far as the ICA was concerned, however, the question of the Presidency was virtually re solved with Tanner's agreement in January, 1944, that Palmer should become 'Vice-President and Acting President.' At the first meeting of the Central Committee after the War held in Zurich in 1946, Tanner's resignation, formally conveyed to Palmer in a letter of September, 1945, was accepted. Palmer, now Lord Rusholme, became President of the ICA in his own right.[68]

R.A. Palmer (Lord Rusholme)
1891 - 1977

Tanner's wartime years had undoubtedly been controversial, but they illustrated how intense the personal and political dilemmas of public figures can be during war. From our present and kinder perspective we can perhaps conclude that, above all, Tanner was a Finnish patriot.

Returning now to other parts of the ICA during the war, we should note the role of the Secretariat.

The Wartime ICA Secretariat Staff

At the beginning of the war ICA staff numbered 20. By February, 1941, this had dropped to eight due to redundancies, bombing injuries, internment, and army call up.[69] There had also been the resignation of W. P. Watkins[70] because of disagreement with the way that Miss Polley and Palmer appeared to be running the Alliance, with other members of staff being little consulted or involved.[71] Later, Watkins was to be-

M/H.

21st September, 1939.

Dear Mr. Tanner,

  At last I am writing to give you some idea of the situation of the work of the I.C.A., of the measures I have taken, and the suggestions I have to make for the continuance of our work.

  First let me say that the population here is at present taking life in a manner as near to the normal as is possible, in view of the nightly "black-out" which has been in operation since the Germans invaded Poland, two days before the declaration of war by Great Britain and France. Our people are not in the least excited, at least in their demeanour and actions, but they are resolute, quiet, and purposeful.

  If Neville Chamberlain had not declared war at the moment he did, he would have had to face a revulsion of feeling against himself that might have swept him from power. It is wonderful how he held the mass of the population in favour of his Peace Policy, up to a certain point, and then how quick was their reaction against its failure. But, of course, the final influence which tipped the scale, or turned the balance in favour of war, was the savagery of action and the loathsome tactics and policy of Hitler and his whelps.

  We are preparing steadily - not by any means hysterically - for the commencement of the war in this country. We are intensely sympathetic and full of admiration for the Poles, who have been doubly double-crossed, in their marvellous fight for Freedom. In London we are barricaded, and are barricading still more against aerial bombardment, and any other bestiality which may come from the Berlin Apostles of Peace!

  Now as to the Alliance. Well, it is no use disguising the fact that we have not only lost another National Movement from our ranks, but that the activities of the Alliance are now seriously handicapped until the war is over. I imagine, however, that the existing members will wish that I should use every endeavour to keep the flag flying and the work progressing during the conflict. To this end I have taken preliminary steps.

  <u>ARCHIVES.</u> The most important records of the Alliance, its early minute books, copies of Congress Reports, and other valuable papers, have been deposited with the C.W.S. Bank for safe custody until after the war.

  <u>STAFF.</u> The war conditions will inevitably reduce the amount of work we are able to do. At present I cannot even form an opinion of any value as to the work which can go on. In any case, I think the staff will have to be reduced before very long - say, at the end of the year. Meanwhile, three members have gone out in ordinary ways, reducing our number to sixteen, exclusive of myself. At least three more must go shortly, unless they were all prepared to accept short time and corresponding wages. But that is a solution for a later stage. At present I hope to keep all going till the end of the year. With regard to myself, I will put my decision in a separate letter.

Part of last letter from Henry J. May, ICA Secretary-General, to Väinö Tanner, ICA President, 21 September 1939.

come the Alliance's Director between 1951 and 1963. Another resignation illustrated how war issues divided ICA staff. In the autumn of 1941 problems arose over the Research Officer, Dr Shenkman. Ostensibly like Watkins, he was unhappy about the organisation of office work, believing that his work was hampered by insufficient information because the ICA's correspondence was 'entirely' in Miss Polley's hands. However, it is likely that Shenkman's main disaffection arose over the British Central Committee members' attitude to Tanner. Writing to Palmer, Shenkman accepted that they could not remove the President, but he did feel that they should have more strongly disassociated the Alliance from him.

Something of Miss Polley's attitudes are revealed in Shenkman's letter of resignation, in which he claimed that Tanner's 'pernicious' influence on the secretariat had led to:

'the anti-soviet attitude which Miss Polley as the administrative Secretary, who is in fact in charge of the office, is determined to pursue. It cannot be considered as unintentional that no article has been published in the Review .... during the last four months dealing with the Nazi war against the Soviet Union and that any attempt to deal with current events in the economic and co-operative life of the USSR in a sympathetic, though perfectly objective manner, are strongly resisted, while the collaboration of the Co-operative Movements with the Nazis and the Fascist Governments in other countries is glossed over.[72]

Shenkman, who was Russian, was undoubtedly wrong about Miss Polley's attitudes but his disagreement over what was going, or not going, into the Review leads us to take a detailed look at how it functioned during the war.

Review of International Co-operation during the War

It will be recalled that Henry May had argued that the *Review of International Co-operation* should be one of the main points of contact between the Alliance and its members during the war, and he had planned to increase its practical value by dealing with a whole range of problems under the heading of 'War-Time Economic Control'. He also proposed a regular War-Time Chronicle of co-operative activities. Palmer supported both ideas and added, when he wrote to Miss Polley in November, 1940[73] that he believed that the Review should also try to remain topical by publishing items of immediate interest, and that it should act as a means of maintaining goodwill by keeping the Alliance in touch with international co-operative affairs. An analysis of the Review during the war shows that these objectives were met. Some changes, though, were inevitable. For example, the customary reports of the meetings of the Executive and Central Committees could not be produced because neither was meeting. However, the traditional messages at New Year and for International Co-operatives Day on the first Saturday on each July were continued.

Despite wartime difficulties, a fairly wide international coverage was maintained, with news items appearing from Argentina, Australia, Belgium, Canada, China, Ceylon (Sri Lanka), Colombia, Estonia, Finland, France, Germany, Great Britain, Holland, India, Norway, Palestine (Israel), Romania, Sweden, Switzerland, the USA, the USSR, Venezuela and Yugoslavia. Towards the end of the war articles began appearing on co-operatives in British colonies. For example, in the Review for July, 1943, A. Creech Jones, MP., who was to become a Colonial Secretary in the post-war Labour Government, wrote an article examining 'Co-operation as a Factor in Colonial Progress'.

Regular features included Book Reviews, International Women's Notes and Educational Notes, and an obituaries section. One of the most moving of these was written by R. A. Palmer for his fellow Vice-President, Ernest Poisson, who had died aged 60 in March, 1942. Palmer traced Poisson's early years, his collaboration with L'Humanité, the famous journal of socialist Jean Jaurès, with whom Poisson was sitting when he was assassinated on the eve of the First World War, and also of Poisson's close association with Charles Gide and Albert Thomas.[74]

During the war the Secretariat was unable to maintain research at previous levels, which meant that there were fewer items in the Review on the statistics of member movements. It is interesting to note, however, that new items were introduced which reflected wartime conditions, including reports on 'British Co-operative Trade Associations Under

Wartime Conditions', 'International Commodity Controls', and 'Wartime Economic Control'. The Review also recorded the Alliance's efforts to be associated with moves to establish the United Nations and with post-war relief and reconstruction. These are large issues which will be treated separately. Before doing so, we should perhaps note other activities of the ICA secretariat during the war. At the end of this section, though, we should perhaps note that Shenkman's criticism may not have been entirely unfounded. To have met his wishes could have weakened the Alliance's neutrality but, as we have seen, the Review effectively maintained this during the war.

Other Activities of the Wartime ICA Secretariat

Many traditional functions survived, although the documentation for meetings was limited to that required for the meetings of the British members of the Central Committee. The handling of membership applications and withdrawals was somewhat reduced, and finances focused more on the administration of Relief Funds.

A new responsibility was that of ensuring the protection of the ICA archives and library during the war. Writing to ICA member organisations and members of the Central Committee in July, 1940, Miss Polley indicated that Mr May had already deposited the most valuable records with the CWS Bank.

Additional arrangements were later made for the safekeeping of 'original publications and documentation relating to the history of the ICA and the Co-operative Movement in the different countries, many of which are out of print and irreplaceable'.[75] Subsequently, the ICA library and other effects were insured under the War Damage Act.

We have previously noted that Henry May foresaw possible damage from air raids. Great Smith Street was damaged but the ICA offices were relatively unscathed. One legend has come down among Alliance staff of how, after one bombing and with the street cordoned off by police and ARP (Air Raid Precaution) wardens, Miss Polley, umbrella in hand, insisted on stepping over the cordon to get into the ICA offices. Certainly, she wrote to Mr M. Osmay of the Co-operative Service, International Labour Organisation at McGill University, Montreal, Canada, on 21st March, 1941:

'We have never thought of giving up or even of leaving here, though like everybody in London and, in fact, all parts of the country, we have many difficulties.'[76]

The ILO office had evacuated from Geneva to Montreal during the war. An anticipated wartime problem had been the disruption of communications but, by early 1941, the position appeared less bad than had been feared. Apart from co-operative organisations in occupied countries, communications had been maintained with all other members of the Alliance. Moreover, the Head Office was still receiving 79 co-operative journals from member movements on a regular basis.[77]

Information about Centrosoyus seems to have been the most difficult to come by, and great efforts were made to learn what was happening in Moscow. Besides writing to Centrosoyus direct [78], Miss Polley approached the highest Soviet Authorities in London', and Sir Stafford Cripps, the Labour politician, who was appointed British ambassador to Moscow.[79]

Perhaps the most notable achievement of the Secretariat during the war was the continued publication of the *Review of International Co-operation*. It not only provided the kind of communications that both May and Palmer had envisaged, but also offered a forum for debate that was important for the Alliance in the absence of the Executive and Central Committees and the ICA Congress. We have already noted that the issue of co-operative development within existing colonies had been raised. At this time, a number of the ICA's most important co-operative movements were in countries that were still major colonial powers including Britain, France and Holland. The growth of co-operatives as a mechanism for development within ex-colonial powers, would have considerable significance after the war.

In the meantime, the *Review* hosted another debate that had equally long-term importance. Because of the quality of that debate, and because it showed that the Alliance's ideological base was shifting once more, it is now considered separately.

Review Debate on Co-operatives and the State

At the outset, we should remind ourselves that earlier ICA leaders such as Gide, Thomas, Oerne and May had believed that voluntary co-operation, through the vehicle of consumer co-operatives, had the capacity to transform large sections of private enterprise into democratic co-operative social ownership. They believed that this transformation could be achieved without Government interference, and by the free operation of the market in which the co-operatives' ability to meet their members' needs most economically encouraged ever stronger and wider adherence.

As we have seen, though, there was a close, and often overlapping, relationship between co-operation and socialism, in both personal and philosophical terms. Under the arrangement reached at the Congress of the Socialist International in 1910, co-operatives maintained their separate but complementary existence. Earlier ICA leaders, confident in the thrusting dynamic of co-operative organisation among the populous working classes of the first part of this century, perhaps failed to see that the State socialism advocated by other socialists could possibly inhibit co-operative growth. Within the ICA, the issues thrown up by the Russian Revolution had been largely glossed over. We have seen, though, that the Alliance's last pre-war Congress had begun to address the issues arising from the recognition that co-operatives operated in different economic and political systems.

Now, the war itself provided a new impetus towards greater State involvement in economic and social life. For example, it led to a kind of 'wartime socialism', where goods were rationed to ensure fair distribution, and health became an important question if armies were to have able-bodied recruits.

Together with the effect of mounting national war efforts, they led to a dramatic increase in the power of the State. In some countries, such as Britain, it seemed that the State would keep some of its new powers after the war. In Britain, for example, proposals were being drawn up for a welfare State and in July, 1943, the *Review of International Co-operation* published an article on the Beveridge Plan, outlining a national system of social security.[80]

Such proposals coincided with the ICA's discussion of its 'wartime tasks'. It will be recalled that the ICA Executive, at its meeting in Paris in March, 1940, had approved Henry May's programme and initiated steps to carry it out.[81] These included inviting affiliated organisations to give their views on May's six points, but particularly on which ICA activities could be renewed after the war (point 3), and on the kind of peace settlement to be sought and how co-operative movements could influence it (points 4 and 5).

The most robust answer came from J. P. Warbasse, of the Co-operative League of the USA, who feared that increasing *'statism..... will come in serious conflict with the expansion of the co-operative movement.'* [82]

'It is my opinion that the encouragement which socialists have unanimously given to the expansion of government is destined..... to redound to the disadvantage of the co-operative movement. In Great Britain for example, the philosophy of co-operation..... has come largely from socialists in the back of whose minds, and indeed underlying whose minds, was always the idea of the ultimate political state. People like the Webbs saw the political state as the final agency to solve the economic problem. They have looked upon the co-operative movement as a minor device for serving the minor needs of consumers, ultimately to make its contribution to the aggrandizement of the state.'

Warbasse continued:

'We have refused to accept the Italian co-operative movement into member ship in the Alliance because it was dominated by the fascist state. What shall we do if we should find the British movement not only dominated by the British Government, but swallowed up by the state and made a part of the functions of the state?'

Warbasse developed arguments in a polemic article in the *Review of International Co-operation* in May, 1943, entitled 'Co-operatives to be absorbed by the State'.[83] In this, he argued that the British Co-operative Movement was helping to plan its own destruction by supporting the Beveridge proposals and by approving plans for the state control of 'land, transport, shipping, power, fuel and light, as well as housing and building materials, and medical and health services. Warbasse feared that the British Co-operative Insurance Society, and the CWS's coal mines and flour mills, could be adversely affected, and he was critical of a British co-operative official who had argued that when we get socialism we shall not need the Co-operative Movement'.

To some extent, Warbasse's arguments reflect a difference between Great Britain and the USA. Indeed, he went on to acknowledge that in the United States there was a much stronger distinction between socialism and co-operation, with the American working class being in general 'hostile to socialism but friendly to co-operation'.

In line with other ICA leaders, Warbasse was anti-capitalist. While happy to see the decay of capitalism, he feared that one of the dangers arising from this was that, in order to secure employment and supply consumers, Governments would intervene. They would do so first to financially shore up failing businesses, but finally they would take them over.

'Thus the bodies of dead profit businesses do not bestrew the ground and the socialising state serves apparently to keep capitalism going. The opportunity of Co-operation is to enter the fields vacated by ineffective capitalism, rather than to belittle the effectiveness of Co-operation and shift the responsibility to the Government.'[84]

Warbasse argued that the co-operative movement had shown that people were capable of doing things for themselves quite as much as acting as citizens or subjects of the State. Moreover, through co-operation they could supply themselves with goods and services that would otherwise be provided by private or State enterprise. He went on to say:

'Co-operation is private business. Whether a Co-operative Society consists of a family, buying club of a score of persons, or an aggregation of Rochdale Co-operators, it represents the private undertaking of the members. Private business may run for profit or for service. Co-operation is the service form of private business.'

Warbasse concluded his article by reminding readers of the areas that co-operatives had moved into in different countries: farming, tea plantations, bus services, shipping, coal mines, oil wells and refineries, electric light, telephone services, banking, insurance, building and building materials, medical services, schools, colleges and housing. Of the last mentioned he said:

'Co-operative housing, so beautifully illustrated in the Scandinavian countries, offers contrast to political housing..... Housing is not at its best when it becomes a part of the paraphernalia of a political party, as in Vienna ten years ago, when the municipal houses were cannonaded by the opposing political regime. Like all State business, it is antithetical to the Co-operative idea.'

By way of reply to Warbasse, the *Review of International Co-operation* printed an article headed 'The British Movement and the Beveridge Plan' by C. W. Fulker, Acting Secretary, Joint Parliamentary Committee of the Co-operative Congress, two months later. This confirmed the British co-operative movement's whole-hearted support for the Beveridge Plan.[85] It also illustrated the pressures that a co-operative movement came under as a result of war.

Fulker argued that, had the British movement attempted to 'contract out' in respect of its own insurance interests, the fundamental basis of the Beveridge Plan would have been weakened.

'Instead, the British Movement has taken the only possible course of giving whole-hearted support to the Plan, even though it may suffer some loss. The benefits to the community as a whole under the Plan are so tremendous that it would be sheer folly for one section of the working-class Movement to seek special exemption.'

Fulker concluded that there was plenty of room for 'voluntary' co-operation alongside the 'compulsory' co-operation on matters affecting everyone in the community.

His article showed the interaction of wartime influences on social policies when he mentioned that the Beveridge Plan had received enthusiastic support from members of the British armed forces who wanted to avoid a recurrence of the unemployment that had followed demobilisation in 1919.

However, the most robust rebuttal of Warbasse came not from Europe, but from Latin America. In the January, 1944 issue of the *Review of International Co-operation*, Prof. A. Fabra-Ribas, a Spanish exile in Bolivia[86], criticised the alarming tone of Warbasse's article,[87] which had 'greatly surprised many Latin American co-operators'. He argued that within many economies there were state, private enterprises and co-operative sectors which were continually readjusting themselves to one another. In his article headed Relations between Co-operative Societies and the State', Fabra-Ribas recalled the argument of the British Professor and co-operative writer, C. R. Fay.[88]

'....... in a balanced society there are three sectors, a private, a co-operative, and a state sector. We then say that the middle way of Co-operation is preferable because, unlike the private sector, it rests on altruism and, unlike the State sector, on persuasion. Altruism being superior to self-interest and per suasion superior to compulsion, it is desirable to do by voluntary Co-operation as much as is technically possible.'

Prof. Fabra-Ribas was obviously less worried about the State than Warbasse. Whereas Warbasse appeared to view the State as being static, Fabra-Ribas suggested that it differed according to circumstances of time and place. Therefore, one should not be against the State per se but have attitudes towards distinct types of State, such as 'fascist, Nazi or democratic'. He believed that the majority of co-operators traditionally saw the State in dynamic terms, an idea that had been illustrated by Väinö Tanner's paper at the 1937 Paris Congress from which Fabra-Ribas quoted:

'*Co-operation, as a form of expression in social activity of its own, is possible and necessary in all the different kinds of economic and political systems, even though its tasks and importance vary in different systems, principally depending upon the character of the social groups which have obtained possession of the State power.'*

Fabra-Ribas also quoted the late Albert Thomas, that the aim of co-operatives was 'to make men', who then went on to create States. But, Fabra-Ribas warned:

'Just as all men are not alike so also there are States and States. The State, as it is known to all the countries of Latin America, is both in origin and character quite different from those in ancient Europe and that of the United States.'

The Professor then went on to describe a number of Latin American States Peru, Venezuela, Brazil, and Colombia - and their attitudes towards the co-operative movements in their countries. Some of these helped the State to carry out its functions and, in doing so, then had no qualms about accepting assistance. While Prof. Fabra-Ribas ac knowledged that such a top-down approach was at variance with the bottom-up approach of co-operatives in Europe and North America, he believed that:

'the growth and importance of the Co-operative Movement throughout the world does not permit its confinement within a framework of too-rigid out lines or stereotyped formulas. When this dreadful war ends we shall be con fronted with a world in ruins and shall be obliged to tackle many new problems, not to rebuild the old world..... but a new and better one in which advantage can be taken of the great scientific and technical progress made in recent years, especially during the war. We cannot claim to adapt this new world to the pre-war conditions of the Co-operative Movement.'

Fabra-Ribas supported the view of an unnamed but 'clear-sighted' English co-operator, who had argued that the question was not so much of what the State should control as to who should control the State.

Two months later, in the *Review of International Co-operation*, R. A. Palmer wrote a more prosaic article than either those of Warbasse or Fabra Ribas. Under the heading 'British Co-operation and the State'[89], Palmer made it quite clear that the British Co-operative Movement did not ever see itself taking over functions such as education, national transport, post and telegraphic services and the control of land, for which it believed that the State should become responsible: these essential services were not 'suitable' for voluntary co-operative control. Similarly, the British movement believed that there were other functions best performed by local Government, including municipal transport, electric and gas lighting and water supplies. As far as mining, iron, steel and all branches of heavy and extractive industries were concerned, Palmer indicated that the British movement felt these should be controlled by 'Special Boards' representative of consumers, workers and the State.

He suggested that co-operatives should limit themselves to those things for which they were particularly suited. They should also not hinder the operations that were not specially theirs from being brought under non-profit making State control.

'But all such forms of organisation must conform to the outstanding co-operative principles that they should give but a limited return as interest on capital, that they are controlled by those whose needs they serve, and that any benefit from increasing efficiency returns to the consumer. This must apply whether the organisation be the Co-operative Society, the municipality, the public utility, or the State.'

The Warbasse/Fabra-Ribas/Palmer debate, prompted by the Beveridge Plan proposals in Britain, was limited to the *Review of International Co-operation*, although the question of Co-operation and State and Public Authorities was to figure prominently in post-war ICA Congresses.[90] It was significant for a number of reasons. One was that it showed that co-operative theory was changing with a new generation of ICA leaders, as well as the pressures of total war. Charles Gide, G. J. D. C. Goedhart, Albert Thomas, and perhaps even H. J. May, were not likely to have accepted the barriers to co-operative expansion that Palmer did now. This raises the question of whether British co-operation, which traditionally played such a large role within the ICA, was not now closer to British Labour politics than to Rochdale Co-operation. In Chapter 2 we saw that British co-operatives had jettisoned two of the original Rochdale Principles, political neutrality and cash trading. We have also seen in this Chapter the active part it played in the National Council of Labour bringing together British Trades Unions, the Labour Party, and the Co-operative Union. We should also recall that Fulker had firmly included British co-operatives within the 'working class movement'.

Something not mentioned previously, but having relevance here, was Henry May's concern about the politicisation of the British Co-operative Movement. In 'personal and private' letters to G. J. D. C. Goedhart, past President of the Alliance, he was critical of the British Co-operative Party. In March, 1935, May wrote to Goedhart that some British co-operative leaders 'started from the political stand-point of the Co-operative Party' and were no longer concerned about what was a true co-operative principle, but of interpreting a principle to fit in with present activities.[91] In an earlier letter May had criticised British co-operative politicians who were so eager to talk about the dead past of the Rochdale Principles'.[92]

Such comments were made in private. They never surfaced in official debates or documentation within the ICA. May might disapprove, but he was a realist in accepting the importance of the British movement to the ICA in terms of subscriptions and other support. His private comments do, however, indicate a shift among British co-operators, which is likely to have made it easier for them to accept limits on potential co-operative growth as a result of the growth of State ownership than it was for Warbasse.

As we have seen from Fabra-Ribas's intervention, the question also impinged on co-operatives' attitudes to, and position within, different kinds of State, which is a central theme of this study. Although we have looked most closely at those relationships within Fascist and Communist States, we should also take into account the expansion of State enterprise within other kinds of regime.

The Warbasse/Fabra-Ribas/Palmer debate was essentially about the shape of the co-operative movement in the post-war world. Linked to this were the important questions of post-war relief and reconstruction. Through the Secretariat's close links with British Labour politicians, it was able to keep abreast of developments among Allied Governments on their plans for these. We now move on to the ICA's initiatives in these areas.

The ICA and Post-War Relief and Reconstruction

As early as 1941 the ICA noted the moves of the British Foreign Secretary, Mr Anthony Eden, in conjunction with other Allied Governments, in London, to consider possible post-war problems.[93] R. A. Palmer, as Vice-President, and Miss Polley, as Administrative Secretary, immediately wrote to Eden on behalf of the ICA seeking to become involved

'...... in the name of the International Co-operative Alliance, for the recognition of the Principles of the Rochdale System of Co-operation as the ideal basis for a New World Order capable of replacing the capitalist and individualist profit-making system, of guaranteeing good relations between all peoples, and of assuring the equitable distribution of the resources of the world. Co-operative economy differs from capitalist economy in that it substitutes the service of the community with the profit of the individual, and establishes a genuine interdependence between its members throughout the world and a means, through international association, of achieving equilibrium in the economic sphere between the needs of the people and world resources.' [94]

Palmer and Polley emphasised the Alliance's past stand on peace, and its participation in world events, including the World Economic Conference at Geneva in 1927. The ICA was, they declared, a 'neutral ground on which people holding the most varied opinions and professing the most diverse creeds may meet and act in common'.

They also asserted that, because the ICA united over 100 million co-operators in 40 States, it was 'the Real League of the Peoples' and they hoped that as such it would be invited to join the discussion of economic and social problems relating to the coming Peace Settlement'.

Although implementing one of the wartime tasks identified by May, namely becoming involved in the peace settlements, Palmer and Polley deserved credit for the way in which they had seized opportunity, which was undoubtedly assisted by proximity to an important centre of wartime decision-making. We should note, though, that their claim was based on the 'Rochdale System of Co-operation and the fact that co-operative economy was different from capitalist economy in seeking to achieve an equilibrium between people's needs and the world's resources, an aim that has contemporary significance half a century later.

To help formulate an ICA post-war reconstruction policy, Palmer proposed calling an 'informal conference' of the British members of the Central Committee, together with representatives of those national co-operative movements that were exiled in, or visiting, London, as well as a number of experts.

In addition to the impetus given by the Eden initiative, encouragement seems to have come from a resolution on the Peace Settlement and Reconstruction passed by the conference of the International Labour Organisation in Washington in November, 1941. This urged the ICA to present a case to Allied and Neutral Governments that it should be allowed to become associated with post-war reconstruction. The ILO Conference had further urged the Alliance to seek representation in any 'Peace or Reconstruction Conference' convened after the war. At national levels, it suggested that the ICA should try to ensure that national and international co-operative organisations were consulted on questions of economic and social needs.[95].

Further impetus for the British Conference might well have come from moves within the Co-operative League of the USA (CLUSA). A question that arises about the meetings of the British members of the Central Committee was what would have been the constitutional position had any other national delegation to the Central Committee, such as CLUSA, acted similarly. While they could not have had the relationship with the London-based ICA Secretariat that the British members had, they could still have had a hand in shaping future ICA policy. This seemed set to happen in the USA.

In 1942, together with co-operative leaders from other movements exiled in the States, the Co-operative League of the USA set up a Committee for International Co-operative Reconstruction.[96] Its Chairman was the redoubtable Dr Warbasse, and the two main purposes of the Committee were to assist the rebuilding of co-operatives after the war, and to link up with the various post-war Commissions so as to contribute co-operative ideas to their work. The committee soon focused on four main areas: (i) 'Immediate Action - in the USA and in Europe; (ii) Preparation of post-war action; (iii) Public Relations; (iv) Development of Co-operatives and Co-operative Action'. It could be argued that CLUSA was taking on the work of the ICA itself, and this seems to have been how it was viewed back in London.

While the British members of the ICA Central Committee welcomed the American initiatives, they expressed the view that it was vitally important for post-war problems and solutions to be agreed by as many as possible of the affiliated National Co-operative Organisations'. They therefore advised CLUSA that the ICA was seeking the views of those members who could be contacted, and that these views would be collated and discussed at the earliest possible date after the cessation of hostilities'. It is clear that the British members believed they were acting as the ICA when they said that, although heartily welcoming the American move,

'ICA cannot see its way to be represented on the Committee set up in New York under the chairmanship of Dr. Warbasse - a member of the Central Committee of the Alliance - or to regard it as an affiliate ....'[97]

The British conference was held in Manchester in June, 1942, and was attended by UK members of the Central Committee, as well as Prof. Louis de Brouckere (Belgium), Rudolf Kreisky and W. Brauner (Czechoslovakia), F. Gabrovshek (Yugoslavia) and E. Mynderup (Scandinavian Co-operative Wholesale and International Co-operative Trading Agency).

Among the questions discussed was that of how far surviving co-operative facilities could be used to distribute relief supplies in liberated countries in the transitional period following the 'Armistice'. Another question concerned relief, and was whether the International Co-operative Movement should act through the ICA or through other international relief bodies. A third question was whether ICA member organisations in free and neutral countries should be asked to take steps to organise money, goods or loans to help liberated co-operative movements as soon as the war ended.[98]

On the first point, it was agreed to write to the National Governments of occupied countries based in London, in an attempt to get them to acknowledge the role that national co-operative movements could play in post-war reconstruction, as well as their more traditional roles in distributing food and other vital supplies. It was also agreed that a similar message should be sent to the Inter-Allied Committee for Post War Reconstruction.

On the second and third points, the Manchester meeting felt that the International Co-operative Movement, through the ICA, should act independently of other international relief bodies in helping to restore co-operative movements in occupied countries, and further agreed to set up an International Co-operative Relief Fund.

The next meeting of the British members, held in November, 1942, learned that the Canadian and British Co-operative Movements had made representations to their respective Governments to seek support for the involvement of the International Co-operative Movement in the Peace and Reconstruction Conference likely to be called after the war, and that favourable responses were expected. The Swiss movement had indicated that it felt unable to take any action because of Switzerland's neutrality.

Palmer and Miss Polley also reported that they had approached representatives of Governments exiled in London, urging their support for the International Co-operative Movement's involvement in the coming Peace Settlement, and that favourable replies had been received from the Polish and Yugoslav Ministries.

On the question of representation on the Inter-Allied Committee for Post-War Reconstruction, it was reported that a letter had been sent expressing the hope that there would be an opportunity to discuss the co-operative movement's involvement in post-war relief. In the hope of gaining their support, copies of this letter had also been sent to the Prime Ministers of the exiled Governments of Poland, Czechoslovakia, Yugoslavia, Norway, the Netherlands and Belgium.[99]

As far as the actual Inter-Allied Committee for Post-War Reconstruction itself was concerned, Mr Palmer, Miss Polley and Mr Mynderup subsequently reported to the British members of the Central Committee that they had met Mr J. H. Gorvin. He was the Head of the Allied Post-War Requirements Bureau. Initially, Gorvin's interest centred on how the ICA could assist the Allied Agricultural Advisory Committee. Palmer and Miss Polley pointed out, however, 'that the Alliance was not primarily interested in agricultural problems'. [100] Gorvin then suggested that it would be helpful if the Alliance produced a survey of consumer co-operative movements in European countries to show their strength and activities, and the part they might be able to play in distributing relief supplies. He also asked the ICA to identify the classes of people with whom 'Co-operative Societies tended to replace private enterprise.' The Secretariat produced a document, which described co-operative movements in the occupied countries of Europe and the Balkans and included sketch maps showing their geographical distribution.[101] Additionally, Gorvin asked the ICA to consider whether it, or its member organisations, could provide field kitchens or ambulances. The British members of the Central Committee, although recognising the propaganda value of these, rejected the idea because they felt that co-operators should provide a more permanent form of relief.

In addition to the approaches that they made to the Inter-Allied Committee for Post-War Reconstruction, Palmer and Miss Polley also proposed co-operative collaboration with the Ministers of Reconstruction in Allied Governments. A number of meetings were held, and among the ideas generated was one that the ICA should hold a Conference of all the co-operative leaders then in Britain. The Conference was held in London in November, 1943, and, because of its importance, we will consider it later in conjunction with a similar conference in the USA.

A further body that the ICA attempted to influence was the Allied Military Government of Occupied Territories. Soon after it was set up in 1943, Palmer and Miss Polley sought a meeting with Mr Stopford, Chief of the Civil Affairs Department of the British War Office. He also sought information about co-operative movements in occupied countries and asked for a 'confidential list of co-operative leaders and other reliable co-operators in each country who could be contacted and consulted by the Military Authorities'. [102]

Palmer and Miss Polley provided this list, and later learned that it had been forwarded to the responsible officers in the European and Middle East theatres of operations'. At a later meeting with the Allied Military Government of Occupied Territories (AMGOT), when army officers were present, Palmer and Miss Polley asked for, but failed to get, assurances that co-operatives would be used during the period of military occupation immediately after the war. The AMGOT thought it even less likely that representatives of the International Co-operative Movement would be taken on to the staffs of Allied Military Missions. However, this changed after the election of a British Labour Government in 1945. The following year, Mr W. P. Watkins was appointed to help re-establish the German Co-operative Movement.[103] In 1943, however, there seemed to be reluctance to use co-operative figures, although not those from private trade. Palmer and Polley had better success with the American Office of Foreign Relief and Rehabilitation, which was more prepared to use co-operative personnel in developing its post-war programmes. They met Mr F. K. Hoehler on a number of occasions, and responded to his suggestion that they pass on names of British co-operative specialists in the fields of textile production, food processing and agriculture, and of experts in management and distribution. Hoehler also asked whether British co-operative factories would be able to process and manufacture the 'primary goods' that would be required by countries once they were liberated.

Responses from the English and Scottish Co-operative Wholesale Societies, the Co-operative Productive Federation, and 30 of the largest British retail co-operative societies to whom these questions were passed [104] were uncertain. Both wholesales anticipated that they would have staff shortages after the war. As far as panels of experts were concerned, they feared that there could be language difficulties because British technicians had little familiarity with foreign languages. They therefore suggested that European co-operative refugees might be better able to help.

It was through Hoehler that the ICA came into active contact with UNRRA, the United Nations Relief and Rehabilitation Administration, which was established before the formal setting up of the UN in 1945.

In 1941, President Roosevelt had coined the term 'United Nations' to describe those countries fighting the Axis powers. The term was first officially used on 1st January, 1942, when 26 States joined the United Nations Declaration in which they pledged to continue their joint war effort, and not to make peace separately, [105]

UNRRA was the forerunner of the UN, and an example of wartime international action: its Director General, Mr Herbert Lehman, had been the former Head of the United States Department of Foreign Relief and Rehabilitation at Washington. It was from there that Mr F. K. Hoehler passed on to him the information he had received from the ICA on co-operative movements in occupied countries. [106]

In December, 1943, the ICA formally requested representation on both the UNRRA's Council of Administration and on its European Regional Committee. The Alliance further asked that co-operative movements in occupied countries, as well as those in free and neutral ones, should be invited to assist in the relief and rebuilding of Europe. [107] Despite fulsome assurances about the likely place that co-operatives would have in post-war relief and reconstruction, the first request was rejected because only member Governments could appoint official representatives. Moreover, although it was suggested that the ICA might be invited to send Observers to the European Committee or its sub committees when items of special interest to the co-operative movement were being discussed, this possibility never materialised. Nevertheless, UNRRA appears to have had some interest in co-operatives because it went on to appoint a Consultant on Co-operatives, Mr Lincoln Clark, [108] an appointment that may have been due to American co-operative pressure. According to the Co-operative Builder for 25th November, 1943, the American International Committee for Post-War Co-operative Reconstruction had sent a telegram to Lehman, offering its assistance to the UNRRA and proposing that it should have a Co-operative Division administered by experienced persons who had a long association with co-operatives.[109]

Closely linked to the Alliance's efforts to work with relief and reconstruction agencies was the ICA's own Appeal Fund. In February, 1943, the British members of the Central Committee launched, in the name of the ICA, an 'appeal to the co-operators of all free nations' for contributions towards the rehabilitation of co-operative movements in 'war stricken and occupied countries'.

By the end of 1945, around £300,000 had been raised, augmented by gifts in kind donated by some national co-operative organisations, such as the Swiss and Swedish.[110] Earlier, in separate appeals for Spanish, Czechoslovak and Finnish co-operators, the ICA had raised more than another £50,000.[111]

Returning now to the suggestion, made during meetings with exiled Governments' Ministers of Reconstruction, that the ICA should call a conference of co-operative leaders in London, arrangements were made for this to be held in November, 1943. One of its unspoken aims seems to have been to show that the ICA was more than just a body representing consumer co-operatives. The conference was called the 'International Conference of Representatives of Consumers' and Agricultural Co-operative Organisations.'[112] The calling of the conference should also be viewed in the light of the politicking between British and American co-operative interests, and also those of their respective Governments. At their meeting in London in June, 1943, the British members of the Central Committee held a long discussion on their relations with CLUSA's International Committee for Post-War Reconstruction. The ICA had received several letters, and a memorandum under the title of 'Co-operatives in Post-War Relief and Reconstruction', from Mr Howard Cowden, Chairman of the American Committee.

While the British members welcomed the fact 'that the Alliance might have the fullest collaboration of the American Movement in relief and reconstruction planning' and 'great interest and admiration' for its work, concern was expressed over the Committee's relations with the US Government.

'In the light of what was understood to be the intention of the Governments of Great Britain and the USA regarding the administration of the occupied coun-

tries immediately they are liberated, however, the Committee* felt that it would be very difficult for the American Committee to realise its aims, but, at the same time, they felt that, in view of the close relationship of the American Movement with the Government of the USA, and the fact that Mr. Murray Lincoln, President of the Co-operative League, was one of the USA Government's representatives at the United Nation's Food Conference at Hot Springs, the American Committee would not be likely to issue any statement of aims which would be in opposition to the attitude of the (American) Government.'[113]

*British Members of the Central Committee.

It was against this background that the British members of the ICA Central Committee learned that the American Committee planned to hold a conference of co-operative leaders in October, 1943. They arranged for a telegram of greetings be sent 'in the name of the Alliance', although they later learned that the conference had had to be postponed until January, 1944.[114] This meant that the British and American conferences on Post-War Co-operative Reconstruction were held within two months of each other. We are therefore able to consider them together, thus helping us to get a transatlantic picture of co-operative ideas as the war entered its final years.

The London conference was attended by the British members of the Central Committee, now increasingly referred to as 'the Executive', Consumer representatives came from the British Co-operative Union and the English and Scottish Co-operative Wholesales, and former leaders and representatives of consumer movements in Belgium, Czechoslovakia, Poland and Palestine. Agriculture representatives came from the Horace Plunkett Foundation, the Welsh and Irish Agricultural Organisation Societies, the New Zealand Producers' Association, the Overseas Farmers' Co-operative Federations, and leaders from Czechoslovakia, Poland and Yugoslavia.[115]

We should compare this list with those attending the Washington Conference. Representatives at that came from the American co-operatives, as well as some from Canada, China, Holland, Palestine, Sweden, and Yugoslavia. These were joined by the New York and Winnipeg representatives of the English and Scottish Co-operative Wholesale Societies, and a number of Secretaries and Counsellors of Embassies and Legations in Washington. Also, and most significantly, in attendance was Sir Arthur Salter, Senior Deputy Director-General of UNRRA [116] Even more interesting, and indicating co-operative sympathies at the highest American levels, was a message from President Roosevelt. This read:

'It is fitting that the centennial of the truly democratic Rochdale Principles is being celebrated. The Weavers* balanced independence with interdependence, self-interest with goodwill, and action with foresight. Any effective handling of the problem of relief and rehabilitation of the victims of axis aggression must be based upon these same considerations. The Co-operative Movement, which belongs to no one nation but has its roots in the traditions of all democratic peoples, is, therefore, one of the appropriate instruments to be used in this task.'

*Rochdale Pioneers

Let us now compare the matters considered by each conference. That in London was more focused and concentrated on only two issues. It was chaired by R. A. Palmer who, as Acting President of the Alliance, reiterated the ICA's claim to be represented at any Peace Settlement Conference on the grounds that it was *'the greatest economic and social organisation of the peoples of the world.'*[117]

There were two papers at the London conference. One looked at 'The Place of Co-operation in the Post-War Economy' and was delivered by Mr J. A. Hough, M.A., Economic Adviser to the British Co-operative Union. The other was the 'Relations Between Co-operative Organisations of Consumers and Agricultural Producers', presented by Mr George Walworth, M.A., Agricultural Adviser to the British Co-operative Union.

These papers led to two resolutions being passed. The first, on 'The Place of Co-operation in the Post-War Economy', argued that the role of the co-operative movement should be to create and 'organise a collective economy based upon mutuality and self-help..... and called for freedom of people to 'organise co-operatively'. It also called for the freedom of movement of people and goods between all countries; and the prohibition of cartels, monopolies and capitalist agreements that benefited private enterprise at the expense of the consumer. The resolution also called for the application of co-operative principles in the exploitation and distribution of the world's natural resources, and in the organisation of international trade and transport. Finally, it called for the establishment of an International Co-operative Wholesale Society, together with its complementary organisations of Bank and Assurance Society, an idea that, like closer relations between consumer and agricultural co-operatives, had been around in the ICA since before the First World War.

The second resolution, on 'Relations Between Co-operative Consumers' and Agricultural Producers' Organisations', called for the 'unification of all National Co-operative Organisations, but with a definite division of functions between consumer and agricultural interests. It advocated that common action should be taken in areas such as Education, Propaganda, Common Defence and Scientific Research. The aim of the resolution appears to have been to help post-war rehabilitation by rationalising co-operative organisation at national levels.

Even today, fifty years later, the papers by Hough and Walworth deserve re-reading, not only for their clear articulation of contemporary co-operative theory but also for their power of analysis, particularly in projecting post-war problems.

Unfortunately, the ICA archives do not have copies of the papers presented to the Washington Conference. However, from a report in the *Review of International Co-operation*,[118] it would seem that there were more, but less in-depth, papers. Their subjects included Producer/Marketing Co-operatives in the USA, American Consumer/Purchasing Co-operatives, The International Co-operative Movement, How Government and Co-operatives can work together for a lasting peace, Co-operatives in International Relief and Rehabilitation, and International Trade and Manufacturing. Speakers included Dr J. P. Warbasse, President Emeritus of CLUSA, E. R. Bowen, CLUSA's General Secretary, Murray D. Lincoln, its President, and Howard A. Cowden, President and General Manager of the Consumers' Co-operative Association and Chairman of the Committee on International Co-operative Reconstruction. Speakers from outside the co-operative movement included Sir Arthur Salter, Senior Deputy Director-General of UNRRA, who spoke of that organisation's plans for post-war recovery; Dr Joseph G. Knapp of the USA Farm Credit Administration, Washington; and Mr M. Colombian, Chief of the Co-operative Section of the International Labour Organisation. We had already noted that the ILO had moved from Geneva to Montreal during the war. Fortunately, in the sense that embarrassment was avoided, the Washington Conference's Recommendations mirrored those of the London Conference. In fact, the *Review of International Co-operation* reported that some were taken from the first conference and that they were subsequently adopted by a Joint Meeting of the Boards of the Co-operative League and National Co-operatives, Inc., the National Co-operative Wholesale Society.

Recommendations fell into three main areas: International Co-operative Collaboration; Relief and Reconstruction, which had not been treated separately in London; and Co-operative Policy. Within the first of these, and in line with the London Conference, the Washington Conference included proposals to establish an International Co-operative Trading and Manufacturing Association, expansion of international co-operative business between producer and consumer co-operatives, and the facilitation of the movement of goods between Producer Marketing Co-operatives and Consumer Purchasing Co-operatives. Recommendations stated more explicitly in Washington than in London concerned post-war Relief and Reconstruction, and centred largely on co-operative collaboration with UNRRA, including the request that that organisation should set up a Co-operative Division, establish a Central Loan Fund to rehabilitate co-operatives in occupied countries, and launch a Freedom Fund, raised by popular subscriptions, to help co-operatives in the liberated countries. In the third area, that of Co-operative Policy, recommendations were very similar to those of the London Conference and included the freedom and international movement of people, goods and currencies; curbs on cartels and monopolies; and the application of Co-operative Principles in ownership, development and distribution of the world's natural resources.

When we consider the London and Washington Conferences it is likely that comparisons with the three Inter-Allied and Neutral Conferences called by the French Co-operative Movement in 1916 and 1919 arise. Like those Conferences, the London and Washington Conferences helped to set up the post-war agenda of the International Co-operative Alliance. They, and particularly the Washington Conference, strengthened links between the ICA and Government and pre-UN agencies, helping to pave the way for eventual UN recognition of the ICA.

In passing, we should note that the Co-operative League of the USA had an easier relationship with its Government than did the ICA Secretariat in London with the British Government. This could have presaged future American Government influence on the ICA through CLUSA, but it also suggests that the American Government did not see co-operatives in quite the class terms that the British Government did. We have noted the difficulties in understanding, or reluctance to use co-operatives, by the British War Office and the Allied Military Government of Occupied Territories. However, with the fledgling United Nations taking form in the United States, and having good relations with the American Government, CLUSA was well-placed to help the ICA to become recognised by the UN.

The struggle to achieve this status formed a large part of the ICA'S work in the later stages of the 1939-45 war. We now end this Chapter by taking a brief look at the stages through which eventual recognition was achieved.

The ICA and the United Nations

We have already noted the ICA's abortive attempt to gain observer status on UNRRA's European Economic and Social Committee, and its efforts to achieve some kind of status with other relief and post war reconstruction agencies. We should also, perhaps, note that, as far back as April, 1940, the Alliance, through Miss Polley, had written to Mr J. Avenol, Secretary-General of the League of Nations, expressing the hope that the Alliance would be invited to join the League's Central Committee for Economic and Social Problems.119 In 1920 the Alli-

INTERNATIONAL CO-OPERATIVE ALLIANCE.

Internationaler Genossenschaftsbund.

ALLIANCE COOPÉRATIVE INTERNATIONALE.

TELEPHONE NO. 7487 VICTORIA
TELEGRAPHIC ADDRESS
   INLAND—INTERALLIA, PARL LONDON
   FOREIGN—INTERALLIA, LONDON

"Orchard House,"
14, Great Smith Street,
LONDON. S.W. 1.

    THE INTERNATIONAL CO-OPERATIVE ALLIANCE presents to the Governments of Great Britain, of the United States of America, of the Soviet Union, and of China, a request for consultative representation at the forthcoming United Nations Conference at San Francisco, and also upon the Economic and Social Council which was envisaged at Dumbarton Oaks Conference as part of the structure of the International Organisation to maintain peace and security, whose Charter the forthcoming Conference will prepare.

    The aims of the International Co-operative Alliance are economic, social and humanitarian in the fullest sense, and the whole of its activity during the past 50 years constitutes a campaign for economic and political peace.

    With its affiliated National Federations in 35 countries, in which approximately 75 million co-operators are organised, the I.C.A. is by far the most powerful Voluntary International Organisation.

    Moreover, as it represents the Co-operative Organisations of all types whose members are drawn from every social and economic section of the people as well as from every political party and religious denomination, it rightly claims to be the most representative Organisation of the People.

    Its wide international character gives the Alliance an unique position in world affairs, and although, being a non-official Organisation, it could not have representation within the League of Nations, the significance of its views in regard to international problems has always been recognised by the League. The Alliance received an invitation from the Council of the League to the International Economic Conference in 1927, and it participated in a consultative capacity in the Economic Consultative Committee which was subsequently formed.

    The authorities and members of the International Co-operative Alliance have observed with profound gratification that the historic Declarations made during the war by the Leaders of the Great Powers, concerning the future basis of world peace, ratify the claims of Co-operators that the application of the Fundamental Principles of the Voluntary Co-operative Movement offers an assurance of peace and understanding.

    The International Co-operative Alliance is, therefore, confident that its request, as the representative of the World Co-operative Movement, to consultative representation at the San Francisco Conference and upon the Economic and Social Council of the new World Organisation, will receive both sympathetic and favourable consideration by the Governments of the Four Great Nations which are convening the Conference.

    On behalf of the International Co-operative Alliance,

Acting President I.C.A.   Administrative Secretary I.C.A.

20th March, 1945.

Copy of letter sent on 20 March 1945 to the Governments of Great Britain, United States of America, the USSR and China.

ance had been unsuccessful its attempt to gain representation with the League. This time around its efforts were to be successful, due not only to a greater readiness of the UN to accommodate Non-Governmental Organisations, but also to the ICA's effective lobbying in London and Washington.

To some extent, the ICA got into the UN on the coat tails of the International Federation of Trade Unions, although the ICA's strong determination in the matter is underlined by the way that it monitored early UN developments. Besides its representations to UNRRA, it had followed the UN Conference on Food and Agriculture held at Hot Springs, USA, in May and June, 1943, the forerunner of the UN's Food and Agricultural Organisation. After the Conference the Alliance had written to the Conference's Secretary-General, welcoming the recognition that the Conference had given to the part that co-operatives could play in 'attaining the goal of Freedom from Want in the post-war period in relation to food and agriculture'. The Alliance asked to become associated with this work, offering its services in the supply of information about co-operatives.[120]

How the ICA actually gained recognition by the UN can be traced through its correspondence, Memoranda on Agenda, Minutes, and contemporary reports in the *Review of International Co-operation*. Putting these together, we can draw up the following table of events.

On 19th February, 1945, Albin Johansson in Sweden sent a telegram to Palmer, advising him that Swedish news agencies had reported trade union moves to be represented on a consultative basis at the coming conference in San Francisco to establish the UN.[121] This spurred the ICA into similar action. On 20th March, 1945, Palmer as Acting President, and Miss Polley, as Administrative Secretary, wrote to the Governments of Great Britain, United States of America, the USSR and China, seeking representation at San Francisco.

Co-operative movements in the four countries were asked to lobby their Governments.[122] When the British members of the Central Committee learned of these moves they urged that additional pressure should be put on the British Government, because they believed that this would influence the other Governments. [123] It was agreed to ask Mr A. V. Alexander, First Lord of the Admiralty, but still Parliamentary Secretary to the British Co-operative Union, if he could help to arrange for an ICA delegation to meet the British Prime Minster, Winston Churchill, 'so as to put the case the for the ICA to be represented both at San Francisco and in the New World Organisation'.

However, when Miss Polley met A. V. Alexander on 22nd March, 1945, he said that he thought there was 'no possibility of representation for the ICA at the coming Conference'. He also did not think it an opportune moment to seek a meeting with Churchill. Instead, it might be easier to arrange one with Clement Attlee, Deputy Prime Minister, one of the 'two Principal British Government representatives at San Francisco'. This move also appears to have been unsuccessful, as neither the International Co-operative Alliance nor the International Federation of Trade Unions gained direct representation at the Conference at San Francisco. However, the ICA closely followed all moves leading to the setting up of the UN. It asked CLUSA if it could 'select a delegate' to attend the San Francisco Conference, and they appointed Wallace J. Campbell, their Assistant Secretary. Because neither CLUSA nor the ICA 'was well enough known in the US State Department to qualify as important non-Governmental organisations' CLUSA suggested that Campbell should attend the Conference on his press pass, which would allow him to observe more sessions than he could as an NGO representative.

Campbell's remit was to table a statement on behalf of the ICA. This was circulated to all the delegates attending the Conference and very closely resembled the statement that Palmer and Polley had sent to the British, American, Soviet and Chinese Governments.

Campbell wrote a fascinating account of his representation of the ICA at the UN's founding conference in the *Review of International Co-operation in 1983*.[124]

UN recognition of the ICA could not come at its founding Conference, and action to achieve it thus moved back to London once more.

A very detailed account of how the ICA achieved Grade A Consultative status at the UN, including voting figures for and against motions and amendments, and the countries involved, was told in the *Review of International Co-operation* in February, 1946.[125] The ICA's success was closely related to that of the World Federation of Trade Unions. The relevant UN Resolution was prefaced by the statement:

'In accordance with the requests of the World Federation of Trade Unions, the American Federation of Labour, the International Co-operative Alliance, and other non-governmental organisations, that their representatives shall be allowed to take part in the work of the Economic and Social Council, and in accordance with article 71 of the Charter.....'

The ICA appears to have experienced difficulties in achieving this status because of the similar, but larger, claims made by the World Federation of Trade Unions. The WFTU sought a seat not only on the Economic and Social Committee but also on the UN General Assembly, and asked for participation with voting rights in both bodies. Although these demands had strong Soviet support, they aroused opposition elsewhere on the grounds that they were contrary to the concept of the UN as a Union of Nations. These moves were accompanied by others which seemed to have been aimed at excluding the ICA.

The *Review of International Co-operation* reported:

'The motive of those delegations which voted for the Soviet amendment was to secure and enhance the status of the World Federation of Trade Unions in U.N.O. But this desire is hardly an explanation for refusing the International Co-operative Alliance not only equality of status with the W.F.T.U. BUT ANY STATUS* in U.N.O., at least for the time being. The reasons for the desired exclusion of the ICA were never stated. No doubt its members in the countries concerned will be asked by the Executive of the Alliance to seek an explanation from their Governments.'

*Review editor's capitals

Soviet moves in late 1945 and early 1946 to enhance the status of the World Federation of Trade Unions at the possible expense of the International Co-operative Alliance suggests that the USSR saw trade unions, and their international body, as being more significant than co-operatives and their international representative, the ICA. This question will be explored more fully in the next chapter.

Moves on behalf of the ICA were made elsewhere. In London, Palmer and Miss Polley sought an interview with Mr Philip Noel Baker, British Minister of State and one of the principal members of the British delegation to the UN.[126] The help that Philip Noel Baker subsequently gave was acknowledged at the ICA's first post-war Congress at Zurich in 1946, as was that of Mr Peter Fraser, Prime Minister of New Zealand, and Senator Connally, of the US delegation to the UN, 'although he openly confessed that he knew nothing of the ICA'. This almost throw away remark could suggest that Connally and USA support were not so much for the ICA as against a position taken by the USSR in the UN.

In the end, the ICA was successful in being one of the first three named organisations achieving Category A consultative status with the UN. We have seen, on a number of occasions, the strong links that existed between the ICA and the International Labour Organisation. This productive relationship may also have been a reason for the ICA's success with the UN, a success that was to open up new areas of collaboration for the Alliance.

Conclusions

Recounting the ICA's success with the UN has taken us beyond the end of the Second World War, which has been the main concern of this Chapter. However, it illustrates strengths and abilities in the ICA which had also enabled it to survive the war. Although there were contingent reasons for that success, such as the location of the Alliance's Secretariat and the national co-operative movement most able to help it in an unoccupied country, we can see that other factors were also at work. Important among these were the Alliance's organisational capacity, and an ideology which gave it focus and cohesion.

Examining this claim in greater detail, and turning first to organisational aspects, we note that the Alliance had the maturity to overcome the crisis created by Henry May's death. It was also shown to be flexible enough, and sufficiently capable of improvisation, to turn the British members of the Central Committee into a kind of Executive. While there was always the danger that such action could be considered unconstitutional, because the ICA Constitution made no such provision, British members were awake to this charge and approached all issues sensitively, particularly that of the ICA Presidency. On occasion, though, as in relation with their American counterparts, they stood on their dignity, and we noted that the British members increasingly came to refer to themselves as 'The Executive'.

Two points should be made in mitigation. One was that there was no readily-available alternative. The other was that, along with the Secretariat, the British members of the Central Committee reported back, and handed over responsibility as soon as they could, to the ICA's reconstituted Central Committee and first post-war Congress.

During the period of the Second World War the Secretariat showed many abilities, ranging from that of maintaining the publication of the *Review of International Co-operation* to the lobbying which took the ICA into the UN. It also established and administered relief funds, and effectively sought collaboration with relief and rehabilitation bodies and with the Allied Military Government of Occupied Countries.

On the ideological front, it seems reasonable to claim that the Alliance was helped by the fact that the Allies' war aims were broadly in line with those of the ICA; also by the fact that there was a fair degree of cohesion within ICA membership. Apart from some ambivalence among the Finns, the majority of ICA member organisations subscribed to the Allies' cause. The Germans, Italians, Austrians and Japanese were no longer members of the Alliance.

We have also observed that the war encouraged a number of shifts in ICA thinking. Although Rochdale still had pride of place, and was steadily mentioned in declarations throughout the war, agricultural co-operatives assumed increased importance alongside consumer co-operatives in the Alliance. Greater emphasis was made in statements that the Alliance represented all kinds of co-operative.

The war had also caused the State to become more actively involved in economic and welfare questions, a situation that seemed set to continue in the post-war world. Ramifications of this had led to a lively debate in the *Review of International Co-operation*, and would continue in post-war Congresses. The result was that co-operatives had begun to accept limits to their expansion that earlier ICA leaders would not have countenanced; but the latter had not experienced total war of the kind that the 1939-45 War proved to be. We have already noted that, at the beginning of the war, Henry May had realised that its nature would be different from that of the First World War.

In many ways it can be argued that Warbasse was correct. But we should also recognise that the war had created new societal and political pressures which were bound to influence wartime co-operative leaders. In such questions there is always the need to weigh advantages against disadvantages. On the one hand, the Alliance's close links with the British co-operative movement, enhanced by war-time dependence, made it more open to the political ideas that permeated the British movement. On the other hand, such links undoubtedly had a political justification as far as the Alliance's relations with relief and rehabilitation organisations were concerned and its eventual admission to the UN.

It is in the Alliance's attempts to be taken seriously by UNRRA, etc., and the embryonic UN that we find the best statements of its philosophy during the war. Its claim to be the real League of the People, which dated back to just after the First World War, was repeated on a number of occasions. Now there were new ones, two of which were particularly significant. One was the call from the London and Washington Conferences for the application of co-operative principles to the exploitation and distribution of the world's natural resources. In the next Chapter we will see how this led to an ICA initiative concerning the world's oil supplies. Another shift was represented in the welcome that the Alliance gave for the call from the UN's 1943 Hot Springs Conference for 'Freedom from Want'. Wartime situations encourage sloganising, but this was one upon which the co-operative movement would build strategies as far as the Third World was concerned. It presaged the Alliance's concern with co-operatives in developing countries in the post-war world.

Despite wartime ravages and dislocations, it would seem that the Alliance emerged from the end of the war in a stronger position than it had been at the beginning. However, Cold War tensions developed within a very short time. These were to bring quite new and dangerous challenges to the organisation, in terms both of its constitution and of its ideology.

Notes

1. WATKINS, W. P., Recorded interview, 17th September, 1991.
2. International Co-operative Alliance, *Review of International Co-operation*, No. 12, December, 1939, p. 585.
3. ICA Archives, Letters from Henry May to Väinö Tanner, 8th June, 22nd June, 3rd July, 1939.
4. ICA Archives, Letter from Henry May to Väinö Tanner, 28th September, 1938.
5. ICA Archives, Letter from Henry May to members of the ICA Central Committee, 7th November, 1939.
6. International Co-operative Alliance, *Review of International Co-operation*, No. 11, November, 1939, p. 513.
7. This Study, Chapter 3, pp. 113-114.
8. This Study, Chapter 2, p. 50.
9. WATKINS, W. P, Taped interviews with W. P. Watkins, 11th September, 1989, and Lord Gallacher of Enfield, Interview, 22nd February, 1990.
10. This Study, Chapter 5, p. 200.
11. ICA Archives, Letter from Henry May to G. J. D. C. Goedhart, ex-President of ICA, 27th September, 1928.
12. ICA Archives, Letter from Henry May to G. J. D. C. Goedhart, ex-President of ICA, 27th August, 1929.
13. International Co-operative Alliance, *Minutes of the ICA Executive, Geneva, 28th October, 1932*, p. 2.
14. International Co-operative Alliance, *ibid.*, p. 2.
15. International Co-operative Alliance, *Report to ICA Congress, Paris, 1937*, pp. 7-8.

16. International Co-operative Alliance, *Minutes of meeting of ICA Executive, Paris, 15th March, 1940*, p. 2.
17. International Co-operative Alliance, *Review of International Co-operation*, No. 12, December, 1939.
18. International Co-operative Alliance, *Minutes of meeting of ICA Executive, Paris, 15th March, 1940*, p. 1..
19. WATKINS, W. P, op. cit., p. 231, and pp. 243-244. After the Second World War the Henry J. May Foundation Centre for the Study of International Co-operation was founded.
20. International Co-operative Alliance, *Minutes of meeting of ICA Executive, Paris, 15th March, 1940*, p. 2.
21. International Co-operative Alliance, *ibid.*, p. 2.
22. This Study, Chapter 5, pp. 198-202.
23. This Study, Chapter 5, pp. 215-217, 225-228, and Chapter 6.
24. International Co-operative Alliance, *Report of the ICA Congress, Vienna, 1930*, pp. 36-40;
Report of the ICA Congress, London, 1934, pp. 38-43;
Report of the ICA Congress, Paris, 1937, pp. 38-43;
Report of the ICA Congress, Paris, 1937, pp. 185-210
25. This Study, Chapter 5, p. 217.
26. ICA Archives, Letter from Väinö Tanner to Henry May, 17th November, 1933.
27. ICA Archives, Letter from Väinö Tanner to Henry May, 19th December, 1932.
28. ICA Archives, Letter from Väinö Tanner to Henry May, 8th June, 1932.
29. ICA Archives, Letter from Väinö Tanner to Henry May, 23rd June, 1933.
30. ICA Archives, Letter from Väinö Tanner to Henry May, 30th August, 1933.
31. ICA Archives, Letter from Väinö Tanner to Henry May, 1st September, 1933.
32. International Co-operative Alliance, *Review of International Co-operation*, No. 11, November, 1939, p. 522.
33. ICA Archives, Telegram from Henry May to Väinö Tanner, c/o Finnish Legation, Moscow, 2.40 p.m., 23rd October, 1939; and Telegram from Henry May to Väinö Tanner, c/o Centrosoyus, Moscow, 11.00 a.m., 23rd October, 1939.

34. ICA Archives, Telegram from Henry May to Vice-President Khokhlov, Centrosoyus, Moscow, 11.00 a.m., 23rd October, 1939.
35. International Co-operative Alliance, *Review of International Co-operation,* No. 1, January, 1940, p. 4.
36. PALMER, Alan, *Dictionary of Modern History, op. cit.*, p. 115.
37. International Co-operative Alliance, *Minutes of ICA Executive Meeting, Paris, March, 1940*, p. 7.
38. ROBERTS, J. M., *Europe 1880-1945*, Longman Group UK Limited, New York, 1989, p. 550 and p. 565.
39. International Co-operative Alliance, *Report of Discussion at meeting of British members of ICA Central Committee, Manchester, 8th October, 1941*, p. 3.
40. International Co-operative Alliance, *ibid.*, p. 3.
41. International Co-operative Alliance, *Minutes of meeting of ICA Executive, 15th March, 1940*, p. 3.
42. International Co-operative Alliance, *Minutes of British members of ICA Central Committee, 26th February, 1941*, p. 7.
43. International Co-operative Alliance, Report on discussion of ICA attitude to Väinö Tanner, *Minutes of the Meeting of British members, ICA Central Committee, Manchester, 8th October, 1941*.
44. International Co-operative Alliance, Report on discussion of ICA attitude to Väinö Tanner, *ibid.*, p. 1.
45. International Co-operative Alliance, Report of Discussion on ICA Attitude to Väinö Tanner, *op. cit.*, p. 2.
46. ICA Archives, Press cutting, *Manchester Guardian*, 6th October, 1941, report headed 'No Peace with Soviet Rulers'.
47. International Co-operative Alliance, Report of discussion on ICA attitude to Väinö Tanner, *op. cit.*, p. 2..
48. International Co-operative Alliance, *Minutes of the meeting of British members of ICA Central Committee, Manchester, 8th October, 1941*, p. 2.
49. ICA Archives, Press cutting, *Manchester Guardian*, 9th October, 1941, item headed 'Co-operators Criticise Mr Tanner'.
50. International Co-operative Alliance, *Minutes of meeting of British members of ICA Central Committee, Manchester, 4th November, 1942*, p. 1.

51. International Co-operative Alliance, *ibid.*, p. 2.
52. International Co-operative Alliance, *ibid.*, p. 2.
53. ICA Archives, Press cutting, *Western Producer*, Canada, 30th April, 1942.
54. ICA Archives, Press cuttings.
55. ICA Archives, Press cutting *Evening Standard*, undated but near time of Palmer and Tanner's broadcasts to which it refers.
56. ICA Archives, Press cutting, *The Times*, 17th September 1941
57. ICA Archives, Press cutting, *Scottish Co-operator,* 7th March, 1942.
58. ICA Archives, Press cutting, *Tribune*, 31st March, 1942.
59. International Co-operative Alliance, *Minutes of meeting of British members of ICA Central Committee, 23rd June, 1943*, p. 3.
60. ICA Archives, Press cutting, *Daily Herald*, 13th February, 1944, item headed 'Four Finns who matter most'.
61. International Co-operative Alliance, *Minutes of Meeting of British members of ICA Central Committee, op. cit.*, p. 4.
62. International Co-operative Alliance, *ibid.*, p. 4.
63. ICA Archives, Letter from Miss Polley, 13th July, 1943, to some members of ICA Central Committee. No distribution list indicated.
64. International Co-operative Alliance, *Minutes of meeting of British members of ICA Central Committee, Manchester, 5th January, 1944.*
65. ICA Archives, Press cutting, *The Times*, 24th October, 1944, heading 'Party Split in Finland - aftermath of war'.
66. ICA Archives, Unattributed article headed 'A Hundred Years since the Birth of the Finnish Co-operator Väinö Tanner (1881-1966)', p. 3.
67. ICA Archives, *ibid.*, p. 4.
68. International Co-operative Alliance, *Report of ICA Congress, Zurich, 1946*, pp. 57-58.
69. International Co-operative Alliance, Memorandum on Agenda of meeting of British members of ICA Central Committee, 20th February, 1941, pp. 1-2.
70. International Co-operative Alliance, *Minutes of meeting of*

British members of ICA Central Committee, 20th February, 1941, p.1.

71. WATKINS, W. P, Taped interview with W. P. Watkins, 17th September, 1991.

72. ICA Archives, Letter from Dr Shenkman to R. A. Palmer, 3rd November, 1941.

73. ICA Archives, Letter from R. A. Palmer to Miss G. F. Polley, 25th November, 1940.

74. International Co-operative Alliance, *Review of International Co-operation*, July, 1942, p. 97.

75. ICA Archives, Letter from Miss G. F. Polley to ICA Member Organisations and Central Committee Members, 16th July, 1940.

76. ICA Archives, Letter from Miss G. F. Polley to Mr M. Osmay, Co-operative Service, International Labour Organisation, 21st March, 1941.

77. International Co-operative Alliance, *Minutes of meeting of British members of ICA Central Committee, 26th February, 1941*, P. 5.

78. ICA Archives, Letter from Miss G. F. Polley to Centrosoyus, 11th August, 1941.

79. ICA Archives, Letter from Miss G. F. Polley to Sir Stafford Cripps, 26th March, 1941.

80. International Co-operative Alliance, *Review of International Co-operation,* No. 7, July, 1943, p. 78.

81. International Co-operative Alliance, *Minutes of ICA Executive Meeting, Paris, 15th March, 1940*, pp. 7-8.

82. ICA Archives, Letter from J. P. Warbasse, President of the Co-operative League of the USA, 24th April, 1941.

83. International Co-operative Alliance, *Review of International Co-operation*, No. 5, May, 1943, p. 51.

84. International Co-operative Alliance, *ibid.*

85. International Co-operative Alliance, *Review of International Co-operation,* No. 7, July, 1943, p. 878.

86. International Co-operative Alliance, *Report of the ICA Congress, Zurich, 1946*, p. 37.

87. International Co-operative Alliance, *Review of International Co-operation*, No. 1, January, 1944, pp. 12-15.

88. DIGBY, Margaret, *The Little Nut Tree*, The Plunkett Foundation, Oxford, 1979, p. 69 and p. 149.

89. International Co-operative Alliance, *Review of International Co-operation*, No. 3, March, 1944, pp. 37-39.

90. International Co-operative Alliance, *Report of ICA Congress, Zurich, 1946*, pp. 150-176; and *Report of ICA Congress, Prague, 1948*, pp. 160-189.

91. ICA Archives, Letter from Henry J. May to G. J. D. C. Goedhart, 29th March, 1935.

92. ICA Archives, Letter from Henry J. May to G. J. D. C. Goedhart, 30th January, 1935.

93. International Co-operative Alliance, *Minutes of meeting of British members of ICA Central Council, Manchester, 8th October, 1941*.

94. ICA Archives, Letter from Mr R. A. Palmer and Miss G. F. Polley to Mr Anthony Eden, British Foreign Secretary, 18th September, 1941.

95. International Co-operative Alliance, *Minutes of meeting of British members of ICA Central Committee, Manchester, 1st April, 1942*, p. 5.

96. International Co-operative Alliance, *ibid.*, p. 5.

97. International Co-operative Alliance, *ibid.*, p. 6.

98. International Co-operative Alliance, *Verbatim Report of Proceedings of meeting of British members of ICA Central P Committee and representatives of National Movements overseas, Manchester, 24th June, 1954.*

99. International Co-operative Alliance, *Minutes of meeting of British members of ICA Central Committee, 4th November, 1942*, PP. 3-4.

100. International Co-operative Alliance, *ibid.*, p. 4.

101. International Co-operative Alliance, *Report of ICA Congress, Zurich, 1946*, p. 45.

102. International Co-operative Alliance, *Minutes of meeting of British Members of ICA Central Committee, 5th January, 1944*, PP. 5-6.

103. WATKINS, W. P. Interview with W. P. Watkins, 3rd September, 1972.

104. International Co-operative Alliance, *Minutes of meeting of British members of ICA Central Committee, Manchester, 5th January, 1944*, pp. 6-7.
105. Penguin Books Ltd., *The Penguin Concise Columbia Encyclopedia*, Penguin Books Ltd., Harmondsworth, Middlesex, England, 1987, p. 873.
106. International Co-operative Alliance, *Minutes of meeting of British members of ICA Central Committee, Manchester, 5th January, 1944*, p. 6.
107. International Co-operative Alliance, *Report of ICA Congress, Zurich*, 1946, pp. 45-46.
108. ICA Archives, Letter from Mr. Lincoln Clark, UNRRA Consultant on Co-operatives, to Miss G. F. Polley, 23rd January, 1945.
109. International Co-operative Alliance, *Minutes of meeting of British members of ICA Central Committee, Manchester, 5th January, 1944*, p. 8.
110. International Co-operative Alliance, *Report of ICA Congress, Zurich, 1946*, p. 47.
111. WATKINS, W. P., *op. cit.*, p. 219.
112. International Co-operative Alliance, *Report of ICA Congress, Zurich, 1946*, p. 42.
113. International Co-operative Alliance, *Minutes of meeting of British members of ICA Central Committee, London, 2nd June, 1943*, pp. 6-7.
114. International Co-operative Alliance, *Minutes of meeting of British members of ICA Central Committee, 5th January, 1944*, p. 8.
115. International Co-operative Alliance, *Review of International Co-operation*, Nos. 11 and 12 November/December, 1943, p. 190.
116. International Co-operative Alliance, *Review of International Co-operation*, No. 2, February, 1944, p. 21.
117. International Co-operative Alliance, *Review of International Co-operation*, Nos. 11 and 12, November and December, 1943, P. 191.
118. International Co-operative Alliance, *Review of International Co-operation*, No. 2, February, 1944, pp. 21-22.
119. ICA Archives, Letter from Miss G. F. Polley, to Mr J. Avenol,

Secretary General, League of Nations, 1st April, 1940.

120. International Co-operative Alliance, *Minutes of meeting of British members of ICA Central Committee, Manchester, 5th January, 1944*, p. 7.

121. International Co-operative Alliance, *Minutes of meeting of British members of ICA Central Committee, London, 7th March, 1945*.

122. ICA Archives, Letter from Miss G. F. Polley to R. A. Palmer, 20th March, 1945.

123. ICA Archives, *ibid*.

124. ICA Archives, Original typescript of article appearing in *Review of International Co-operation*, Vol. 76, No. 2, 1983, pp. 18-25 of original.

125. International Co-operative Alliance, *Review of International Co-operation*, No. 2, February, 1946, pp. 21-24.

126. International Co-operative Alliance, Memorandum on the Agenda of ICA Executive Meeting, Copenhagen, 18th and 19th March, 1946, p. 2.

Chapter eight

The ICA and the Cold War

Introduction

The ICA had survived the Second World War but, almost immediately, it faced the problems of the Cold War. This time it very nearly did not survive. Previously the Alliance had been on the side of Allies in opposing right-wing authoritarian regimes, but this time the world divide between communists and non-communists came right into the ICA itself. Therefore, the problems it faced were different from those that it had had to surmount in the two World Wars. The way it over came them is the subject matter of this Chapter.

The Immediate Post-War Period

Despite postal problems, the ICA Secretariat had maintained varying degrees of contact with co-operative leaders in occupied countries. Finding out how their co-operative movements had survived the war became an early priority in 1945. In fact, an ICA fact-finding mission visited France even before the end of the war. In February, 1945, R. A. Palmer, Neil Beaton, a British member of the Central Committee, and Miss Polley spent eight days in Paris with permission from the British Foreign Office.

They visited French consumer, agricultural and workers' co-operatives, and reported on the visit to the British Members of the ICA Central Committee at their meeting in London in March, 1945.[1] The British members placed £25,000 from the ICA's Relief Fund at the immediate disposal of the French consumer co-operatives, and also made attempts to find 50 lorries to help them distribute their goods, stipulating that these were not to be requisitioned by the French Government to help overcome its transport needs. In addition, the British Members of the Central Committee approached Co-operative Wholesale Societies in Britain and elsewhere, asking if they could provide credits to the French Co-operative Insurance Society and whether they would consider opening branches in Paris. Larger British retail societies were encouraged to adopt French co-operatives.[2]

Although no ICA delegation went to Moscow, a British Co-operative Delegation had visited Centrosoyus in late 1944. Its members included R. A. Palmer, T. H. Gill and P. J. Agnew, who, also being members of the ICA Central Committee, reported on the visit to a meeting of the British Members of the Central Committee in Manchester in November, 1944.[3] There questions were raised about Centrosoyus's likely attitude to the ICA after the war. Mr N. Sidorov, President of Centrosoyus, had assured the British delegation that the Soviet Union would take a full part in the Alliance's post-war work.

Information about other war-affected co-operative movements - Belgium, Romania, Finland, Poland, Bulgaria, Yugoslavia, Holland, Denmark, and Norway - came through more haphazardly during the first year after the war. Very often, their greatest need was for transport. A Dutch representative wrote:

'You can imagine that the co-operative bakeries are situated centrally and that bread cannot be brought to the surrounding villages. As a result the members must buy their bread at the local middle-class shop. Many people will continue buying there if this situation lasts a long time - hence that supplication for transport material.[4]*'*

This quotation reflects not only a pressing post-war need but also the working class nature of the Dutch movement, characteristics repeated elsewhere in Western European consumer co-operative movements at the time.

Of all the war-torn movements, the Polish seemed to make the quickest and most spirited recovery.[5]

By 1946 £311,215 (sterling) had been raised in the ICA's Relief Fund. British co-operatives, through the Co-operative Union, made the largest contribution of £257,011, while Switzerland gave £28,818, the USA £21,750 and Iceland £3,116. Smaller amounts were received from co-operative organisations in Argentina, Australia, Canada, India, New Zealand and, touchingly, exiled Sudeten German Co-operators living in Britain.[6]

The previously noted need for transport became the area targeted for most assistance. France received 53 lorries, as well as 50 typewriters, huts and shop fittings. Norway received four lorries and lorry accessories, in addition to sieves for flour mills. Between them, Holland and Austria received 12 cars, while Poland received agricultural implements, as well as 100 pairs of scales, building materials and concrete mixers.[7]

The areas of biggest need, however, lay among co-operatives in Germany and Austria, where aid was only one issue and was complicated by the French, British, American and Soviet military occupation of both countries. The ICA sought guardian and trustee roles for both movements during the de-Nazification process which began immediately after the war. Before that, it had tried to send a delegation to Germany, and had expressed its hopes to the British Foreign Office that a voluntary consumers' co-operative movement would be rebuilt once German workers were again granted the rights of free association.[8] Prior to that, the Alliance suggested there was an urgent need for an orderly return of German co-operative assets and, as we have noted, it applied for trusteeship of these.

As early as the end of May, 1945, the British Military Government began, at least as far as its own zone was concerned, the restoration of the German Co-operative Movement: it allowed the Hamburg-based Wholesale Society of German Consumers' Societies to reform and appointed, by order, Henry Everling to be its Managing Director.[9] In Chapter 5 we followed the efforts of Everling and Klepzig to save the German Co-operative Movement from Nazi takeover and their relations with the ICA during that period.

After the war, the ICA's *Review of International Co-operation* noted an awareness in London and Hamburg of the potentiality of the co-operatives as part of a new democratic structure'. [10] Now, with a British Labour Government, R. A. Palmer and Miss Polley found that they could make representations at the highest levels. In January, 1946, they met John Hynd, Chancellor of the Duchy of Lancaster and also Chief of the Control Office for Germany and Austria, who was anxious for an ICA delegation to visit the two countries.[11]

He asked Palmer, who had recently been elevated to the British Peer age and had taken the title of Lord Rusholme, to head a delegation comprising Marcel Brot (France), Albin Johansson (Sweden), Frederick Nielsen (Denmark), and Miss Polley.[12] The delegation arrived in Hamburg, following the meeting of the ICA Executive in Copenhagen in March, 1946. Its first meeting, with Henry Everling and other co-operative leaders, was followed by four days of discussion and fact-finding trips throughout the British Zone. They learned that, after the collapse of the Nazi regime, a number of previous co-operators had tried to take control of former co-operative properties and *'... everywhere Nazis were turned out'*.

They also learned of a notice laying down the conditions under which German co-operative societies could re-establish. These were very much in line with traditional co-operative practices. Their membership had to be voluntary and open to all, each member was to have only one vote, and membership rules must contain no conditions on the religious or political view of members. Even so, *'No person who was an active Nazi shall hold any official position in any Society'*.

Profits were to be distributed among members in proportion to their purchases, and rates of interest on members' investments, as distinct from dividends on purchases, were to be limited. Future wholesale societies had to be related to retail societies in accordance with Co-operative Principles, and finally co-operatives should provide education in those Principles for their members.[13]

After their visit to Germany, Lord Rusholme, Miss Polley and Marcel Brot travelled to Vienna. The resumption of relations between Austrian co-operators and the ICA was already underway as the result of an Austrian initiative at the highest level.

At the first post-war meeting of the ICA Central Committee, held in Zurich in January, 1946, Lord Rusholme received a personal message from Dr Karl Renner, now Chancellor of the Provisional Austrian Government and shortly to become Austria's first post-war President.[14] Renner asked if Rusholme could meet Dr Vukowitch, of the Central

Union of Austrian Consumers' Societies, and Dr Strobl, from the Austrian Agricultural Co-operative Movement, at Dornbirn, on the Austrian-Swiss border. He was unable to go, but asked the Swiss Co-operative Movement if it could help. The Swiss arranged for a Dr Mühlemann to meet Vukowitch and Strobl.[15]

Mühlemann's report to Miss Polley in London provides a graphic account of Austrian co-operatives' post-war difficulties. The Allies' four zones of military occupation in Austria were:

'..... *isolated hermetically. Only by surmounting enormous difficulties can one cross the lines of demarcation. It is characteristic that up to the recent past the temporary Central Management of the Austrian Co-operative Movement, which lies in the hands of the two above-named gentlemen (Dr. Vukowitch and Dr. Strobl), as well as of Mr. Korp and another co-operator from Vienna, were only able to get in touch with their adherent Consumers' Co-operative Societies by functionaries risking their lives when travelling from one zone to another without permit, and to whom it very often happened to be robbed. Austrian economy as a whole is almost paralysed.*'[16]

Dr Mühlemann said that Vukowitch and Strobl estimated that approximately 65 per cent of the assets of Austrian consumer co-operatives had been lost through societies' being absorbed into the German system, bombing, war action and pillaging.

'*A great part of the warehouses... have been destroyed or heavily damaged. The warehouses of the Wholesale, as far as they still exist, are situated in the Russian zone of Vienna where they have been completely robbed by the occupants and moreover, severely damaged. The same is true of the wine cellars. The Co-operative Society of Vienna....... lost 160 out of their 320 stores by military action.*'

Thus, when the ICA delegation arrived in Vienna on 27th March, 1946, they were partly prepared for what they would find. Problems were compounded by a crippling lack of transport and difficulties in restoring co-operative property. Although the Provisional Austrian Government had agreed that assets stolen from the Roman Catholic Church, the Trade Unions and the Co-operative Movement should be restored, impediments remained as far as co-operatives were concerned.

One was that Austrian co-operative property had become part of the assets of the German Labour Front. But the offices controlling these had been in Hamburg, and no disposal of German assets in Austria could be made without the consent of the Allied Powers in Germany, including the USSR. This was further complicated by the fact that, under the Potsdam Declaration of the previous year, the USSR had the right to a share of German foreign assets in Eastern Austria. However, this could change if a pending decision acknowledged that Austria had been the first victim of Hitler's aggression. But, even if the Potsdam decision were upheld, there were plans to introduce legislation restoring trade union and co-operative property on the grounds that the Potsdam Declaration should not apply to the property of 'workers' organisations'.

The ICA Delegation found that, whereas the British Military Government in Germany had laid down the framework for the re-establishment of German co-operatives, no similar action had taken in Austria. So far only four Trustees - Korp, Vukowitch, Strobl and Beck - had been appointed to administer co-operative property, although they had drafted model rules including one requiring 'Cash Trading' in all societies. The ICA delegation also learned that every co-operative meeting held since the end of the war had voted in favour of political neutrality. However, the Delegation found that this was not necessarily protecting the fledgling consumer societies from the hostility of private traders, which was reported to be as strong as ever it had been before 1934.

Dr Karl Renner had become President of Austria by the time that the ICA delegation arrived, but he found time to receive them twice. He then spoke about the difficulties that Austria faced and his hopes for the future. He also asked a number of questions about the Alliance, showing

'... that his interest in its work and its future progress is as great today as during the long years when he was a member of its Central Committee'[17].

At the time that the ICA delegations visited Germany and Austria, the position in Italy was far less well known: there had been no direct

Subscriptions received for the years 1946 and 1947

	1946.			1947.		
	£	s.	d.	£	s.	d.
Argentina	14	0	0	82	0	0
Australia	20	0	0	20	0	0
Austria	—			215	0	0
Belgium	220	0	0	240	0	0
Bulgaria	—			—		
Canada	33	0	0	86	0	0
China	50	0	0	80	0	0
Czechoslovakia	*			600	0	0
Denmark	220	0	0	480	0	0
Finland	652	15	0	816	15	0
France	269	8	0	1,667	4	0
Greece	*			80	0	0
Great Britain	4,696	17	0	7,504	0	0
Holland	221	5	0	381	15	0
Iceland	38	12	0	80	0	0
India	—			—		
Israel	100	0	0	100	0	0
Italy	*			—		
Norway	124	18	0	230	3	0
Poland	380	0	0	1,151	9	0
Roumania	*			*		
South Africa	—			6	0	0
Sweden	1,065	0	0	1,216	18	0
Switzerland	634	3	0	573	19	0
U.S.A.	77	13	0	600	0	0
U.S.S.R.	3,500	0	0	5,000	0	0
Yugoslavia	40	0	0	80	0	0
	12,357	11	0	21,291	3	0

* Organisations not in membership in 1946.

213

contact between Italian co-operators and the Alliance. However, the resurrected ICA Executive Committee, meeting in Copenhagen in March, 1946, received indirect news through the Swiss Co-operative Union. The Union had received two issues of *La Cooperzione Italiana*, one of which reported the first post-war meeting of the ICA Central Committee at Zurich the previous January. It also gave a brief history of the Alliance, so that 'especially the younger generation may realise the significance of the meeting' and recalled past actions of the Alliance on behalf of the Lega. [18]

The other issue of *La Cooperazione* Italiana had called for unity among Italian co-operatives.[19] However, from John Earle's book *The Italian Co-operative Movement*, we learn that hopes for a unified Italian co-operative movement were dashed when the Catholic Confederation's Co-operative Italiano re-established itself, but declined to merge with the Lega.[20] Later, against the background of Cold War politics in Italy, this failure to achieve an amalgamation would have significance within the ICA.

Before looking at how the German, Austrian and Italian Co-operative Movements rejoined the ICA, we should perhaps look at the rest of the ICA's membership in the immediate post-war period, and at the reconstitution of the Executive and Central Committees. Page 302 gives a subscription list which was reported to the 1948 Congress in Prague.[21] The increase in Argentinean membership was largely due to the work of Czechoslovak exile, and past member of the ICA Executive, Emil Lustig, [22]

Elsewhere, the Co-operative League of China, established in 1940, joined the Alliance in 1945 [23] and, earlier that year, the Co-operative Federation of Australia had also affiliated. [24]

Furthermore, we can gather from the table that Austria and Italy had been readmitted. Despite some delays in payment of subscriptions the ICA's membership base was being reconstituted.

303

When it came to representation on the Central Committee it was found that only 29 of the 57 members in 1939 were still nominated in 1945,[25] The Committee therefore had to be reconstituted, and ICA member organisations were invited to nominate temporary representatives to sit on it until the first Congress was held.

We saw in the last Chapter that the British Movement, like Centrosoyus, was anxious that the Committee should meet as soon as possible, and notices for a meeting were sent out on 26th May, 1945, only 18 days after the end of the War in Europe.[26]

However, it could not strictly be a meeting of the Central Committee, which was still in the process of being reconstituted. Consequently, it came to be known as the 'London Conference', and attendance was on the basis of those member organisations which were able to send representatives to London. These numbered 56 from co-operative movements in Belgium, Denmark, Finland, France, Great Britain, Iceland, Holland, Norway, Palestine (Israel), Poland, Sweden, Switzerland, the USA and the USSR. The speed with which the conference was called, and the number who attended at a time when there were still many travel problems, indicated the degree of enthusiasm that ICA member movements felt for renewing links and activities.

Because the London Conference was not an official organ of the ICA it could not determine policy. It did, however, laydown markers. Two important 'statements' were discussed and adopted. The first, submitted by the Swedish and American delegations, was based on the Atlantic Charter,[27] which had laid down the fundamental principles for the post-war world and had been agreed by Roosevelt and Churchill in 1941. The Swedish and American statement also reflected a post war concern over raw materials and urged the newly established United Nations to take measures to restrain monopolies and cartels. This would enable co-operatives to obtain equitable shares of raw materials in order to realise the people's aspirations for freedom from want.[28]

The second statement, proposed by the Swedish delegation alone, reflected post-war issues. It argued that a prerequisite of the full employment of all productive resources was an expansion of the economy and, included within it, the Co-operative movement. To attain these goals it was necessary to stabilise currency and exchange rates; eliminate obstacles to international trade; abolish quota systems for raw materials and imported goods; and ban restrictive and monopolistic policies.[29]

French delegates also submitted a statement but, because it was opposed, it was remitted to the first meeting of the Central Committee, at which it was amended and passed. It is quoted here in full because it leads on from the Warbasse/Fabra-Ribas/Palmer debate in the last Chapter, and heralds subsequent debates at the Zurich and Prague Congresses, in 1946 and 1948, concerning the relationship between co-operatives and the State. The statement shows two important things as far as the ICA's philosophical base is concerned. One was that it could be flexible, yet pragmatic, in the face of social and economic changes hastened by the war. The other was its belief that the State should embrace the co-operative idea of 'an economy of service above an economy of profit'.

'Considering that the evolution of liberal capitalism into a capitalism of cartels and trusts, as well as the situation resulting from the war, imposes on the State the task of ensuring, by deliberate measures of organisation, the restoration of national economies and of international economy;

Considering that this imposes on the Co-operative Movement the necessity of defining its position with regard to those changes which the action of the State is bringing about in the structure of the economy;

Recognises that there is identity of aims between co-operative action and the action of the State, provided that the latter be freed from any coalition of private interests, and that it corresponds to the necessity of an organisation which places an economy of service above an economy of profit, both from a national and an international point of view. The Co-operative Movement is aware that the State is being led to take measures in order to assume the direction of the whole sphere of economy. But the action of the State necessarily has limits, and in its efforts towards the general organisation of economy it cannot do without the collaboration of co-operative institutions of all kinds. Co-operation, being an organisation built up from below, and which groups, in federated organisations, units of a personal and family character, which are at the basis of economic and social life both in towns and in the country, is the only organisation capable of linking those units organically with any plan embracing the whole economy.

Once this is recognised there will be no opposition, but rather a judicious distribution of tasks and a reciprocal collaboration between the activities of the State and those of Co-operative organisations that must be associated with the State activities.

The Co-operative Movement is, therefore, entitled to claim from the public authorities the liberty of its full development in the large fields of economic life where co-operation succeeds in reconciling order, efficiency, and liberty, by a freely accepted discipline, and the putting into practice of the principles of self-help and mutuality.' [30]

From the above it can be seen that together the London Conference of September, 1945, and the first meeting of the reconstituted Central Committee four months later, marked a robust resumption of ICA policy-making. In this it was matched by vigorous re-establishment of the organisational side of the Alliance. The Central Committee elected a new President and Vice-Presidents, and considered the appointment of a new General Secretary. On this last question the Executive was asked to advertise the position and invite member organisations to make nominations.[31]

The question of the Presidency could be decided more quickly. Lord Rusholme was elected unanimously and new Vice-Presidents were also soon elected. Whereas these were traditionally French and British, a widening in the balance of power within the Alliance could be detected with the election of Albin Johansson (Sweden), and Mr N. Sidorov of the USSR.[32] This trend was also shown in the elections to the Executive Committee to which an American, Murray D. Lincoln, was elected for the first time.

The first post-war Congress was held in 1946, and took place in Zurich. Perhaps not surprisingly, the *Review of International Co-operation* waxed lyrical about the dignity and beauty of the Zurich Krongresshaus adorned by rainbow flags and other 'co-operative symbols', which provided a striking setting for delegates from war-scarred and devastated countries', who could enjoy the spiritual rehabilitation at being again on the terrain of the ICA.[33]

367 delegates came from Austria, Belgium, Bulgaria, Canada, Czechoslovakia, Denmark, Finland, France, Great Britain, Holland, Iceland, Norway, Palestine (Israel), Poland, Sweden, Switzerland, the USA, the USSR and Yugoslavia.[34] Twelve of those 19 countries had been occupied during the war.

The ICA's Zurich Congress of 1946 is significant for what it tells us about the Alliance's post-war thinking. For example, how much of this would be a carry-over from before the war, and how much would be due to the war and events immediately afterwards? In the latter category we can already place the ICA's evolving attitude to the State and nationalisation. Similarly, the effect of bitter wartime experiences: Centrosoyus was not only hostile to Väinö Tanner, but critical of the Alliance for not having done more to try to prevent the war.[35] N. P. Sidorov, one of the Alliance's new Vice-Presidents, attributed much of this ineffectualness to Väinö Tanner's influence as the Alliance's President, a view strongly contested by Lord Rusholme.

Despite this heated exchange, the debate on the Central Committee's Report, covering the years 1937-1946, was remarkably free from post war acrimony; it was also constructive and forward-looking. The proposal to form an auxiliary committee for workers' co-operatives was welcomed by Mr A. Antoni (France). Mr S. Apelquist (Sweden) urged the need to develop co-operative insurance societies to compete with private companies, and the United Nations was kept well to the fore both with the presence of a UN Observer, Miss Catherine Rolfe, and the suggestion by Murray Lincoln (USA) that the ICA should appoint permanent representatives to the UN. Mr Ch. H. Barbier, on behalf of the Swiss Movement, proposed the setting up of an International Co-operative Press Agency, among whose objectives would be the promotion of peace.

The rest of the Congress agenda was also forward-looking with four big set debates: "The Future Programme and Policy of the ICA"; the 'International Exchange of Goods from the Consumers' Point of View'; 'Co-operation and Public Authorities'; and a resolution concerning 'The Control of the World's Oil Resources'. This last initiative showed that the new generation of ICA leaders could be as dynamic and forward looking as earlier ones had been, but it ran almost immediately into wider political difficulties. Wanting more time to consider the implications, the Soviet delegates moved that the question be referred to the Central Committee. This was defeated, and the resulting resolution read:

'Whereas equal access to natural resources, as set out in the Atlantic Charter, must be considered an irrevocable condition of economic construction, or re-building free interchange of goods among nations and of the maintenance of peace; and

'Whereas experience has proved that international rivalry over raw material resources either on the part of predatory private monopolists or on the part of imperialistic governments, or both, lead to an unbalance in economic affairs, inevitable conflicts, and the jeopardising of peace, such as we have witnessed recently, for example, in the struggle for control of oil resources in the Middle East; and

'Whereas development of such natural resources by consumer Co-operatives will operate to checkmate monopolistic concentrations and tend to lead away from rather than towards war, conflicts over oil resources being an ever-present threat to world peace; now, therefore be it.

'Resolved that with a view to implementing the Atlantic Charter and safe guarding the supply of this vital raw material for all national households - the 16th Congress of the International Co-operative Alliance emphasizes in strongest terms the immediate need of placing control and administration of the oil resources of the world under an authority of the United Nations, and,

as a first step in that direction, the oil resources of the Middle East, by and with the consent of the States involved, these resources to be administered in such a way that Co-operative Organisations can be assured of receiving an equitable share'.

In passing, we should observe that the growing significance of oil supplies had been noted within the ICA a decade earlier. A proposal for an International Petroleum Association had surfaced at the Alliance's Congress in Paris in 1937, although conditions were not then considered right for proceeding. During the intervening years, American co-operatives had developed the production and distribution of petroleum products to an extent that they had become the largest independent distributor and owned nearly 500 oil wells. After forming the Co-operative Oil Association they had been able to reduce petrol prices by around 50 per cent, and had overcome difficulties with oil combines. As a result, at Zurich, Howard A. Cowden, Vice-President of the Co-operative League of the USA could say that:

'.... the oil combines are not all-powerful, that they are not as powerful as they would have us think they are, and that the common people themselves have in their own hands the tools to shape their own destiny.'

But he acknowledged that part of American co-operatives' success in oil was due to a 'good friend', President Roosevelt.

Cowden reported that plans were well advanced for an International Co-operative Petroleum Association, which had a start-up capital of $15 million, and whose founding members would be co-operative organisations in Belgium, China, Cuba, France, Scotland, Sweden, the United States, Switzerland, Canada, Australia, South Africa, Iceland, Norway, Finland, Egypt, Palestine (Israel), Italy, Tunisia and Siam (Thailand). Cowden said:

'... I hope the time will come when tankers with the Rainbow Flag at the masthead will sail the seven seas, carrying a message of peace and goodwill and Co-operation, as contrasted with the exploitation of cartels.'

We can perhaps stay with this issue and follow it through later moves, although doing so takes us beyond the immediate post-war period. They are important in as much as they illustrate the difficulties of an international NGO operating within the UN system during its early stages.

The oil resolution passed at the Zurich Congress was forwarded to the Secretary-General of the UN[36] and, in an attempt to gain governmental support, co-operative movements in Czechoslovakia, Great Britain and Norway forwarded copies of the resolution to their own governments.[37]

When the ICA Central Committee held its next meeting in Avignon in May, 1947, it reaffirmed the Zurich resolution. It also acted on Murray Lincoln's proposal at the Zurich Congress, and accepted the offer of Sweden's Kooperativa Forbundet to second Thorsten Odhe to become the Alliance's Permanent Representative at the UN in New York. One of Odhe's first jobs was to prepare a memorandum supporting the ICA resolution and submitting it for inclusion on the agenda of the next session of the UN's Economic and Social Council.[38]

It soon became clear that some governments were cautious of, or even hostile to, the ICA's proposals. When these were discussed by the Economic and Social Council on 12th August, 1947, the Soviet Union, although sympathetic to parts of the proposal that criticised monopolistic oil interests, was not prepared to support it. The Lebanon strongly opposed it. However, the outcome turned on the British view that the proposal 'was unripe for action by the United Nations'. They proposed a resolution, passed by eight votes to two with eight abstentions, that the Council should merely take note of the ICA's case.[39]

We should, perhaps, remind ourselves that the British view was that of a Labour Government and that it may not have been as unsympathetic as it appeared. At the meeting of the ICA Executive in Amsterdam in January, 1948, Lord Rusholme and Miss Polley reported:

'We... had the great advantage of a private and confidential talk with Mr. Ernest Bevin, British Foreign Secretary, who explained to us the reasons for

the attitude of the British delegates at the last meeting of the Economic and Social Council towards the ICA Resolution. We were all greatly impressed with the meeting, which suggested possible new lines of thought both as regards the Resolution and I.C.P.A.* action'.[40]

* *International Co-operative Petroleum Association*

Bevin's advice seems likely to have included suggested modifications to the original ICA resolution because the Executive reintroduced the question at the next meeting of the Central Committee. When a new resolution was submitted to the Committee at its meeting in Rome in May, 1947, it decided that, because the original resolution had been passed by one Congress, the new resolution should go before the next Congress, now only four months away[41]. It was there, in Prague, 1948, that a new resolution was proposed, reflecting a widening from oil to raw materials generally.

'The 17th Congress of the International Co-operative Alliance stresses the urgent necessity of an effective implementation of the principle of the Atlantic Charter of free and equal access to the raw material resources of the world for the maintenance of a lasting peace;

Further, that these raw material resources to an ever-increasing extent are being exploited by monopolistic combinations, cartels and trusts, active in the national or international field, with a view to deriving excessive profit by restricting production and establishing domination of the markets of distribution;

Also that this development, in the case of certain important raw materials such as petroleum, has had the effect that, in spite of abundant potential resources, the supply available during periods of particularly heavy demand cannot satisfy the growing needs, with the result that, in the present situation, a world shortage of petroleum has arisen.

'The Congress, therefore, emphasises the urgency that this development be submitted for study to a suitable organ or specialised agency within the frame work of the United Nations Organization to serve as a basis for measures to be taken with a view to safeguarding, by international agreement, the expan-

sion of production and free access to petroleum, also to providing for the consumers all reasonable facilities cover their needs through organisations of their own.'

The British delegate moving it, Mr J. M. Davidson, provided an insight into the interests watching ICA developments. Recalling the observers from the major oil companies who had sat in the galleries at the Zurich Congress, he said:

The fact that the Congress of the ICA attracted hundreds of leaders from more than a score of countries, and that the ICA has permanent consultative status with the United Nations, not only impressed but disturbed the oil companies. The efforts of Co-operators to emphasise the need to study the question and to place the control and administration of oil resources of the world under the authority of the United Nations, have been more effective in high places than most of us realise.[42]

An amendment, proposed by the International Co-operative Petroleum Association, suggested the insertion of the words 'private and State capitalistic' following being 'exploited by' in paragraph 2. This drew opposition from the Soviet delegation, which moved that the word 'capitalistic' should be inserted before the word 'monopolistic' in paragraph 2. They also disagreed with the proposal to establish a specialised agency within the UN.

In opposing both Soviet suggestions, T. H. Gill (Great Britain), who was shortly to be elected President of the ICA, argued that Congress would make a tremendous mistake if it agreed that oil owned by the State should be excluded from any enquiry.

The ICPA amendment was then carried, and the Soviet one defeated. A second resolution on control of world resources was then passed and resubmitted to the UN's Economic and Social Council. There it became caught up in various mishaps. A 'technical error' arose from the fact that the documentation in which it should have been included was not distributed to delegates in time, and this led to the question being deferred until the next session of the Council. It was then deferred on two more occasions, and only reached the Council at its meeting in Chile in 1951. There the British delegation successfully moved that, because an oil shortage no longer existed, the question should be dropped. Unfortunately, the matter arose at a stage in the agenda when Non-Governmental Organisations' representatives were not entitled to address the Council.

In his history of the ICA, W. P. Watkins, who by this time in 1951 had become Director of the Alliance, wrote that the ICA Central Committee could only express its regret. He suspected, though:

'that in reality none of the major powers had been really happy that a question so full of political "dynamite" had been submitted at all' [43]

The ICA's initiative on the world's oil supplies shows that the ICA was prepared to act on important issues. However, the experience indicated that, where the interests of major States were involved, the influence of Non-Governmental Organisations would be severely limited within the UN. In tracing the outcome of this question we have gone beyond the immediate post-war period. We should now briefly conclude this section by noting changes within ICA leadership which were about to become significant as Cold War politics burst in on the ICA.

An organisation's ability to move from one generation to the next suggests that its philosophy and values transcend the personalities of its leaders. When we examine the ICA leadership after 1945 we see that, in personal terms, there had been considerable changes. May, Poisson, Goedhart, Suter, Jaeggi and Serwy had died and Väinö Tanner was in prison. Against these losses, however, we should note that, in terms of the member co-operative movements which led the ICA, there had been little change. The most important of these movements were still the British, French, and Swedish, but it had become clear during the war that the American movement might seek to play a more influential role. As far as the Soviet movement was concerned, it was still unclear in 1945-46 how far it would use its undoubted weight as far as subscriptions and votes were concerned. Despite its size, Centrosoyus had not played as large a role in the pre-war ICA as had traditional Alliance leaders, the British, French and Swedes.

We should note that, whatever American aspirations might have been, in terms of membership and subscriptions to the ICA the American movement was small. During the war its subscription had ranged from £74 to £149.[44] This rose dramatically to £600 in 1947,[45] indicating perhaps that the Americans intended to increase their influence within the Alliance. But this was still way below the £5,000 paid by Centrosoyus, which had nine members on the Central Committee compared to the Americans' two. However, we shall find that, as we go on to consider the ICA and the Cold War, it was Western European co-operative movements, rather than their American counterpart, that resisted the Communist designs on the Alliance.

The ICA and The Cold - Introduction

At the outset we should note that the problems created for the ICA by the Cold War were far more internal than those posed by the two World Wars. As we have seen, the Alliance considered itself to be hardly part of the 1914-18 war, while during the 1939-45 war it was firmly on the side of the Allies. But, with a Cold War, stemming from the clash between the American capitalism and Soviet Communism, the ICA could not remain similarly detached. The Co-operative League of the USA had affiliated to the ICA in 1917, while Centrosoyus's membership went back even further to 1903. At least by the time that the Second World War began, the Italian, German and Austrian co-operative movements were no longer members of the ICA, and at no time had they approached the size or significance of the Soviet movement.

Unlike the two World Wars, the Cold War did not begin on a particular day with declarations of war between specific nations. Instead, suspicious and hostile attitudes built up between Western democracies, headed by the USA, and the Eastern socialist countries, led by the USSR. Although a momentum gathered in the later 1940s, perceptions that a Cold War existed developed only gradually both within the ICA and elsewhere. Wilfried Loth, in his book, The Division of The World 1941-1955, suggests that the Cold War could be taken to have begun and ended at different times, depending from which point of view the question was approached. If the Cold War was seen as the way that people perceived events, or the terms in which they spoke, it could be said to have begun in 1947. If, however, it was seen as the conflict between the USA and the USSR and its resultant impact on Europe, the starting date was likely to have been 1917 and the Russian Revolution. Should the Cold War be taken to be the actual antagonism between the USA and USSR and its impact on the international system, then its starting date was likely to have been 1943.[46]

Loth suggests that:

'... these uses of the term 'Cold War' are so imprecise in terms of content that in the interests of precise conceptualisation it would be advisable to limit the term to the central process from 1941 to 1955...'

He then went on to describe the Cold War as being the establishment of a new international order after the Second World War, based on the formation of blocs. On one side was the liberal-capitalist system of the USA which was:

'set on establishing a tendentious world-wide system of free trade in order to avoid profound economic crises and secure its socio-political status-quo, being at the same time set on the unlimited economic expansion of the USA'.

On the other side:

'The Soviet mobilisation dictatorship oriented itself according to its claim to be centre of a world revolutionary movement and could only survive by protecting itself from these liberal principles, by opposing the forward economic march of the USA with a counteracting force and by freeing itself from the pressure of aggressive neighbouring states in its western forefield'.

The above appear to be good working definitions as far as this study is concerned. Without going into too much detail as to how these opposing forces worked out in practice, we should at least note their effect on the ICA's post-war policy.

Germany was to be a pivotal area as East-West suspicions grew. C. J. Bartlett, in his book, The Global Conflict 1880-1970, agreed that whereas the British and American Governments wished to ensure that their

German occupation zones created as small a drain as possible on local economies, the Soviets saw their Zone as a means of speeding up their own recovery through reparations. As Bartlett observed:

'The incompatibility of allied economic interests is evident, and competition could only worsen once attention turned to the long-term future of a people who could not be trusted to determine their own destiny but whose exclusive control by Russia or the western powers would have the most serious impact upon the balance of power in Europe'.[47]

We should, therefore, begin our examination of the Cold War and the ICA by looking at how relations developed between the Alliance and co-operatives in Germany. By September, 1946, the Central Committee's Report to the Zurich Congress, indicated that the 'economic', 'political' and 'legal and administrative difficulties' of re-establishing co-operatives in Germany were 'closely linked with the general political problems of East West tension.'[48]

'So far as the political difficulties are concerned, they are mainly a result of the zonal frontiers between Eastern and Western Germany, which were never meant to be trade barriers, but tend to become ever stronger barriers to trade, also to ideas, news, etc. the more the gap widens between the economic and political structures of the Eastern and Western Zones. Germany lives in a field of tension between two ideologies and between two political systems, between two fundamentally different conceptions of what is the place of man in that society.'

We can see from this that trying to harmonise co-operative redevelopment in the four occupation zones was going to prove difficult. However, the ICA Executive was still hoping to achieve this, as can be seen from its meeting at Avignon in April, 1947,[49] when Lord Rusholme said that there was 'a unanimous desire' for the 'rebuilding of a unified Co-operative Movement, with a Central Union and Wholesale'.

Difficulties in achieving this led to the British, French and American zones of occupation agreeing to the re-establishment of the German Wholesale Society (GEG) in April, 1948. This became a three-zoned co-operative organisation, which immediately applied to join the ICA.

Sidorov (USSR) opposed this on the grounds that the full unification of the German movement should precede this, but, at its meeting in Rome in May, 1948, the Executive agreed to the admission.[50]

At the following Central Committee meeting the next day, Sidorov repeated his arguments and was now supported by J. Zerbowski and J. Jasinki (Poland), J. Moravec (Czechoslovakia) and Mr Orekhanow from the Centrosoyus delegation. Even so, the admission was endorsed by 30 votes to 14.[51] As the combined Soviet, Polish and Czechoslovak delegates numbered 14, we can deduce that they voted as a block. We should also note that GEG's admission to the ICA was achieved at great speed, and that Centrosoyus's representatives seem to have been taken by surprise. In many ways, the admission of the GEG, based on three of the four zones of occupation in Germany, marked the arrival of the Cold War in the ICA.

There is a sad irony that countries which had been threatened by the Nazis in the 1930s were similarly threatened by Soviet Communism in the late 1940s. Wilfried Loth, in his book, The Division of the World, shows that this development had not been inevitable, but was a consequence of the worsening relations between the USA and the USSR.[52] The latter felt that her power and security were once again threatened, 'if not acutely... at least potentially and in the long term'. Soviet responses had the effect of limiting East European countries' room for manoeuvre.

Loth further suggested that:
'Without any definite concept for the future social order in the countries of this region, the Soviet Government had attempted, by means of swift economic stabilisation after its initial plundering, partial democratic reforms ...... and a definite share of Communists in power to create guarantees for a policy that would not be hostile to the Soviet Union'.

As this policy developed, it affected countries seeking their own political stability in the wake of Nazi occupation and post-war dislocation. Moreover, some groups in these countries were receptive to American talk of self-determination, and were not necessarily convinced that they should fall into step with Soviet strategy. Where such doubts existed, local Communists tried to tighten their political hold, sometimes even with the help of the Red Army. By also manipulating elections and weakening the hold of Peasant parties, and with occasional terrorist acts, Communists gained control in Bulgaria in 1946, and Po land, Romania and Hungary in 1947.[53]

Recognition elsewhere that a Soviet bloc was developing was reinforced by Soviet and East European reactions to the USA's proposed Marshall Plan. Alarmed at slow economic recovery in Western Europe, America proposed the Marshall Plan, through which America would channel aid throughout the whole of Europe as a 'co-ordinated European programme of reconstruction'.[54]

Although the USSR was cautious, some East European countries responded favourably, thus leading the Soviet leadership to instruct East European Governments, 'under massive pressure', not to proceed.

Similar pressure was also put on Communist parties in the West: initially the French, Italian and Belgian Communist parties had welcomed the Marshall Plan. In September, 1947, Soviet leaders called a conference of Yugoslav, Bulgarian, Romanian, Hungarian, Czechoslovak, French and Italian Communists, at which a stronger anti-American stance emerged. Instead of being seen as a benevolent power, the USA was accused of leading those countries that were preparing for a new imperialist war against socialism and democracy, and of supporting reactionary pro-fascist regimes and movements. Moscow now argued that the Marshall Plan was part of an aggressive course of economic expansion which was designed to enslave Europe by binding a block of States to American monopoly power. This was aimed at bringing the 'impoverished victorious countries.... into dependence on the restored economic power of Germany and German imperialism'. Soviet leaders argued that it was necessary to counter this and, to do so, develop an 'anti-imperialist democratic camp' under Soviet leadership.

The conference ended with the decision to set up a joint Communist Information Bureau, or Cominform, which would draw up a common platform and design tactics against 'American imperialism, against its

English and French allies, against Right-wing Socialists, above all in England and France.' [55]

Three observations should be made about the effect of these developments on the ICA. The first is that by the end of 1947 two power blocks had emerged in the post-war world. Their leaders, the USA and the USSR, had co-operative organisations that were members of the ICA, creating the danger of the ICA becoming polarised between the Co-operative League of the USA and Centrosoyus. The second point is that the right-wing socialists', who were castigated as being part of the imperialist conspiracy, were the very ones with whom ICA leaders had traditional affinity. The third point is that the organisation of the Cominform covered not only the Communist parties in East European countries, but also those in Western Europe. Consequently, Soviet influence extended into more pluralist countries, affecting their co-operative movements and, through them, the ICA. This indirect Soviet influence was most notable with the left-wing Italian Lega Nazionale delle Cooperative e Mutue, referred to subsequently as the Lega. After its re-affiliation to the ICA in January, 1947 [56], the Lega frequently voted in line with Soviet delegates and caused problems on several issues. In addition to those countries, such as Poland, Hungary and Czechoslovakia, that were now brought under Soviet domination, there were others such as Estonia, Latvia and Lithuania, which had enjoyed a short-lived independence between the two wars but which were now reabsorbed into the USSR. In consequence, their co-operative movements became part of Centrosoyus.

While these developments raised concern in the ICA they led to no direct action, unless the unusually quick admission of West Germany's GEG be interpreted in this way. However, the question of whether the location of the next ICA Congress, scheduled to be held in Prague in September 1948, should be changed was raised at the Central Committee's meeting in Rome the previous May.

Mr J. J. A. Charbo (Holland) said that:
...in the opinion of nearly all of my compatriots, Czechoslovakia is considered as to be a country where freedom is no longer sufficiently existing and

that, by consequence, the Prague sphere should be considered as to be unfavourable for the Congress of the worldwide Co-operative Movement which is based upon freedom and voluntarism'.

Charbo emphasised that he wanted to avoid any political discussion, but felt that if a Dutch delegation took part in the Congress it would be seen as

'an explicit demonstration..... in favour of the political ideology dominating now in Czechoslovakia as cannot be in accordance with the absolute political neutrality of our Movement' [57]

Rather surprisingly, Charbo received no support. Indeed, Mr. J. M. Davidson (Great Britain) argued that:

'The ICA should not concern itself with the political set-up in any country and should go to Prague irrespective of the political regime within Czechoslovakia' [58]

It is difficult to imagine a similar statement having been made about holding a Congress in Italy, Germany or Spain in the 1930s. No vote was taken and Prague thus remained the venue of the next Congress.[59] The episode suggests that, with no clear declaration of war, the ICA was cautious about assuming that one existed.

The Dutch were ahead of the rest of the Alliance in taking an overtly anti-communist position. While the Executive and Central Committees were more cautious, they soon became resolute, and adept, at deflecting increasing Soviet attempts to gain control of the Alliance.

As we shall see, the Soviet block within the ICA wanted to control rather than to divide. The issue therefore became whether non-communist resistance to such attempts could be effective or whether a split became inevitable, as happened in very similar circumstances in the World Federation of Trade Unions in 1949. Soviet pressures within the ICA manifested themselves in four main areas: attempts to shape ICA agendas; proposals to amend the Alliance's Rules and, closely related to this, the increased affiliation of communist co-operative movements;

attempts to exercise greater control over the ICA Secretariat; and, above all, efforts to shape the Alliance's policy on peace.

We will examine each of these in turn, although there is some artificiality in doing so because all were closely inter-related and often over lapped in time.

Communist Attempts to Determine ICA Agendas

The Central Committee's meeting in Rome, 1948, marked a heightening of tension within the Alliance.

In addition to considering the re-admission of GEG, the Central Committee was required under the ICA's Constitution to determine the Agenda of the coming Congress in Prague, finalise its report to the Congress, and consider proposals for amendments to ICA Rules that would go before Congress, the first major revision since the 1937 Paris Congress.

By mid-1948 Centrosoyus invariably had distinct points of view on most issues coming before the Central Committee. This soon proved to be the case in Rome, when Centrosoyus delegates criticised the draft Manifesto due to be issued on the 26th International Co-operative Day on 3rd July, 1948. They had prepared an alternative calling on national co-operative movements to celebrate the day by organising mass meetings to support the

'struggle for lasting peace and democracy, against the incendiaries of the new imperialist war, against the mass executions of Greek patriots, who had been fighting against German invaders and now being executed by the Government of Athens, of protest against support of fascist regime of Franco in Spain by the Governments of the USA, England and France, and for the improvement of the economic position of the toilers'.

The Swedes soon invoked the Alliance's political neutrality. Albin Johansson reminded the Central Committee that International Co-operative Day was the occasion when co-operators reaffirmed faith in their principles, but there was no mention of these in Centrosoyus's alternative Manifesto. Instead, it contained only 'political questions which were not the concern of the ICA'. The Central Committee agreed, and went on to endorse the version of the Manifesto prepared by the Secretariat and approved by the Executive, by 26 votes to 15.[60]

The question of the Congress' agenda had still to be settled at the Rome meeting and, in the proposals from Sidorov, we can see Centrosoyus's sharpened thrust in support of peace and the workers. Sidorov moved that the agreed paper on 'The Future Policy and Programme of the ICA' should be replaced by one considering The Tasks of the International Co-operative Movement in the Struggle for Peace', and that the paper to be prepared by Albin Johansson (Sweden) on The Practical Formation of International Co-operation in the Economic Sphere' should be substituted by one on The Tasks of Co-operation in Defence of the Economic and Social Rights of the Toilers'. Sidorov also proposed a completely new paper on The Development of Co-operation in Colonial and Undeveloped Territories'.[61]

As we shall find on later occasions, the Executive and Central Committees used procedural, or constitutional, tactics to resist Soviet moves. The Rome meeting provided good examples. While indicating the Executive's agreement on a paper on Co-operation in the Colonies, the President said that the Executive believed that Albin Johansson's paper should proceed because it was being prepared at the request of the Central Committee and would, in any event, propose measures to 'improve the economic position of the peoples as a whole'. As to the paper on the ICA's Future Policy and Programme, Rusholme suggested that removing it would go against a decision of the Zurich Congress, which had requested the report. In the end, the Soviet delegates did not force the issue, but then moved to attack the Central Committee's Draft Report to Congress. Soviet, Italian and Polish delegates strongly criticised those parts referring to Germany, while Soviet delegates urged that more should be said about what the ICA had done on peace and the improvement of the people's lives.[62]

At the end of the debate a vote was avoided by the expedient of asking the Secretariat to revise the report in the light of the discussion and to send new sections to members of the Central Committee for them to approve by post.

The Rome meeting was not the only occasion when Soviet delegates tried to shape ICA agendas. This happened many times throughout the Cold war, and we shall find other examples as we deal with related issues. We now move on to the next of these, namely changes to ICA Rules.

Soviet Proposals for ICA Rules Revision, 1948

We should note that no major changes had been made to the ICA Rules for over a decade. Some limited ones, made at the Zurich Congress, 1946, had concerned only the Alliance's finances.[63] Because of the war no other major changes had been possible since the Congress in Paris in 1937. Then the eligibility for ICA membership had been redefined in the light of the review of Co-operative Principles which had been concluded at that Congress. Rules changes in 1937 had also redefined membership of the Central Committee and restricted it to representatives from 'Affiliated National Organisations in the different countries or unions of countries and elected by the Congress'. No country, or union of countries could have more than nine representatives.[64]

More than ten years later the Central Committee, at its meeting in Rome in May, 1948, proposed changes that would go before the Congress in Prague the following September. The aim of these proposals seems to have been to ensure that the Rules were more precise, and in line with each other and recent developments, rather than to make fundamental changes. In other words, the status quo was to be maintained. Centrosoyus had other ideas and submitted alternative proposals at the last minute. They had not notified the Alliance that they would be proposing changes; instead their delegates brought a large number of amendments with them to Rome.[65] The aim of these was clearly to change ICA structures and the decision-making processes of its authorities.

A feature of this period that we should perhaps note, was that the right to substitute delegates was exercised to a greater degree by co-operative movements in the Communist countries than by other ICA member organisations. This may have been due to the fact that, whereas the latter delegations were fairly settled, the former were changing as more hard-line regimes took over or as the Soviet line hardened in Moscow. We have several examples at the Rome Central Committee meeting, including that of Mr Orekhanov, who proposed Centrosoyus's suggested Rules' amendments. So unknown was he in the ICA that the Minutes do not give his initials. Orekhanov began by arguing that the ICA was not a 'neutral Organisation'. Centrosoyus therefore proposed that Article 7 of the existing Rules under the title 'Neutrality' should be headed 'Independence' and have the title of 'Unity of the Co-operative Movement. There would follow a completely new text, which would read:

'The ICA regards Co-operation as a Movement in which people of the most diverse creeds and opinions may meet and act together, except fascists whose views are contradictory to the Co-operative Movement. This unity must be based on free exchange of opinions'.[66]

Centrosoyus also proposed that Article 17 of the existing Rules, or 18 under the Central Committee's proposals, and headed 'Authorities' under both, should be renamed 'Structure of the ICA'. Besides listing the Congress, Central Committee, and Executive Committee as ICA authorities, the new rule would include a 'Management Bureau', which would exclude the post of Director included in the Central Committee's proposal, but include the post of General Secretary, featured in both. The Management Bureau would comprise the President and three, rather than the existing two, Vice-Presidents. Together these would oversee the work of the General Secretary. Centrosoyus saw no need for a Director, whose functions would be difficult to divide from those of the General Secretary. Instead, Centrosoyus proposed that the latter should have two Assistant Secretaries, who would be appointed from the biggest National Movements'. Had this proposal been implemented it would have meant that one of these would have come from Centrosoyus. The General Secretary and two assistant secretaries would have been required to work closely with the Management Bureau. Financial responsibilities would also have been moved, under the Centrosoyus proposals, from the Secretariat and Executive Committee to an Auditing Committee.[67]

We can see that, had these proposals been accepted, they would have created fundamental changes to the Alliance's structure and in its methods of accountability and control. For example, the role of the Executive Committee would have been downgraded because of its loss of financial responsibilities, while the executive functions of President and three Vice-Presidents would have been increased. Such a setup is likely to have been what Centrosoyus was familiar with, but it differed considerably from the structures of Western European national co-operative organisations on which the ICA had been originally based. Had the Centrosoyus amendments been accepted, the Alliance would have been opened up to much greater Soviet influence.

When put to the vote in the Central Committee in Rome, the Centrosoyus amendments were defeated. Votes on each proposal varied, with the largest split being 10 for and 28 against, while the smallest was 14 for to 24 against. These figures indicate the existence of a distinct Centrosoyus voting block in the Central Committee, and this was carried over into the Congress in Prague four months later. Then, Centrosoyus's proposals were voted upon en bloc and rejected by 435 votes for to 556 against.[68]

Before leaving the actual rules revision, we should note an additional Centrosoyus proposal concerning the Article dealing with the Methods' by which the ICA achieved its 'Objects'. Centrosoyus proposed that this should include a clause stating:

'By collaboration with the Trade Union Federation and other democratic organisations which are struggling for peace and security all over the world'.[69]

This would be reinforced in the Article dealing with 'Duties of the Executive' by Centrosoyus's proposal of a clause stating:

'To direct the collaboration of the ICA with the W. F. T. U. * and other international democratic organisations which are fighting for lasting peace and security all over the world' [70]

* World Federation of Trade Unions

Previously we have noted that the ICA and the WFTU, and its predecessor the International Federation of Trade Unions, had worked together on an ad hoc basis when questions of shared interest were involved. However, such collaboration had not been spelled out in ICA Rules, the nearest thing being the clause in the 1937 Rules which, under the Article on Methods, stated:

'By special collaboration with other International Organisations pursuing aims of importance to Co-operation'.[71]

We should note the emphasis on 'Co-operation', which would have been weakened by the widening effect of the Centrosoyus proposals. Undoubtedly, the Soviet Government wished to be able to influence mass working-class movements. So far it had not succeeded in subverting the ICA, but its attempts to do so in the World Federation of Trade Unions led directly to that organisation dividing in 1949, and to the subsequent creation of the non-Communist organisation, the International Confederation of Free Trade Unions.

Between the end of the Second World War and this split, the Alliance had developed good relations with the WFTU. At its meeting in Copenhagen in March, 1946, the ICA Executive had agreed to contact the WFTU, to see how closer relations might be developed,[72] thus acting on the call made six months earlier at the London Conference for closer relations between the two internationals.[73] Similarly, the Zurich Congress, 1946, encouraged these with the following resolution:

'Taking into consideration that the World Federation of Trade Unions is created for the realisation of the social progress and improvement of conditions of life and labour of the people of all the World, and that analogical aims are facing the ICA, and also that the Co-operative Movement, by reason of its penetration into industrial and agricultural production, is an employer of labour on a large scale -

The 16th Congress of the ICA is firmly convinced of the necessity of the establishment of the closest possible relations and of mutual collaboration between the International Co-operative Alliance and the World Federation of Trade Unions.

'It is also convinced of the importance of the establishment of equally close relations between the International Co-operative Alliance and the Co-operative Organisations of Agricultural Production.

'The Congress therefore instructs the Central Committee of the Alliance to take the necessary steps to give effect to the purpose of this Resolution'.[74]

An example of practical collaboration soon occurred when the WFTU strongly supported the Alliance in its attempts to get the question of the international control of world oil resources on the agenda of the UN's Economic and Social Council.[75]

For all this, talk about the changed constitution of the WFTU' led the Alliance to hang back from closer collaboration with the organisation. After the WFTU's division in 1949 the Alliance began to develop new relations with its non-Communist counterpart, the International Con federation of Free Trade Unions.

We have seen that Centrosoyus had tried a number of initiatives that had not gone very far. One that seemed likely to go further was its attempt to increase ICA membership among co-operative movements in the Communist bloc. This issue became very much linked to interpretation of ICA Rules relating to membership. It was not only a matter of admitting new members, but also of what to do when an existing member movement, like the Polish, found its Rules altered under a new Communist regime, or when others, like the Bulgarian and Romanian movements, wished to increase their affiliated membership.

Had these changes been allowed, Soviet delegates could have expected that the ICA would soon come under their control. They may even have been surprised that their moves were resisted because, after all, Centrosoyus had been allowed to remain affiliated after its status had changed following the Russian Revolution. Under Cold War pressures, though, strong resistance developed, and the eventual success of this depended on a number of tactics: re-stating traditional co-operative philosophy; constitutional prevarication; and, figuratively speaking, moving the goal posts by sharpening the 'interpretation' of Article 8 of the Rules covering membership eligibility.

ICA Rules and Membership Applications

During 1949 the problem of handling membership applications from East European co-operative movements became critical. In January, the ICA Executive had before it applications from five Hungarian co-operative organisations. Previously, the Hungarian General Co-operative Council had applied but, while waiting to be admitted, it wrote asking for its application to be adjourned because Hungarian representation was being reorganised.[76] The application was never renewed. Instead, five other Hungarian bodies applied to become members of the ICA.

The custom in the ICA was that a copy of the Rules of any organisation applying to join had to be sent to the Alliance to ensure that they were in line with Article 8 of the Alliance's Constitution and with Co-operative Principles. A photocopy of Article 8 follows on page 329 [77], taken from the Rules as amended by the 1948 Prague Congress.

The Rules of the five Hungarian applicants showed that they did not meet ICA requirements on 'Democratic Control' and 'Open Membership', and that their status as free independent co-operative organisations was also in doubt.

The Hungarian applications created a clear split in the Executive. On one side was Sidorov (USSR), who argued that the Hungarian organisations 'fully observed the Rochdale Principles', and Cerreti (Italy), who reported that a recent Lega delegation to Hungary had found the Co-operative Law there acceptable; moreover, the Italians had thought it appropriate that Hungarian co-operatives were coming under State control because the Hungarian Government favoured the co-operative movement. The views of Sidorov and Cerreti were supported by the Czechoslovak member. On the other side were the eight members of the Executive from Britain, Switzerland, Sweden, France, the Netherlands and Belgium, who opposed the Hungarian admissions. After the vote of four in favour to eight against [78] Sidorov (USSR) claimed that the Executive had acted incorrectly because they were not fully

Amendments to the Rules of the ICA

Article 8. Eligibility.

Associations of persons or Organisations shall be eligible for membership of the I.C.A., provided that they observe the Objects of the I.C.A. and the Policy laid down by its Congress, and conform to the Principles of Rochdale, particularly as regards—

Voluntary membership.

Democratic control (election of the administrative organs by the members freely and on the basis of equality).

Distribution of the surplus to the members in proportion to their participation in the social transactions or the social services of the Association or Organisation.

Limited interest on capital.

Subject to compliance with these conditions, the types of Association eligible for membership shall include the following:—

(a) National Unions of Co-operative Societies.
(b) National Federations of Co-operative Unions.
(c) Regional Unions of Co-operative Societies.
(d) Recognised Auxiliary Organisations of affiliated National Unions or Federations.
(e) Consumers' Co-operative Societies, Retail or Wholesale.
(f) Co-operative Societies of Industrial Producers or Artisanal Co-operatives.
(g) Agricultural or Fishery Co-operative Societies.
(h) Co-operative Credit Societies, Co-operative Banks, Co-operative Assurance Societies.
(i) Housing and Building Societies.
(j) Other associations of persons or Organisations whose juridical status may be different from that of Co-operative Associations.

conversant with the Hungarian Co-operative Law and said that he would raise the question at the next meeting of the Central Committee.

The new President of the Alliance, Mr T. H. Gill (Great Britain), who had been elected at the first meeting of the Central Committee following the Prague Congress and after the retirement of Lord Rusholme,[79] tried to be flexible. While, under ICA Rules, and a tradition of collective responsibility within the Alliance, he could have asked Sidorov not to do so, he took a more conciliatory line emphasising that the decision had been taken in accordance with the Rules, and that he had no desire to prevent the Russian or any other delegation from raising the question'.[80]

By the next meeting of the Executive Sidorov's case had been weakened on two counts. One was that none of the five Hungarian co-operative organisations had appealed against their non-admission, as they were entitled to do under Article 10 of the ICA's Rules. The other was that one of the organisations had been dissolved by a Government decree. Consequently, Sidorov's protest was merely 'noted'.[81]

However, far greater controversy arose when membership applications were received from six Regional Co-operative Unions in Eastern Germany. Miss Polley reported that they had been received only nine days before a meeting of the Executive in Stockholm and that there had been too little time to study the applications, and their accompanying Rules, for 'an adequate report' to be prepared for the Executive. As a result, the Executive decided to delay consideration until their next meeting.[82]

There must be some doubt whether Miss Polley's case was genuine, if we remember the speed with which GEG was re-admitted. Such doubt is reinforced by the deferment of an associated item of business. At the Prague Congress the Czechoslovak delegation had called for the Central Committee to summon 'as soon as possible, before October, 1948 at the latest', a meeting of the co-operative representatives in all the four German zones for the purposes of discussing the membership of the whole German movement. Now that the applications of the six

East German unions had been deferred until the next meeting of the Executive, the President proposed, and it was agreed, that the question of a joint conference should also be adjourned until decisions had been reached on those applications.[83]

The East German question eventually came before the Executive at its meeting in Paris in November, 1949. By that time, the details of the six Regional Unions, and their Rules, had been translated into English and circulated. Although their almost identical Rules showed that they were broadly in line with Article 8 of the ICA's Rules, copies of their enclosed Annual Reports showed that they were State controlled.[84]

For some unexplained reason the two Soviet members of the Executive were not present at the meeting in Paris, neither was the Czechoslovak member. This meant that the communist bloc was represented only by the Italian Cerreti, and that he had to try to deflect a non-communist move obviously aimed at preventing the admission of the East German Co-operative Unions. The move was based on an attempt to determine the 'principles of essential genuine co-operative activity' against which applications for ICA membership could be judged.[85]

Ostensibly, the question had been raised as a result of the work of the Policy Sub-Committee, but there must be some doubt about this. The Sub-Committee had already reported to the Zurich and Prague Congresses, but was only now suggesting that clarification of Article 8 was required because:

'The unity of the International Co-operative Movement cannot be established unless the most important general principles of Co-operation are strictly observed by all the affiliated Organisations. These principles, without which any genuine co-operative activity is impossible, are:

1. Co-operative Organisations must be open to everybody who desires and is able to employ their services, without any discrimination on political, religious or racial grounds.
2. The Organisations of Co-operatives must be democratic; this is to say, they must have the right to elect their committee or other governing bodies without any intervention or pressure from outside, and all members of Co-

operatives must have the same rights and be able to form and express their opinions freely.

3. Co-operative Organisations must be completely free and independent and must be able to take up a position with regard to all the problems which affect their own interests, or the general interests, independent of the State and public authorities generally, as well as of private organisations (political par ties).

In countries where a dictatorship exists, and where there is substantially only one party and a single political movement, where the right of free association is denied and where any divergent opinions are suppressed, free and independent Co-operative Organisations cannot exist.

It is only in this way that the Co-operative Movement can be in a position to fight against oppression in all its forms and for the liberation of all the social groups, and thus contribute to ensure peace.'[86]

Initially appointed by the Central Committee in 1946, the Policy Sub Committee comprised the ICA President, at first Lord Rusholme but later T. H. Gill, Mr J. McFadyen (Great Britain), Prof. Louis de Brouckere (Belgium), Mr Johannes Hüber (Switzerland) and Dr Mauritz Bonow (Sweden). The Sub-Committee's Western European nature can readily be seen, providing another pointer to the fact that the above statement emerged not so much as a result of the Committee's work as in response to increasing Communist pressures in the ICA.

There are two reasons for believing this. One was that this clarification was not sought or made when a major rules revision was carried out at the Prague Congress the previous year. The other was the Executive's decision, by ten votes to one, that the clarification issue should be resolved before the Hungarian and East German applications were considered.

A question was not being faced in the Alliance and had been fudged in the inter-war years: namely, how could the Communist principles, under which Centrosoyus operated, be reconciled with the Co-operative Principles which governed ICA. That question had been avoided right from the time of the Basle Congress, 1921, when

Centrosoyus had been allowed to remain an ICA member. But, in addition to this, practical difficulties also arose.

One was whether the above interpretation of Co-operative Principles would apply only to new applications, or whether it should apply retrospectively to existing members such as Centrosoyus. There was an immediate realisation that the question of whether the Alliance split or remained in its present form hung on how this issue was handled. Cerreti (Italy) believed that the Executive was trying to split the Alliance. Because of this, and also because he believed that the statement had political overtones, he argued that it should be dealt with by the Central Committee rather than by the Executive. Dr Bonow (Sweden) also recognised that there could be a split, but seemed more ready to accept it. He said:

'Although it had been possible for the authorities of the ICA to secure agreement as between the majority and the minority regarding the wording of certain resolutions and thus to reach a unanimous decision, this unanimity had in some case been purely formal. For instance, a resolution which affirmed faith of Co-operators in democracy covered two entirely different concepts, one of democracy in the sense of the proposition before the Executive, the other of a system in which there is only one party that decisively influences the policy of the country, and cannot be turned out of power by a free vote of the citizens, also in which the citizens have no right to oppose the principles for which such a dominating party stands'.

Dr Bonow argued that:
'... it was impossible for the ICA to go on trying to reconcile the wide difference of opinion which exists by purely formal expressions covering two different and mutually exclusive concepts with the same word'.

Before the Executive voted upon the Policy Sub-Committee's proposal it approved the following statement unanimously, which meant that Cerreti voted with other Western European co-operative representatives.

'The Executive Committee whose duty it is to decide on admissions to membership of the ICA consider it necessary to clarify the provisions of Article 8

of the Rules as they understand they would be applied considering that the unity of the International Co-operative Movement......'

When it came to voting for the Policy Sub-Committee's proposal, the Executive approved the first paragraph unanimously. Likewise the second, after the addition of the words 'at all levels' after 'racial grounds'. The third paragraph was agreed by ten votes to one, as was the penultimate paragraph after the deletion of the words 'where a dictatorship exists and where there is substantially only one party and a single political movement.' The final paragraph was also approved by ten votes to one after the addition of the words and in this way only it will materialise a real co-operative system based upon mutual self-help'.

It is worth noting that, had the two Soviet and one Czechoslovak members of the Executive been present, the above votes would still have been likely to have been ten to four, meaning that there would have been a sizeable majority in favour of the clarification.

The first real test of this could have come immediately, when the Executive began consideration of the East German Cerreti moved their admission. But he was thwarted when Marcel Brot (France) moved, and Robert Southern (Great Britain) seconded, the adjournment of the question because of pressure other Executive business. This must be interpreted as a stall, particularly as Southern went on to request more information on the origins of the East German Regional Unions and 'the order of the Soviet Union which approved the basis for the foundation of Co-operative Societies in the Eastern Zone of Germany'.

Members of the Executive received this information in the Memorandum on the Agenda of their meeting in Basle in March, 1950.[87] The two Soviet and one Czechoslovak members absent at the last meeting were now present, quickly protested against the re-definition of principles which had then taken place and demanded a reopening of the discussion. This was resisted by eight votes to four.[88]

Giulio Cerreti (Italy)　　　　　　Robert Southern (Great Britain)

At the last meeting there had been the first hint that Robert Southern (Great Britain) would take a more aggressive line against Communist representatives, and this became even more apparent at the Basle meeting.

As soon as the item on the Agenda dealing with Applications for Membership was reached, Southern moved that, in view of the copies of the Order (No. 176) of Marshall Zhukov, dated 18th December, 1945, on the 'Re-establishment of Consumers' Society in the Soviet Occupation Zone, the German Organisations ...

'were not in conformity with the operative principles laid down by the Executive at the last meeting for its own guidance in considering future applications for membership, these applications could not be considered. He, therefore, moved "that we pass to the next business" so that the remaining applications might be considered'.

A more conciliatory tone was taken by Marcel Brot (France), but it had the same effect as Southern's move. Brot suggested that, as the principles laid down at the last meeting had been disputed by some members of the Executive, and as it had been requested - by Sidorov - that they be referred to the Central Committee, the Executive should not examine the present, or any new applications for membership.

However, the debate continued. Sidorov (USSR) said that there were 'several political parties' and 'full freedom of expression and of political life' in East Germany, where the Co-operative Movement was 'perfectly democratic in the sense of the Rules of the ICA' and he saw no reason to reject their applications which, if it happened, 'would definitely mean a split within the ICA'

Despite speeches by A. Zmrhal (Czechoslovakia) and A. Klimov (USSR) elaborating points made by Sidorov, and with the addition of aspersions against Southern, with questions such as 'for whom he was working and at what he was aiming', the Executive agreed by eight votes to four that no applications should be considered until the Central Committee had decided upon the principles laid down by the Executive at its Paris meeting.

Before the Central Committee met in Helsinki in August, 1950, a new development aggravated deteriorating East-West relations in the ICA. In April, 1950, the Secretariat learned of changes in 'Spolem', the ICA's Polish affiliate. With its name changed, and its rules amended, it had been merged with a State Trading Company to form a State-owned Foodstuffs Central Organisation.[89]

At their meeting in Helsinki, immediately before that of the Central Committee, the Executive accepted the case made by Serwy (Belgium), son of the earlier Serwy, Bonow (Sweden), and Barbier (Switzerland) that there had been a fundamental change in the Polish movement, and asked the Secretariat to investigate the position 'thoroughly'. [90]

Thus, at Helsinki, the question of the admission of the East German Co-operative Organisations became bound up with that of the changed status of the Polish movement. The German question was not raised at the Executive's meeting because it had already been referred to the Central Committee, but Spolem, and the whole question of admissions from Central and Eastern Europe, arose in another way.

By now it must have become clear to both camps in the Alliance that the pressure for admissions from the East was being resisted by the West, either through delays or re-defining of the Rules. On the last point, it could be argued that the Swedes, French, Swiss, Belgians and British were only reaffirming traditional Co-operative Principles. The weakness in their position was that they had allowed these to be flouted by tolerating the membership of Centrosoyus since 1921.

Past ICA leaders should not necessarily be criticised for this. Their tolerance could be explained by the strong sense of fraternity in the Alliance, and by the fact that the Russian Central Union had joined the ICA as early as 1903, and had played an active part in it before the First World War. In any event, the eventual nature of the Soviet regime could not have been foreseen in 1921. By the late 1940s, however, Soviet Communism had become Stalinist, and it was not just a question about Centrosoyus, but of whether other latter-day Communist dominated co-operative organisations should be allowed to join the Alliance. Non-Communist members of the Executive and Central Committees should not be criticised for believing that their best defence against this pressure was a restatement of traditional Co-operative Principles. As we have seen, other weapons were also being used.

That battle was joined was illustrated by Soviet readiness to counter attack. At Helsinki, the Executive learned of strong attacks on the President, Sir Harry Gill, who had recently been knighted, Robert Southern (Great Britain) and Dr Weber (Switzerland) in the Soviet journal TRUD. The article in which the attacks appeared had been written by the two Soviet members of the ICA Executive, Sidorov and Klimov.

It was in remonstrating about the article that the Executive found that the German question was raised in any event.

The tone of Sidorov's and Klimov's attack in the article can be gathered from the fact that they accused 'Woods, of England' of 'making a venomous speech in the spirit of the Anglo-American warmongers'.[91] In posthumous defence of Woods, it should be mentioned that he was a religious minister, believed to have been the only one to have served on the Central Committee and, far from being a 'warmonger' or making 'venomous speeches', his contributions appear to have been rather pedestrian, or mainly on points of procedure. At the Helsinki Executive meeting, Ch. H. Barbier (Switzerland) protested strongly against the charge that Gill, Southern and Weber had made an 'illegal amendment of the statutes... presented in another form'.[92]

Barbier wanted the Executive to protest at the article, and affirm its full confidence in Gill, Southern and Weber. He also asked Sidorov and Klimov to appreciate that 'such polemics in the press against members of the Executive were not designed to improve relations within the Committee'.

Dr Bonow (Sweden) supported Barbier, saying that it was one thing for different members of the Executive to hold different opinions, but quite another for a member to use abusive language about another member in a way that reflected on their honour.

In their defence, Sidorov and Kilmov said that their article only repeated arguments that they had used in the Executive, 'so that there was nothing new in it'. They claimed, though, that it was their duty to 'inform the Soviet masses about what the ICA was doing to preserve and to protect their interests'.

When Marcel Brot (France) moved a resolution regretting the 'unfounded and injurious statements' and expressing sympathy with, and confidence in, those attacked it was passed by seven votes to two, with the President, Dr Weber and Southern not voting.

All this was only a prelude to the trouble which was to break out at the meeting of the Central Committee which followed. Besides the text on Article 8 adopted by the Executive in Paris the previous November, there were three resolutions which had been tabled by Centrosoyus, the Polish Central Co-operative Union, and the Italian Lega, all condemning, or attempting to revoke the Executive's decision and claiming that it was intended to split the Alliance.[93]

Sir Harry Gill responded by arguing that the Paris resolution was not an amendment but 'merely a decision to set up for.... guidance a definition of the principles already in the Rules in order to assure uniformity of treatment for all applicants...... '

One of the longest and hardest-hitting debates in the ICA then took place. Thanks to the almost verbatim Minutes, covering 17 foolscap pages, we can trace it blow by blow, with at times passionate speeches from 13 members of the Central Committee.

The debate is important because it puts into sharp perspective the issues facing the ICA at the start of the Cold War. It also confirms earlier impressions that the Communists wanted to keep the ICA together and that any split would be due to non-Communist forces' breaking away, as they had done in the World Federation of Trade Unions.

Klimov moved the Centrosoyus resolution and reminded the Central Committee that Article 3 of the Rules laid down that one of the objects of the ICA was to be the 'universal representative' of all kinds of co-operative. But the Paris decision, besides being illegal would split the Alliance because it

'aimed at making the ICA representative only of Movements in the bourgeois countries, and discriminated against countries having social and democratic aims'.

Cerreti (Italy) argued that the Executive had exceeded its powers and had even pre-judged those of the Central Committee. He further claimed that partiality and discrimination now affected the admission of members, and recalled that the German GEG had been admitted without any preliminary enquiries or supplementary documentation', and only opposed by some 'from the point of view of the unity of the German Co-operative Movement'. While Cerreti was not sorry that GEG had been admitted, he did regret the discrimination shown in regard to subsequent applications. He proposed that ICA Commissions be sent to countries where the position of national co-operative movements was unclear.

Dr Weber (Switzerland) denied that the Executive had exceeded its powers, and 'emphatically asserted' that it was fully competent to deal with the question. Moreover, under the Rules, if an organisation was not satisfied with the Executive's decision about its application for membership it could appeal to the Central Committee, whose ruling was final. Weber further argued that the Executive had to ensure 'the continuity of the interpretation of Article 8', and the Paris resolution had been passed to assist in this.

Moving on to co-operative theory, and to the meaning of democracy, Weber argued that it extended beyond what applied in Article 8 to co-operatives' internal workings, and included the system under which co-operatives operated.

'... it was not only necessary to have free elections but for the organisations to be in a country where freedom of association existed, where it was possible to have freedom of speech and to be able to speak in opposition. If these conditions did not exist there was no real freedom, either from the point of the Rochdale Principles or from the point of view of true democracy.'

Weber thus touched on the point that Bonow had made at Paris. He continued that in a true co-operative, people should be free to enter or not to enter. Free and voluntary membership could not apply if people had to join because that was the only way that they would obtain rationed goods. Moreover, democracy was far more than the 'possibility of electing representatives whom one could not choose'.

While agreeing with Cerreti (Italy) that the whole issue was one of politics, Weber argued that the Executive had taken their stand in Paris to prevent the Alliance from 'becoming a political organisation'. The Executive, and those who supported their resolution, had no desire to have things forced upon them,

'either in the ICA or in their own countries. They favoured tolerance, but tolerance did not mean that they would allow themselves to be wiped out'.

By this time the Soviet and Polish resolutions had been withdrawn, leaving only the Italian. In concluding his speech Weber moved an amendment to this, which stated simply that the Central Committee noted the interpretation of Principles related to the Rules on admission of members, made by the Executive at their meeting in Paris on 17th and 18th November, 1949, and declared that it had been within the competence of the Executive to take this decision and that the Central Committee now approved it as being 'in conformity with the Rules'.

Perhaps the most powerful speech in support of the Executive was made by Robert Southern, who had followed Lord Rusholme as General Secretary of the British Co-operative Union. Southern gave the clearest insight yet into the fears of the non-Communist members of the Executive. He challenged the kind of 'democracy' that was being created in the 'new democracies' and claimed that it could not be the same as that which had developed over hundreds of years elsewhere, which was based on free elections, a judiciary that was not controlled by the State, and a variety of people and parties representing different opinions and sections of the community. Southern also questioned how far the recent co-operative growth in Communist countries was genuine. He believed that the Alliance was entitled to an explanation of 'the rapid and tremendous increase in membership which was claimed'. He suggested that one reason for this growth was that co-operative organisations were being used to build up a completely new economy in which co-operative shops became agencies for the distribution of essential goods. Southern feared that 'compulsory co-operation was developing'. Coming right to the heart of why the Executive had acted as it had, Southern said:

'These and other features had caused the Executive much concern. Co-operative Organisations had disappeared overnight and new organisations had been established and presented as genuine Co-operatives eligible for membership of the ICA. Real democracy did not work so quickly, and in such countries Co-operation was entering into a new phase, that new forms were emerging which were not comparable with the traditional forms of Co-operation and did not conform to the basic principles set forth in the rules of the ICA.'

At the end of his speech Southern said:
'... the majority of the members of the Executive recognised their duty to the existing members of the ICA and that duty was far greater than any duty they might have in promoting the aspirations of new and different Organisations which were attempting to enter the Alliance'.

Southern's stand was supported by Dr Bonow (Sweden), Marcel Brot (France) and Ch. H. Barbier (Switzerland), who replied on behalf of the Executive at the end of the debate. In between there were opposing speeches from Bulgarian and Romanian delegates, who protested at the delay in allowing them to increase their affiliated membership in the Alliance, and from Mr A. Zmrhal (Czechoslovakia). In looking at their contributions, three features of the debate should be mentioned. One was that both sides were familiar with the earlier history of the Alliance and quoted it when it seemed to support their arguments. Another were references to contemporary events, which help us to place the debate in a particular period of the Cold War. The third feature was the speakers' grasp of the philosophical and political theories permeating the issue. Both Zmrhal (Czechoslovakia) and Brot (France) referred to the French Revolution. Zmrhal argued that it had 'put democracy on a much broader basis; at that time the bourgeoisie were starting to rule, whereas today it was a rule of monopolies, cartels and trusts. Without economic democracy there was no political democracy. Only where the workers were guaranteed against unemployment and misery was there democracy'.

However, Brot suggested that its principles of political freedom meant that there must be economic freedom as well. For that reason, he argued:
'... many of us are Socialists, because we believe that political liberty without economic liberty is unreal, but the Socialism we want to see is Socialism which will reinforce economic liberty and make political liberty effective, not something which will stifle freedom of opinion under the pretext of Socialism'.

Zmrhal had also voiced a fear that a decision to exclude new members from Eastern Europe might prejudice Centrosoyus's continuing membership because some believed that Soviet Co-operation now contained 'dangerous possibilities and influences'. He said:

'The dangers now referred to.... had not been foreseen when the Rules were drawn up in 1948'.

This statement well illustrates the speed with which international relations had deteriorated and had affected the ICA. Certainly the debate showed how the different systems in the East and West viewed each other. Earlier we quoted how Southern, Bonow and Weber saw Communist regimes and the co-operatives within them. It is equally interesting to note the Soviet view of capitalist countries, as expressed by Sidorov. He said that:

'...autonomous parties with opposing interests were only in existence where there were capitalists, and where there were poor and rich classes. In the Soviet Union, where the only classes were the worker and the peasants, only one party could exist, the Communist Party, which defended their interests.... in bourgeois countries democracy was in the hands of the strong, whereas in the popular democracies it was in the hands of the people.'

Sidorov also argued that in the bourgeois countries, co-operatives
'were entirely dependent upon the capitalists, who held in their hands the instrument of production, which was the decisive factor in the economic situation, and thus might at any time apply coercive measures against the Co-operatives'.

Ch. H.Barbier (Switzerland) replied to the debate on behalf of the Executive and his speech provides insight into personal feelings among non-Communist ICA leaders. Barbier said:

'For many years I and others have shown the greatest patience. For years we have thought that it was necessary to give the Movements in Eastern Europe time to take stock of themselves, and time for those strictly co-operative values which should inspire the Movement to prevail. But we have come to the conclusion that the action of those movements has not been in the direction of the values in which we have confidence. We do not pretend that in our countries which are called a little too simply 'capitalist' but are countries in which, though capitalism does play a role, it is not alone in doing so, because we have a public sector and a co-operative sector which are of considerable

importance - everything is for the best in the best of all possible worlds. We know well that in the egotistical form of civilisation in which we live we, as co-operators, must try to develop a sense of the community, a sense of solidarity and the need for joint action'.

Concluding his reply to the debate Barbier said that:
'everyone hoped for the unity of the ICA but the majority saw things now more clearly than before.'

The Central Committee's debate in Helsinki, August, 1950, showed that the Communists and non-Communists now had clear ideas about each other, with the mutual recognition that the former wished to gain control of the Alliance while the latter were equally resolved to resist. In this context, the remarks at the end of the speech by Marcel Brot (France) became significant because they point to future toleration.

'To the extent to which we can live together, let us seek to preserve in this last International Organisation, which has guarded unity, the unity that we have. Let us preserve our tolerance and friendship, even for those organisations which do not come strictly within our Rules - but that tolerance should not lead us to admit new Organisations which are not entirely voluntary Organisations and are not entirely free of State control. '

Although this begs the question of what, then, should the Alliance's attitude be to existing members, such as Centrosoyus, which did not measure up to these criteria, Brot's appeal suggests a way ahead. It became even more significant when, five years later, Brot because President of the Alliance. His wish to preserve the 'last International Organisation' by 'tolerance and friendship' must be considered a factor in the ICA's survival.

The membership question was settled decisively, and for a number of years, in Helsinki by approval of the Executive's interpretation of Rule 8 by 43 votes to 25. Before summing up this section we can perhaps look at what happened later to the issue.

At the Paris Congress of 1954 Centrosoyus called for reconsideration of the membership applications from the Polish, Albanian, Hungarian and East German Co-operative Movements, but this was rejected by 671 votes to 366[94]. However, the Paris Congress did agree a new Rule which provided for Associate Membership in the Alliance. It seems likely that this move was an attempt by Western co-operators to try to accommodate a less pure form of co-operative organisation within the Alliance.

The new Rule allowed for co-operatives which did not yet qualify under Article 8 because, being in the early stages of development and receiving external support, they did not yet have complete control of their affairs, to apply for Associate Membership. The debate on this proposal recalls echoes of the earlier ICA debate at the Budapest Congress of 1904 on whether it was appropriate for fledgling co-operatives to receive State assistance. Under the new Rule, Associate Members could receive a number of benefits such as ICA publications and the right to nominate observers to attend meetings of the Central Committee, but without the right to speak or to vote. Similarly, they could send observers to ICA Congresses where, with the consent of Congress, they could speak but still not vote.[95]

This position was reaffirmed at the Congress in Lausanne in 1960, after Centrosoyus had made another attempt to re-open the question.[96] Associate Membership was obviously a device to maintain ICA relations with co-operative movements in Communist countries. As such, it succeeded in carrying the Alliance through the worst of the Cold War. It should be observed, though, that readiness to use such a method stemmed from the Alliance's traditions of 'tolerance and friendship', or solidarity if we use the terms of earlier working-class rhetoric.

Equally, we should observe that it enabled the Rochdale tradition of co-operation to continue to predominate in the Alliance. However, the readiness of Western co-operative movements to allow coexistence with a less pure form paved the way for the time when, from the 1960s onwards, increasing numbers of applications for ICA membership came from co-operative movements in developing countries. Many of these were State-promoted under national schemes of development, and had not yet become autonomous or independent.

This Chapter, and the study, end with an examination of the effect of the Cold War on the question of peace within the Alliance. We have already noted in Chapter 2[97] that the quest for peace was an important part in ICA ideology. In previous threats to world peace the Alliance, and its members, could blame external forces such as the imperialists or the Fascists and Nazis, but in the Cold War representatives of the main protagonists had ICA membership. There was, therefore, no way in which the Alliance could avoid the tensions stemming from these opposing forces of capitalism and communism. For most of the Cold War there was the risk that the situation could suddenly deteriorate to become World War Three.

As we have seen, from its very early years the Alliance passed resolutions or declarations in support of peace. It also joined with other organisations in campaigning for peace. During the Cold War Centrosoyus made strong efforts to shape ICA policy on peace and its implementation. We will now follow these moves and their ramifications.

The ICA and World Peace

Closely related to the question, as to all those considered in connection with the Cold War, is the impact of deteriorating East-West relations on the ICA Secretariat. In November, 1948, those working for the ICA numbered 12.[98] Of these, only Miss Polley, General Secretary, and Thorsten Odhe, who had been appointed Director in 1948, had any political role. It may be recalled that Odhe had originally been seconded by the Swedes to become the Alliance's first Permanent Representative with the United Nations. Both he and Miss Polley came under immense pressures. Those on her perhaps owed more to Centrosoyus's efforts to circumscribe the position of General Secretary rather than to genuine complaints. She was criticised, along with Lord Rusholme, for violating 'the principle of collegiency' by not agreeing agendas etc. with 'all' the members of the Executive and Central Committees.[99]

A running battle also developed over the accuracy of the Minutes of Executive and Central Committee meetings, but Miss Polley showed remarkable spirit and was not easily intimidated. On each occasion that Minutes were challenged she argued their accuracy by reference to the English and French shorthand notes taken during the meetings. She was also criticised for her drafting of the International Co-operative Day Manifestos, particularly those parts referring to peace. Odhe's problems were also closely linked to peace issues, such as those arising from the Peace Resolution passed at the 1948 Prague Congress.

Before explaining that, we should note that, even by the Zurich Congress of 1946, Soviet delegates were taking a harder line than other delegates on the question of peace and related issues. For example, and as we have noted previously, they suggested that the Alliance had not done all that it could have done to have prevented the 1939-45 war; neither had it worked as effectively as it might have done for the defeat of the Nazi enemy and the establishment of peace once war had broken out.[100] However, it was still possible at the Zurich Congress to composite two Peace Resolutions, one received from the British Co-operative Union and the other from Centrosoyus, and to pass the resolution unanimously.[101] In 1946, also, little controversy was aroused over the International Co-operative Day Manifesto, drafted by Miss Polley and approved by the Executive and Central Committees.[102] Again, in 1947, the Manifesto was passed in the same manner and without problems.[103] By 1948, though, matters were becoming more difficult. The draft that year stated familiar sentiments such as Co-operation becoming one of the most powerful forces in preserving world peace if only nations' economic and social life were organised 'according to the Co-operative Principles'.[104] Nevertheless, Mr N. Sidorov, on behalf of Centrosoyus, submitted an alternative draft which called for national co-operative movements to organise mass meetings with trade unions and other democratic organisations to call for peace and democracy and to oppose those threatening a new imperialist war. The mass meetings should also criticise those Governments supporting Franco's regime in Spain and protest against political executions in Athens. The President proposed rejection of the Soviet draft on the grounds that it was a political, rather than a co-operative, statement. All the Executive, except Sidorov, agreed.

Soviet disagreement with the 1948 International Co-operative Day Manifesto should be seen as part of a long-term strategy to produce an ICA peace policy that was in line with Soviet thinking. At the centre of this was the Peace Resolution to be passed at the ICA's Prague Congress. As we shall see, this would be capable of being used in various ways, including the justification of the proposal that the ICA should participate in the World Congress of Partisans for Peace, and in shaping future International Co-operative Day Manifestos.

Initially, two Peace Resolutions were tabled for the Prague Congress, one by the Central Committee and the other by Centrosoyus. Because of their 'irreconcilability' it was decided that both should go before the Congress. At this point it seems likely that the Communist bloc realised that the Central Committee's resolution, rather than its own, would be passed because no vote in the ICA Executive and Central Committees, or in a Congress, had yet gone the Soviet way. Such doubt may have prompted Centrosoyus to compromise, because overnight personal negotiations were held between members of the French, Swiss and Soviet delegations resulting in the following composite motion:

'The 17th Congress of the ICA emphasises anew that the strivings for the maintenance of a lasting peace are indissolubly inherent in the Co-operative Movement, which has been making steady progress since the last Congress, and unites ever-growing numbers of the broad masses of people in all Continents.

The Congress strongly stresses that it is the duty of Co-operation, in the present international situation even more than previously, to work for peace with all resources and energies at its disposal, make all contributions necessary for reconciliation and understanding between the peoples of the world, and unite in an unbreakable front against all forces active in weakening the foundations of a lasting peace.

The Congress recommends the National Organisations to strain their efforts to make the activities of the United Nations Organization known to the fullest extent in all countries, and to bring pressure to bear on their Governments to make their contributions towards bringing them into full effect.

The promotion of peace has been the task of Co-operation from its first origins and has found its expression in all its principles, its objectives and its activities. The barbarism of war, with its repercussions on the work of material and cultural progress of humanity, is also disastrous for the upholding of the ideals of freedom and democracy and for the realisation of the peaceful and democratic programme of the Co-operative Movement itself, as well as for the international collaboration within the co-operative ranks embodied within the International Co-operative Alliance. For the sake of human progress and to save the broad masses in all countries from unspeakable sufferings and destitution, Co-operators must, therefore, stand prepared to fight war by untiring united efforts.

The Congress urgently appeals to the Co-operators of the world to raise their voices in the defence of peace, free progressive development of all the Co-operative Movement, independence of nations and close collaboration between all peoples.

The Congress calls all National Co-operative Organisations to celebrate the traditional International Co-operative Day by mass meetings in their respective countries in support of peace and democracy and the raising of the standard of living of the toilers, and recommends them to take up the fight for peace in collaboration with Trade Unions and other democratic organisations. [105]

We can deduce the Soviet motives, but those of the French and Swiss are less clear. It seems reasonable to suggest, however, that Marcel Brot's conciliatory tendencies influenced the French delegation at least. Whatever motivation lay behind it, the Peace Resolution was passed unanimously.

When the Manifesto for the 1949 International Co-operative Day came to be discussed by the Executive on January, 1949, Brot suggested that it should be based on the Prague Congress Peace Resolution. [106] By now, Sidorov (USSR) and Cerreti (Italy) wanted a stronger line supporting an United Nations Disarmament resolution, and the naming of 'war mongers' and the 'enemies of peace and co-operation'.

Procedural procrastination, that had been developed to a fine art in the ICA during the Cold War, was now brought into play. After much discussion it was agreed that the Secretariat should prepare a draft which would be approved by an Executive Sub-Committee set up in January, 1947, to deal with staff and organisational matters.[107] It must therefore have been a strange vehicle for drafting the Manifesto. The move is likely to be explained, though, by the fact that, apart from Cerreti, there were no Eastern bloc members on the Sub-Committee.[108] Moreover, as there would be no meeting of the full Executive before the Manifesto was distributed, the Executive Sub-Committee could virtually have the final say.

When the Sub-Committee met in London in March, 1949, it approved a draft calling on Co-operators throughout the world to 'make a powerful demonstration in support of the ideals of Free and Voluntary Co-operation'. It also urged them to show their wish for peace by joining like-minded others in denouncing the hindrances to its realisation. The Manifesto then denounced economic nationalism, combines and cartels, and argued that the Co-operative System provided the best chance for peace. Finally it pledged the ICA's full support for the programme of the United Nations.[109]

This text was a clever piece of drafting, emphasising free and voluntary co-operation, but still keeping in line with Sidorov and Cerreti's demands. Even so, it was strongly attacked at the Central Committee's meeting in Stockholm in June, 1949, with Polish, Italian and Czechoslovak ICA member organisations complaining that the Manifesto did not fully comply with the Peace Resolution of the Prague Congress'. Moreover, the Poles proposed an amended text, which was supported by the Italians and Czechoslovaks.[110]

By the time that the Central Committee convened the next day the Soviet delegation had handed in a text of a telegram which they also wished to propose, and which would replace the Polish text. The Soviet draft telegram, to be sent all ICA member organisations, called for national co-operative organisations to demonstrate in 'defence of peace, for democratic collaboration between peoples against fascism. ... against capitalist monopolies and trusts and against the instigators of a new war'. Such demonstrations should be made in 'collaboration with trade unions affiliated to the World Federation of Trade Unions'.[111]

When put to the vote, the original text of the Manifesto was agreed by 44 votes to 24, and the Soviet proposed telegram rejected by 42 votes to 23. Although the thrust of the Communist bloc's criticism of the Manifesto was that it had not been sufficiently based on the Prague Congress's Peace Resolution, its members showed that elsewhere they were using the resolution in ways not intended or envisaged by Western co-operative movements. One such incident led to considerable controversy surrounding the new Director of the Alliance, and may have been a factor in Thorsten Odhe's early departure from that position after only three years.

In connection with the Executive's meeting in Stockholm in June, 1949, Odhe sent a memorandum drawing attention to what he considered was the Italian Lega's improper use of the Prague Congress's Peace Resolution. He argued that they had used the resolution in a national political struggle to imply ICA 'condemnation of the Atlantic Pact'. Believing that such actions breached the ICA's political neutrality, Odhe said:

'This (Italian Lega) campaign has also been connected with grave accusations against other democratic countries of preparing for, or inciting to, war, in which connection the contents of the Peace Resolution of the Alliance have been used for creating a background for these accusations'.[112]

Not surprisingly, Odhe's memorandum prompted a heated discussion.

Sidorov (USSR) reminded the Executive that the title of Article 7 of the Rules had been changed at Prague from 'Neutrality' to 'Independence'. This should have allowed the ICA to have become a meeting place for people of different religious and political faiths. Consequently, if the Lega thought that the Atlantic Pact was a threat to peace, it should be free to say so. And, if it did, Sidorov saw no contradiction between that and ICA Rules. He therefore suggested that the matter be dropped, a view supported by A. Klimov also of the USSR.

The President, Sir Harry Gill, pointed out that the question was not the action taken by the Lega, but its misuse of the ICA's name and Congress resolution. Marcel Brot (France) endorsed this and proposed a motion which emphasised that the Alliance was neutral ground on which people of varying opinions could meet, but urgently recommending its member organisations 'not to use or interpret ICA Resolutions for internal domestic political purposes'. The ICA did not deny them the right, on their 'own responsibility', to take decisions relating to their country. As usual, Robert Southern (Great Britain) took a stronger line. He also proposed a motion recommending that the Central Committee should inform the Lega that, by attributing to the ICA an attitude in opposition to the Atlantic Pact, it had misused the Prague Congress Peace Resolution. Moreover, that the resolution could 'not possibly be interpreted' in the way that the Lega had done, and that such misuse was not in conformity with the Lega's obligations to the ICA.

Both resolutions were carried, Brot's by six votes to three, and Southern's by six votes to four, and both were sent to the Central Committee meeting the following day. There, some confusion prevailed, arising to some extent from a lack of collective responsibility in the Executive. Marcel Brot stated that he thought Southern's resolution would be merely communicated to the Lega, and not passed to the Central Committee. He now appealed to the British to withdraw their resolution. Speaking on their behalf, Southern said they declined to do so on the grounds that the first recommendation did not deal with the specific question raised by Odhe, and that the Central Committee could ignore neither the Director's memorandum nor events in Italy. Central Committee was then adjourned, so that a special meeting of the Executive could be convened to iron out procedure and air recriminations about lack of collective responsibility.[113] The more general resolution proposed by Brot, containing no criticism of the Lega, was then returned to the Central Committee and passed, the British Motion having been withdrawn.[114]

This incident raises a number of questions. The main one was whether Marcel Brot (France) was genuinely confused, or whether he was trying to avert a worsening in relations that Southern's motion could cause. Because of the clarity of the Executive's Minutes, whose accuracy was not challenged, and Brot's subsequent admissions, it seems to have been the latter.

A worsening of relations resulted anyway, with Thorsten Odhe becoming the chief victim. The Executive of the Italian Lega passed a resolution strongly objecting to events in Stockholm, and to Odhe's part in them.[115] The resolution, considered by the ICA Executive at their meeting in Paris in November, 1949, also called for Odhe to be censured on the grounds that he had lacked 'the feelings of equanimity and impartiality' to be expected of the Director of an international organisation. [116]

It soon became clear that, since the Stockholm meetings five months earlier, the views of the non-Communist members of the Executive had hardened: they had now had time to read the articles referred to in Odhe's original memorandum and proceeded to pass the succinctly expressed following resolution:

'That the request of the Lega Nazionale delle Cooperative be rejected; that the Executive confirm the correctness of the action of the Director in bringing before it in an objective and proper way a matter concerning the political independence of the International Co-operative Alliance; and express their regret at the expressions used in the official organ of Lega Nazionale. '[117]

In particular, it became clear that Brot's position had shifted. He now said he regretted that, despite 'an effort at appeasement' at Stockholm and the great effort of conciliation' then made, the matter had not been settled. He hoped that it would now be closed and not be reopened in the Central Committee, a warning that was heeded. The matter was closed without Odhe being censured.

This hardening among non-Communist members of the Executive was accompanied by two features which we should note. In addition to the French, headed by Marcel Brot, the Swedes also began to play a more prominent role in the Alliance, even though their nominated ICA Director, Odhe, resigned in 1950. Alongside this, the Secretariat was shown to become increasingly adept at surviving the effects of Cold

War politics. This last aspect was well illustrated when attempts were made to get the Alliance to support a Soviet-sponsored peace organisation. In March, 1949 A. Khoklov (USSR) sent a telegram to the ICA Secretariat reporting that Centrosoyus supported the convening of the World Congress of Partisans of Peace, and urging the ICA and its member co-operative movements to do likewise. The Director, Thorston Odhe, and General Secretary, Miss Polley, replied to Khoklov that they had consulted members of the Executive, and while four had favoured participation ten had not. Therefore, the Alliance would not be represented. [118]

Klimov (USSR) then raised the question at the meeting of the Central Committee in Stockholm in June, 1949, claiming that the reason why ten members of the Executive had not been in favour of the Peace Congress at Paris was that the General Secretary had given insufficient information about the Congress. He criticised Miss Polley for not having taken the trouble to supply them with the kind of material that would have helped them to have come to the 'right decision'. Klimov now proposed that the ICA should send a representative to the Permanent Committee of the World Congress of the Partisans for Peace. Miss Polley's reply was as robust as it was succinct. She read out the telegram received from Khoklov on 23rd March, and then that sent out to the Executive the following day illustrating how closely the latter had been based on the former. Miss Polley said that the only additional information that the Secretariat had was that gained from the British Press, and she had not imagined that 'Mr Klimov would have approved the sending of this to the Executive'. Miss Polley ended by saying that, while the ICA had received appeals that it should participate in the Congress from co-operative organisations in Poland, Czechoslovakia, Bulgaria, Romania and Italy, it had not received an invitation from the Peace Congress itself.

The Central Committee went on to defeat the proposal that the ICA should affiliate to the Peace Congress by 23 votes for to 43 against.

The increasing role of the Swedes in the Alliance was illustrated when, at the Central Committee's meeting in Helsinki in August, 1950, not one, but four, Peace Resolutions appeared on the Agenda, and the

Swedish delegates led the non-Communists within the meeting. We should note that the Helsinki meeting was held two months after the outbreak of the Korean War, which had the effect of intensifying the Cold War in Europe and leading to an increase in the production of armaments. The four Peace Resolutions seem to have been prompted by the Korean War and had been sent in by Centrosoyus, the new central co-operative organisation in Poland still in ICA membership, the Italian Lega and the Swedish delegates. By the time the Central Committee actually convened, the Soviet and Italian Peace resolutions had been withdrawn in favour of the Polish. This, and the Swedish resolution, thus represented the Communist and non-Communist views in the Central Committee at this time.

The Polish resolution stated that many millions of 'rank and file co-operators' had joined in the campaign for peace, despite the fact that the ICA had declined to participate in the Peace Congress. By limiting itself to purely formal declarations, the ICA, according to the Poles, had acted contrary to the 'interests of the broad masses organised in Co-operative Societies'. The resolution appealed to co-operators throughout the world to 'actively struggle' against preparations for a new war and to demand the prohibition of atomic weapons. It also endorsed the declaration of the International Red Cross appealing for the prohibition of atomic weapons, and supported the similar decision taken by the Stockholm Session of the Permanent Committee of the Partisans of Peace (Peace Congress). Finally, the Polish resolution appealed to co-operative organisations throughout the world to demand that their Governments should take steps against 'war propaganda' by branding and unmasking in the 'co-operative and in the education press the criminal schemes of warmongers', and to assist the broad working masses in their heroic fight for the frustration of imperialist schemes.....'[119]

By contrast, the wording of the Swedish resolution was gentler and more in the tradition of ICA Peace Resolutions. It recalled the Prague Congress Peace Resolution, and reaffirmed its call to national co-operative organisations to 'strain their efforts' to make known the activities of the UN and to bring pressure to bear on their Governments to give full effect to UN decisions.

The Swedish resolution endorsed the recent unanimous proposal made by the UN's International Legal Commission that any use of armed force not made in self-defence or in executing a commission for the UN should be considered 'a crime against peace and the security of mankind'. The Swedish resolution called for 'certain prerequisites for peace', such as people's rights to 'freedom of thought, freedom of speech, freedom of movement, freedom to elect their Governments by democratic methods', as well as the freedom 'to create, administer and control their co-operative organisations according to the principles of Rochdale'. Prerequisites of peace also included raising living and economic standards in developed and under-developed countries, 'particularly by the promotion of co-operation', and the development of full international co-operation in the economic field by abolishing excessive trade barriers. A further prerequisite was that countries that were members of the UN should collaborate 'harmoniously' in fulfilling the aims of the UN in 'the spirit of the Atlantic Charter, particularly as regards the implementation of the principles of free access to the raw material resources of the world' and curbing monopolistic cartels and combines. Finally, the Swedish resolution called for effective international control of armaments production, including that of atomic bombs. The Swedish resolution seemed to be an effective summation of many ICA policies since the end of the First World War.

The debate on the two resolutions was relatively short, although none the less pithy. It was clear that by now both sides were familiar with each other's well-rehearsed arguments.

Although the Soviet resolution had been withdrawn in favour of that of the Poles, the first speaker was N. P. Sidorov (USSR), who claimed that more than 270 million people had signed a peace petition, the Stockholm Peace Appeal, which had been organised by the Peace Congress, and that these signatures included those of many co-operators'. E. Pszczolkowski (Poland) supported this assertion by claiming that in Poland 18.5 million had signed, including five million co-operators. This did not impress Nils Thedin, moving the Swedish resolution, who said that signing the Stockholm Peace Appeal did not necessarily mean that signatories would not take up 'arms against world peace'. By way of example he quoted the four million Koreans who had signed the Appeal, but who were at the same time helping their country to prepare for war. Thedin said that the Swedes did not believe that a further Peace Resolution was necessary, because the one passed by the Prague Congress should be sufficient. They were, therefore, prepared to withdraw their resolution, but only if the Poles also withdrew theirs.

When this did not happen, Thedin went on the attack. He said that the Polish resolution was 'entirely unacceptable' because it demanded the prohibition of the atom bomb but made no similar demand for 'bacteriological warfare'. He reminded Central Committee members that the UN had already called for the prohibition of atomic weapons as well as all other weapons as a means of aggression. While the Polish resolution called for the first Government to use atomic weapons to be 'declared a war criminal', the Swedish delegation believed that the first Government to use any weapon to solve an international problem should be declared guilty of a 'crime' against humanity.

Thedin then returned to the Korean crisis, saying that it was not merely a question that four million North Koreans had signed the Stockholm Appeal, but that they were now waging war against

'the world peace organisation, the United Nations; it showed also the importance of reiterating the pledge given in the Prague Peace Resolution, in which the members of the ICA pledged themselves to give their full support to the United Nations'.

When the vote was taken the Polish resolution was defeated by 35 votes against to 25 votes for. The Swedish resolution was then carried by 37 votes to 23 against.

We can thus observe that, whereas once the ICA had a united peace policy, it was now divided. This was to continue for the next three decades or so. Although the Alliance continued its pro-peace policy, its subsequent peace resolutions and International Co-operative Day Manifestos were dulled by compromise. However, a new element entered into ICA peace demands when strongly pro-peace Japanese co-operators returned to the ICA in 1952.[120]

Although future statements needed to be worded in ways that were acceptable to East and West, this readiness to compromise reflected both toleration and a wish that the ICA should continue as an international co-operative forum.

Conclusion

The Cold War represented a greater threat to the unity of the International Co-operative Alliance than either of the two World Wars. We have seen that the 1914-18 War was viewed by ICA members as an imperialist war which involved workers as combatants, but was not begun by them. Consequently, ICA activities could resume with relatively little rancour. The 1939-45 War was somewhat different. Besides having different origins, it became the most total war in history, justifiably being labelled the people's war. Even so the ICA was little affected because, basically, all its members were on the same side: Fascist or Nazi co-operative movements had left the Alliance earlier and had not attempted to subvert it.

If we look at the 20th century in terms of its competing ideologies of Fascism and Communism, it is possible to argue that the former appeared to be defeated in 1945, while Communism remained to agitate non-Communist States into hostility and the Cold War. A Communist co-operative movement, Centrosoyus, had long been a member of the ICA, and this meant that the Alliance was therefore open to Communist pressure in a way that it had not been to Fascist and Nazi pressure. As we have demonstrated previously, one of the unanswered questions in the ICA is why Centrosoyus was allowed to remain a member.

Another unanswered question is why the Co-operative League of the USA played virtually no role in the events described in this Chapter. Perhaps this was a good thing, otherwise the Alliance might have been in even greater danger of splitting. It is strange, though, that, having played such a prominent role during the war, CLUSA did not continue to do so after the war. It becomes even more inexplicable when we contrast this with the leading role that the Americans played in the World Federation of Trade Unions and later the International Confederation of Free Trade Unions. The question arises as to whether the

Americans considered co-operatives less significant than trade unions in the Cold War.

It is interesting to note that CLUSA's representation in the Executive and Central Committee was thin and patchy during the period 1945-50, probably because of the costs and distances involved. CLUSA's period of highest activity in the ICA occurred during the war. Even though Murray D. Lincoln became a Vice-President of the Alliance between 1946-48, Minutes show that he did not attend any meetings. Mr H. A. Cowden, elected to the Executive in 1948, attended no meeting of the Committee between then and 1950, when this study closes. Moreover, few Americans attended other ICA meetings. Indeed, their representation declined from 20 delegates at the 1946 Zurich Congress[121] to only four at the Prague Congress in 1948,[122]

It seems reasonable to suppose that there would have been greater polarisation in the Alliance had the Americans been more active in the ICA during the Cold War.

This being so, it indicates the need to take into account negative, or contingent, reasons for the ICA's survival, quite as much as those that can be readily deduced. Other examples of contingent factors will be explored in the final Chapter.

In the meantime, we should conclude this Chapter by noting that, despite the immense pressures created by the Cold War, no group in the ICA wanted to split the organisation. For instance, Centrosoyus had a strong interest in having access to a mixed international forum. While traditional co-operators were ready to countenance a split, they did not seek to bring it about; instead, they successfully resisted Communists' various attempts to gain control of the Alliance.

As a result an uneasy coexistence emerged, aided by toleration and friendship, and also by the fact that the Alliance had become a mature organisation with a fair degree of continuity in its Secretariat.

Notes

1. ICA Archives, *Confidential Report of ICA Delegation to Paris, February, 1945*, p. 1.
2. International Co-operative Alliance, *Minutes of the British Members of the Central Committee, London, 7th March, 1945*, PP. 6 & 7.
3. International Co-operative Alliance, *Minutes of the meeting of the British Members of the Central Committee Manchester, 22nd November, 1944*, pp. 1 & 2.
4. International Co-operative Alliance, Memorandum on the Agenda of the Meeting of the Meeting of the British Members of the Central Committee, London, 18th July, 1945, p. 7.
5. International Co-operative Alliance, Memorandum on the Agenda of the Meeting of the British Members of the Central Committee, 18th July, 1945, p. 8.
6. International Co-operative Alliance, *Report of ICA Congress, Zurich, 1946*, Appendix vi.
7. *Ibid*
8. International Co-operative Alliance, *Review of International Co-operation*, Nos. 3 & 4 March-April, 1946, p. 43.
9. *Ibid.*, p. 43.
10. *Ibid.*, p. 43.
11. International Co-operative Alliance, Memorandum on the Agenda of the meeting of the ICA Executive, 18-19th March, 1946, p. 1.
12. *Ibid.*, p. 11.
13. International Co-operative Alliance, *Review of International Co-operation*, Nos. 3 & 4 March-April, 1946, p. 45.
14. CHAMBERS, W. & R. Ltd., *Chambers Biographical Dictionary*, p. 1120.
15. International Co-operative Alliance, Memorandum on the Agenda of the Meeting of the ICA Executive, Copenhagen, 18-19th March, 1946, pp. 12-16.
16. *Ibid.*, p. 12.
17. International Co-operative Alliance, *Review of International Co-operation*, Nos. 3 & 4, March-April, 1946, p. 59.

18. International Co-operative Alliance, *Ibid.*, p. 17.
19. International Co-operative Alliance, Memorandum on the Agenda of the meeting of the ICA Executive, Copenhagen, 18th-19th March, 1946, p. 17.
20. Earle, John, *The Italian Co-operative Movement*, Allen & Unwin, London, 1986, p. 30 and p. 46.
21. International Co-operative Alliance, *Report of ICA Congress, Prague, 1948*, Appendix viii, p. 213.
22. International Co-operative Alliance, *Report of ICA Congress, Zurich, 1946*, p. 37.
23. International Co-operative Alliance, Memorandum on the Agenda of the Meeting of the British Members of the O Central Committee, London, July, 1945, p. 1.
24. International Co-operative Alliance, *Minutes of the British Members of the Central Committee, London, 7th March, 1945*, p. 3.
25. International Co-operative Alliance, *Report of ICA Congress, Zurich, 1946*, p. 57.
26. International Co-operative Alliance, *Report of ICA Congress, Zurich, 1946*, p. 53.
27. PALMER, *Alan, Dictionary of Modern History 1789-1945* pp. 34-35.
28. International Co-operative Alliance, *Report of ICA Congress, Zurich, 1946*, pp. 54-55.
29. Ibid., pp. 55-56.
30. International Co-operative Alliance, *Report of ICA Congress, Zurich, 1946*, p. 56.
31. *Ibid.*, p. 58.
32. *Ibid.*, p. 58.
33. International Co-operative Alliance, *Review of International Co-operation*, Nos. 10 & 11, October/November, 1946, p. 157.
34. International Co-operative Alliance, *Report of ICA Congress, Zurich, 1946*, pp. viii - xiv.
35. *Ibid.*, pp. 83-84.
36. International Co-operative Alliance, *Minutes of the meeting of the ICA Executive, Brussels, 15-17 January, 1947*, p. 2.
37. International Co-operative Alliance, Memorandum on the Agenda of the meeting of the Central Committee, Avignon, 1st - 2nd May, 1947, p. 14.

38. International Co-operative Alliance, Memorandum on the Agenda of the meeting of the ICA Executive, Prague, 2nd & 3rd September, 1947, p. 10.
39. International Co-operative Alliance, *Review of International Co-operation,* No. 8 August, 1947, p. 115.
40. International Co-operative Alliance, Memorandum on the Agenda of the meeting of the ICA Executive, Amsterdam, 23 - 24 January, 1948, p. 23.
41. International Co-operative Alliance, *Minutes of the ICA Central Committee, Rome, 26-28 May, 1948*, pp. 25-26.
42. International Co-operative Alliance, *Report of the ICA Congress, Prague, 1948*, p. 92.
43. WATKINS, W. P., *The International Co-operative Alliance 1895-1970*, The International Co-operative Alliance, London, 1970, p. 205.
44. International Co-operative Alliance, Report of ICA Congress, Zurich, 1946, p. 142.
45. International Co-operative Alliance, *Report of ICA Congress, Prague, 1948*, p. 213.
46. LOTH, Wilfried, *The Division of the World 1941-1955*, Routledge, London, 1988, p. 305.
47. BARTLETT, C. J., *The Global Conflict 1880-1970*, Longman Group UK Limited, Harlow, 1984, p. 258.
48. International Co-operative Alliance, *Report of ICA Congress, Prague, 1948*, p. 35.
49. International Co-operative Alliance, *Minutes the meeting of the ICA Executive, Avignon, 27-28 April, 1947*, pp. 7-8.
50. International Co-operative Alliance, *Minutes of the meeting of the ICA Executive, Rome, 24-25 May, 1948*, pp. 5-8.
51. International Co-operative Alliance, *Minutes of the meeting of the ICA Central Committee, Rome, 26-28 May, 1948*, p. 9.
52. LOTH, Wilfried, *op. cit.*, pp. 125-129, and pp. 135-164.
53. *Ibid.*, pp. 126-127.
54. *Ibid.*, p. 145.
55. *Ibid.*, pp. 160-162.
56. International Co-operative Alliance, *Minutes of the meeting of the ICA Executive, Brussels, 16-17 January, 1947*, p. 12.

57. International Co-operative Alliance, *Minutes of the meeting of the ICA Central Committee, Rome, 26-28 May, 1948*, pp. 10-11.
58. *Ibid.*, p. 11.
59. *Ibid.*, p. 11.
60. *Ibid.*, pp. 21-22.
61. *Ibid.*, pp. 11-12.
62. *Ibid.*, pp. 12-16.
63. International Co-operative Alliance, *Report of the ICA Congress, Zurich, 1946*, pp. 119-121.
64. International Co-operative Alliance, *Report of the ICA Congress, Paris, 1937*, pp. 175 - 181.
65. International Co-operative Alliance, *Minutes of the meeting of the ICA Executive, Rome, 24-25 May, 1948*, p. 10.
66. International Co-operative Alliance, *Minutes of the meeting of the ICA Central Committee, Rome, 26-28 May, 1948*, p. 16.
67. *Ibid.*, pp. 16-17.
68. International Co-operative Alliance, *Report of the ICA Congress, Prague, 1948*, pp. 106-110.
69. *Ibid.*, p. 106.
70. *Ibid.*, p. 108.
71. *Ibid.*, p. 112.
72. International Co-operative Alliance, *Minutes of the meeting of the ICA Executive, Copenhagen, 18-19th March, 1946*, p. 1.
73. International Co-operative Alliance, *Review of International Co-operation*, Nos. 9 and 10, September/October, 1945, pp. 146,149 and 153.
74. International Co-operative Alliance, *Report of the ICA Congress, Zurich, 1946*, p. 180.
75. International Co-operative Alliance, *Report of the ICA, Congress, Prague, 1948*, p. 32.
76. International Co-operative Alliance, *Minutes of the meeting of the ICA Executive, Zurich, 28-30th January, 1949*, p. 16.
77. International Co-operative Alliance, *Report of the ICA Congress, 1948*, p. 115.
78. International Co-operative Alliance, *Minutes of the meeting of the ICA Executive, Zurich, 28-30th January, 1949*, p. 1.
79. International Co-operative Alliance, *Minutes of the meeting of the ICA Central Committee, Prague, 29th September, 1948*, p. 2.

80. International Co-operative Alliance, *Minutes of the meeting of the ICA Executive, Zurich, 28-30 January, 1949*, p. 18.
81. International Co-operative Alliance, *Minutes of the meeting of the ICA Central Committee, Stockholm, 25-27 June, 1949*, p. 14.
82. International Co-operative Alliance, *Minutes of the meeting of the ICA Executive, Stockholm, 23-24 June, 1949*, p. 7.
83. International Co-operative Alliance, *Minutes of the meeting of the ICA Central Committee, 25-27 June, 1949*, p. 14.
84. International Co-operative Alliance, Memorandum on the Agenda of the meeting of the ICA Executive, Paris, 17-18. November, 1949, Item 7, pp. 1-8.
85. International Co-operative Alliance, *Minutes of the meeting of the ICA Executive, Paris, 17-18 November, 1949*, pp. 1-2.
86. *Ibid.*, pp. 12-13.
87. International Co-operative Alliance, Memorandum on the Agenda of the meeting of the ICA Executive, Basle, 23-25 March, 1950, Item 8, pp. 1-2.
88. International Co-operative Alliance, *Minutes of the Executive, Basle, 23-25 March, 1950*, p. 1.
89. International Co-operative Alliance, Memorandum on the Agenda of the meeting of the ICA Executive, Helsinki, 14-15 August, 1950, Item 4, p. 1.
90. International Co-operative Alliance, *Minutes of ICA Executive, Helsinki, 14-15 August, 1950*, pp. 4-5.
91. ICA Archives, Photocopy of English translation of an article Towards a United International Co-operative Movement' by N. Sidorov and A. Klimov, in TRUD, 21 June, 1950, p. 1.
92. International Co-operative Alliance, *Minutes of ICA Executive, Helsinki, 14-15 August, 1950*, pp. 8-10.
93. International Co-operative Alliance, *Minutes of the ICA Central Committee, Helsinki, 16-18 August, 1950*, pp. 8-12.
94. WATKINS, W. P., *op. cit.*, pp. 274-5.
95. *Ibid.*, p. 275.
96. *Ibid.*, p. 300-301.
97. This study, Chapter 2, pp. 77-80.
98. International Co-operative Alliance, Memorandum on the Agenda of the meeting of the ICA Executive Sub-Committee, London, 4th November, 1946, p. 1.

99. International Co-operative Alliance, *Minutes of ICA Central Committee, Rome, 26-28 May, 1948*, p. 5.

100. International Co-operative Alliance, *Report of ICA Congress, Zurich, 1946*, p. 83.

101. *Ibid.*, pp. 178-179.

102. International Co-operative Alliance, *Minutes of the meeting of the ICA Executive, 25-26 June, 1946*, p. 11, and *Minutes of the meeting of the ICA Central Committee, Bridge of Allan, 27-28 June, 1946*, p. 14.

103. International Co-operative Alliance, *Review of International Co-operation, No.6, June, 1947*, p. 69.

104. International Co-operative Alliance, *Minutes of the meeting the ICA Executive, Rome, 24-25 May, 1948*, p. 13.

105. International Co-operative Alliance, *Report of ICA Congress, Prague, 1948*, pp. 189-190.

106. International Co-operative Alliance, *Minutes of the meeting of the ICA Executive, Zurich, 28-30 January, 1949*, p. 23.

107. International Co-operative Alliance, *Minutes of the meeting of the ICA Executive, Brussels, 15-17 January, 1947*, p. 1.

108. International Co-operative Alliance, *Minutes of the ICA Executive Sub-Committee, London, 30th March, 1949*, p. 1.

109. *Ibid.*, p. 5.

110. International Co-operative Alliance, *Minutes of the meeting of the ICA Executive, Stockholm, 23-24 June, 1949*, p. 8.

111. International Co-operative Alliance, *Minutes of the meeting of the ICA Central Committee, Stockholm, 25-27 June, 1949*, p. 17.

112. International Co-operative Alliance, Memorandum from ICA Director, Thorsten Odhe, to ICA Executive meeting, Stockholm, 23-24 June, 1949, p. 4.

113. International Co-operative Alliance, *Minutes of Special Session of ICA Executive, Stockholm, 20th June, 1950*, pp. 1-2.

114. International Co-operative Alliance, *Minutes of the meeting of the ICA Central Committee, Stockholm, 25-27 June, 1949*, p. 8.

115. International Co-operative Alliance, Memorandum on the Agenda of the meeting of the ICA Executive, Paris, 17-18 November, 1949, Item 2, p. 6.

116. International Co-operative Alliance, *Minutes of the meeting of the ICA Executive, Paris, 17-18 November, 1949*, p. 3.
117. *Ibid.*, p. 7.
118. International Co-operative Alliance, *Minutes of the ICA Central Committee, Stockholm, 25-27th June, 1949*, p. 8.
119. International Co-operative Alliance, *Minutes of the meeting of the ICA Central Committee, Helsinki, 16-18 August, 1950*, p. 32.
120. ICA Archives, List of Members Since 1904.
121. International Co-operative Alliance, *Report of the ICA Congress, Zurich, 1946*, p. xiv.
122. International Co-operative Alliance, *Report of ICA Congress, Prague, 1946*, p. xvii.

Chapter nine

Suggested Reasons why the ICA Survived the Two World Wars and the Cold War

Introduction

This Chapter, which concludes the study, is divided into two main parts. The first seeks to establish that, during the period studied, the International Co-operative Alliance was an international working-class organisation. The second will advance the main reasons for the Alliance's survival and attempt to identify secondary reasons.

Was the International Co-operative Alliance an International Working-Class Organisation between 1910 and 1950?

I have always seen the International Co-operative Alliance as having been an international working-class organisation during the period 1910-1950. This view has not been unchallenged. The most significant reservations arose in discussions with Mr W. P. Watkins, whose views were given weight by the fact that he had been Director of the Alliance from 1951 to 1963, and had previously been employed by the ICA between 1929 and 1940. He also wrote a history of the Alliance between 1895 and 1970. However, I believe that his views represent a caveat to, rather than a rejection of, the idea that the Alliance was a working class organisation. Watkins argued that the peasants' interests, represented in agricultural and thrift and credit co-operatives affiliated to the Alliance, meant that it was not exclusively a workers' body.

A similar view was expressed by Mr Robert Beasley, Director of the Alliance from 1984- 1988. It is believed, though, that his view may have been coloured by the fact that he is American, and therefore from a country whose working-class culture differed somewhat from that in Europe, and by his previous career in American agricultural co-operation.

Nevertheless, it is necessary to answer these reservations. If the argument that the ICA was an international working-class organisation cannot be substantiated, we cannot legitimately compare it with similar international bodies and ask how and why it survived and they did not. First of all, it is necessary to define what is meant by 'working-class organisation'.

In the case of the ICA, it was a body whose affiliated membership was predominantly made up of wage-earners, who subscribed to the working-class culture of the period and often participated in trade unions and workers' political parties. Their co-operative membership was mainly in the large-scale consumer societies of industrialised Europe. ICA statistics, reported in the March edition of the *Review of International Co-operation*, 1929,[1] show that the Alliance's overall membership in 1927 was 42,992, 068. Of that figure, agricultural co-operatives accounted for 11,644,318 and consumer co-operatives just over 31 million. Twenty-one years later, in 1948, the Report to the Prague Congress showed that total ICA membership had increased to 98,705,646. Within that, agricultural co-operatives numbered just over 9,500,000 and consumer co-operatives almost 56 million.[2] Photocopies of the tables appear on pages 370-374.

From these figures we can see that agricultural co-operative representation in the Alliance had fallen, both in terms of actual members and as a proportion of overall ICA membership.

We should also note that the numerical strength of consumer co-operatives translated itself into voting power in the election of ICA leaders and in policy determination. All the leaders mentioned in this study - Maxwell, Goedhart, Kaufmann, Serwy, Gide, Thomas, Poisson, Suter, Jaeggi, Tanner, Lustig, Freundlich, Renner, Oerne, Johansson, Warbasse, Palmer, Southern, May, Polley, and Odhe came from, or represented, consumer co-operative movements. To them, but particularly to Henry May, Co-operation was largely synonymous with consumer co-operation. This had ideological implications, as in the emphasis on 'open membership' as a basic Co-operative Principle. It will be recalled that the invocation of this principle played a prominent part in the debate on the Central Committee's 'Interpretation' of Article 8 in 1950.[3]

Beside its predominantly working-class affiliated membership, the aims of the ICA also suggest that it should be classified as an international

APPENDIX VI.

INTERNATIONAL

TYPES OF CONSTITUENT SOCIETIES: NUMBER

Country and Organisation*.	Year.	Consumers'.		Workers' Productive and Artisanal.		Agricultural.	
		(1)	(2)	(1)	(2)	(1)	(2)
EUROPE.							
AUSTRIA	1947	30	130,000	...	...	...	...
BELGIUM	1946	66	427,600	19	2,704	...	...
S.G.C.	1946	40	327,600	19	2,704	...	...
Fédération Coopératives Chrétiennes...	1946	26	100,000	...	...	...	...
BULGARIA(b)	1946	213	339,123	1,331	123,765	1,179	449,463
General Union	1946	213	339,123	1,331	123,765	1,179	449,463
Union des Banques	1945	...	...	...	...	...	...
CZECHOSLOVAKIA	1946	65	725,814	1,408 (d)795	221,586 (d)128,411	4,209	803,584
DENMARK	1946	1,957	440,000	82	...	5,506	790,548
Samvirkende Andelsselskaber	1946	1,957	440,000	...	...	5,506	790,548
Kooperative Faellesforbund	1946	50	97,819	82 (d)33	...	...	...
FINLAND	1946	491	841,476	...	...	...	...
K.K.	1946	121	425,163	...	...	...	...
Y.O.L.	1946	370	416,313	...	...	...	...
FRANCE	1946	1,026	2,008,832	647	41,000	13,100	1,400,000
F.N.C.C.	1946	1,026	2,008,832	...	...	...	...
Confédération des Sociétés Ouvrières de Production	1946	...	...	647	41,000	...	...
Fédération de la Mutualité Agricole...	1946	...	...	...	...	13,100	1,400,000
Caisse de Crédit Agricole	1946	...	...	...	...	...	...
Fédération Agricole	1946	...	...	...	...	(e)22	...
GERMANY(c)	1948	284	500,000	...	...	...	...
GREAT BRITAIN	1946	1,004	9,730,140	46	15,296	...	...
Co-operative Union	1946	1,004	9,730,140	46	15,296	...	...
Co-operative Productive Federation...	1946	...	...	46	13,862	...	...
GREECE	1946	...	...	...	...	4,257	420,160
HOLLAND	1946	288	278,000	...	...	...	...
ICELAND	1946	53	26,694	...	...	2	431
ITALY	1946–48	6,365	2,260,727	4,078	310,703	4,487	666,260
Lega Nazionale delle Cooperative	1946	3,865	1,758,787	2,841	248,853	2,259	220,660
Confederazione Cooperativa Italiana...	1948	2,500	501.940	1,237	61,850	2,228	445,600
NORWAY	1946	1,001	239,854	...	...	...	...
POLAND	1946	4,994	1,424,995	1,419 (d)80	64,092 (d)6,467	3,137	1,211,495
ROUMANIA	1946	273	448,429	261 (d)93	35,849 (d)12,329	5,190	1,689,124
SWEDEN	1946	705	851,576	...	...	...	...
SWITZERLAND	1946	893	516,311	...	...	...	...
V.S.K.	1946	552	489,159	...	...	...	...
V.O.L.G.	1946	341	27,152	...	...	...	...
U.S.S.R.	1947	28,000	32,000,000	...	...	...	...
YUGOSLAVIA	1946	839	576,837	794	21,335	9,493	1,735,056
TOTAL—EUROPE	1946	48,547 (19)	53,766,408 (19)	10,085 (10)	836,330 (9)	50,560 (10)	9,166,121 (10)
Number of Countries							

* In countries where only one Organisation is affiliated, their names are not given here but will be found in Appendix V.
(a) U.N. Monthly Bulletin of Statistics, April—October, 1948.
(b) Official Statistics.
(c) Societies in Three Western Zones affiliated to G.E.G.

CO-OPERATIVE ALLIANCE.

OF SOCIETIES (1). INDIVIDUAL MEMBERSHIP (2).

Building.		Miscellaneous.		Credit.		Total.		Population Estimates, 1946(a).
(1)	(2)	(1)	(2)	(1)	(2)	(1)	(2)	
...	...	...	...	...	...	30	130,000	7,009,000
...	...	10	...	...	...	95	430,304	8,389,000
...	...	10	...	...	...	70	330,304	...
...	...	...	...	...	...	26	100,000	...
...	...	15	4,502	3,152	903,890	5,890	1,820,743	6,993,000
...	...	15	4,502	3,152	903,890	5,890	1,820,743	...
...	...	...	...	245	326,032	245	326,032	...
711	75,315	192	20,000	4,074	1,227,863	10,659	3,074,162	13,091,000
157	31,812	86	...	47	25,094	7,835	1,287,454	4,101,000
...	...	...	...	...	...	7,463	1,230,548	...
157	31,812	86	...	...	...	375	129,631	...
...	...	...	...	...	...	491	841,476	3,847,000
...	...	...	...	...	...	121	425,163	...
...	...	...	...	...	...	370	416,313	...
...	...	...	...	4,397	629,500	19,170	4,079,332	40,000,000
...	...	...	...	...	...	1,026	2,008,832	...
...	...	...	...	...	...	647	41,000	...
...	...	...	...	...	...	13,100	1,400,000	...
...	...	...	...	4,397	629,500	4,397	629,500	...
...	...	...	...	...	...	(e)22		
...	...	...	...	...	...	284	500,000	(f)65,911,000
...	...	...	...	...	...	1,050	9,745,436	49,318,000
...	...	...	...	...	...	1,050	9,745,436	...
...	...	...	...	...	...	46	13,862	...
...	...	...	...	...	...	4,257	420,160	7,450,000
...	...	...	...	...	...	288	278,000	9,420,000
...	...	...	...	...	...	55	27,125	132,000
507	56,816	1,292	302,348	895	227,948	17,624	3,824,802	45,486,000
264	32,516	539	189,398	4	1,745	9,772	2,451,959	...
243	24,300	753	112,950	891	226,203	7,852	1,372,843	...
...	...	...	...	...	...	1,001	239,854	3,105,000
...	...	303	49,809	1,222	447,164	11,075	3,197,555	(g)23,930,000
...	...	102	36,811	3,076	1,034,370	8,902	3,244,583	16,472,000
...	...	...	...	...	...	705	851,576	6,719,000
...	...	...	...	...	...	893	516,311	4,466,000
...	...	...	...	...	...	552	489,159	...
...	...	...	...	...	...	341	27,152	...
...	...	...	...	...	...	28,000	32,000,000	193,000,000
228	18,066	443	21,796	1,401	114,276	13,198	2,487,366	14,800,000
1,603	182,009	2,443	435,266	18,264	4,610,105	131,502	68,996,239	523,639,000
(4)	(4)	(8)	(6)	(8)	(8)	(20)	(20)	(20)

(d) Artisanal Societies included in Workers' Productive Societies.
(e) Specialised Federations or National Unions.
(f) Population enumerated in four zones of occupation, including Berlin.
(g) Pre-war Territory.

APPENDIX VI. (continued)

TYPES OF CONSTITUENT SOCIETIES: NUMBER

Country and Organisation.*	Year.	Consumers'.		Workers' Productive and Artisanal.		Agricultural.	
		(1)	(2)	(1)	(2)	(1)	(2)
AMERICA.							
CANADA	1943	269	219,738	...	...	6	167,837
U.S.A.	1946	2,603	646,000	...	...	...	...
ARGENTINA	1946	91	117,402	...	...	...	...
COLOMBIA	1946	1	3,025	...	...	...	...
Total	1946	2,964	986,165	...	...	6	167,837
ASIA.							
CHINA	1946	...	...	...	...	...	...
INDIA†	1944–45	43,364	960,624	...	...	...	...
Agricultural	1944–45	...	...	...	...	...	...
Non-Agricultural	1944–45	...	...	...	...	...	...
ISRAEL	1946	200	110,000	86	2,800	235	31,156
" Hevrat Ovdim "	1946	200	110,000	86	2,800	235	31,156
" Merkaz "	1946	...	...	...	...	...	...
Total	1944–46	43,564	1,070,624	86	2,800	235	31,156
OCEANIA.							
AUSTRALIA‡	1941–42	90	110,565	...	...	440	206,604
NEW ZEALAND	1947	28	11,500	...	...	...	...
Total	1941–47	118	122,065	...	...	440	206,604
SOUTH AFRICA	1946	1	3,000	...	...	...	...
CONTINENTAL TOTALS.							
EUROPE	1946	48,547	53,766,408	10,085	836,330	50,560	9,166,121
AMERICA	1946	2,964	986,165	...	...	6	167,837
ASIA	1946	43,564	1,070,624	86	2,800	235	31,156
OCEANIA	1941–47	118	122,065	...	...	440	206,604
SOUTH AFRICA	1946	1	3,000	...	...	...	...
WORLD TOTAL	1946	95,194	55,948,262	10,171	839,130	51,241	9,571,718
Number of Countries	...	(28)	(28)	(11)	(10)	(13)	(13)

* In countries where only one Organisation is affiliated, their names are not given here but will be found in Appendix V.
† Official Statistics.
‡ Mainly Credit Societies.

OF SOCIETIES (1). INDIVIDUAL MEMBERSHIP (2).

Building.		Miscellaneous.		Credit.		Total.		Population Estimates, 1946.
(1)	(2)	(1)	(2)	(1)	(2)	(1)	(2)	
...	...	...	...	...	...	275	387,575	12,307,000
...	...	...	...	...	...	2,603	646,000	141,229,000
...	...	...	...	...	...	91	117,402	16,032,000
...	...	...	...	...	...	1	3,025	10,318,000
...	...	...	...	...	...	2,970	1,154,002	179,886,000
...	...	...	...	...	...	160,222	19,624,599	455,592,000
...	...	...	...	116,269‡	7,394,556‡	159,633	8,355,180	366,500,000§
...	...	...	...	...	...	137,692	5,152,070	...
...	...	...	...	...	...	21,941	3,203,110	...
57	10,130	43	...	63	89,871	684	243,957	1,912,000
57	10,130	43	...	20	31,165	641	185,251	...
...	...	...	...	43	58,706	43	58,706	...
57	10,130	43	...	116,332	7,484,427	320,539	28,223,736	824,004,000
...	...	...	...	...	...	530	317,169	7,466,000
...	...	...	...	...	...	28	11,500	1,761,000
...	...	...	...	...	...	558	328,669	9,227,000
...	...	...	...	...	...	1	3,000	11,420,000
1,603	182,009	2,443	435,266	18,264	4,610,105	131,502	68,996,239	523,639,000
...	...	...	...	...	...	2,970	1,154,002	179,886,000
57	10,130	43	...	116,332	7,484,427	320,539	28,223,736	824,004,000
...	...	...	...	...	...	558	328,669	9,227,000
...	...	...	...	...	...	1	3,000	11,420,000
1,660	192,139	2,486	435,266	134,596	12,094,532	455,570	98,705,646	1,548,176,000
(5)	(5)	(9)	(6)	(10)	(10)	(30)	(30)	(30)

§ *Estimated population of Provinces and States included in Statistics.*

Statistics of Affiliated National Organisations (1927)

General Summary of the Tables.
(Membership, Trade and other operations)

Societies.	Societies Affiliated.	Societies Furnishing Statistics.	Individual Members.	a Sales to Members. b Sale of Produce of Members. c Total.	Value of Own Productions.
				£	£
1. Consumers. 33 Countries: 39 Organisations.	43,498	42,434	31,101,954	a 1,211,134,498 b 74,367,056 c 1,312,234,089	119,225,586
2. Wholesale. 27 Countries: 35 Organisations.	—	—	—	a 317,081,520 b 34,075,993 c 362,714,413	65,177,696
3a. Workers' Productive. 11 Countries: 14 Organisations.	2,102	1,361	174,962	a — b 8,623,011 c 13,849,652	11,181,973
3b. Federated Productive. 9 Countries: 20 Organisations.	—	—	—	a 1,214,954 b 29,472 c 6,324,067	4,204,543
4. Agricultural. 18 Countries: 21 Organisations.	93,926	51,960	11,644,318	a 112,525,388 b 308,342,921 c 421,276,642	66,014,206
5. Miscellaneous. 7 Countries: 9 Organisations.	657	498	70,834	a 748,006 b 122,000 c 1,233,341	66,370
Total	140,183	96,253	42,992,068	a 1,642,704,366 b 425,560,453 c 2,117,632,204	265,870,374

working-class organisation. A major aim and recurring theme of the study has been the Alliance's goal of assisting in the improvement of co-operative members' living standards, i.e. those of the workers. This aim led it to collaborate with a number of bodies with similar aspirations, in particular, the International Labour Organisation and the International Federation of Trade Unions and its successors.

Moreover, the first Article of the Alliance's original Constitution included the objective of the 'amelioration of the lot of the working classes.'[4] Although this wording was dropped from later Constitutions it can be argued that the aim was maintained in various other forms of words.

We can also see the working-class nature of the Alliance from the political affiliations of its leaders. It must be said at this point that many of those leaders, and particularly Goedhart, Gide, Thomas, Suter and Freundlich, appeared to have middle-class backgrounds, discernible in the degree of education they showed. Maxwell and May came from more humble origins and their initial training was in the form of industrial apprenticeships, Maxwell in coach building and May in engineering. However, it can be argued that many ICA leaders showed left-wing political affiliations. For example, we have noted that Henry May stood, unsuccessfully, as a Co-operative Candidate in the 1918 British General Election. Albert Thomas and Karl Renner were left wing ministers in French and Austrian Governments respectively, as was socialist Väinö Tanner in Finland. In addition, less politically eminent ICA leaders such as Victor Serwy (Belgium), Ernest Poisson (France), Lord Rusholme (Great Britain), Emil Lustig (Czechoslovakia) and Emmy Freundlich (Austria) all had close links with workers' parties as, of course, did the ICA delegates from the USSR's Centrosoyus and other Communist co-operative movements. In the last Chapter we noted their description of the workers as 'the toilers'.

Another influence that we should keep in mind was that of the British Co-operative Movement. Besides being the strongest voluntary movement in the ICA, it was also the one with the closest links to a political party. Through the Co-operative Union, British consumer co-operatives constituted one of the three wings of the British National Council of Labour, the other two being the Labour Party and the Trades Unions Congress. Such links helped the Alliance to lobby effectively on issues such as its representation in the UN[5] and its proposals about the world's oil supplies.[6]

Quite apart from the company that its major voluntary member organisation kept, we should remind ourselves of the bodies with which the Alliance itself associated. We have already noted that its strongest and most consistent relationship was with the International Labour Organisation. But it also had links with the International Federation of Trade Unions and, before the 1914-18 War, with the Socialist International.

We can therefore conclude this section by noting that, in terms of its affiliated membership, its aims and policies, the political complexion of its leadership and the organisations with which it worked, the Alliance was an international working-class organisation. We are then faced with the question of why it survived the two World Wars and the Cold War when its close associates, the Socialist International and the International Federation of Trade Unions, did not. The International Labour Organisation was a different kind of body, being part of first the League of Nations system and later the United Nations.

In the final section we will examine what are believed to be the main reasons for the Alliance's survival, namely its ideology and organisation.

Reasons for the ICA's Survival

Having traced the ICA through the two World Wars and the Cold War, which, in view of the fate of other international working-class organisations, must have constituted the biggest threat to the Alliance's existence, we are led to the conclusion that ideology explained 'why' the Alliance survived and its organisation 'how' it did so. It is also necessary to explore other haphazard, or contingent, reasons why the Alliance survived, but we shall find that these did not form as distinct a pattern as the two main reasons.

Ideology

As we saw in the first two Chapters, the Alliance resulted from the internationalism of national co-operative movements. These subscribed to a distinct view of society characterised by the moral and communitarian ideas of Robert Owen and Saint Simon, which stemmed from their belief that, in economic and social activities, co-operation was superior to competition. Many of the national co-operative movements coming together to form the International Co-operative Alliance in 1895 had also adopted the economic teachings and practices of Dr William King and the Rochdale Pioneers, focusing on self-help and mutual aid, and on undertaking economic activity for service rather than for profit. As part of their wish to do away with the profit motive, early co-operators experimented with profit-sharing, or co-partnership and, initially, the Alliance was an organisation 'to promote co-operation and profit-sharing in all their forms'.

Throughout the period studied, the Alliance claimed that it was based on Rochdale Co-operation. However, we have noted the rise of other influences, particularly the changing role of the State. Although its ideology and organisation played the major part in the Alliance's survival, other features also contributed, including an ability to evolve and change. Even so, the Alliance retained a sentimental attachment to Rochdale despite changing economic and social conditions which required co-operatives to develop new practices. Because of this, the ICA tended to have a developing philosophy and shifting rhetoric throughout the period - but always one with a strong moral tone. The result was that ICA ideology did not become fossilised in an earlier period. To a large extent it seems that the ICA informally subscribed to the views of Dr Georges Fauquet (France), expressed at the Paris Congress in 1937, that co-operatives were 'living organisms', and therefore the co-operative spirit' permeating them was more important than a set of Principles.[7] Such flexibility made it possible to confer the co-operative spirit elsewhere. Thus, R. A. Palmer argued in the 1943 debate between himself, Dr Warbasse and Prof. Fabra-Ribas that co-operatives could acknowledge a place for nationalised industries, but that these should operate, as co-operatives did, for service rather than profit and that their benefits to consumers and workers should have priority over their returns to capital.[8]

Other ideas were also grafted on to the Alliance's Rochdale-oriented philosophy. One that has relevance to this study was the belief that the ICA, rather than the League of Nations or United Nations was the real League of the People. While this reflected the populist and working class bias of the organisation, it also illustrated the fact that it had a clear picture of its place in international relations.

In addition to the ICA's ideology considered in this study, we should take into account other aspects which may also have had a bearing on the organisation's survival, but which have been little explored in this context. One example is the principle of co-operation between co-operatives. While not enunciated until the Vienna Congress of 1966, it had long been recognised as a distinct feature of co-operative activity. Indeed, the Alliance was an international expression of it. But its most usual form occurred in co-operatives trading with each other. This was an area of ICA preoccupation pre-dating the 1914-18 War and included attempts to establish an International Co-operative Wholesale Society and, later, the International Co-operative Trading Agency.[9] It is reasonable to suggest that co-operatives' trade provided a cohesiveness, or identity of interests, within the Alliance that assisted its survival. The point that should be underlined is that this strand of development had an ideological basis. Initially such trade was based on identified consumer needs. Therefore, the production it called forth was not speculative. Such trade also helped to increase economies of scale, and to make more economic use of natural resources. We should re mind ourselves that this was an important element in the 1946 Zurich Congress debate on the world's oil supplies.

Work on this study has suggested a number of areas for subsequent research, and the place of inter-co-operative trading within the ICA is one of these.

A consequence of ICA ideology revealed by this study is that delegates to ICA meetings and Congresses appeared to think of themselves first as Co-operators and secondly as Britons, French, Swedes or other nationalities. As a result, ICA meetings and Congresses were remark ably free of chauvinism, a fact that is reflected also in Minutes, Reports and letters. This even continued during the Cold War, although Communist bloc members referred more frequently to external events, specific countries, or people from them. The most notable example we have quoted was their reference to Woods of England... making a venomous speech in the spirit of the Anglo-American warmongers'.[10] Again, in its alternative draft of the 1948 International Co-operative Day Manifesto, Centrosoyus referred to the 'mass executions of Greek patriots' and protested against the support of the Franco regime in Spain by the Governments of the USA, England and France'.[11] Despite such incidents, the big debates in the ICA during the Cold War were invariably conducted on co-operative terms and were essentially about the Western and Eastern systems of co-operation within the Alliance. They therefore had a strong philosophical element.

One reason for this concentration on co-operative, rather than national, matters appears to have stemmed from the Alliance's attempts to remain politically neutral. As we saw in Chapter 2, religious and political neutrality was an important part of ICA ideology. Efforts to observe such neutrality are likely to have reduced the potential for controversy within the Alliance, and again assisted its survival. Examples of the principle being evoked include the rejection of the Communist draft for the 1948 International Co-operative Day Manifesto because it was not politically neutral and because it insufficiently reaffirmed faith in co-operative principles,[12] and the rejection of the Dutch proposal that the 1948 Congress should not proceed in Prague because of the Communist takeover of Czechoslovakia earlier that year.[13]

But we have also seen that avoiding a political judgement was sometimes very difficult. The most tortured example was the debate at the 1937 Congress on the Spanish Civil War.[14]

Despite all its attempts to be politically neutral, the Alliance was consistently anti-Fascist or anti-Nazi. Its views on Communism were more ambiguous, but hardened as Communism became more Stalinist. Even so, after the most dangerous period of the Cold War, the Alliance learned to co-exist with Communist co-operators.

We have also noted that the ICA's pursuit of peace brought it into political areas. In particular, we have seen that the Alliance took positive stands in support of the League of Nations, and later the United Nations, seeking representation in both. They, and the International Labour Organisation with which the ICA also worked closely, and later organisations such as the UN's Food and Agricultural Organisation, represented a new international order, based on social, economic and political justice, that the ICA actively supported.

To conclude this section, we should note that the ICA tempered its overall ideology with some degree of pragmatism and flexibility. There were, however, a number of central ideas that provided an important sense of identity and cohesion within the Alliance. Moreover, we should observe that the ICA's ideology helped to shape the organisation's Constitution. It has already been observed that this remained remarkably constant during the period of this study, and even withstood Centrosoyus's attempts to revise it at the 1948 Congress. The only effect the Cold War had on the Rules was the perceived need to clarify Article 8 and to create Associate Membership in 1954.

We noted the main points of the ICA's Constitution in Chapter 2[15]. Having since traced the ICA's survival through two World Wars and the Cold War, we are now better able to assess the aspects of ICA organisation that contributed to that achievement.

Organisation

By organisation we mean the ICA's Constitution plus the workings of its authorities, namely the Congress, Central and Executive Committees and the Secretariat.

We have already noted how themes in this study, such as the working class nature of the Alliance and its pursuit of world peace, were reflected in ICA Rules. The aim of this section is, therefore, to illustrate particular events or developments and to show how the ICA Rules helped shape these. It is also hoped to show that, being a typical working-class organisation of the period, the ICA always closely observed its Constitution yet used it in sophisticated ways.

We have seen that the Alliance achieved a constitutional resumption of its activities after the two World Wars. On both occasions these were likely to have been assisted by the fact that, apart from Centrosoyus's long sustained hostility to Väinö Tanner, ICA member organisations exhibited few post-war recriminations. Nevertheless, fear of such recriminations caused the all-British Executive to delay calling meetings of the Central Committee in 1919. Consequently, the first Central Committee Meeting was not held until 1920 and the first Congress was not convened until a year later.

Throughout the period studied, but particularly during the two World Wars, one gains the impression that the ICA Constitution, like the organisation's ideology, provided another element of cohesion. For example, national co-operative movements, often from different traditions, as we have seen with the Scandinavians and British, found that the Constitution guaranteed them both equity and legitimacy within the Alliance.

By the way that the Constitution was observed we can see that ICA member movements had confidence in it. It was noted that the French, during the First World War[16], and the Americans, in the Second World War[17], created initiatives on a number of policy issues that a British based Executive, or substitute, felt unable to make. Yet, in both cases, the French and Americans handed over their initiatives to the Alliance as soon as it was able to pursue them.

The most notable organisational achievement in the Alliance came in 1939, when it surmounted three simultaneous crises: the outbreak of the Second World War, the death of its General Secretary, and the isolation of its President. Each crisis was overcome with some degree of sophistication typical of a mature organisation, but always within its Constitution.

Overcoming the crises was also assisted by a marked degree of continuity. While Miss Polley was not given the status of General Secretary, she was able to continue her administration in much the same way as she had previously, but reporting to R. A. Palmer and the British members of the Central Committee rather than to Henry May and the Executive and Central Committees. There was no change in the way that Minutes, reports and ICA finances were handled, apart from changes imposed by wartime conditions. In connection with these, we should note that, although Dr Shenkman and Mr W. P. Watkins left the Alliance in disagreement over the way that Miss Polley and Mr R. A. Palmer ran the Secretariat and, in particular, the way they handled information, it seems reasonable to suggest that the war increased the need for confidentiality on a number of issues.

Another example of the Secretariat operating largely as it had done before the war can be found in the continued production of the *Review of International Co-operation*. Only in the final year of the war did worsening newsprint shortages force occasional editions to be produced bi-monthly rather than monthly.

The problems surrounding the Presidency were far more intractable. They also illustrated the strict constitutionalism that permeated the Alliance. There was no provision in ICA Rules for a single country's delegation to the ICA Central Committee to act alone on behalf of the Committee. Yet, had the British members not acted as they did there could have been a dangerous vacuum in the Alliance. Throughout their wartime meetings, though, they had an eye to their eventual account ability, both to the full Central Committee and to the ICA Congress. That constitutional correctness was particularly evident in the handling of the question of the Presidency.[18]

Only in 1943, two years after the matter became pressing, did the British members move to appoint R. A. Palmer as 'Vice-President and Acting President'. Until then, their consistent line had been that only the full Central Committee had the power to re-elect an existing President or elect a new one. There is good reason to believe that the factor which finally caused them to move from this position was the need for documents to be signed on behalf of the ICA to enable it to become officially involved in schemes for post-war relief and rehabilitation. Even then, as we have noted, the move was not made before those co-operative leaders who could be contacted were consulted. Even then, among these Dr Warbasse in the United States opposed the move on the grounds that there was no provision in the ICA Rules for an Acting President. [19]

When we move into the Cold War period we find that the main bastion against a Communist take-over of the Alliance was its Constitution. Centrosoyus and the co-operative organisations in Eastern and Central Europe obviously recognised this. Hence their proposals for large-scale amendments during the 1948 Rules Revision.[20] Again we see the mark of a mature organisation in the sophisticated, but constitutional, ways in which that, and other initiatives, were resisted by Western co-operative movements. The one caveat to that should be the clarification of Article 8. But, even here, the issue was raised constitutionally through the Policy Sub-Committee,[21] and it was always claimed to be a 'clarification' or 'reinterpretation' rather than an amendment. We have noted doubts about this, but it must be listed as an important reason why the ICA came through the Cold War as a single organisation and not divided, as was the World Federation of Trade Unions.

We should remind ourselves, though, that the move was defensive, and was made to resist Soviet attempts to flood the Alliance with the membership of Communist-controlled co-operative movements whose rules and status had been changed, or whose membership had been inflated through compulsion rather than by voluntary choice. In this connection, we should recall Robert Southern's telling argument that the Alliance's duty was to its 'existing members' rather than to dubiously-constituted co-operative organisations applying for membership.[22]

In concluding this section, we could perhaps speculate that the very longevity of the ICA's Constitution, which had allowed member organisations to develop familiarity and confidence in it, was a reason why the ICA survived. This possibility can be seen more clearly when we contrast the Alliance with the World Federation of Trade Unions, which was re-established in 1945. That organisation then had little time to develop a similar confidence in its Constitution. This may have been a factor in its not being as successful as the ICA in withstanding Soviet pressures during the Cold War.

As important as the ICA's ideology and organisation were in helping it survive the crises surrounding 20th century wars, other more contingent reasons also played a part. We will now examine each of these in turn.

Contingent Reasons for Survival
Location of Secretariat.

An important reason must have been the location of the Secretariat. During both World Wars, it was a coincidence that it was in one of the few Western European countries to escape invasion; moreover, that this was also the home to the Alliance's largest voluntary member movement and the one that was closest, geographically and historically, to Rochdale. During the wars, though, it was the practical help which the British movement could give that was particularly significant.

It helped to strengthen the benefits arising from the accident that, during the First World War, the Alliance still had an all-British Executive: The war might have had a more divisive effect had the Executive comprised a wider membership and increased the risk of wartime antagonisms coming into the heart of the Alliance. A similar situation applied in the Second World War, when the British members of the Central Committee became, in effect, the ICA Executive. During both wars the all-British arrangement was never exclusive: observers, or representatives, from exiled co-operative movements were always welcomed at meetings if able to attend.

Another benefit arising from the all-British arrangement was that the Secretariat did not operate in a vacuum. It was able to report its actions, be held accountable and receive practical advice. Without these constitutional mechanisms its legitimacy would have become more suspect both inside and outside the Alliance. The smooth resumption of ICA activities after each war might not then have taken place, and the Secretariat's initiatives to involve the Alliance in relief and rehabilitation, and to seek membership of the United Nations might not have proceeded as far as they did. Moreover, the success of these must have given a boost to the resumption of Alliance activities after 1945. Another advantage derived from the ICA's being based in London was that, in both wars, the ICA Secretariat and Executive were near to the Government of a leading Allied country. We have noted that this benefit was enhanced by personal acquaintances, particularly among Labour members of the British wartime coalition Government during the 1939-45 War.[23]

Reduced American Influence

It was observed that, rather surprisingly, CLUSA's participation in the Alliance declined during the Cold War.[24] Throughout the study we have, perhaps, made little mention of the constraints of communications and travel applying between 1910 and 1950. Given that ICA meetings were in Europe during that period, it seems likely that the cost and time involved in crossing the Atlantic had an inhibiting effect on the Americans. Even so, we noted that CLUSA's representation declined in the late 1940s compared with what it had been immediately after the war. While it is difficult to suggest reasons for this, it is likely that the Alliance would have been in greater danger of splitting had the American presence been stronger.

It is felt that this is another area of ICA history that would repay further research.

Lack of Nationalism

We have previously referred to the fact that nationalistic sentiments seldom entered ICA debates. It did not become clear that this might constitute a contingent reason for the Alliance's survival until the end of the research and the writing of this study. By then, certain patterns had become discernible; this particular one was sharpened by an article in History Today, which appeared in September, 1990.[25] Written by Denis McShane, it argued that one of the reasons for the division of the World Federation of Trade Unions was the emergence of divergent national priorities among member trade union movements. By this McShane meant that, at moments of crisis, such as the two World Wars and the Cold War, trade unions saw events very much from the point of view of their own countries. Moreover, they sought to answer problems, such as the relief of poverty, in terms of national, rather than international, solutions. In other words, the existence of strong nation States militated against trade union cohesion at an international level. McShane further suggested that a sound trade union international was unlikely to emerge while trade unions continued to identify with the nation State. Only in recent years did he feel that this position had begun to change in Europe, with the development of the European Community.

As we have found, a similar analysis cannot be said to have applied to co-operatives during the same period. Not only did they exhibit a strong thrust towards internationalism throughout the whole period of this study, but an analysis of ICA Minutes and Reports, etc., reveal an absence of nationalistic sentiments to a marked degree.

Obviously, the nature of their activities helps to explain the difference between co-operatives and trade unions in this area. We have already suggested that further research into the contribution that co-operative trade made to ICA cohesiveness would be enlightening. Allied to the question of the lack of nationalism in the ICA was the obvious presence of fraternity and toleration within the organisation. These emanated from co-operative ideology but their practice played a significant role, particularly during the Cold War. It seems likely that, throughout the period, they helped to sustain the 'co-operative spirit' that was always prominent in the Alliance.

Conclusion

This second edition was prompted by the war in Ukraine and questions being raised about earlier ICA responses to War and Peace. The first edition was published in 1995 since which time the Alliance has become more regionalised and developed stronger sectoral structures. Its membership has grown making it truly worldwide. The period covered in this book therefore becomes less significant in terms of years but it offers important lessons.

Between 1910 and 1950 the International Co-operative Alliance was an international working-class organisation. It was the only one such to survive the two World Wars and the Cold War. At the centre of this success were a number of closely inter-related factors: the Alliance's ideology, and its organisation based on its Constitution and assisted by the workings of its authorities, namely the Congress, Central and Executive Committees and the Secretariat. These two overriding reasons were assisted by more haphazard factors, such as the Alliance's location, a declining participation by an important national delegation, and the absence of nationalism, as well as the more positive features of tolerance and fraternity that imbued ICA leaders.

In addition to these reasons, we might also speculate whether the Alliance might not have survived because it was capable of the occasional fudge, such as over the issue of whether Centrosoyus should remain a member. Had it not done so, and had Centrosoyus left, the Alliance could have split as early as 1921.

Undoubtedly, the ICA's survival was a remarkable achievement, given the propensity of working-class movements to split. However, we need to ask whether it was worthwhile.

The answer to that must be an unequivocal yes. While working-class people were not so successful in their other international organisations, in the Alliance they showed that they could organise effectively and operate at an international level. They also proved that, over a long period of time, they could promote alternative views on international economic and social issues and, most importantly, on questions war and peace. Equally significant, the ICA's survival enabled it to go on to promote co-operation as means of national development in many Third World countries from the 1960s onwards. Thus, in this later work the Alliance showed the ability it had demonstrated throughout its history to adapt and to respond positively to world changes.

Laying of the stone for the Regional Office for Asia and the Pacific - Marcel Brot (France, 1887-1966) was very active in preventing the ICA from splitting between 1948 and 1950. This photograph represents the link between the ICA's survival and its ability to contribute to Third World Development.

Notes

1. International Co-operative Alliance, *Review of International Co-operation*, No. 3, March, 1929, p. 89.
2. International Co-operative Alliance, *Report of the ICA Congress, Prague, 1948*, Appendix vi.
3. This Study, Chapter 8.
4. WATKINS, W. P., *op. cit., The International Co-operative Alliance*, p. 48.
5. This Study, Chapter 7. pp 279-284
6. This Study, Chapter 8, pp 308-313
7. This Study, Chapter 2, pp 60-63
8. This Study, Chapter 7, p. 245
9. WATKINS, W. P., *op. cit., The International Co-operative Alliance*, pp. 124, 143, 157, 159, 164, 166-168, 191-194, 208-209, 227, 245 and 246 (International Co-operative Wholesale Society), pp. 209, 217, 234, 245-246, 248, 252, 256 and 264 (International Co-operative Trading Agency).
10. This Study, Chapter 8, pp. 337-338
11. This Study, Chapter 8, p. 321
12. This Study, Ibid.
13. This Study, Chapter 8, pp. 319-320
14. This Study, Chapter 6, pp. 198-204
15. This Study, Chapter 2, pp. 34-46
16. This Study, Chapter 3, pp. 83-85
17. This Study, Chapter 7, pp. 274-279
18. This Study, Chapter 7, pp. 236-262
19. This Study, Chapter 7, p. 251
20. This Study, Chapter 8, pp. 323-328
21. This Study, Chapter 8, pp. 331-344
22. This Study, Chapter 8, p. 342
23. This Study, Chapter 7, pp. 243, 267 and 282
24. This Study, Chapter 8, pp. 358-359
25. MCSHANE, Denis, *'The World Federation of Trade Unions', History Today*, September, 1990.

Index

International organisations are arranged under their own names. National organisations are arranged under their country, with the exception of Centrosoyus (Russia), The Co-operative League of the USA (USA), The Co-operative Union (Great Britain), and Lega Nazionale delle Cooperative e Mutue (Italy), which are discussed in detail in the text, and have their own entries in the Index.

Acción Cooperatista, 212
Agnew, P. J., 297
agricultural co-operation, 26, 153-154, 277, 285, 369
Albania, 344
Alexander, A. V., 282
Allen, Sir T. W., 45, 109, 129, 155, 160
Allied Agricultural Advisory Committee, 271
Allied Military Government of Occupied Territories, 271-272, 285
Allied Post-War Requirements Bureau, 271
American Office of Foreign Relief & Rehabilitation, 272
Anton, Juan Salas, 196
Antoni, A., 307
Apelquist, S., 307
Argentina, 21, 297, 303
Armenia, 77, 118
Atlantic Charter, 304, 308, 311, 356
Atlantic Pact, 351-352
Attlee, Clement, 243, 282
Austria
    agricultural co-operatives, 184, 185
    aid from ICA, 186, 188-189
    appeal to British Government, 181
    Austrian situation of 1934, 178-191
    co-operative movement, 77, 78, 80, 163, 180-190, 298-301
    Co-operative Unions, 180, 182, 183, 185, 186.
    Co-operative Wholesale Society, 180, 182, 184-185, 186, 189

        early support for ICA, 21
        government control of co-operatives, 180-190
        Labour Bank, 184, 185
        links with Czechoslovakia, 205
        membership of ICA, 26, 180, 189, 303
        memorandum to Federal Government, 182-183
        merger of Germany and Austria, 163, 179, 190, 191
        Union of German-Austrian Consumers' Societies, 180
        Vienna Co-operative Society, 182, 184, 185, 189, 190
Australia, 21, 35, 297, 303
Avenol, J., 279
Azerbaijan, 118

Baker, Philip Noel, 284
Baldwin, Stanley, 137
Barbados, 24, 35
Barbier, Ch. H., 307, 336, 338, 342, 343-344
Barnes, Alf, 199-200, 201-202
Basle Congress 1921, 38, 51, 64, 65, 86, 101, 102-109, 113, 129-130,131, 135
Bastlein, Hugo, 161
Beasley, Robert, 368
Beaton, Neil, 235, 296
Beck, 182, 301
Belgium
        appeal for war relief, 82
        First World War, 77, 80-81
        members of Central Committee, 23
        representation at Congresses, 20, 21, 24
        representation at London Conference 1943, 275
        Second World War, 297
Benes, Dr. Edward, 206, 213
Berkenheim, 101
Bevin, E., 243, 310-311
Birkbeck, Dr., 4
Blanc, Louis, 13-14
Boer, K. de, 235

Bonow, Dr. Mauritz, 332, 333, 336, 338, 342
Bowen, E. R., 277
Boyve, Edouard de, 17, 19, 76
Brauner, W., 269
Brot, Marcel, 299, 334, 336, 338, 342, 344, 349, 352, 353
Brouckere, Prof. Louis de, 269, 332
Buchez, Philippe, 13,60
Buchlein, Georg, 161
Budapest Congress 1904, 26, 150
Bulgaria, 297, 327,342
Bulletin of International Co-operation (later Review of International Co-operation), 72, 74-77

Cabrini, M., 142, 145
Campbell, Wallace J., 282
Canada, 77, 246-247, 270, 275, 297
Canadian Co-operator, 247
cash trading, 7, 58, 60, 61, 265, 301
Cecil, Lord, 215
Central Committee
    appeal fund for Austria, 188-189
    frequency of meetings, 37
    German participation, 161
    meetings post First World War, 81, 84-86, 380
    meeting Copenhagen 1921, 111
    meeting Milan 1922, 116
    meeting Essen 1922, 117
    meeting Paris 1925, 53-54, 117
    meeting Rotterdam 1934, 187-188, 189
    meeting Paris 1937, 200
    meeting Zurich 1939, 209
    meetings not held during Second World War, 210, 228, 231
    meeting of British members Manchester 1941, 240-241, 243,245-246
    meeting of British members 1942, 270
    British Conference 1942, 268-270
    meeting of British members London 1943, 249-250, 274-275

British Conference 1943, 271, 274, 275, 276-277
meeting of British members Manchester 1944, 252, 297
meeting of British members London 1945, 296
London Conference 1945, 304-306, 326
meeting Zurich 1946, 299-300, 303, 305, 306
meeting Avignon 1947, 310
meeting Rome 1947, 311, 319-320
meeting Rome 1948, 317, 319-320, 321, 323
meeting Prague 1948, 330
meeting Stockholm 1949, 350-352, 354
meeting Helsinki 1950, 336-344, 354-355
members, 23, 35, 39, 40, 41, 47, 102, 104, 113, 118, 139, 150, 161, 303, 304
minutes, 346-347
plans for war-time work, 229
proposed boycott of Japanese goods, 192-193
report 1937-1946, 307
resolution on German movement, 167-168
resolution on Russian representation, 103-105
resolution on Spain, 198-204
responsibilities, 37-38,
right to speak at Congress, 37

Centrosoyus

Cold War, 319
congresses, 308, 322
co-operative leaders in exile and imprisoned, 94, 101
co-operative movement in socialist republics, 116-118
criticism of ICA inability to prevent war, 307
criticism of International Co-operative Day message, 321, 378
foundation, 95
government representation on board, 97, 98, 113
international trade, 101.
members of Central Committee, 102, 113, 313
membership of ICA, 39, 40, 95, 102-112, 120, 313-314, 327, 332, 337, 344, 386
peace resolution, 65, 347-349, 355
political party, 52, 79

       post revolution board, 112-114
       proposals for ICA rule amendments, 41, 119, 320, 323-327, 380
       resolution on ICA membership, 338-339, 345
       Russo-Finnish War, 239
       Second World War, 258, 297
       subscriptions to ICA, 119-120
       view on Italian fascism, 137
       view on political neutrality, 121-122
       World Congress of Partisans of Peace, 354
Cerreti, 328, 331, 333, 335, 339, 349, 350
Charbo, J. J. A., 319-320
China, 192-195, 275, 303
Christian Social Union, 21
Christian Socialists, 11, 12-13
Churchill, Winston, 282, 304
Clark, Lincoln, 273
Codd, J. H. H., 202, 203
Cold War
       effect on ICA, 66, 314-359, 384-385
       location of Congress 1948, 319-320
       origins, 314-318
Columbain, M., 278
       Committee on International Co-operative Reconstruction, 243, 268, 269, 274-276, 277-279
communism (see also Russia; Centrosoyus)
       attempts to determine ICA agendas, 321-323
       Cold War, 314-359
       Communist Information Bureau, 318-319
       Communist International, 110
       eastern European applications for ICA membership, 328-346, 383
       ICA response, 52, 100-112, 340
       Russian Revolution, 52, 91, 95-100, 115
Congresses of the ICA
       general, 35, 36, 37, 155, 181, 231
       limitation of voting powers, 39, 42, 47, 108
       powers, 37

Paris 1895, 20, 21-22
Paris 1896, 24-25, 67
Manchester 1902, 29
Budapest 1904, 26, 150
Cremona 1907, 27, 36, 134
Hamburg 1910, 36, 48-49, 218.
Glasgow 1913, 28-30, 49, 64, 65, 113
Basle 1921, 38, 51, 64, 65, 86, 101, 102-109, 113, 129-130, 131, 135
Ghent 1924, 39, 52-53, 121, 135
Stockholm 1927, 39-40, 64, 65, 119, 148
Vienna 1930, 40, 57, 119, 236
London 1934, 40, 59-61, 65, 120, 189, 196, 235
Paris 1937, 40-41, 61, 65-66, 188, 190, 198-204, 210, 236, 244, 263, 377
Zurich 1946, 41, 307-310, 316, 331, 347, 359, 378
Prague 1948, 41, 303, 311-312, 319-320, 321, 322-323, 325, 326, 330, 331, 347-349, 351, 355, 359, 369, 379, 380
Paris 1954, 344-345
Lausanne 1960, 345
Vienna 1966, 377

Connally, Senator, 284

consumer co-operation (see also countries)
    producer/consumer co-operatives in ICA membership, 20, 24, 25, 26, 38, 47-50, 62, 369
    socialism, 47-50, 259
    use of co-operative principles, 61

co-operation between co-operatives, 23, 58, 146, 277, 278, 377-378

co-operative banking, 96, 98, 135

Co-operative Builder, 252, 273

co-operative communities, 10-11

co-operative housing, 262

Co-operative League of the USA
    Cold War, 319, 358-359, 384-385
    Committee on International Co-operative Reconstruction, 243, 268-269, 274-276, 277-279
    delegate to UN conference, 282

    membership of ICA, 85, 314
    relationship with Government, 279
    support for Finland, 239
co-operative principles
    definition, 7-8, 23, 47, 267, 369, 377
    fascism contrary to, 128
    requirement for ICA membership, 38, 40, 164, 166, 323, 328, 331-332, 337-339, 340
    review, 40, 55-64
Co-operative Union
    early aims, 12
    Foreign Enquiry Committee, 17, 18, 21
    International Peace Congress, 215
    membership of ICA, 24
    memorial to Henry J. May, 235-236
    National Council of Labour, 265
    peace resolution, 64-65, 346.
    Propaganda Department, 121
    support for Belgian co-operatives, 82
    war time ICA Executive, 241, 275
Cooperazione Italiana, 303
    Cowden, Howard, 274, 277, 309, 359
credit
    cash trading, 7, 58, 60, 61, 265, 301
    German consumer co-operatives, 151
Creech Jones, A., 256
Cremona Congress 1907, 27, 36, 134
Cripps, Sir Stafford, 258
Cruger, Dr., 150
Czechoslovakia
    cecession to Germany, 205, 208, 209
    Cold War, 319-320
    co-operative movement, 77, 80, 205-211, 319
    Co-operative Unions, 205-206, 207, 209
    Co-operative Wholesale Societies, 207, 209
    Czechoslovak situation, 204-211
    delegates' views on political neutrality, 53

    General Co-operative Bank, 207
    ICA relief fund, 205, 206, 209
    International Co-operative Day manifesto, 349
    links with Austria, 205
    medal presented to Henry J. May, 220
    membership of ICA, 80, 206
    representation at London Conference, 1943, 275
    view on German ICA membership, 160, 330-331
Daude-Bancel, 76
Davidson, J. M., 312, 320
Denmark, 21, 65, 77, 297
Dietl, Anton, 182, 183, 186, 188
dividend, 7, 8, 9, 57, 58, 63
Dollfuss, Englebert, 180, 182, 183, 186-188, 190
Downie, J., 235

Eden, Anthony, 267
Elm, Adolf Von, 30, 73
Estonia, 80, 118
Everling, 143, 161, 165, 167, 298, 299
Executive
    aid for Italian co-operators, 139
    appeal for Czechoslovakia, 206
    benefits of all British membership, 81
    Centrosoyus subscription agreement, 119-120
    co-operatives and the state paper, 210
    duties, 38
    Executive Bureau, 23, 35, 36
    German participation, 161
    letter of protest to Mussolini, 133-134
    meeting London 1915, 75, 82
    meeting Britain 1918, 92-93
    meeting Geneva 1919, 84
    meeting London 1920, 147
    meeting Brussels 1922, 113,
    meeting Milan 1922, 116 116
    meeting Ghent 1923, 134

meeting Stockholm 1925, 53
meeting Strasbourg 1927, 147
meeting Bremen 1928, 66
meeting Geneva 1928, 144
meeting Paris 1931, 119-120
meeting Geneva 1932, 120, 234
meeting Basle 1933, 155
meeting Vienna 1933, 162
meeting Miramar D'esterel 1934, 164
meeting Rotterdam 1934, 187
meeting Paris 1935, 154, 165-166
meeting Prague 1935, 167-168
meeting Warsaw 1936, 213, 214
meeting Paris 1937, 198
meeting Strasbourg 1937, 214
meeting Amsterdam 1938, 206, 207
meeting Glasgow 1938, 212-213, 216
meeting Zurich 1939, 209
meeting Paris 1940, 44, 235, 240, 260
meetings not held during Second World War, 231
meeting Copenhagen 1946, 303, 326
meeting Avignon 1947, 316
meeting Amsterdam 1948, 310-311
meeting Rome 1948, 317
meeting Stockholm 1949, 330, 351-353
meeting Paris 1949, 331, 336, 338-339, 341, 353
meeting Zurich 1949, 349
meeting Basle 1950, 334
meeting Helsinki 1950, 336-337, 338
members, 21, 37, 115, 154, 235, 303, 306, 338
minutes, 346-347, 352
picture, 44-45
proposal on Russian representation, 102-103, 109
protest by Emmy Freundlich at remarks of Ernest Poisson, 211
role and activities, 36, 324-325
sending Henry J. May to Italy, 139-141
status of German delegation to special conference, 155-156, 158

       sub-committee, 240, 349-350
       substitute members, 40
       wartime Executive, 240-241

Fabra-Ribas, Prof. A., 263-266, 377
fascism
       Austrian situation, 178-191
       Czechoslovak situation, 204-211
       european shift to the right, 128-129
       German Nazism, 149-168
       ICA attitude, 52
       Italian fascism, 128-145
       Sino-Japanese War, 192-195
       Spanish Civil War, 196-204
Fauquet, Dr. Georges, 55-56, 60, 142, 143, 377
Fay, C. R., 263
Finland
       co-operative movement, 77, 80, 239
       ICA appeal, 239-240
       Kulutusosuuskuntien Keskusliitto, 148
       membership of ICA, 41, 118, 148
       Russo-Finnish War, 238-240
       Second World War, 241, 243-252, 297
       Union Keskuskunta, 148
First World War
       appeals for war relief, 82-83
       Bulletin of International Co-operation, 72, 74-77
       changes in co-operatives' capital base, 80
       outbreak, 30-31
       maintenance of links between countries, 72-73, 76, 92, 229, 231
       Peace Conference, 85, 208
       peace settlements, 79-80, 232
       post war ICA activities, 81-86
       Reports of the Central Organisations on their Activities During the War, 77-81, 92, 94
Fourier, Charles, 13
France
consumer co-operatives, 17, 81, 83

Co-operative Congress, 18
co-operative movement, 13-14
First World War, 77, 78, 80, 81
French Consultative Chamber of Workers' Productive Societies, 25
French National Federation of Consumer Co-operatives, 81,83-84, 161
London Conference 1945, 305-306
members of Central Committee, 23, 35
membership of ICA, 41, 313
peace resolution, 348-349
producer co-operatives, 12, 17, 25
representation at ICA Congresses, 20, 21, 24
review of co-operative principles, 55-56, 60
Second World War, 296, 297, 298

Franco, 197, 203, 347, 378
Fraser, Peter, 284
Freundlich, Emmy
- Austrian situation of 1934, 178, 179, 180, 181, 187, 188, 189-190
- Executive member, 235
- International Co-operative Women's Guild, 76, 190
- opposition to German delegation at Special Conference, 155 159
- picture, 45
- protest at remarks of Ernest Poisson, 211-213, 217
- socialist leader, 52, 375

Fulker, C. W., 262, 265

Gabrovshek, F., 269
Georgia, 77, 80, 116-117
Germany
- attacks on co-operative movement, 152, 167
- *Bulletin of International Co-operation* German edition, 75
- secession of Czechoslovakia, 205, 208, 209
- Central Union of German Consumer Societies, 150, 151, 152, 154, 161, 163-164
- Cold War, 315-317

concern about neutrality, 53, 150
Congresses, 14, 151, 206
consumers co-operatives, 26, 150, 151
Consumers' Co-operation Under the Nazi Regime, 168
co-operative movement, 14-15, 149-168, 316-317
Co-operative Wholesale, 150, 154, 298, 316
Deutsche Arbeitsfront, 149
early involvement with ICA, 20, 24
effects of Hitler's rise to power, 151
First World War, 77, 80
General Union of Industrial & Economic Societies, 14, 26, 150
Grosseinkaufs Gesellschafts D. Consumvereine, 143
members of Central Committee, 23, 35, 161
membership of ICA, 41, 150, 158, 161, 162, 164, 316-317, 330, 331, 334-339, 345
merger of Germany and Austria, 163, 179, 190, 191
National Consumers' Organisation, 163
reconstruction of co-operative movement, 272, 298, 299, 301, 316-317
Reichsbund of German Consumer Societies, 161, 162, 164, 165
Reichsvervand, 158
Rundschau, 152, 159
Second World War, 298-299
Special Conference Basle, 154-157
state aid for co-operatives, 153-154
state control of co-operatives, 163-164
thrift and credit societies, 14, 26, 150
views on Italian fascism, 143-144
Volksfusorge, 154
Ghent Congress 1924, 39, 52-53, 121, 135
Gide, Prof. Charles
    articles, 76
    association with Ernest Poisson, 256
    background, 18, 375
    Congress, 129
    consumer co-operatives, 48
    co-operative principles, 55

       ICA socialist period, 26, 50
       League of Nations, 51, 64
       rainbow flag, 67
       Russia, 117
Gill, T. H. (later Sir Harry), 46, 297, 312, 330, 332, 337, 351
Glasgow Congress 1913, 28-30, 49, 64, 65, 113
Goedhart, G. J. D. C.
       Congress, 104, 107, 135
       correspondence with Henry J. May, 43, 136, 148, 217, 234, 266
       election as President, 43-44
       government office, 78
       maintenance of links during First World War, 72-76, 87
       middle class background, 375
       picture, 46
       proposals, 29, 67, 129,
       resignation as President, 145-146
       telegram to Mussolini, 136-137
Gorvin, J. H., 271
Grahl, Erich, 155, 157, 161
Gray, J. C., 23, 36
Great Britain (*see also* Central Committee; Co-operative Union)
       aid for Spain, 199-200
       appeal for government aid for Austria, 181
       attitudes to Russia, 108-112
       Beveridge Plan, 260, 262, 265
       Brighton Co-operative Benevolent Association, 4
       Cold War, 315-316
       congresses, 5-7, 17, 79, 110
       co-operation and the state, 264-265
       Co-operative Bank, 209, 257
       Co-operative Insurance Society, 261
       co-operative movement in war, 77, 80, 270, 272
       Co-operative Party, 52, 60, 79, 199, 203, 266, 374
       Co-operative Wholesale Society, 12, 19, 60, 146, 160, 261, 272, 275
       Co-operative Women's Guild, 20, 65
       Independent Labour Party, 21

      influence at Basle Congress 1921, 108-109
      influence on ICA, 375, 384
      Labour Co-partnership Association, 19, 29
      legislation, 12
      members of Central Committee, 23, 35, 275
      members of Executive Bureau, 23
      membership of ICA, 39, 41, 313
      Methil Co-operative Society, 241, 243
      motion at Ghent Congress 1924, 121
      motion on German co-operatives, 166
      National Council of Labour, 243, 265, 374
      nationalisation, 261
      representation at ICA Congresses, 20, 21, 24
      relationship with labour movement, 265
      resolution on neutrality, 53
      review of co-operative principles, 60, 63
      Scottish Co-operative Wholesale Society, 12, 60, 250, 272, 275
Greece, 347, 378
Greening, E. O., 20, 21, 22, 23
Greenwood, A., 243
Grey, Albert (later Lord), 20, 21, 23

Hall, Prof., 129
Hamburg Congress 1910, 36, 48-49, 218
Hayward, Sir Fred, 166, 167-168, 240
Henderson, Rt. Hon. Arthur, 65
Hess, Mr. 167
Hitler, Adolf
      Czechoslovakia, 205
      German co-operative movement, 167, 168
      petition from Central Union, 152-153
      rise to power, 149, 150, 151
      Second World War, 248
Hoehler, F. K., 272, 273
Holland
      anti-communist position, 319-320, 379
      representation at ICA Congress 1895, 20, 21

representation at Washington conference, 275
war, 77, 297, 298
Holyoake, George Jacob, 20, 22
Hough, J. A., 276, 277
Hüber, Johannes, 332
Hughes, Thomas, 19
Hungary, 77, 319, 328-330, 344
Hynd, John, 298-299

Iceland, 297
India, 21, 297
Inter-Allied Committee for Post War Reconstruction, 270-271
Inter-Allied Conference, 83-84, 231, 279
International Conference of Representatives of Consumers' &
    Agricultural Co-operative Organisations, 271, 274, 275, 276, 277
International Conference on Disarmament, 65
International Co-operative Alliance (*see also* Central Committee; Executive;
    countries; subjects such as Congresses and membership).
    aims and objects, 23
    appointment of Director, 41, 42, 255
    appointment of General Secretary, 27, 28, 37, 46, 233-235, 236, 306
    articles, 22-23, 24, 324, 328, 334
    Austrian appeal fund, 188-189
    auxiliary committee for workers' co-operatives, 307
    collection of publications, 34, 257, 258
    Committee of Honour, 38, 134, 196
    communications, 72-73, 76, 92, 128
    constitution, 22-23, 24, 34, 36, 369, 380-383
    duties of Administrative Secretary, 42, 236
    duties of President, 38
    early activities, 18, 22
    early relations with international organisations, 51, 54, 83-84
    election of President 36, 46, 145-149, 244, 250, 251, 253, 306
    first President, 20

>foundation, 13, 15-21
>headquarters, 35, 39, 82, 257, 383-384
>ideology, 47-67, 376-380
>independence from socialist movement, 27
>lack of nationalism, 385-386
>'league of the people', 51, 87, 267, 286
>misuse of ICA name and resolutions, 351-353
>name agreed, 20
>Policy Sub-Committee, 331-334, 382
>Preliminary Committee, 19-20, 21
>publications, 27, 63, 72, 74-81, 230, 231
>Regional Office for Asia & the Pacific, 386.
>relationship between General Secretary and President, 43, 46, 148, 166
>responsibilities of General Secretary, 39, 42, 43, 324
>rules, 37, 39, 40, 41, 43, 119, 321, 323-346, 380-383
>Secretariat, 42, 43, 236, 253, 255, 256, 257-258, 346, 381, 383-384
>Spanish appeal fund, 198-199
>structure, 324-325
>subscriptions, 23, 35, 39, 40, 41, 80, 118, 119-120, 243, 302
>Vice-Presidents, 38
>working class organisation, 24, 50, 122, 368, 373-376, 377

International Co-operative Day
>manifesto, 216, 218, 249, 256, 321-322, 347-348, 349-350, 357, 378, 379
>introduction, 67

International Co-operative Petroleum Association, 309, 311, 312
International Co-operative Press Agency, 308
International Co-operative Relief Fund, 270
International Co-operative Trading Association, 378
International Co-operative Trading & Manufacturing Association, 278
International Co-operative Wholesale Society, 146, 277, 377
International Co-operative Women's Guild, 65, 190, 211
International Federation of Trade Unions, 52, 54, 64, 110, 137, 281, 369, 375-376
International Labour Organisation

        conference, 268
        Co-operative Section, 49
        establishment, 49, 51, 112
        headquarters, 258
        ICA support for, 52, 179, 369, 379
        views on Italian fascism, 139
International Peace Bureau, 29, 64
International Peace Campaign, 64, 66, 213-216
International Peace Congress, 29, 213-215
International Red Cross, 355
International Socialist Congress, 27, 48
International Union of Red Co-operatives, 110
Ireland, 20
Italy (see also Lega Nazionale delle Cooperative e Mutue)
        Communist Party, 130
        Confederazione delle Cooperative, 130
        Cooperative Italiano, 303
        co-operative movement, 18, 128-145.
        Ente Nazionale della Cooperazione, 135, 140, 141, 142-144
        fascism, 128-145
        fascist co-operative movement, 130
        Fascist Party, 130, 141
        First World War, 77
        ICA donation to Vergnanini memorial, 145
        International Co-operative Day manifesto, 350
        members of Central Committee, 35
        membership of ICA, 130, 142-144, 260, 303
        representation at ICA Congresses, 20, 21, 24
        Second World War, 303
        Sindicato Nazionale delle Cooperative, 130
        violence against co-operatives, 129-130, 131, 132-134, 136, 140

Jaeggi, Bernhardt, 138, 146-147, 155, 165, 166, 235
Japan, 192-195, 357
Jasinki, J., 317
Johansson, Albin
        Congress paper, 322

    constitution, 251, 252
    delegation, 299
    International Co-operative Day, 321
    picture, 45
    Second World War, 210
    United Nations, 281
    Vice-President, 306
Juell, A, 201

    Kagawa, 194-195
Kaufmann, Heinrich
    First World War, 73, 75, 76, 87
    leader of Central Union, 150, 158
    nomination of President, 146, 147
Keen, Mr., 246-247
Khinchuk, 102, 137
Khoklov, A., 353-354
Khoklov, I. S., 235, 239
King, Dr. William, 4, 24, 47, 375
Kissin, A. A., 116
Klepzig, Vollrath
    calculation on deposits, 151
    correspondence with Henry J. May, 152, 153-154, 161
    Executive, 154, 162
    meeting with Väinö Tanner, 165, 167
    picture, 45
    Special Conference, 154-157, 157-159
Klimov, A., 336, 337-338, 339, 351, 354
Knapp, Dr. Joseph G., 278
Komeda, Karl, 207
Korean War, 354-355, 356, 357
Korobof, Mr., 94, 101, 111
Korp, Andreas, 182, 183-184, 186, 189, 300, 301
Krassin, 102
Kreisky, Rudolf, 269
Kukhtin, A. P., 202-203

Labadessa, Roasario, 142, 143, 144
Latin America, 263-264
Latvia, 80, 118
Lausanne Congress 1960, 345
Lavruklin, 94, 111
Lawrenson, Mrs., 20
League of Nations
    ICA support for, 51, 52, 64, 66, 112, 179, 212, 232, 279, 379
    peace, 65, 214
    Lega Nazionale delle Cooperative e Mutue (formerly Federazione frale Cooperative Italiane)
    delegation to Hungary, 328-330
    dissolution, 130, 131-132, 136-137, 139-141
    improper use of peace resolution, 351-353
    ICA support for, 53, 129-130, 131-144
    membership of ICA, 130, 131, 319
    resolution on ICA membership, 339-340, 341
    voting with soviet delegates, 319
Lenin, 97, 98, 99-100, 110
Lenskaya, Mme, 101
Lessiak, F., 182
Levy, Gaston, 135
Ley, Robert, 149, 163, 167
Lezhava, 101, 106
Lincoln, Murray, 275, 277, 306, 307, 310, 359
liquidation of co-operative societies, 59
Lithuania, 80, 118
Litvinoff, 102
London Congress 1934, 40, 59-61, 65, 120, 189, 196, 235
Lorenz, Heinrich, 105-106, 108, 109, 150, 151, 161
Lozovsky, 137
Ludlow, J. M., 12, 14
Lustig, Emil
    Austrian situation, 181-182, 188
    Czechoslovak situation, 209, 210
    opposition to aid for German co-operatives, 166
    opposition to German delegation to special conference, 155, 159

        picture, 45
        Second World War, 235, 303
        socialist leader, 52, 374
Luzzatti, Luigi, 130, 134, 135, 141

McFadyen, J., 332
Manchester Congress 1902, 29
Mann, Tom, 19
Maresch, Dr. Otto, 185, 186
Marshall Plan, 318.
Maxwell, Sir William, 15, 17, 27, 29, 36, 43, 76, 110, 218, 375
May, Henry J.
        appointment as General Secretary, 28, 42-43
        Austria, 180-190, 191
        change of President, 146, 147
        combination of positions, 82-83, 112
        conferences, 84, 142
        correspondence for ICA, 30-31, 35, 101, 110, 132, 133-134, 136-137
        correspondence with Bernhardt Jaeggi, 165
        correspondence with G. J. D. C. Goedhart, 43, 136, 148, 217, 234, 266
        correspondence with Väinö Tanner, 152, 164, 190, 206, 215, 237, 238, 239, 242, 254
        correspondence with Vollrath Klepzig, 152, 153-154, 161
        Czechoslovakia, 206-210, 220
        death, 43, 86, 228, 233-236, 285
        engineering apprenticeship, 375
        First World War, 72-76, 87
        general election candidate, 79
        German co-operative movement, 154, 162, 166, 167
        Italy, 139-141, 142-144
        memoranda, 53-55, 85
        Moscow, 114-115, 117-118, 122
        peace, 214, 216, 217, 218, 219
        picture, 42
        review of co-operative principles, 57-58

Review of International Co-operation, 63, 122, 168, 193-194, 214, 215, 216-217, 218, 219, 228-233
Russian revolution, 103-105, 109
Russian trade delegation, 102, 111
Second World War, 213, 228-233, 257, 260
Sino-Japanese War, 192-195
Spain, 196, 197
Special Conference at Basle,155-158, 160-162
view on elections to Executive, 39
view on political neutrality, 217
membership of co-operative societies, 9, 58, 62, 78, 113, 119, 153, 259, 340, 369

membership of ICA
- Associate Membership, 345, 380
- co-operative principles as requirement, 38, 40, 164, 166, 323, 328, 331-332, 337-339, 340
- expulsion, 35
- general, 23, 34, 35-37, 38, 40, 80, 160, 233, 303, 327, 328-346, 369, 373-376
- individual, 23, 35-36, 37, 38
- producer/consumer co-operatives, 20, 24, 25, 26, 38, 47-50, 62, 369

Mercer, Thomas William, 63
Mitchell, J. T. W., 19
Moravec, J., 317
Mühlemann, Dr., 300
Müller, Director, 185.
Müller, Dr. Hans, 27
Müller, Karl, 161, 164, 167
Munich Agreement, 205, 207
Musnetsof, 94, 111.
Mussolini, Benito, 53, 130, 131, 133-135, 136-137, 141
Mynderup, E., 269, 270

Neale, Edward Vansittart, 11, 12, 18, 19, 20, 21
Netherlands (see Holland)
New Zealand, 275, 297

Nielsen, Frederick, 299
Nitobe, Dr. I., 178
Nobel Peace Prize, 66
Nogin, 102
Norway, 77, 78, 297, 298

Obreggor, Prof., 185
Odhe, Thorsten, 43, 346, 351, 352, 353, 354
Oerne, Anders, 52, 56
oil resources, 286, 308-313, 378
Orekhanow, Mr., 317, 324
Osmay, M., 257-258
Owen, Robert, 3-4, 5, 8, 9, 14, 15, 376

Palestine, 275
Palmer, R.A. (later Lord Rusholme)
    Acting President, 46, 251-252, 381, 382
    co-operatives and the state, 264-265, 377
    Congress, 322
    correspondence, 255, 256, 267, 280-281
    criticism of actions, 346
    delegations, 296, 297
    Executive, 155, 235, 240, 241, 243-246, 247
    links with workers, 375
    London Conference, 276
    meetings, 284, 298-300, 307, 310, 316
    peace, 270-272
    picture, 253
    President, 46, 253, 306, 332
    retirement, 330
    war time control of Secretariat, 241, 381
Pantulu, Hon. V. Ramadas, 251-252
Pare, William, 15
Paretchny, M., 101
Paris Congress 1895, 20, 21-22
Paris Congress 1896, 24-25, 67
Paris Congress 1937, 40-41, 61, 65-66, 188, 190, 198-204, 210, 236, 244, 263, 377

Paris Congress 1954, 344-345
Passio, Rafael, 252-253
peace
    activities of ICA, 18, 51, 64-67, 211-221, 267, 346-357
    International Conference on Disarmament, 65
    International Peace Bureau, 29, 64
    International Peace Campaign, 64, 66, 213-216
    International Peace Congress, 29, 213-215
    Nobel Peace Prize, 66
    Peace Congress, 213-214
    peace declaration, 218
    peace resolutions, 28-30, 49, 64, 347-349, 351-352, 354-357
    Peace Society, 21
    Permanent Committee of the Partisans of Peace, 355
    Stockholm Peace Appeal, 356
    World Congress of Partisans for Peace, 348, 354, 355, 356
Poincare, M., 146
Poisson, E.
    change of President, 147
    debate on Russian membership, 104-105
    First World War, 73, 77
    German situation, 159-160, 166
    International Peace Campaign, 213, 214
    Italian fascism, 129, 136-137, 139
    picture, 45
    protest by Emmy Freundlich at remarks, 211-213
    review of co-operative principles, 55
    Second World War, 235, 240, 256
    socialist leader, 52, 375
    Spanish Civil War, 201, 203
Poland, 80, 118, 275, 297, 298, 319, 327, 336, 338-339
political neutrality
    Austria, 301
    co-operative principle, 23, 58, 265
    co-operative societies, 78-79
    Germany, 150
    Great Britain, 203

ICA constitution, 25, 50, 321, 324, 351
ICA 'political' stands, 51-55, 66, 193, 199, 202, 379
Spain, 197
wartime, 229
Polley, Gertrude F.
   appointment as Administrative Secretary, 42-43
   early role in ICA, 147
   correspondence, 255, 256, 257-258, 267, 279, 280-281, 300, 354
   criticism of actions, 346-347
   delegations, 296, 299
   meetings, 282, 284, 298, 310, 330
   minutes, 346-347
   no right to sucession to General Secretary, 234-235, 381
   peace, 270-272
   picture, 42
   response to criticism of Väinö Tanner, 250-251
   war time control of Secretariat, 43, 46, 241, 253
Polovtseva, Dr., 106-107
Potter, Beatrice, 13.
Prague Congress 1948, 41, 303, 311-312, 319-320, 321, 322-323, 325, 326, 330, 331, 347-349, 351, 355, 359, 369, 379, 380
Pratt, Hodgson, 19
producer co-operatives
   French, 12, 17, 25
   producer/consumer co-operatives in ICA membership, 20, 24, 25, 26, 38, 47-50, 62, 369
profit-sharing, 9, 25, 47, 49.
Pszczolkowski, E, 356

Rae, W. R., 121
Raiffeisen, Freidrich, 14, 60
rainbow flag, 67
Rapacki, Prof., 235
rationing, 77-78, 340
raw material resources, 286, 308-313, 378
religious neutrality, 23, 25, 53, 54-55, 58, 379
Renner, Dr. Karl,

Austrian situation of 1934, 178-179, 180, 181, 187, 188, 189-190
government office, 51, 78, 179, 299, 301, 375
picture, 45

Review of International Co-operation (previously *Bulletin of International Co-operation*)
Austrian situation, 179
Congress 1946, 307
co-operative movement in Russia, 122
co-operative principles, 63, 218
co-operatives and the state, 259-266, 286
dictatorships, 193-194
ICA statistics, 373
International Co-operative Women's Guild reports 143-144, 211
Italian propaganda campaign, 141
memorial to Henry J. May, 86, 235
obituary of Albert Thomas, 107-108
peace, 213, 214, 216, 217, 218
Russo-Finnish War, 238-239
Second World War, 168, 210, 211, 219, 228-233, 255-257, 258, 285, 298, 381
Sino-Japanese War, 194-195
United Nations, 281, 282
Washington Conference, 277-278

Ricardo, David, 9
Robens, Alf, 202, 203
Robert, Charles, 22
Rochdale Pioneers (*see also* co-operative principles)
centenary, 276
foundation, 7-10
Henry J. May's visit, 58
influences on development, 4-6, 376
photograph, 6
share certificate, 6
Roig, J. Ventosa, 196, 197, 201
Rolfe, Catherine, 307
Roosevelt, Eleanor, 218

Roosevelt, President, 273, 276, 304, 309
Rosovsky, 102
Romania, 21, 297, 327, 342
Rundschau, 152, 159
Rusholme, Lord (*see* Palmer R. A.)
Russia (*see also* Centrosoyus)
    Allied Supreme Council blockade, 93, 100
    Big Artel Transbaikal, 94
    civil war, 99, 100
    Cold War, 314-359
    condemnation of dividend, 57, 63
    co-operative delegation to Russia, 93
    co-operative movement, 91-123
    co-operative movement in the socialist republics, 116-118
    Co-operative People's Bank, 96, 98
    Co-operative Trade Delegation, 93, 102, 111
    co-operatives converted to consumer communes, 98
    delegate's comment on political neutrality, 53
    First World War, 77, 78, 92, 94, 95-96
    ICA delegation to Moscow, 114-116
    ICA response to post revolution changes, 110-112
    International Co-operative Day manifesto, 350
    international trade, 101, 111, 114
    membership of ICA, 41, 102-112, 118, 313
    Moscow Union of Consumer Societies, 95
    oil resources, 308, 310
    political activity, 52, 79
    post revolution co-operative movement, 56, 95-112
    Potsdam Declaration, 301
    representation at ICA Congress, 21
    representation on Central Committee, 39, 118
    representation on Executive, 115
    revolutions, 52, 91, 95-100, 115
    Russo-Finnish War, 238-240, 244
    soviet view of capitalist countries, 343
    state control of co-operatives, 96-100, 111
    treatment of USSR as one country, 118

United Nations, 283, 284
Workers International Russian relief, 110
view on issues, 39-40
Russo-Finnish War, 238-240, 244

Salter, Sir Arthur, 276, 278
Scandinavia, 52, 54
Schact, Dr., 168
Schnopf, 182
Scholesser, Robert, 155, 156-158, 161
Schrier, S., 207
Schüller, Dr., 186
Schultze-Delitzsch, Hermann, 14, 26, 94
Scottish Co-operator, 248
Second World War
    co-operative movements in occupied countries, 271-272, 296
    debate on co-operatives and the state, 259-266
    effects on ICA, 228, 235-259, 380-382
    immediate post war period, 296-314, 384
    ICA appeal fund, 273-274, 297-298
    ICA freedom fund, 250
    outbreak, 66
    peace settlement, 231, 232, 251, 267, 270
    post war activities, 231
    post war relief and reconstruction, 267-279, 318
    view of Henry J. May on tasks, 228-233, 260
Selheim, 94, 101
Serwy, 336
Serwy, Victor
    delegation to Georgia, 116-117
    German developments, 167-168
    opposition to German delegation to Special Conference, 155, 159
    picture, 45
    Sino-Japanese War, 194
    socialist leader, 52, 375
Shenkman, Dr., 255, 381

Sidorov, N.
- attacks on President, 337-338
- attitude to Väinö Tanner, 307
- Centrosoyus post war attitude to ICA, 297
- Congress, 322
- German co-operative movement, 317, 336
- Hungarian co-operative movement, 328-330
- International Co-operative Day manifesto, 347, 349
- neutrality, 351
- peace, 356
- Soviet view of capitalist countries, 343
- Vice-President, 306

Simon, Saint, 13, 376
Sino-Japanese War, 192-195
Smith, Adam, 8.
Social Democratic Federation, 21
Socialist International, 110, 259, 375-376
Socialist International Congress, 27, 48
Southern, Robert, 334, 335, 336, 337, 341-342, 352, 383
Soviet War News, 248
Spain
- appeal fund, 198-199, 212
- Catalonian Co-operative Federation, 212-213
- Central Wholesale Society, 197, 198
- congress, 197
- co-operative movement, 196-204
- First World War, 77
- membership of ICA, 196
- Regional Chamber of Co-operative Societies of Catalonia & Balearic Islands, 196
- Spanish Civil War, 196-204
- Spanish National Federation of Co-operatives, 196, 197, 198

Special Committee
- review of co-operative principles, 57-63

Special Conference in Basle, 154-157, 237
Stalin, 249
state
- debate on co-operatives and the cate, 259-266, 305-306

state control of co-operatives, 96-100, 111, 163-164, 180-190
Staudinger, Prof., 129
Stewart, Sir Robert, 155
Stockholm Congress 1927, 39-40, 64, 65, 119, 148
Stopford, Mr., 271
Strobl, Dr. Ludwig, 185, 186, 189, 300, 301
Suter, Dr.
    aid for Italy, 131, 132-133, 139, 147
    background, 375
    Congress, 129
    correspondence with Henry J. May, 136, 137
    picture, 138
Sweden
    activity in ICA, 353, 354
    Kooperative Forbundet, 210
    membership of ICA, 41, 313
    peace resolution, 354-357
    representation at Washington Conference, 275
    review of co-operative principles, 60
    statements at London Conference 1945, 304-305 VI, 246
Switzerland
    Bulletin of International Co-operation French edition, 76
    congresses, 190
    co-operative movement, in war, 77, 80, 270
    Co-operative Union, 76, 139, 303
    early support for ICA, 21, 24
    ICA relief fund, 297
    peace resolution, 348-349
    Union of Swiss Distributive Societies, 27

Tanner, Väinö
    accusation of pro-Nazi sympathy, 243, 253, 255, 380
    Austrian situation, 180, 181, 189, 190
    Congress paper, 263
    correspondence with Henry J. May, 152, 164, 190, 206, 215, 237, 238, 239, 242, 254

    Czechoslovak situation, 206
    election as President, 46, 145, 147-149, 244
    German co-operative movement, 158-159, 164-165, 167, 237
    government office, 52, 78, 148, 158, 237, 240, 244, 249, 374
    isolation during Second World War, 228, 235, 236-240, 241, 243-253, 307
    peace declaration, 218
    picture, 45, 138
    Place of Co-operatives in Different Economic Systems, 210
    plans for war time work, 229
    Spanish Civil War, 200-201

Thedin, Nils, 356-357

Thomas, Albert
    aim of co-operatives, 264
    association with Ernest Poisson, 256
    Congresses, 104, 107-108
    co-operative activities, 49
    co-operative principles, 56
    government office, 78, 374
    International Labour Office, 49, 139, 142, 179
    peace, 29-30, 218
    picture, 138
    war, 81

Tillet, Ben, 19

Totomianz, Prof., 94, 129

Tournier, Miss, 20

trade
    Allied Supreme Council blockade of Russia, 93, 100, 111
    cash trading, 7, 58, 60, 61, 265, 301
    co-operation between co-operatives, 23, 58, 146, 277, 278, 377-378
    international trade, 308
    oil resources, 286, 308-313

trade unions
    International Federation of Trade Unions, 52, 54, 64, 110, 137, 281, 369, 375-376
    model conditions within co-operatives, 49

World Federation of Trade Unions, 283, 320, 325-327, 350, 383, 385
Trud, 336
Tschaikowsky, 93

Ukraine, 77, 80, 118.
USSR (see Russia)
United Nations
    food conference, 275, 281
    formation, 257, 272-273, 281-283
    ICA consultative status, 41, 284
    ICA involvement, 279-284, 286, 310, 348, 350, 379, 384
    ICA permanent representative, 310, 346
    Korean War, 357
    proposal on armed force, 355-356
    raw materials, 310-313
    Relief & Rehabilitation Administration, 272-273, 278, 279, 281
United States of America (*see also* Co-operative League of the USA)
    American Office of Foreign Relief & Rehabilitation, 272
    Central Co-operative Wholesale Wisconsin, 252
    Cold War, 314-359
    Co-operative Oil Association, 309
    early support for ICA, 21
    First World War, 77
    ICA relief fund, 297
    members of Central Committee, 23, 314
    membership of ICA, 35, 314
    National Co-operatives Inc, 278
    reduced American influence on ICA, 358-359, 384-385
    statement at London Conference, 304

Vergnanini, Antonio, 131-132, 134, 136, 137, 139, 141, 142, 145
VI, 246
Vienna Congress 1930, 40, 57, 119, 236
Vienna Congress 1966, 377
Vivian, Henry, 19
Vukowitch, Dr. Andreas, 182, 183-184, 186, 189, 299, 300, 301

Walworth, George, 276, 277
war *see* individual wars
Warbasse, Dr. James Peter
    Committee for International Co-operative Reconstruction, 268, 269
    Congress, 86
    constitution, 251, 252, 382
    co-operatives and the state, 260-262, 266, 377
    Second World War, 286
Watkins, W. P., 122-123, 135, 253-254, 272, 313, 368, 381
Webb, Beatrice, 13
Weber, Dr., 337, 340-341
Western Producer, 247
White Russia, 118.
Whitehead, A., 147
Williams, Aneurin, 23, 29, 78, 84
Williams, Dr. & Mrs. Harold, 92-93
Wolff, Henry W., 20, 21, 22, 23, 36
women
    Co-operative Women's Guild, 20, 65
    International Co-operative Women's Guild, 65, 190, 211
    positions of authority, 190, 234-235
Woods, 337-338, 378
working classes
    ICA as a working class organisation, 24, 50, 122, 368, 373-376, 377
World Congress of Partisans for Peace, 348, 354, 355
World Economic Conference, 51
World Federation of Trade Unions, 283, 320, 325-327, 350, 383, 385

Yakhimstroff, 101
Yugoslavia, 270, 275, 297

Zerbowski, J., 317
Zhukov, Marshall, 335.
Zmrhal, A., 336, 342-343
Zurich Congress 1946, 41, 307-310, 316, 331, 347, 359, 378

BIBLIOGRAPHY

In addition to the archival primary sources used in this book reference was also made to the following books and journals:

ARMSTRONG, David, *The Rise of the International Organisation*, Macmillan Education, London, 1982.

BARTLETT, C. J., *The Global Conflict 1880-1970*, Longman Group UK Limited, Harlow, 1984.

BELL, P. M. H., *The Origins of the Second World War in Europe*, Longman Group UK Limited, Harlow, 1986.

BONNER, Arnold, *British Co-operation, Co-operative Union Ltd*, Manchester, 1961.

CHAMBERS, W. & R. Ltd., *Chambers Biographical Dictionary*, Edinborough, 1988.

CRAIG, Gordon A., *Germany 1866-1945*, Oxford University Press, 1987.

EARLE, John, *The Italian Co-operative Movement*, Allen and Unwin Ltd., London, 1986.

DIGBY, Margaret, *The Little Nut Tree*, The Plunkett Foundation, Oxford, 1979.

FAUQUET, Dr Georges, *The Co-operative Sector*, Co-operative Union Ltd, Manchester, 1942.

GIDE, Prof. Charles, *The International Co-operative Alliance*, The International Co-operative Alliance, London, 1920.

INTERNATIONAL CO-OPERATIVE ALLIANCE: *REPORTS OF ICA CONGRESSES*, published by ICA, London, year of Congress Glasgow, 1913; Basle, 1921; Ghent, 1924; Stockholm, 1927; Vienna, 1930; London, 1934; Paris, 1937; Zurich, 1946; Prague,1948.

INTERNATIONAL CO-OPERATIVE ALLIANCE: *Bulletin of International Co-operation* 1914-1928.

INTERNATIONAL CO-OPERATIVE ALLIANCE: *Review of International Co-operation*, 1928 - 1983

KING, Dr William, *The Co-operator*

KRASHENINNIKOV, A. I., *The International Co-operative Alliance-Past, Present and Future*, Centrosoyus, Moscow, 1988.

LOTH, Wilfried, *The Division of the World 1941-1955*, Routledge, London, 1988..

OWEN, Robert, *A New View of Society, Association of all Classes and Nations*

PALMER, Alan, The Penguin Dictionary of Modern History 1789 - 1945, Penguin Books, London, 1988.

PENGUIN BOOKS Ltd., *The Penguin Concise Columbia Encyclopedia*, Penguin Books Ltd, Harmondsworth, 1987

POTTER, Beatrice, later Webb, *The Co-operative Movement*

ROBERTS, J. M., *Europe 1980-1945*, Longman Group UK Ltd., Harlow, 1989.

SMITH, Adam, *Wealth of Nations*

TAYLOR, James and SHAW, Warren, *A Dictionary of the Third Reich*, Grafton Books, Collins Publishing Group, Glasgow, 1988.

WATKINS, W. P., *The International Co-operative Alliance*, The International Co-operative Alliance, London, 1970.

Additional documents and journals in the public domain to which references are made:

Andelsbadet - Denmark
Atlantic Charter
"The Austrian Co-operatives Under Dictatorship", report produced by the Austrian Socialists
Canadian Co-operator - Canada
Co-operative Builder - USA
Emancipation - France
Evening Standard - UK
Die Konsumgenossenschaft - Czechoslovakia
Manchester Guradian - UK
Rochdale Pioneers, "Law the First" and "Almanac 1860"
Rundschau - Germany Schweiz Konsumvereine - Switzerland
Scottish Co-operator - UK
Soviet War News - USSR
Soviet Weekly News - USSR
Stockholm Peace Appeal
Trud - USSR
The Times UK
Western Producer - Canada

www.ingramcontent.com/pod-product-compliance
Lightning Source LLC
Chambersburg PA
CBHW071443220526
45472CB00003B/649